D1599482

Hippocrates Cried

Hippocrates Cried
The Decline of American Psychiatry

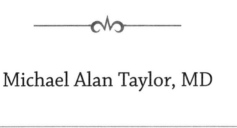

Michael Alan Taylor, MD

OXFORD
UNIVERSITY PRESS

OXFORD
UNIVERSITY PRESS

Oxford University Press is a department of the University of Oxford.
It furthers the University's objective of excellence in research, scholarship,
and education by publishing worldwide.

Oxford   New York

Auckland   Cape Town   Dar es Salaam   Hong Kong   Karachi
Kuala Lumpur   Madrid   Melbourne   Mexico City   Nairobi
New Delhi   Shanghai   Taipei   Toronto

With offices in

Argentina   Austria   Brazil   Chile   Czech Republic   France   Greece
Guatemala   Hungary   Italy   Japan   Poland   Portugal   Singapore
South Korea   Switzerland   Thailand   Turkey   Ukraine   Vietnam

Oxford is a registered trademark of Oxford University Press
in the UK and certain other countries.

Published in the United States of America by
Oxford University Press
198 Madison Avenue, New York, NY 10016

© Michael Alan Taylor 2013

Library of Congress Cataloging-in-Publication Data
Taylor, Michael Alan, 1940–
Hippocrates cried : the decline of American psychiatry / Michael A. Taylor.
p. cm.
Includes bibliographical references and index.
ISBN 978–0–19–994806–2 (hardcover : alk. paper)   1. Psychiatry —United States —
History.   2. Neurosciences —United States —History.   3. Diagnostic and statistical
manual of mental disorders.   I. Title.   II. Title: Decline of American psychiatry.
RC339.A1T39 2013
616.89 —dc23
2012030771

9 8 7 6 5 4 3 2 1
Printed in the United States of America
on acid-free paper

To Ellen

CONTENTS

INTRODUCTION

This is a series of personal essays. It is a 45-year eyewitness account of the decline of American psychiatry. It is not a broad social history or an in-depth memoir or an autobiography of my personal life. Other than my mother, most observers found that last sequence of events less than exciting. I experienced no great journeys to the ends of the earth or to enlightenment. I made no great discoveries that changed the course of human events. Nothing happened in my life that would inspire a novelist or a playwright. Although my wife and two kids are the kind of people who bring out the best in others and who you don't want to let down, and although I gave them priority over academic political advancement, they are not central to this account. This chronicle is a narrative of what I witnessed over almost half a century of the degrading of a branch of medicine as old as Western Civilization.[1] This book is a personal account of that debasement. It is an effort to show what has happened to psychiatry in the United States over the past 50 years through personal memories, from the stories of patients I have tried to help, and from what the science of the field reveals. The decline has occurred in the ability to effectively diagnose and care for patients, and it has been fueled in part by a moral decline, as many in our field sold their souls to the pharmaceutical industry. The debasement is not a pretty picture. Of course, like all eyewitness accounts, this one is the product of the distillation of memory flavored by opinion and aging.

The aging occurred over four decades of seeing thousands of patients, training hundreds of residents and many more medical students, directing acute-treatment psychiatric inpatient units in different parts of the country, chairing a department of psychiatry, and founding a doctorate-level department of psychology, with both departments focusing on brain and behavior interactions. I've done my share of research, founded a scientific journal, published peer-reviewed papers, some of which have made a difference, and I have written or co-authored a number of textbooks. For the past 12 years I have been on the psychiatry faculty of the University of Michigan where I see patients as a neuropsychiatrist and as a member of the electroconvulsive therapy team. But as I look back at the events sur-rounding those professional biographic milestones, I see a deterioration in patient care and in the skills and knowledge psychiatrists were supposed to have acquired when I started out. I am both saddened and angry by the decline of my slice of medicine.

Over those years, the field has learned much about brain chemistry and its neurotransmitters and their receptors among laboratory animals and in Petri dishes, but it has mostly ignored how it all works in the patient's brain at the bedside. Almost any psychiatry resident and many practicing psychiatrists can tell you which neurotransmitter system a specific psychi-atric medication is supposed to alter, but few can tell you which parts of the brain those transmitters subserve and what those brain areas do in generating normal or abnormal behavior. Almost all psychiatric residents can recite at least in approximation the diagnostic criteria for depression, mania, and the other "big-ticket" items in the present diagnostic system, but few have heard and even less can recognize the wealth of diagnostically revealing psychopathology not listed in the diagnostic manual and so they miss the illness the patient in fact has as they offer the label that has little relevance to what needs to be done to successfully treat the patient. Alas, most of their teachers are no better.

It is, of course, presumptuous to relate some of the events of your life for others to consider. But I was a tenured professor for decades. I profess. And, without realizing it, I have followed the injunction offered by D. H. Lawrence: *"When genuine passion moves you, say what you've got to say, and say it hot."* Righteous indignation fuels the narrative. Once, many years ago, in a log house in a serene valley in Montana, I was in conversation with several neighbors. One neighbor was a minister in her real-world life. At one point, she stopped the discourse and said to me, "You have lots of strong opinions, don't you?" I responded, "Sure, I'm 55 years old, and if I don't have a lot of opinions at my age I've been wasting my time." She liked that response well enough to ask if I minded if she used it in a sermon. Well, I'm now 72 years old and I haven't been wasting my time, so the opinions have amassed. Somewhere the tipping point occurred and I started to write this book.

In putting down in print the events I have witnessed and in describing the stories of some of the patients I have met that highlight the decline of my field, I recognize that this is my account. A historian would likely tell a somewhat different story. I also don't know what psychiatry is like elsewhere on the planet. It may be better. I doubt it, but I've been wrong before. Even if they do it better elsewhere on the globe, that doesn't help those in the United States with psychiatric illness. It also doesn't help those who care for them.

So, I am writing, presumptuous and opinionated, hoping that those new to my field may learn what has happened to psychiatry in the United States and from that insight make better choices in their education. They are the future and have the ability to reverse the decline. To encourage them, I have relied heavily on the patients I have met, as the best lessons are taught by the sufferers of illness. But readers should keep in mind the caveat of William Osler, the most influential North American physician of his time: *"No human being is constituted to know the truth, the whole truth, and nothing but the truth; and even the best of men must be content with fragments, with partial glimpses, never the full fruition."* Alas, this caveat applies to me too.[2]

I also hope the general reader will discover this book, and so I have written it in common usage English, not in technical jargon. When a technical term is unavoidable, I offer an explanation. Because almost all the experience of general readers about psychiatry comes from movies and TV, my hope is that they will learn that those screen images do not reflect the reality of psychiatry in the United States. Hollywood has gotten it wrong and in presenting a false picture of psychiatry has done much damage. They have indirectly killed sufferers of psychiatric illness by falsely indicating what works (psychoanalysis) and what doesn't work (electroconvulsive therapy). They have shown us as nineteenth-century mesmerists rather than as the medical doctors that many of us are. To the general reader who has had a psychiatric illness or who has a friend or loved-one who has had a psychiatric illness, this is also a warning label. Most of what's on the psychiatric supermarket shelf is not worth purchasing and is in fact bad for your health.

HIPPOCRATES

Hippocrates, I am told, was born around 460 BCE on the Greek island of Kos. He forcefully argued that diseases were caused naturally and were not the result of supernatural forces. He separated the discipline of medicine from religion, which is never a popular position as stem cell researchers in the United States know only too well. Hippocrates considered disease not to be a punishment inflicted by the gods, but rather the result of environmental factors, poor diet, and unhealthy living habits. Twenty-five hundred years later physicians are still trying to convince folks that these factors are counterproductive to good health. In his treatise, *On the Physician*, he recommended that physicians always be well-kempt (clean), honest, calm, understanding, and serious. Physician hand washing is still the most important factor in reducing hospital-related infections. He considered the physician to be a professional.

Hippocrates' novel opinions about disease and treatments got him into hot water with the Hellenistic powers that were and he was imprisoned for 20 years. He did not waste this time, however, and spent it writing several of his most famous treatises such as *The Complicated Body*. His contributions to medical diagnosis and patient care have a modern ring and he is considered to be the "Father of Medicine." Hippocrates taught and practiced medicine throughout his life, traveling widely. He likely died in his 80s, probably at the hands of another physician.

The quotes at the beginning of chapters attributed to Hippocrates come from brainyquote.com.

THE HIPPOCRATIC OATHS

There are several versions of the Hippocratic Oath.[3] The first that I ran across, translated from old Greek, invokes Apollo and other ancient celebrities, and incorporates anachronisms such as not doing surgical procedures, then reserved for practitioners other than the physician. On the other hand, the old version first and foremost requires the new physician to promise to "never do harm." Isn't it odd that future iterations of the oath do not include this phrase? Could that be recognition that we all make mistakes or is it the result of a lawyer's tweaking a verbal contract to avoid future liability?

The next version of the oath, also considered old, was the one I took in June 1965 as I graduated from medical school in front of parents, family members and guests, teachers and fellow graduates, and Robert F. Wagner, the mayor of New York City and our commencement speaker. I don't recall a thing he said. But as I stood in that auditorium with the other 100 or so members of my graduating class, I, an atheist, swore to Apollo as if interactions with discarded deities were okay while conversations with the newer fellas (they are now of course all male) were somehow a reflection of superstition. Given the substantial changes in medicine in the intervening millennia between the old oath and the one I avowed, it is also not surprising that I was required to first and foremost pledge my support to teachers and other members of the organization rather than to patients. I swore to

> hold him who has taught me this art as equal to my parents and to live my life in partnership with him, and if he is in need of money to give him a share of mine, and to regard his offspring as equal to my brothers in male lineage and to teach them this art—if they desire to learn it—without fee and covenant; to give a share of precepts and oral instruction and all the other learning to my sons and to the sons of him who has instructed me and to pupils who have signed the covenant and have taken the oath according to medical law, but to no one else.

I can only imagine that this degree of loyalty required of us to join the MD club was of similar rigor to the requirements for signing up to the Cosa Nostra. It also did not seem to disturb anyone at that ceremony that the club was officially male, even though there were four women in our class. Were they and their offspring eligible for the club's perks and to some of my money if needed? Such concern is of course moot since today over half of medical students are women and the last time a well-healed doc chipped in to help out a financially strapped colleague Eisenhower was a corporal.

The oath went on:

> Whatever houses I may visit, I will come for the benefit of the sick, remaining free of all intentional injustice, of all mischief and in particular of sexual relations with both female and male persons, be they free or slaves.

To the modern ear these requirements sound almost un-American. If they could be charted, I'd bet that as the number of house calls has plummeted over the decades the incident of doctor–patient fornication has proportionately risen. Priorities have changed. My grandfather had a general practice in New York City and for 50 years made regular and emergency house calls to patients in Manhattan and the Bronx. But except as an intern on an ambulance run, I have never made a house call other than to check out a friend or relative. During my time at bat, I can name more incidents of a doctor diddling a patient than a doctor making a house call.

Recent renditions of the oath offer corrections to the flaws of the past. Students now pledge to

> ...respect the hard-won scientific gains...gladly share such knowledge with those who are to follow...remember that there is art to medicine as well as science, and that warmth, sympathy, and understanding may outweigh the surgeon's knife or the chemist's drug...not be ashamed to say 'I know not,' nor will I fail to call in my colleagues when the skills of another are needed for a patient's recovery...remember not to treat a fever chart, a cancerous growth, but a sick human being, whose illness may affect the person's family and economic stability. My responsibility includes these related problems, if I am to care adequately for the sick...

And

> I will prevent disease whenever I can, for prevention is preferable to cure. I will remember that I remain a member of society, with special obligations to all my fellow human beings, those sound of mind and body as well as the infirm.

From my experience, I can only conclude that a lot of doctors did not pay attention to what they were reciting during their graduation ceremony with the new version. Maybe they were dreaming about their drives and putts or the new set of wheels that would carry them down life's highway. Somewhere along the way the wheels started to come off that car, and now psychiatric medicine, at least as practiced in the United States, has structurally discarded the pledges made to Apollo and to ourselves. The field has devolved and it's a close call as to whether present-day psychiatry in the United States does more harm than good.

The chapters that follow are my recollections of the decline. Will the telling make a difference or change the outcome? A pessimist might answer, "How many people read books with no sex, violence, car chases, or evil shadow societies subverting the world?" On the other hand, the patients I describe were real people who experienced real suffering. The doctors that did well by them or poorly were real doctors in real medical settings. The things related really happened.

PATIENT STORIES

Throughout this book I illustrate my concerns about psychiatry in the United States with stories of patients I have met over the years. I have detailed many of these patients in seminars and lectures, and these patients will be familiar to those physicians who attended and stayed awake. Several of these stories have also been published in one form or another in the following textbooks referenced at the end of this book: Fink and Taylor (2003), Atre Vaidya and Taylor (2004), Taylor and Fink (2006), and Taylor and Atre Vaidya (2009). These stories, however, have been superficially altered rather than presented in their original prose. Several patients have not been previously described. In all cases the identity of the patient is masked. These patients and several thousand others have taught me much more than I have taught others.

ACKNOWLEDGMENTS

This book could not have been conceived without help and inspiration. The inspiration came from the patients I have met, professors who offered encouragement, peers who challenged me, and students and residents who kept me double checking the facts that "validated" my opinions. Several of the patients whose stories motivated me are described in the chapters that follow. Among the professors who shared their knowledge and gave support, Max Fink stands out. I first met him in 1966 and he still has much to teach. Among my peers, Bob Levine insisted that we all adhere to evidence-based practice before the phrase became popular and the standard was recognized as a worthwhile endeavor. Dick Abrams was most important in my development as a psychiatrist. We trained together, learned together, and then worked together for decades.

The help came from several people. Michael Schrift, director of neuro-psychiatry at the University of Illinois at Chicago and co-director of their behavioral neurology and neuropsychiatry fellowship, carefully read the manuscript and offered many specific and helpful suggestions. He wanted more discussion about the advances in cognitive and basic neuroscience as they apply to clinical psychiatry. I'm sure I fell short in this regard. My excuse is that such a worthy endeavor is a different book better written by others. Nutan Atre Vaidya, a neuropsychiatrist at The Rosalind Franklin University of Medicine and Science, also read the manuscript and offered good advice. She wanted more personal stories and less patient stories. Although I did prune some stories, my excuse for not doing more of that, and offering more personal experiences, is that the patients I describe are more interesting and instructive than I am.

Edward "Ned" Shorter, Professor of History of Medicine at the University of Toronto, also reviewed the manuscript. As always, his enthusiasm was energizing. Any historical errors in the text are certainly not his. Max Fink also read the manuscript and checked for any missteps in which my foot ended up in my mouth. Any remaining *faux pas* are mine. My editor at Oxford University Press, Craig Panner, kept me in the middle of the road.

His suggestions about the structure of the book were critical to its readability. Kathryn Winder and Emily Perry at Oxford offered sound guidance throughout the production process. Nancy Russo, my sister-in-law, read most of the early chapters and was heroic at curbing my creative spelling and unique approach to grammar. She was a public school teacher much of her life. Ellen S. Taylor read everything several times. I think I would have given up in many ways were it not for her.

Hippocrates Cried

CHAPTER 1

❦

The Origins of Indignation

Indignation: strong displeasure or anger aroused by something unjust, unworthy or mean.
Webster's Collegiate Dictionary

"Science is the father of knowledge, but opinion breeds ignorance."
Hippocrates

The first patient ever assigned to my care died at the moment of our introduction. I don't mean around the moment; I mean that as the words of presentation from the resident in charge of our little band of student interns were still bouncing about the two-bed hospital room, the patient's head slowly sank onto his left shoulder and he into oblivion. I don't remember the patient's name, but I can still see that head sinking.

You might imagine that we all became distraught, overwhelmed by empathic sorrow or terror. It is not every day that you see the actual act of dying other than on TV or in the movies. These frauds, however, don't count. But we were not distressed. For me, surprise would fit better, for up to then life had always been easy, mostly due to the efforts of others. The patient's apparent response to the news that I was to be his doctor was definitely a speed bump. Some folks would surely have taken the event as an omen, a signal from some higher power to consider alternative schooling. But my philosophic perspective then did not include destiny as playing a role in human endeavor. It wasn't fate, but it was a hell of a coincidence.

So minimally perturbed, I just stared at the patient as his chin slowly descended to his left shoulder and the sheets over his chest stopped moving. And that was that. There were no sudden alarms or codes. No hospital personnel in different colored pajamas came running with a crash cart and other paraphernalia to bring the patient back from wherever he was heading. No effort at all occurred, other than a quick confirmation of death by the supervising resident.

At that moment the lack of effort and concern did not seem strange to me. It seems extraordinary now. At least a pause to mark the passing would have been a lesson in humility and a model of empathy. But in the New York City-run hospital where this event occurred, death was a common occurrence. Resuscitation codes were rarely called. Many patients arrived at our doors too far gone to be saved by the medical interventions of the 1960s. There was no such thing as organ transplants. Billy Holiday died of liver failure in a pauper's bed on our medical service. So, instead of drama, our little group moved on and I was assigned another patient, leaving the nursing staff with the clean-up.

LESSONS LEARNED IN A TEACHING HOSPITAL

The individual who accepted that callus response of our little group to the death of that almost-first patient is no more. Lesser events today trigger righteous indignation.[1] The change derives from experiencing the tragedies of many patients written by their physicians who should have known better and cared more. Most of these incidents occurred at "teaching hospitals." Teaching hospitals are created to ideally provide the best model of care and through that model teach medical students, resident physicians, and other health care professionals how to be good at what they do. Teaching hospitals also offer many other kinds of lessons.

The Poor Do Not Ride in First Class

To appreciate U.S. psychiatry of the 1960s you need to get a flavor of the medical world of that era. New York City then pretty much reflected the medical urban landscape across the United States and offered the best and the worst of medical care. Most residency programs were located in cities. The best in New York were at some of the academic private pavilions dotting Manhattan such as Mount Sinai hospital. The worst were at some of the small cash-cow private hospitals in "the neighborhoods." In addition, the city operated 19 municipal hospitals across the five boroughs and several had academic affiliations. The quality of training and care in this system was spotty. The hospital I trained in offers a picture of care for the poor and what U.S. psychiatry was like then. The less common psychoanalytic country club retreats and the many well-appointed offices of urban private practice psychiatrists offered leisurely psychotherapy to a limited number of financially well-off patients. This image of psychiatry in the United States is still presented by Hollywood, but it is outmoded.

My medical school, New York Medical College, was then located in Manhattan and was decades away from purchase by the New York Catholic Archdiocese and its move to bucolic Westchester county north of the city.[2] The school was affiliated with two hospitals, Flower Hospital on Fifth Avenue and 106th Street for the rich and famous, and Metropolitan Hospital, a city-owned affair off First Avenue and 101st Street for the poor, Hispanic, and people of color.

Pleading minimal funding and with the medical school's acquiescence, Metropolitan Hospital had no interns (persons who had graduated from medical school but who had a restricted license requiring more training), and so they used medical students as substitutes. We had no degrees, no licenses, and no salaries: the cheapest labor. We paid the school for the privilege of working 80 hour weeks as we rotated through the hospital's various clinical services. Exploitation of house staff (interns, residents, and postresidency fellows) continued into the twenty-first century throughout the country with limits on work hours to reduce medical error from fatigue only recently becoming a national requirement.[3]

The More Things Change the More They Stay the Same

There were many lessons to learn as a fourth year medical student at a city-run hospital in the 1960s. The conflicts surrounding the lessons are still central to the national debate almost a half century later. On the Ob-gyn service we saw 10–20 young women every night who came to our emergency room suffering with an incomplete abortion. Abortions were then illegal. If you were rich, however, you went to a fancy hospital where your doc "winked" and said your periods were too heavy and that you needed a "D and C," dilatation and curettage. That procedure removed any pregnancy. If you were poor and from East Harlem, you went to one of the butcher-women on East 101st or 102nd Street and took some toxic brew or had a coat-hanger procedure. The latter was as you imagine it and removed part of the pregnancy. Then the survivor was sent off to our hospital for the rest. If the woman was lucky, we did the D and C and all was well. Some had a ruptured uterus and the surgeons removed it. They also removed the ovaries making young women suddenly postmenopausal. Few received hormone replacement therapy. The really unlucky women ended their trip from the abortionist with blood poisoning, went into toxic shock, and died. The women who went to the abortionist knew the risks they were running but they still went. I have no doubt that poor young women will do so again should abortions once again become illegal. The present debates over abortion ignore them.

The Ob docs were not distraught by this carnage. They did not seem to like women. One Ob resident almost sexually assaulted a prostitute in mild heroin withdrawal who had a ruptured uterus from an abortion on 101st Street. She was in terrible pain and feared the pelvic examination. He didn't care and told her to spread her legs with the encouraging, *"you do that for a living."*

Poor people then as now do not have their own private physician. When sick they delay seeking help until the illness is too disabling and then they go to their local emergency room. No one today who is advocating cutting Medicaid or who is against adequate health care for all is poor. Like many of the city's hospitals it was routine to see young diabetics without toes or lower legs, alcoholics with limb-threatening frostbite, persons with wounds infested with maggots, and cancer patients too far gone with metastases at the first visit. I saw my only patient with leprosy there, making the diagnosis from the classical "leonine" facial features. Patients with tapeworms and other parasitic infestations were regularly encountered at the hospital's clinics. Toddlers with lead poisoning from hungrily eating the sweet lead-laden paint peeling from their tenement's walls had seizures and were rushed to the hospital's pediatric emergency room. The ped-ER was dubbed, *"The Cage."* Babies with rat bites were the worst horror.

Medicaid was created in 1965. It eventually provided more funds to public hospitals and clinics to offer a health care safety net for the poor. Even with it, patients at public hospitals were under duress. As our facility had no air conditioning, patients sweltered in the summer heat. Several died of heat stroke. Fourth year students were assigned to bring patients ice water on particularly hot nights, but the ice melted well before the last patient was hydrated. The medication budget was always short and the psychiatry service ran out of its primary antipsychotic, Thorazine (chlorpromazine) by the 26th of most months.

Patients waited for hours to be seen. As a psychiatric resident, I was told by my supervisors that poor people don't keep appointments, and when they do show up, they come late and don't follow advice. These pronouncements were uttered as if the poor had some genetic defect affecting time management. I was then assigned to a psychiatric medication clinic with

180 enrolled patients almost all of whom had been psychiatrically hospitalized at one time or another. I was told that I could run my clinic any way I wanted. Most of the faculty was interested in psychoanalysis not seriously ill psychiatric patients or psychopharmacology. As long as I didn't kill anyone and professed an interest in psychotherapy, they were content. Today, the supervision of residents is strict. Much of the driving force for this change, however, seems to be about maximizing health insurance reimbursement. Keeping residents from "doing in" the patient population is a bonus.

My residency was considered one of the better ones and was considered progressive for its eclecticism. It presented several versions of psychodynamic theory and practices not just the Freudian perspective, and included what was then almost *avant-garde* group and family therapies. We had extensive training in recognizing and eliciting the signs and symptoms of classic psychiatric disorders. Very few programs then offered the degree of psychopharmacology training we received.

In 1967, like so many psychiatric trainees, I was on my own in that medication clinic. That we had such a clinic was unusual. The only help I received was from my fellow residents or from what I could glean from psychiatric medical journals. For the first month, each Thursday afternoon I faced a packed waiting room. I met with each patient and any family members available and at the end of the visit I told them the date and time I'd see them next. I told them that if they showed up on time I would see them on schedule. There would be no long waits. After 3 months the clinic ran smoothly and the patients came on time. They generally followed my advice.

In those days psychiatric residents were required to spend 6 months seeing patients at a state mental hospital. Our residency sent us to Manhattan State. Anyone driving across the Triborough Bridge or along the upper FDR drive along the East River in Manhattan can't miss the lifeless mass of bone-colored buildings emerging from Wards Island. Manhattan State used to house thousands of patients, some living there for decades. One rather mild-mannered patient had been there for 19 years when I met him because he had committed a crime while psychotic and was sentenced to Manhattan State until he recovered. He apparently never did. His crime was purse snatching. A dietician at Manhattan State proudly told me that they fed all the inmates for seventy-seven cents per person per day. The chronically mentally ill poor have always had it tough.

Manhattan State was a living psychiatric museum. Patients wandered about the grounds, some moaning, others shouting, as if they were inmates in a nineteenth-century European asylum. Sitting in any one of the many lobbies around mid-day, when patients returned for their noon medication dose, was an opportunity to visit the past. Many patients had odd movements that were new to me. I followed the most interesting of these patients to their ward, found out who they were, and then retrieved their records to see what had happened to them. Connecting each odd movement to specific brain impacts in the patient's life, to their other abnormal behaviors, or to a specific diagnosis was a lesson never to be forgotten.[4] No present day high-tech procedure has yet topped skilled observation in the diagnosis of patients with behavioral syndromes. The patient records at Manhattan State were voluminous and detailed. The richness provided an understanding of the patient from almost any theoretical perspective. These patients still exist, but residents today are not required to evaluate and treat them, and thus learn from the chronically psychiatrically impaired. Psychiatric trainees today know little about such illnesses.

Psychiatric residents today also do not know how to write a meaningful description of their patients. The Manhattan State charts were the quality of the efforts of a fine novelist. From them you'd learn the patient's life story and then the story of the patient's illness. The descriptions captured the patient's image and personality. Today, brief notes are standard. A sketch of the patient's symptoms that relate to a few necessary official criteria is considered sufficient. After reading a resident's and often a fellow faculty member's admission note, I often have no idea what the patient is like or what illness he or she actually has. Some leaders of U.S. psychiatry argue that all the detail is not needed; the symptoms listed in the official diagnostic manual (the *DSM* or *Diagnostic and Statistical Manual*) are sufficient. They dismiss the rich descriptions of the past stating that back then, as there were fewer therapeutic interventions, psychiatrists had a lot of free time on their hands and so spent it writing lengthy patient anamneses. But many of the patient stories in this book illustrate the falsehood of these claims. The ability of many in our field to describe a patient well enough to delineate the patient's actual illness to a third party has deteriorated.

DOGMA DERAILS DATA

In the 1960s U.S. psychiatry was dominated by psychoanalytic thinking and psychoanalysts occupied all important positions in medical school departments of psychiatry and on national boards. Only two psychiatry chairmen (they were all male) were not analysts. One's claim to fame was giving LSD to an elephant in an agitated state. The elephant died.[5] Neurochemical systems were just being identified and delineated, so biological psychiatry had yet to fully emerge.

Freudian Orthodoxy Dominated Thinking and Training

The influence of psychoanalysis in the 1960s on the training of psychiatric residents and in the care of psychiatric patients was pervasive. The effectiveness of psychiatric medications and electroconvulsive therapy (ECT) could not be denied, but their effect was considered superficial and not addressing the patient's core problem, which was accepted as psychological. All patients received some form of psychotherapy, even the most psychotic of sufferers. Many "brands" of psychodynamic theory-based therapies emerged (e.g., Adlerian, Jungian, Adaptational), some with and others without the Freudian couch. Their common denominator was the notion of the unconscious mind that harbors various innate drives and structures shaped by childhood experience. Substantial deviations in the interactions among the drives, structures, and external world would lead to symptoms. To resolve the symptoms, the patient, with the help of the therapist, has to understand the deviations and somehow reshape them toward normalcy. None of the brands had or has proven efficacy.

I saw hundreds of patients during my residency. I was required to provide psychodynamic therapy for many of them, but I was never asked to order an electroencephalogram (EEG) assessing the brain's electrical activity as an expression of its functioning. Neurologists had been utilizing this clinical technology for decades. One of the senior faculty members, Max Fink, was an EEG expert and had an EEG research laboratory. The laboratory was housed far from the hospital and he was never asked to discuss EEGs with the residents or consult about a specific patient who might have benefited from such an assessment. The only brain imaging then available was the pneumoencephalogram, a discomforting method of using air and dye to visualize the brain's fluid compartments, its ventricular system, to determine if there was blockage or other abnormalities.[6] I never knew of a psychiatric patient at our hospital who had one. The faculty considered the patient's brain functioning only if the clinical situation was obvious (e.g., the patient had a recent stroke) and that consideration was done so that the patient could be transferred to another service. Other than the Rorschach ink blots and other psychoanalytic-related tests, I was never trained in nor did I see a psychiatric patient during my training receive neuropsychological testing. Intelligence testing had been available since the 1920s and systematic and validated neuropsychological assessment was available since World War II. It was recognized as essential in delineating the effects of traumatic brain injury, but the perspective that behavior results from the brain was not of interest to most in the field.[7]

Many big-city residency training programs were then associated with a psychoanalytic institution. Residents were encouraged to attend. Freud's works were treated as if scripture. Residents were also expected to have analytic training and preferably to also undergo a personal psychoanalysis. A few years after my residency experiences, I was asked as a young faculty member to give one of our department's internal lectures. The topic I chose was the genetics of behavioral disorders. Those in attendance thought well of my effort but those responsible for the residency training program were upset with the lecture's premise that schizophrenia and manic-depression were brain disorders associated with a substantial genetic vulnerability. They organized a "counterlecture" that reviewed the psychological theories of psychiatric disorders. I was not permitted to give another formal internal lecture to the trainees. A few years later, in the mid-1970s, I was a visiting professor at UCLA and was asked to see a patient with the residents and the medical students rotating in psychiatry. The patient was depressed, suffering from melancholia, a severe form of depressive illness. After the examination, the patient returned to her room and I pontificated as required. I opined that she was suffering from a brain disease and required biological interventions. When I finished a resident asked, *"Could you say something about her psychodynamics?"* I responded with, *"she has a brain disease, there isn't any psychodynamics associated with her illness."* The group was shocked, but we talked about it and the conference ended peacefully. Later that day I was in the office assigned to me for my visit when 10 or so faculty came in and asked to speak with me. They could not understand my statement to the trainees. Several said, *"And the residents say how empathic you were with the patient. How can you be like that and not accept a psychoanalytic perspective?"* It reminded me of the questioning of an atheist by a believer. How can a person be ethical and moral and not believe in God? Of course, how can a believer in God be a crook, a murderer, and so on?

Data Debunked Dogma

Psychodynamic theory presents the idea that much of human behavior and certainly personality is an expression of a metaphysical realm. The dynamic unconscious hangs out somewhere in the brain, but psychoanalysts rarely cared about that connection. What was important to them was that the unconscious exists out of our awareness and that it has been shaped by our childhood experiences. Psychoanalytic treatment was expected to reveal the conflicts between a person's unconscious and the real world and in doing so relieve patients of their difficulties. Couch or no couch, all forms of psychodynamic psychotherapy are based on this fundamental notion.

The weight of evidence today does not find classic psychoanalysis or long-term psychotherapies of much benefit.[8] In 1986, after almost a century of dominating psychiatric and Western artistic thinking and being "the face" of psychiatry, an investigator in the United Kingdom[9] reviewed the psychoanalytic literature and concluded that there was little evidence to support its being included as one of the treatments paid for by the British National Health Service. He found that the only studies that showed effects "did not use real patients." He cited several other similar reviews, one of which characterized psychoanalysis as "an expensive placebo."[10] He concluded that it was unethical to use public money to support a treatment without efficacy.

Almost a decade after that assessment, different reviewers of the literature found that the efficacy of psychoanalysis and long-term psychodynamic therapy was an "unresolved issue" because of a "lack of methodologically sound studies."[11] Another examiner of psychotherapeutics stated its use was "based on conviction alone."[12] Treatments of ill persons are not supposed to be placebo or based on conviction alone. Evidence-based treatment is today's standard. Any other medical treatment today with this track record would be taken off the market by the Food and Drug Administration (FDA). Psychiatric residents, however, still learn psychodynamic theory (Freudian and other brands) and must practice individual intensive psychotherapy. No classic couch is needed, visits are weekly rather than three to five times per week, and the therapist interacts more with the patient than does the analyst. But the premise remains that the patient is suffering from some unconscious psychological perturbation and the intervention needs to assist the patient in dealing with it. That's psychoanalysis "lite."

Two more recent and related evaluations of the psychotherapy literature detail all the studies of psychodynamic psychotherapy published between 1960 and 2004.[13] The focus was on randomized controlled trials. This methodology is an acceptable standard for clinical assessment of medical drugs. Subjects are assigned to one of two or more comparison groups by a randomized selection process and features of the groups that might confound the results are accounted for or controlled for in some fashion. This design is needed to avoid comparing apples and oranges. For example, if the study were to evaluate the cognitive functioning of politicians of different political stripes, it would be unfair to compare 60-year-old left-wingers with 40-year-old right-wingers. The two groups should be about the same age as cognition changes over those two decades and usually not for the better. The two investigations assessing psychoanalysis and other long-term psychotherapies found that the studies remained "quasiexperimental," which translates into "no Kewpie doll" or not up to scientific standard. Psychoanalytic therapy was found to be somewhat better than no treatment while there was substantial evidence supporting the use of cognitive behavior therapy for the treatment of some patients with depressive illness. Rather than focusing on the unconscious, cognitive-behavior therapy tries to help the patient deal with his or her distorted notions of life that increase the risks for illness.

The persistent present-day requirement that psychiatry residents be taught psychodynamic psychotherapy demonstrates the continued control of this aspect of the field over training. If psychodynamic therapies were medications, their support by the U.S. psychiatric establishment would be a scandal. Twenty years ago another reviewer who assessed the efficacy of these treatment efforts concluded that "The time has come to relegate psychoanalysis to its proper place as a moment in the historical development of psychiatry and a ripple in 20th century western culture."[14]

THE U.S. NAVY AS A MODEL FOR NEUROPSYCHIATRY

In the latter half of the 1960s the Viet Nam War was heating up and the draft was activated. A young medical doctor had two choices. The first alternative was that the newly minted physician could take his chances and hope that he would not be drafted. This was a bad bet. The risk of this strategy was that if it were unsuccessful, and it almost always was, the doctor would be called up as a general medical officer and the assignments for those physicians were rough. The alternative was to sign up immediately in the *Berry Plan*, guaranteeing entry, but permitting the doctor to finish his specialty training first. When activated, the Berry Planner would go on active duty as a specialist, doing the type of medicine he was fully trained to do.[15] I picked the Berry Plan and the navy. I requested assignment to one of the naval teaching hospitals.

Although U.S. psychiatry in the 1960s was deeply committed to psychodynamic theory and treatments, the U.S. navy of the 1960s was not. I was sent to the Naval Hospital in Oakland, California. It no longer exists. The hospital was the main West Coast receiving facility for naval and marine psychiatric evacuees from the Pacific theater during the Viet Nam War. It was a large hospital and clinic compound labeled as if it were a ship. Walls were bulkheads. Floors were decks. Ceilings were overheads. Hats were covers. Shirts were blouses. We ate in the officer's mess. The little kitchen on the ward was the galley. Beds were berths. Rooms were quarters. I never set foot on a warship while I was in the navy.

The U.S. navy then, and I suspect now, had many lessons to teach. It is an organization that does not easily accept change or individual points of view that are at variance with organizational positions. Yet it was less rigid and more tolerant than the psychoanalytic establishment of U.S. civilian psychiatry in the 1960s and 1970s. The navy was more open to new data-based ideas than civilian clinical psychiatry was then and is now. I obtained my first pneumoencephalogram of a psychiatric patient in the navy documenting his normal pressure hydrocephaly, a condition of enlarged brain ventricles without an increase in cerebrospinal fluid pressure.[16] I was able to obtain EEG studies of patients that I thought needed them. Cognitive testing was available. I was able to assess patients systematically and from a neuropsychiatric perspective without worry about criticism from psychoanalysts. The navy had no use for them other than for special "therapeutic community" projects for patients with a personality disorder. Although my residency training program in New York was highly regarded and produced the best known textbook in psychiatry of its era and the standard source for information needed to pass examinations for several generations of U.S. psychiatric graduates,[17] psychiatry in the navy was whatever the individual psychiatrist wanted it to be. The only clinical standard was that it had to work.

Navy psychiatry as I was able to practice it was neuropsychiatry. The units I ran with another Berry Planner were staffed primarily by corpsmen. I cannot say enough good things about them. They were smart, hard working, and caring. Each unit had a military nurse and a psychologist. We also had navy resident physicians and interns from several nearby San Francisco hospitals. We cared for patients from a medical model perspective. We did general medical examinations as well as behavioral evaluations. We did not rush to treat. We were not forced to prematurely discharge patients. No hospital administrator (senior officers) ever interfered with a specific patient treatment. I asked to establish an ECT program and the captain heading the psychiatry service "made it happen." We were able to systematically diagnose patients and only used the official *Diagnostic and Statistical Manual (DSM-II)* for labels. We were able to complete several clinical research projects on those units. It is extremely difficult to do bedside psychiatric research today at teaching hospitals because without some high-tech component the project will have difficulty obtaining funds. My experiences during the 2 years at the naval hospital established a clinical, research, teaching, and administrative neuropsychiatric model that I describe throughout this book.

Sailors and Marines Suffer from the Same
Conditions as the Rest of Us

During the Viet Nam era the U.S. military still relied on the draft for man-power, although many volunteered for duty in the never declared war. Many college students and young professionals were able to avoid induction and blue-collar folks and the poor were overrepresented among draftees. However, many citizens who were in service at that time had a high school and some college education. The numbers of participants were so large that the patients we treated were sociologically diverse and suffered from all the common psychiatric conditions.[18] We saw many patients. Patients with a drug-induced psychosis, however, were common. In the era of hard rock and Woodstock, many enlisted young men, as their civilian counterparts, used some form of a mind-altering drug beyond nicotine and caffeine. As frightening as it may sound, the heaviest users of marijuana were the parachute packers stationed in Guam. One patient insisted that he and his friends smoked 60 "joints" daily. Their job from morning to night was to repeatedly slowly walk beside a long thin table folding a stretched out para-chute into its carrying harness bag. No one in charge ever considered the dull repetitive act as stressful. No one in charge seemed to notice the cloud of foul-smelling smoke hovering over the parachute tables. Navy pilots, however, did, and performed their own checks to maximize safety. The double-checking offers a good clinical lesson. When I've failed to double-check another clinician's work-up for a patient that I'm asked to treat I've occasionally been unhappily surprised. The story of a young boy in Chapter 5 will illustrate the clinical need to do this.

The availability of mushrooms, LSD, peyote, cannabis, and other exotic Asian mind-altering substances was as common in the Viet Nam Theater as is candy corn on Halloween. U.S. forces used these substances with the gusto of kids trick or treating. The trick was that all these substances can produce brain damage that is permanent. The subtlety of this associa-tion was an important lesson in neuropsychiatry: all behavioral change originates in the brain. Studies show that drugs that substantially distort perceptions and elicit hallucinations can lead to permanent cognitive dys-function. This result is particularly likely if the user has a personal or fam-ily history of psychiatric illness, and thus already has some vulnerability to become ill, or the "dose" of the substance is substantial. The result, however, might not be easily detected if the user starts off with a very good brain. If you have 62 cards in your "deck" and you use drugs that discard 10 of them you're down to 52 and will appear normal. The "deck" nevertheless took a hit. A lot of "smart" kids in the 1960s used drugs and think they "got away with it," but many did not reach their predrug potential.[19]

A Drug That Adversely Alters Behavior Often Damages the Brain

Two people who illustrate the connection between some drug usage and brain damage come to mind. The first such person was a young man without previous psychiatric or neurological problems who was drafted from college. Although many college students received deferrals early in the war, this patient's draft board had a mind of its own, and he was inducted. After only a few months in theater, however, he was air evacuated and arrived at our hospital in an acute drug-induced psychotic state. We treated him with low doses of an antipsychotic drug and he quickly recovered, so his psychosis lasted less than a few weeks. On the unit he seemed socially normal. His vocabulary was good and most of the staff thought that after his discharge he would go back to school. In conversation, however, as the interaction progressed, his responses to our questions and comments became unfocused and not quite on the topic. The more complex the conversation, the more obvious were his difficulties. We decided to assess his cognition. One of the tests we administered was the standard IQ, the Wechsler Adult Intelligence Scale (WAIS), which was originally developed as a neuropsychological assessment of cognitive functioning not just as a measure of intelligence.[20] Using tests of cognition to assess a psychiatric patient's brain function was rarely considered in civilian psychiatry of the 1960s.

Given the patient's vocabulary (which is a rough gauge of preillness intelligence) and his education level, he should have done well.[21] But although his verbal IQ was reasonably high at 115 (100 is average), his performance IQ (involving more spatial functioning and seeing "big pictures") was strikingly low at 87 (100 is average). Previous testing required of all persons entering the navy showed that his performance then had been much more in keeping with his verbal abilities. His brain had taken a substantial hit. We discharged him to the Veteran's Administration (VA) hospital closest to his home and after 6 months he still had no plans to return to school or look for a job.

The second person was one of the corpsmen. He too had been drafted out of college where he was studying to be a high school teacher. A somewhat dour person, he had no personal or family history of psychiatric illness. He did well on our unit until one day when his judgment failed him. A patient of ours was being discharged from the open, step-down unit. To "celebrate," the patient, who had been hospitalized for a drug-induced psychosis, brought in a jug of orange juice and cookies to share with the staff and any patients on the unit. Fortunately no patients and no staff were there, except for the corpsman. He was going off duty and perhaps was distracted. Anyway, he was accommodating and he had a glass of the juice. The corpsman then went outside to the hospital's big lawn for a game of touch football. Within a half hour I received a call to come immediately to the emergency room. There I found the corpsman in restraints, agitated and frightened. He was screaming that the football had lodged in his head and that he was going to die. I gave him a single intramuscular dose of an antipsychotic and within another half hour his psychosis abated. After another hour he seemed back to his usual self, though he was very tired, most likely sedated from the medication. No further treatment was needed. He had no previous history of drug use of any kind. He was not a smoker, and he rarely had more than a beer at a corpsmen party. The orange juice was laced with LSD.

After a few days off, the corpsman returned to work. He had no repeats of his hallucinosis. But he was unable to function as before. He was no longer efficient. He could not sustain his focus on tasks, and although he attended to the details of his tasks, he missed the "big picture." His hallucinations never returned, but after several months, he was medically discharged from the navy. A year later, my family and I were on vacation in Carmel California and we met the ex-corpsman standing alone on a street corner. He seemed distracted. He wasn't waiting for anyone and his responses to us were muted, his emotions dulled. He had no plans to return home to Oregon or to go back to school. One glass of LSD-laced orange juice can ruin a life. Perhaps it was the dose. Perhaps the corpsman's dour demeanor was a trait expression of vulnerability. But there is no doubt in my mind that the LSD damaged his brain. He, like the patient above, would have benefited from the similar type of rehabilitation offered to persons with traumatic brain injury. The injury to the two young men was chemical rather than mechanical, but nevertheless they suffered from a brain injury.

Today, on our hospital's psychiatric service we routinely recommend an evaluation of patients with extensive drug use akin to what is done for patients with brain injury. There is no successful treatment unless the problem is first identified. Unfortunately, there are few psychiatric rehabilitation programs in the country modeled on programs for persons with traumatic brain injury that provide similar treatment for persons who abused drugs. Only if the patient has suffered an obvious traumatic injury will he or she find rehabilitation services.

Despite all the patients from Viet Nam who used drugs and ended up at the naval hospital, most of our patients had the usual distribution of illnesses seen among young men then treated at civilian facilities. Many of our patients had premilitary psychiatric conditions. We learned that one successful Marine Corps recruiting station was established just outside a state mental hospital and that it did a bang-up business signing up newly discharged patients. Recruiters were rewarded for the numbers signed without penalty for those that quickly didn't make it in the service. One of our patients had been hospitalized 19 times for psychiatric reasons before he was recruited into the Marines.

Almost all of our patients recovered and almost all of these were given honorable discharges for medical reasons. Many received benefits as the navy then considered them to have a "service-connected" condition. Posttraumatic stress disorder (PTSD) had not been formulated yet (although "shell-shock" and "war neurosis" were the same idea and were well studied). Over a decade later, when PTSD was established as a psychiatric diagnosis most veterans who applied for benefits had preservice histories of alcohol and substance abuse, violence, and criminality. The behaviors that defined PTSD were present *before* the patient was in the service.[22] One of our hospitalized patients had a necklace of ears from the Vietnamese he had killed. He did not find his collection of trophies to be brutal, and talked about killing as if it were an ordinary task. But this man was always callus and was violent long before he was drafted. Several studies reveal that previous subtle neurological difficulty sometimes expressed as proneness to violence and lack of empathy is a risk factor for enhanced violence when the person is exposed to combat. In a study of identical twins one with and one without PTSD, the twin unexposed to combat still showed the subtle neurological signs also seen in the combat-exposed twin. Both were vulnerable, but only the combat-exposed twin developed PTSD.[23]

DECISION

In the 1970s psychoanalytic theory and psychoanalysts, and therapists of other psychotherapy brands, still dominated U.S. psychiatry. The movement, however, was clearly on the wane. Many studies comparing these therapies to other forms of behavioral interventions found them to be mostly placebo in effect but costly in time and money.[24] These interventions were useless for the severely ill. Psychological explanations for schizophrenia that placed the onus on the mother were found baseless and destructive. The notions that depression was anger inward, gastric ulcer an internalized mother's bite, and other symbolic interpretations were seen to be equally silly and subjective.

My inclination and experiences as a resident and caring for patients in the navy taught me the value of examining psychiatric patients as would any specialist doctor. No couch. No vague responses while letting the patient ramble for a 50-minute hour. What I did then and do now is similar to what neurologists or cardiologists do in their evaluations. I probably spend more time with each patient, but that's likely due to my belief that I need to get the patient's "story" and then the "story" of the patient's illness. The signs and symptoms that I look for are as precise as in any other medical examination. My other inclination and experience indicate that psychiatric disorders are expressions of brain disease and dysfunction. Alexander Luria's *The Working Brain*[25] and other readings in neuropsychology provided the framework for neuropsychiatric practice. Socializing at cocktail and dinner parties was also a good motivator.

Anyone who has been to a cocktail party knows that before everyone is sloshed, newcomers always get asked, *"And, what do you do?"* The answer is defining. As a resident, I naively responded, *"I'm a psychiatrist."* The retelling of the questioner's recent dream was sure to follow with "shrink" jokes next in line. There is nothing as tedious as listening to someone else's dream. It's worse than sitting through slides of their summer vacation because at a cocktail party you can't escape into the dark. As "a shrink" you are supposed to sagely comment on the meaning of the dream. Back from the navy, I changed my response and said I was a behavioral neurologist or a neuropsychiatrist. I told other party-goers that I saw behavioral syndromes as expressions of brain disorder and in addition to seeing patients with mania, depression, psychosis, and other "psychiatric" conditions, I was interested in patients with behavioral problems due to brain injury, epilepsy, stroke, and dementia. That revelation often led to an awkward silence and then a change of subject. Sometimes my area of the room became sparsely populated. But that is what I did and still do. That Hollywood maintains the image of the analyst as the psychiatrist may be of dramatic value, but it doesn't help patients.

For the next 40 plus years I have practiced neuropsychiatry. The patient stories that are detailed in the succeeding chapters come from that experience. My hope is that someday, when some young physician is asked, *"And what do you do?"* the response, *"I'm a neuropsychiatrist,"* will be greeted by an awareness and appreciation of what that is.

CHAPTER 2

꜌꜊ꝏ

First Do No Harm

"And isn't the ignorance, after all, the most shameful kind: thinking you know what you don't."

Socrates in Xenophon's Memorabilia

"Make a habit of two things: to help; or at least to do no harm."

Hippocrates

As a fourth year medical student while acting as an intern but without an MD license a little girl died under my care. I've been told that my ministrations were not the cause of her death. What I know for sure is that during one sultry summer night I was asked to go through a medical-surgical unit to suction patients on respirators or those who had received a tracheostomy to help them breathe.[1] My job was to remove any built-up junk (secretions) from their lungs. Today such patients would be in an intensive care unit (ICU) or critical care unit under constant monitoring and if suction were needed, a qualified nurse or anesthesia person would do it. But it was 1964 in a New York, city-owned public hospital that ran out of money for medications the last week of the month. Who could blame them for using the students as doctors?

I recall wending my way half asleep to use a suction machine I had never used before and for which I had received only cursory instruction. I don't recall doing it correctly. Later that night a slight girl of 8 or 9 years who I had suctioned died. Perhaps it was not of my doing, but what I know for certain is that I did not know what I was doing. I have not allowed myself to be in such a situation again. Not knowing is the first step in learning. Being unaware of not knowing is the first step toward disaster. The most dangerous doctors are those who do not know their shortcomings. I've run across many in psychiatry.

THE DEADLY MIND–BODY DICHOTOMY

One of the more fundamental errors that often goes unrecognized and is repeatedly made by health care providers is the notion that the mind and the body are somehow intrinsically dissimilar, each made of different stuff. If a patient's heart or kidneys go haywire, it is understood that the difficulty results from a physiological or anatomic problem that adversely affects the functioning of those organs. When the mind goes haywire there is the assumption among many physicians and the general public that some psychological perturbation has occurred outside of brain function. Attributing the behavioral difficulty to a pathological brain event is rarely considered first unless the evidence is overwhelming, and even then, maybe not. If the patient's behavioral syndrome emerges amid some environmental turmoil, that uproar is also assumed to be the offender or at least is identified as abetting in the mugging of the patient's psyche. The diagnosis and management of the patient are commonly based on this interpretation of behavioral change. The term *psychiatric*, a mental or metaphysical process, rather than *neurological*, a brain or nerve process, captures the psychological perspective of behavior.

On the surface, these considerations do not seem unreasonable. Substantial stress is not good. Sustained stress has been associated with many medical conditions and may trigger their exacerbation. However, when stress is quickly followed by a stroke, a heart attack, the exacerbation of diabetes, acute thyroid disease, hypertension, and more, no competent physician takes the position that the stroke or heart attack or whatever organ disease emerges is *qualitatively* different from the same organ disease that occurs without a preceding stressful situation. The adverse physiological changes impacting the organ with or without a preceding bad event are considered as the same thing. Similar acute procedures are used to assess and treat the patient. Counseling and education toward minimizing risk factors may be encouraged when stress is a precipitating factor, but no one puts acute cardiac patients without stress in an ICU and those with stress in group therapy. This is not a good business plan. When melancholia, mania, or psychosis emerges during a stressful period of life, however, the stress may surely be the trigger, but it is not the cause. The melancholia, mania, and psychosis are reflections of an exacerbated brain disease. These diseases can't be talked away. The sufferer can't "pull himself together." Just like syndromes reflecting dysfunction of other organs, many behavioral syndromes indicate a brain in a dysfunctional state that requires medical interventions.

In the 1960s, the interpretation of all behavioral syndromes was Freudian or some variation of that theme. Psychiatric medications (psychotropics) and electroconvulsive therapy (ECT), however, were known to be effective at relieving many psychiatric syndromes, and there was grudging recognition that the brain was somehow involved in the etiologies of some psychiatric conditions. Nevertheless, the root causes of the syndromes were still widely considered to be psychological not anatomical or physiological. An underlying metaphysical unconscious was believed to influence behavior and it was accepted that under certain stresses this influence could result in abnormal behavior. Depression was seen as inward-directed anger. Mania was a psychic flight away from depression. The neuroses that encompassed anxiety disorders, obsessions and compulsions, and personality problems were envisioned as an assortment of deviations and fixations in psychosexual development. Schizophrenia and autism were attributed to various parenting short-comings. The effects of psychotropic medications were deemed palliative and not dealing with the "real" problem. ECT's effectiveness was said to be the result of the depressed patient feeling "punished" by the treatment, which in turn led to the relief of the patient's depressive guilt. When "sham" ECT, during which the patient experiences all aspects of the procedure except the seizure and so believes a treatment was given, was shone not to work, the "punishment" theory was reluctantly abandoned.

When the evidence started to amass that patients with behavioral conditions had chemical, physiological, and anatomic perturbations in their brains, the evidence was first ridiculed and its proponents were often demonized. When the evidence became overwhelming for the biological nature of many behavioral syndromes, it was ignored for years by psychoanalysts and psychotherapists who continued to treat such patients as if their difficulties were of the mind and not of the brain. Psychoanalysts were still in dominant positions in the field and denied advancement and positions to psychiatrists identified as "biological" and "anti-Freudian."[2]

But despite the efforts of psychoanalysts to cling to control of U.S. psychiatry, the data were not on their side and today it is not fanciful to state that no matter how complex the thought, emotion, or behavior, no matter how intricate the determinants are of these expressions, they ultimately derive from the brain. This does not change the fact that many physicians today still operate within the mind–body construct. But not to consider abnormal behavior as the result of brain dysfunction in the evaluation of every person with newly emerged behavioral problems is to court disaster. Harm will be done. The following patient encountered in the 1990s sadly illustrates this point.

A Man Who Couldn't Pay Attention to His Left

Over the course of an evening, a young man experienced increasing numbness over the left side of his body. He went to his local emergency room (ER). The ER physician observed that the man was anxious (who wouldn't be under those circumstances?). The man also said that he was under substantial stress at work.

So, there's the patient, stressed-out at work, anxious, and saying that he was numb on the left side of his body. The ER physician's examination revealed that the patient indeed had reduced sensation on his left side, but that the loss of sensation ended sharply at the midline (the imaginary line dividing the body into left and right). In medical school, we are all taught about "dermatomes," strip-like areas along the skin that represent the nerve distributions for sensation. If you can determine which dermatomes show the problem, such as decreased sensation or numbness, then you know which nerves are involved and that information will help toward the diagnosis. The difficulty for the ER physician, however, was that dermatomes do not end at the midline; they interlace like fingers can. In other words, if the patient's distress was a nerve problem, the numbness should have followed a dermatome pattern and not ended abruptly at the midline.

In medical schools today, let alone 15 or so years ago when this patient showed up at his local ER, all students are also taught that if there is no clear anatomic or physiological explanation for the patient's symptoms, the symptoms are psychological. This Freudian notion is still applied in psychiatry's official diagnostic system. We do not fess up to our ignorance, we are taught to blame the patient for being a psychological wimp and not having what it takes to deal with life's slings and arrows. We sometimes call the patient names like hysteric or offer the slander that the patient has a conversion disorder. This term reflects the notion that the perturbed psychic energy (whatever that is) is too difficult for the patient to cope with and so it is converted (thus the term) into a physical symptom. The mind disables the body. So the ER physician concluded that the patient was suffering from a stress-related psychosomatic problem, gave him a minor tranquilizer, and referred him to a shrink. Later that evening the patient died.

Sometimes harm results from an overt act; sometimes harm occurs by omission. What is not commonly taught in medical school is that when a patient has a rather abrupt behavioral change it is *always* the brain until proven otherwise. Also not taught is that while dermatomes cross the midline, one of our brain structures, the centrally located thalamus (and its cortical associates in the parietal lobes of the cerebral hemispheres), pays attention to somatosensory information from the midline out. So groups of nerve cells (nuclei) in the right side of the thalamus pay attention to the left side of the body. The left thalamic nuclei pay attention to the right side. Dysfunction in the thalamus can result in spatial neglect involving the opposite (contralateral) side of the body and external space. Sometimes it is the cortical extension of the thalamus, the parietal lobes, that are dysfunctional. But such neglect always derives from dysfunction in the brain areas subserving this form of attention. When that attention is disrupted the patient may subjectively experience numbness on the side of the body opposite from the trouble. Sometimes, when both sides of the thalamus are affected, the experience can be delusional and the patient feels as if he is dead or that his body has disappeared or has rotted away. Some delusions of nihilism result from lesions in the thalamus or parietal lobe.[3]

The cause of the young man's numbness was an aneurysm that bled into the right side of his thalamus causing the loss of attention and subjective experience of numbness on his left side. Had the ER physician obtained a computed tomography (CT) scan of the patient's head, it would have revealed the bleed and the ER physician would have rushed the patient for life-saving emergency neurosurgery. Bleeding aneurysms can often be safely clipped. Instead, the ER physician referred the patient to a psychiatrist. The official final cause of death of the patient was cerebral hemorrhage, but I think what actually killed the young man was the mind–body dichotomy and the ER physician not knowing what he didn't know. He was and is not alone. The official diagnostic manual for all of U.S. psychiatry and for most of the world for that matter (the *DSM*) has several examples of "conversions" that are anything but.

CONVERSION DISORDER, A CLASSIC PSYCHIATRIC PEJORATIVE

Conversion is a psychodynamic construct that considers the psyche discombobulating the soma by converting psychic energy into a "body" symptom. The definition requires that the symptoms have no anatomic or physiological explanation. The latest *DSM*, *DSM-IV*, requires a "psychological" element to be present, perpetuating the notion. The *DSM* also offers several examples of conversion symptoms that in fact have clear pathological explanations, thus violating its own standard for the diagnosis. The *DSM* doesn't know what it doesn't know, meeting my criteria for a dangerous document. It opines that numbness of the hands and feet (termed stocking-glove anesthesia) is a conversion, although it is a classic sign of peripheral neuropathy often associated with diabetes and other conditions.[4] Astasia abasia is another symptom considered to be a conversion as the patient appears to have no neurological problem while prone but when standing and trying to walk becomes wobbly and slowly falls to the ground, rarely suffering injury. But astasia abasia is associated with migraine and other neurological conditions.[5] These relationships have been understood for many years but present day U.S. psychiatry has lost sight of them.

As disturbing as the young man's death described above, the ER physician's efforts did not meet the definition of malpractice because it did not violate the "general standard of care" requirement. This means that if the procedures accepted by the medical establishment of the community (a vague term that ranges from local to nationwide) have been followed, the patient's outcome may be bad, but it was not due to malpractice, just common practice. If common practice is not good, it needs to be corrected, but the medical community as a whole and the specific physician will be held liable. The general standard of care as expressed by the *DSM* perception of "conversions" and "hysterias" is to treat such conditions as psychological perturbations. The ER physician did what he had been taught to do and what most psychiatrists then and perhaps today would do under similar circumstances.

Some of the greatest harm done to psychiatric patients has been the result of applying the notion of hysteria or "psychogenic disorder" as the explanation for a patient's difficulties. The diagnosis usually involves a male physician (commonly a psychiatrist or a neurologist) who cannot figure out what is wrong with his female patient and so slaps her with a "moving violation." Ignorance and sexism often account for the diagnosis. Nowhere else in medicine is the onus placed upon the patient for the shortcomings of the physician or of the discipline itself. In addition to the conditions above, also incorrectly listed as conversions are limb paralysis or localized weakness (seen with migraine and multiple sclerosis), aphonia (only able to whisper and a feature of catatonia, Parkinson's disease, and several other conditions), difficulty swallowing or the sensation of a lump in the throat (*globus hystericus,* associated with melancholia and multiple sclerosis), and urinary retention (from many medications and subtle genitourinary disease). Loss of touch or pain sensation, double vision, blindness, deafness, and hallucinations have all been considered to be "conversions," but are associated with migraine and other neurological disorders. At one time Parkinson's disease, St. Vitus' dance (the result of strep infection toxins damaging the basal ganglia in the brain), tetanus (lockjaw), and eclampsia (hypertension and its consequences during pregnancy) were considered neurotic disorders and examples of hysteria.[6] Denial of illness supposedly expressed as *la belle indifférence* (French for "I don't care" but literally a beautiful indifference), and hemianesthesia, classic signs of conversion, are associated with thalamic disease. Many so-called nonepileptic fits are in fact partial complex seizures that can be identified by laboratory studies. Anatomically inconsistent pain patterns said to be conversions are often prominent early signs in multiple sclerosis.[7] In addition to its association with migraine, astasia abasia is also associated with dementia[8] and midline cerebellar and corpus callosum lesions. The former structure is a wormy spheroid mass below and behind the cerebral hemispheres and is involved in motor procedural learning and motor regulation. Many physicians are unaware of its cognitive functions. The corpus callosum is a bridge of connecting fibers between the two cerebral hemispheres and is implicated in several unusual symptom patterns unfamiliar to most physicians.

Adding Insult to Injury

Just over a decade ago I met a patient whose experience I believe illustrates the ignorance and bias behind the notion of conversion and the decline of U.S. psychiatry. She was the subject of an academic psychiatric case conference. The patient was a middle-aged never-married health care provider who had left her job to care for her elderly mother who was suffering from cognitive difficulties. After 6 months of this effort the daughter became inattentive, said she no longer had the energy to care for her mother, and was feeling overwhelmed. Her sleep and appetite declined, although she did not lose weight. She was subdued and frequently cried. She felt guilty about her inability to help her mother.

Most psychiatrists reading the above paragraph will instantly recognize that the patient meets *DSM* criteria for depression and fits the image of a person with a psychological dependency problem. The evidence for this notion was her never marrying (although there are a zillion reasonable reasons people don't) and her giving up a professional job to care for her mother who might have been cared for in other ways.

A senior psychiatric resident and his supervisor reached the dependency conclusion, diagnosed the woman as depressed, and prescribed an antidepressant. The medication had minimal effect. Because she was an outpatient and up until that time was in good general medical health, no other assessment was done, which is poor but is now standard psychiatric care throughout the United States. As a resident, I would have been required to provide some assessment of the patient's general medical health and I would have done a general medical and neurological examination. After several months of treatment, however, the resident in this story noted that the patient was exhibiting "odd" movements and referred her to a neurologist.

This superficial and limited psychiatric evaluation is unfortunately common. Thinking only of a psychological depression as the cause of the patient's difficulty was a poor diagnostic assessment. The details of the psychopathology were vague. A physician toward the end of specialty training defining a movement problem in the imprecise, nontechnical term of "odd" is a sign of the field's decline. Although psychiatry in the 1970s and 1980s did not have the advantages of high-tech imaging and sophisticated laboratory testing, residents were expected to be thorough in their history taking and examinations and precise in their descriptions of their patients' symptoms.

The department of neurology at the time of the referral of the woman in this story had a special interest in movement disorders, so the consultation sounded like a good idea. The neurologist observed the following: the patient looked mildly depressed as "anticipated from partial treatment." She exhibited "frontal lobe" cognitive problems attributed "to the depression." Both of these interpretations would have been reasonable, except that the neurologist also noted that the patient's movements were "cerebellar-like." The pattern should have rung the diagnostic bell.[9]

The cerebellum, its name means "little brain," is connected as part of a functional system to the frontal lobes and so cerebellar disease, in addition to characteristic motor features, is associated with frontal lobe cognitive problems and avolitional apathy that can be mistaken for a mild form of depression.[10] The neurologist should have put it all together. Instead, without further evaluation, he concluded that the patient had a "psychogenic disorder." Her depression and overdependency on her mother, her never marrying, and her stopping work to care for her mother all indicated a psychological "conversion disorder, not a neurological disease." Sexism and ignorance trumped data.

The patient returned to the resident physician who accepted the conversion disorder diagnosis as he was taught to do. His psychiatrist supervisor also accepted these conclusions. They tried psychotherapy and different medication combinations but the patient's movements became worse. After a year she was no longer able to care for herself. She was then referred to our case conference, but not to reexamine the diagnosis but rather to assess her ability to be hypnotized for treatment of her conversion. This would have been great stuff in nineteenth-century Paris with Charcot, the famous neurologist, holding court. In a twenty-first century major medical center, it is in my view bizarre.

The psychiatrist leading the conference tried to hypnotize the patient but found her to be a "poor" candidate. In such paradigms, it is never the lack of effectiveness of the treatment or the skill of the practitioner. It is always the fault of the patient. Worse, sitting uncomfortably in front of us was a woman exhibiting not hysteria or conversion but several severe and classic features of cerebellar disease.[11] Her performance on tests of "executive function" (e.g., planning, problem solving, generating ideas, abstract thinking) was within the dementia range.[12] The patient was aware that she had substantial motor and cognitive difficulties and became tearful when discussing them. Because her symptoms were assumed to be "self-inflicted," however, there was initially little empathy or sympathy for her among the conference's participants.

I detailed my alternative understanding of the patient's symptoms as expressions of cerebellar-pontine degeneration (the pons is a brainstem "swelling" below the cerebellum; it means "bridge"). As the condition can run in families, the presenting resident was asked to find out about similar symptoms in the patient's family. After all, the mother did have cognitive problems. To his credit the resident did further work, and reported back to the group the following week that the patient's mother and maternal aunt had similar movement problems and cognitive decline. Brain imaging confirmed the clinical diagnosis of cerebellar-pontine degeneration. There is no cure for familial cerebellar-pontine degeneration, but blaming the patient for her illness was certainly adding insult to the injury of her brain disease.

The "Conversion" Diagnosis as a Substitute for Ignorance

In addition to the conditions mentioned above, catatonia is another syndrome that is often misdiagnosed as a conversion or as a psychogenic movement disorder. Although catatonia is historically linked to the concept of dementia praecox and its modern image as schizophrenia, catatonia is a syndrome that is associated with many conditions, most often mood disorder. The following acutely ill patient who experienced a period of catatonia was transferred from a neurology service to a psychiatry inpatient unit with the diagnosis of conversion disorder.

The patient was an elderly woman who had been living independently until she was diagnosed as being depressed. She was prescribed buproprion (Wellbutrin). Buproprion is a heavily promoted agent and many psychiatrists have bought the erroneous claims that the drug is a good antidepressant and will not induce a mania. In fact, its ability to obtain a remission is no better than a placebo. The switching from a depression into a mania from an antidepressant medication has been overblown and no agent appears to have an advantage at minimizing the change. The manufacturer barely mentions that use of buproprion is associated with seizures.[13]

After a week or so of taking buproprion, the patient progressively lost the ability to care for herself. When she deteriorated into a state of "confusion," her daughter brought her to the hospital's ER. There the patient became mute and immobile, signs of catatonia that can follow a seizure.[14] This association, however, was not considered and no electroencephalogram (EEG) of her brain waves was done. Instead, her symptoms were thought to be the result of a stroke and she was admitted to the neurology service. Brain imaging indicated mild old vascular disease, but provided no explanation of her present condition. The mutism and immobility resolved within an hour of admission, which is consistent with catatonia termed postictal (postseizure) catalepsy (remaining in a prolonged position).

Over the next several hours, however, the patient's condition fluctuated abruptly from "confusion" to apparent alertness. It was "observed" that her episodes of confusion occurred when her daughter was present, but resolved when the daughter left the room. This "observation" was undoubtedly erroneous but when physicians don't know what is going on with a patient they get anxious and either throw all sorts of treatments at the patient hoping one will work, or they come up with all sorts of notions to explain their lack of success. In this case, the mother was considered to be in some sort of psychic turmoil involving the daughter. Thus, the alternating periods of confusion and alertness were interpreted by the neurologists as evidence of hysteria or conversion disorder. The catatonic features noted in the emergency room were also considered to be part of the conversion, and the previous diagnosis of depression was used as "evidence" favoring the psychological diagnosis and justifying the patient's transfer to the psychiatry inpatient unit. By the way, transfers are not unilateral decisions, the consultation psychiatrists and the inpatient psychiatrists were willing to accept the patient as experiencing a psychogenic and not a neurological disorder. The consultation psychiatrists working at that hospital today would not make this mistake.

One of my colleagues on the psychiatric inpatient service, however, was suspicious that the patient was suffering from a neurological disease and not a psychological process, and asked me to see the patient. When I met her, she had just been transferred. She was lucid, but was subdued emotionally and was slow in her movements and responses. She appeared tired. She was pessimistic about her future. Prior to hospitalization, she had been eating and sleeping poorly. Although this picture was consistent with her diagnosis of depression, she retained some humor, which was inconsistent with the degree of her depressive features. As we chatted, she abruptly exhibited the periods of "confusion" that the neurologists mentioned but had never precisely described. By the way, only for psychiatric patients are imprecise terms such as "confusion" accepted. Can you imagine a cardiologist getting away with listening to a patient's heart beat and saying the sounds of the beats are "funny"? In this instance the patient's so-called episodes of confusion turned out to be a speech and language syndrome termed transcortical sensory aphasia. The episodes began and ended abruptly and lasted but a few minutes. Strokes do not produce on and off again aphasia, but seizures do. We obtained an EEG and discovered that the neurology department had transferred a patient to us in status epilepticus (rapidly occurring or continuous seizures). They ignored the brain and opted for a psychological explanation of the patient's symptoms. We treated her with a powerful intravenous anticonvulsant medication and her "conversion" disappeared along with her seizures.

The Psychogenic Myth

Missing the brain disease and interpreting the patient's symptoms as expressions of psychic turmoil are all too common. This misinterpretation is unnecessary as there are many studies that undermine the notions of conversion and psychogenetic disorders.[15] More than 60% of patients labeled as hysteric or as having a conversion are women. Others most likely to be misdiagnosed as "hysterical" are homosexual men, patients with previous psychiatric diagnoses, and those with a plausible psychological explanation for their condition. The biases are obvious. One large study[16] described a number of patients whose diseases were ultimately identified, but who had been initially diagnosed as hysteric because the original doctors couldn't figure out what illnesses the patients actually had.

Many severe neurological conditions are associated with features that initially can elicit the diagnosis of conversion disorder.[17] Among the identified causes of so-called motor conversions are amyotrophic lateral sclerosis (Lou Gehrig's disease) and other motor neuron disorders. A more common explanation for some motor conversions is the Guillain-Barré syndrome.

This is a disorder in which the body's immune system attacks part of the peripheral nervous system causing varying degrees of weakness or tingling sensations in the legs. In many instances, the weakness and abnormal sensations spread to the arms and upper body. These symptoms can increase in intensity until the muscles cannot be used at all and the patient is almost totally paralyzed. The rapidly progressive nature of the condition and its symptom migration upward, rather than in the expected downward march, give Guillain-Barré an exotic quality that can lead clinicians down the metaphysical garden path.

Other conditions that have been mistaken as hysteria or conversion include Huntington's disease, intracranial hemorrhage, malignancy, multiple sclerosis, myasthenia gravis, Parkinson's disease, postencephalitis syndrome, and systemic lupus erythematosis (an autoimmune disease). Mood disorder is another common condition among patients erroneously said to have a psychogenic movement disorder. Patients with melancholia, for example, can appear to have Parkinson's disease, experience tremors, and can be catatonic. All these features, however, resolve with proper treatment of the patient's depressive illness.[18]

Efforts to find some subtle brain perturbation that could explain the few patients who have received the psychogenic or conversion label but for whom no clear neurological or psychiatric cause could be identified have been unsuccessful. The focus has been on trying to understand "psychogenic movement disorders." The diagnosis is made in about 3% of patients who are seen at movement disorder clinics. Neuroimaging and neurophysiological studies including EEG assessing the brain's electrical activity and electromyography (EMG) assessing peripheral nerve functioning have been used. These studies are limited to just a few patients each, often just a single patient. Although modest brain functioning abnormalities are reported in these case reports, the patients in these investigations do not appear to have any clear explanation for their difficulties, and a unified neuroanatomical or neurophysiological pattern of dysfunction has not been identified. Given the lack of a clear understanding of patients with the psychogenic or conversion label and the long list of delineated neurological and metabolic conditions that were once considered psychogenic, it is best to do no harm and to consider these patients in the early stages (prodromes) of general medical or neurological conditions that will eventually emerge. These patients should be carefully evaluated and closely followed medically rather than being given the psychological label and sent for therapy.[19]

It would be nice to say that the patient situations described above and the needless death of the young man with left-sided numbness are rare events. Unfortunately, present-day psychiatric practice is replete with such errors because the field today is essentially no different than it was when I was a resident. In fact it's worse in many ways.

THE DECLINE OF PSYCHIATRIC CARE IN THE UNITED STATES
The Late Nineteenth Century

In the latter part of the nineteenth century U.S. psychiatry, at least in the Northeastern part of the country, was as good as any in the world.[20] Psychiatry was the decipline of neuropsychiatry and most practitioners understood behavioral syndromes to be reflections of brain or nerve dysfunction. The medical model of diagnosis prevailed. The rich tradition of descriptive psychopathology was still an essential part of the patient evaluation process. Neurologists who then cared for many "psychiatric" patients led the way. William Hammond, professor of the diseases of the mind at the Bellevue Hospital Medical College in New York City and President of the American Neurological Association reflected the quality of thinking. Hammond's textbook is a marvel of accurate observation of syndromes and careful consideration of the demographic and epidemiological findings in psychiatric illness. His conclusions rival those of present-day investigations bolstered by stringent methodology. Hammond's work, however, was influential only within the United States and only for a brief period.

Edward Spitzka, a New York City neurologist and President of the New York Neurological Society, considered psychiatric disorders as reflections of different brain diseases that were only waiting the detailing of their neuropathology. He offered a descriptive classification organized by what he understood to be either intrinsic brain disease (primary) or brain dysfunction resulting from disease in other organ systems (secondary). It took psychiatry in the United States another 90 years to recognize the value of this primary–secondary construct. Spitzka introduced the term *coarse brain disease* to characterize behavioral syndromes secondary to what we now define as neurological disease, differing from "mental disorders" only in the coarseness or identifiableness of the brain pathology. Spitzka affirmed that the ultimate understanding of the truth of psychiatric disease would derive from scientific inquiry, but that the goal was generations removed. Among his rich descriptions and classification substantially ahead of his contemporaries, he recognized mania and melancholia with the modern understanding of these conditions. Unlike his European counterparts, he recognized catatonia as having a favorable outcome. Delirium, as we see it today, was included in his classification as was a dementing process of late life suggestive of Alzheimer's disease. He also detailed frontal-temporal dementia decades before it was officially recognized. He described developmental disorders, hysterical insanity, a periodic insanity, and monomania (paranoia or present-day delusional disorder). His demographic and epidemiological conclusions about the major psychiatric syndromes rival present-day understanding.

Hammond and Spitzka and their colleagues provided a foundation for the application of the medical model to behavioral syndromes. Both, however, died before Freudianism took hold of American psychiatry, leaving the neuropsychiatric alternative to the psychoanalytic movement leaderless. American psychiatry stagnated in psychoanalytic thinking for the next 70 years. The rest of medicine moved forward.

By 1910, the diagnosis and management of psychiatric conditions varied greatly across the United States and was recognized as inadequate. In response, the American Medico-Psychological Association and the superintendents of mental hospitals in 1917 agreed on a unifying system that in time was to become the *DSM*. (American Medico-Psychological Association and the National Committee for Mental Hygiene, *Statistical Manual for Use of Institutions for the Insane*, New York, 1918.) In 1921, the association changed its name to the American Psychiatric Association, and through the organizing of the New York Academy of Medicine, the nomenclature of the "superintendent's document" was incorporated into the American Medical Association's classification of disease in 1933.

After World War II, the U.S. Army offered its modification to classification. The World Health Organization quickly followed with the sixth edition of its international classification of disease (*ICD-6*) that included mental disorders for the first time. The categories were psychoses (including mood disorders), psychoneuroses, character disorders, behavior disorders, and deficits in "intelligence."

The efforts to establish a medical classification system, however, floundered as the psychoanalytic movement flourished. The U.S. psychiatric establishment's interest in the signs and symptoms required to make a psychiatric diagnosis (i.e., psychopathology) and in the need to classify psychiatric syndromes waned. Psychiatric syndromes were theorized as expressions of "mental" or "psychological" perturbation and not the results of organ disease. Psychodynamic theory came to dominate American psychiatry, and attention to the biological aspects of psychiatric illness diminished. The field's focus became the dynamic understanding of the individual and not the search for which illness group the patient best fit. Amid great pessimism about the lack of any successful treatment for the psychiatrically ill, many psychiatrists gravitated to the psychoanalytic movement. Within a generation of Freud's 1909 North American lectures, the psychoanalyst became the face of psychiatry in the United States. Think of the movies and TV programs in which a psychiatrist is portrayed. They are almost always therapists and they are often depicted as shady or crazy. Almost all cartoons about psychiatry picture an analyst. As far as I have been able to find, every *New Yorker* cartoon about a psychiatrist, and there are a lot of them, depicts a psychoanalyst. The image of a male psychiatrist (almost always) in a comfortable chair, legs crossed, pad and pencil in hand, and a woman patient (most of the time) on a Freudian couch brings immediate recognition to the viewer. The fact that less than 5% of practicing psychiatrists offer this form of treatment today seems irrelevant to the media.

After Freud, Adolf Meyer was the most influential theorist to shape U.S. psychiatry in the first half of the twentieth century. Meyer emigrated from Switzerland in 1882 and eventually became president of the largest professional organization for U.S. psychiatrists, the American Psychiatric Association (APA). He headed the psychiatry department at Johns Hopkins and in 1912 established the Henry Phipps clinic there as the first psychiatric inpatient facility within a general medical hospital. Before that, and in many places in the United States to the present, psychiatric hospitals were free-standing private facilities or enormous state asylums for the mentally ill who were poor. At that time, John Hopkins was considered the preeminent hospital and medical school in North America, virtually guaranteeing Meyer great influence in the field. Meyer championed the notion that psychiatric disorders were individualized "reactions," or outgrowths of a person's unique biology and experience. In his view, efforts at classification were beside the point because even if patients appeared to have similar clinical features their biographical experiences would be different and so they would require different treatments.

The 1960s

In the 1960s psychiatry was into the second decade of the psychopharmacology era.[21] The first generation of antipsychotic and antidepressant drugs was available and helpful, but psychiatric diagnosis, particularly in the United States, was widely recognized as poor. Almost all patients with severe behavioral symptoms without obvious neurological disease were said to be schizophrenic. This was a far cry from Hammond's and Spitzka's era in which about 5% of patients were said to be hebephrenic, the version of the dementia praecox/schizophrenia construct that was then accepted in the United States as clinically valid. Then, about 50% of hospitalized psychiatric patients were diagnosed as suffering from manic-depression. The flip-flop in the diagnosis of the two major psychiatric syndromes is a prime example of the field's decline. One of my professors opined that he did not think manic-depression existed anymore and wondered whether there had ever been such a disorder. He was one of the core members that formulated the diagnostic system the country was then using, the *DSM-II*.

Every patient hospitalized on our unit who was psychotic, who was experiencing hallucinations or delusions, or who exhibited erratic behavior was diagnosed as schizophrenic. They all received an antipsychotic to quiet them down and to relieve their most prominent symptoms. Many were discharged still somewhat ill. Many were repeatedly rehospitalized as if stuck within a revolving door. Many were transferred to one of the large state mental hospitals in the New York City area where they languished, some for years. This sequence of events is pretty much the same today in many psychiatric settings except that there are many fewer state mental hospitals and many more psychiatric medications, so patients end up overmedicated or living on the streets of our cities.

The 1970s

After I returned from the navy in 1971, I became the director of the same inpatient unit on which I had worked as a resident. With my colleagues, we systematically applied more reliable and precise diagnostic criteria to our admissions (many of whom had been patients hospitalized during the tenure of my professor). We validated our diagnoses based on treatment response, family history of psychiatric illness, and other clinical variables. Rather than zero "manics," as had been the case for the previous decade, we found that almost 30% of acutely psychotic patients were suffering from mania on admission. They were not "excited schizophrenics" or "paranoid schizophrenics" as had been their diagnoses for years. Typically, a patient in a manic episode is irritable and expansive in thinking. The patient can be euphoric or at times distraught. Moods fluctuate rapidly and unpredictably. Their thoughts race. Their speech is rapid as many ideas spill out, overlapping each other, making it difficult to follow what they are saying. They may be delusional and they may hear voices, which is why so many were said to be schizophrenic.

We also found almost three-fold more patients with depressive illness than previously recognized. Schizophrenia dropped from 50% to under 5% of admissions.[22] These diagnostic changes were not just academic. Lithium was now clinically available and was a specific treatment for a patient in acute mania. Lithium's continued use also reduces the risk of recurrence of episodes. When the episode is most severe, ECT can be life-saving for a patient in acute mania.

Time and other studies proved us correct, but in the early 1970s many in the field scoffed at our findings. When we sent a series of papers based on our research to a prestigious psychiatric journal they were all quickly rejected and we were personally criticized by the reviewers. Our claim that schizophrenia was much less common than manic-depression was a threat to all the psychiatrists who made their living treating such patients or who had grants to study schizophrenia.

We did not give up. That first series of papers were constructed with the term "schizophrenia" early in their titles and "manic-depression" near the end. Editors often use the manuscript title to consider which group of reviewers is sent the manuscript because the editors don't have time to read all the submissions thoroughly. We, however, thought our papers were pretty good and should have been given a fair hearing, so we changed the titles around, with "manic-depression" now first and "schizophrenia" near the end. No other changes were made. We sent the papers back to the same editor who most likely automatically sent them on to reviewers who had an interest in manic-depression. These reviewers, of course, were delighted to see more data that showed that they were studying a common condition not a rare one. Grants are in part based on the number of people affected by the condition. Our papers were published in that journal with only minor changes. Today, manic-depression is identified as bipolar disorder in the *DSM*. It is recognized as a common condition.

Later that year the previous director of my unit visited. He was of a mind similar to my old professor and never made the diagnosis of manic-depression. He asked the nurses about several of his former patients and the staff generally offered good reports about them. Our recovery rates were substantially up and readmission rates were substantially down from the past since we were making more refined diagnoses and we were applying more specific treatments. The previous director finally asked about a patient who was then about age 60 and who had been ill for 40 years and had sustained many hospitalizations. She had always been diagnosed as schizophrenic and had always been treated with an antipsychotic.

"*So, how's Alice doing?*" he asked. The nurses beamed with pride. "*Never better,*" they said. For the first time in those 40 years Alice was living in her own apartment, had a job, was getting along well with her daughter, and had not been ill for over a year.

The previous director was taken aback, as such a dramatic change in a schizophrenic was unheard of. He asked about her treatment and the nurses told him that Alice had been prescribed lithium monotherapy during her last hospitalization and had remained on it. We had diagnosed her as manic-depressive not schizophrenic. She had experienced a quick and full recovery and had been well ever since; her daughter said, *"You gave me back my mother."* After a long pause, the previous director shook his head and said, *"Well, I guess some schizophrenics respond to lithium."*

All of the above shows that psychiatry in the United States in the 1960s and 1970s was not very good. The promise of Hammond and Spitzka was clearly unfulfilled. What leads me to conclude that U.S. psychiatry is no better or even worse today?

The 1980s

A colleague from the navy phoned me and asked me to see a friend of his who was hospitalized at our medical school's Veteran's Administration hospital affiliate. The friend was on the hospital's posttraumatic stress disorder (PTSD) unit, but my old colleague thought his friend was depressed. I met the man and found him to be profoundly depressed with melancholia.[23] He was despondent and almost delusional about his failures to help others while on active duty. He was terribly apprehensive and overwhelmed by even mundane chores. He had been recently abusing alcohol. As a EuroAmerican male approaching middle-age in a severe depression and an abuser of alcohol he presented a substantial suicide risk. With his permission, I called the director of the PTSD unit, a clinical psychologist, and conveyed my concerns. I offered to have the man transferred to the hospital's acute psychiatric treatment unit where he would be safe and where we could medically treat him for his melancholia. When he recovered, we would have him go back to the PTSD unit. The director of the PTSD unit, however, dismissed my concerns and said he would continue to treat the man psychologically. A week later the man hung himself. In my experience, almost all suicides can be prevented with proper awareness and treatment.

In the 1980s, the VA was committed to treating patients with the diagnosis of PTSD as if these patients all suffered from the same condition. The commitment was particularly intense for veterans who were in Viet Nam. VA hospitals across the country established specialized PTSD units that offered various psychological and milieu therapies. Almost no attention was paid to the brain functioning of these patients despite decades-old recognition of the incidence of behavioral difficulties resulting from combat-related closed head injuries (the skull remains intact but the brain still takes a beating). The PTSD diagnosis as it was then applied, however, was questionable as most of the patients given that diagnosis by the VA and who sought compensation from the VA during that era were long-time abusers of alcohol and street drugs and many had antisocial personality traits. Veterans in community samples who met the criteria for PTSD but who did not seek compensation, in contrast, were often found not to be antisocial but to have obsessive-compulsive disorder or an anxiety disorder.[24] No one doubted that the stress of combat was severe and that it could elicit symptoms associated with chronic stress. The concern was that all persons with the diagnosis did not suffer from the same illness and that applying treatments as if that were the case, as the PTSD unit director did to the patient who hung himself, was dangerous and was unlikely to benefit many sufferers.

At the height of the VA's focus on PTSD they offered grants to researchers in their system to study patients with the diagnosis. I was on the panel of researchers who reviewed and approved the grant proposals. We were hard-nosed and most applications were rejected as they reflected opinion and political pressures but not science. The system was not happy with us and arranged a workshop for the PTSD VA researchers from across the country to improve their proposals. We met in Washington, DC. Each panel member gave a seminar to the assembled researchers and then we broke up into small groups, each group led by a panel member. We had a lot of tough things to say to the researchers. I remember two incidents vividly.

A well-known physiological psychologist who had published many papers on acute and chronic stress began his presentation with the following anecdote. He told the audience of researchers that they were treating all patients with PTSD as if it reflected a homogeneous process. They were following the *DSM* approach in their research. He said that if they were to be successful they needed to recognize that all persons with war-related symptoms were not alike. He said, *"You have to account for people like me."* It turned out he was a World War II veteran who had fought in Europe and was one of thousands of GIs who entered Germany. He provided several dramatic examples of his combat experiences. He told the audience that a day didn't go by when he did not think about what happened to him during the war, or he had a bad dream about it, or he experienced an acute stress response triggered by some battle-like stimulus. He then told the audience, *"But I am not an alcoholic or drug user. I don't have violent outbursts and I don't have clinical depressions. I'm a tenured professor at a very good university. So your research designs have to consider other factors than just being in combat and the DSM definition of PTSD."*

The second event began as my group of VA researchers was settling in to discuss their research efforts. A late comer rushed in distraught. She was waving a grant application over her head as if it were a weapon. She came up to me and not quite shouting said, *"I just got word that you guys turned down this grant again. I don't understand how you can do that. You all have a bias against PTSD."* Rather than doing what I had planned I decided, with her permission, to review her grant with the other members of the group to see what if any the problems were with her proposal. Two hours later, she grudgingly apologized. The proposal was full of holes.

It would be satisfying to report that our workshop did a great job and that the PTSD grants dramatically improved. They did not. It got so bad that almost none was approved. What did the VA do? They abandoned the review panel and just gave money to any VA researcher willing to study PTSD. The pressures of service groups on the system were too strong to support the standards of science.

One of the results of discarding science for politics was the application of questionable treatments to veterans with the diagnosis of PTSD. Some were akin to snake oil. One fad was based on the idea that because such patients reported nightmares, they therefore had a problem with the dream phase of sleep, rapid eye movement or REM sleep. In response to this notion, the PTSD proponents had fully awake patients rapidly moving their eyes back and forth as if watching a frenetic tennis match. The VA PTSD psychologists told these patients that the procedure worked and would help them. The PTSD psychologists ignored the fact that REM sleep is not just a period of eye movements but a defined physiological state different from wakefulness and other phases of sleep. They also ignored the fact that there was not a shred of evidence supporting the efficacy of the exercise. No one benefited except the perpetrators of this foolish intervention.

Another fad of that era and of nation-wide distribution was the notion of multiple personality. The idea is that one person can harbor many different identities in their psyche. Other than a scattering of patients with seizure disorder who experience what appears to be transient personality changes before or after a seizure, there is no scientific support for the idea. Hollywood, however, loves the concept as it permits the actress or actor involved to chew up the scenery. Specialized units sprung up across the country offering various brands of psychotherapy to treat patients said to have multiple personality. One of the nation's "experts" in this area set up a large unit (I recall 25 beds, but I could be wrong about that number). Even adherents of the notion admitted that multiple personality was not common, so filling up such a large unit could only mean that the expert was himself hearing voices or that he was seeing dollar signs and probably convincing easily suggestible patients that they had the condition. He also encouraged them to adhere to false memories of belonging to satanic cults in other lifetimes. This manipulation of patients for the benefit of the treater was widespread and well-documented in the multiple personality field.[25] He ended up losing his medical license. I believe he served a thera-peutic long jail sentence for overbilling. One story had him billing not by the patient but by each patient's personality. Multiple personality remains a *DSM* bogus diagnosis, but it is now packaged as identity disorder.

The 1990s

In the mid-1990s I was asked to see a 28-year-old woman who had been plagued by episodes of depression since she was 14 years old. She had been treated over the years by a series of social workers for psychotherapy, a psy-chologist or two, and by several psychiatrists prescribing antidepressant medications as she met *DSM* criteria for depression.

In 1980, psychiatric diagnosis became dominated by the American Psychiatric Association's diagnostic manual. A new version (*DSM-5*) will soon be published. In the third version (*DSM-III*) and all subsequent ver-sions of the manual the diagnostic bar for depression was made so low that almost anyone in a funk for 2 weeks or who is chronically disgruntled will meet the criteria. The criteria are designed so that more people are counted as ill (a bigger pie). This artificial increase suits treaters of all stripes who still have to pay their bills as well as the pharmaceutical industry that sees its market for antidepressant drugs ever expanding. In the 1960s and early 1970s, studies identified about 8% of the population as having depressive illness. Today we are told that about 20% have it. We are also told by the National Institute of Mental Illness (NIMH) that about 50% of the U.S. population will experience at least one psychiatric condition. This is hyper-bole made official, but it keeps customers coming into the offices and helps the pharmaceutical industry to stay in business. Paul McHugh, professor at Johns Hopkins and retired chairman, called the 50% figure foolish and the process of diagnosis equivalent to public health investigators studying the prevalence of pneumonia in the United States by calling every instance of cough with a fever and sputum production a case of pneumonia.[26]

Anyway, the young woman had always met the new criteria for depres-sion, justifying her treatments. But over the years the depressive-like episodes increased in their duration and frequency. The various treatments she was pre-scribed didn't work at preventing them and seemed to have little effect on ame-liorating her episodes. As the patient put it, after several weeks the episodes gradually abated, *"like a cold."* She was referred to us for another opinion.

When I met her, it was clear that her depressions were not the same as those of patients who respond to antidepressant medications. In fact, most patients diagnosed as depressed do not respond to antidepressant medications.[27] The *DSM* does not consider its "major depression" category as heterogeneous. So, all patients who meet the criteria are considered to have the same condition and all are treated as if "one size fits all." But the young woman's episodes, although meeting the *DSM* vision of depression, were classic for a type of seizure, the "depressions" occurring after the seizure itself. They were "postictal." She had never been evaluated for epilepsy and no care giver over the almost decade and a half of her difficulties had ever considered the idea that her behavioral problems might reflect a brain problem.[28] From her history I also concluded that she had a vascular abnormality (blood vessels looking like a bag of worms) in her brain, and that the abnormality was the likely focus of her seizures. She had had a small vascular malformation on her lower lip that was surgically removed 10 years earlier, a bit of history that offered the clue to the source of her difficulties. That information, however, was never obtained by her therapists and psychiatrists. A CT scan confirmed the diagnosis. I prescribed an anticonvulsant that relieved her seizures and thus ending her depressions. We also referred her to a neurosurgeon for removal of the vascular malformation in her brain. He reported that although the malformation was undoubtedly surgically removable years before, the vascular malformation was now so large and invasive into other parts of her brain that it was inoperable. We were able to keep the young woman seizure-free and thus depression-free for almost 18 months, the longest period in her life without any of her "depressions." But then one day the abnormal vessels in her brain ruptured and she died. Her death was more than just the result of a diagnostic error. As long as psychiatry thinks of itself as a philosophy and not as a medical specialty, or psychiatrists offer mostly a primary care quick and basic intervention, such deaths will continue to occur. As long as persons licensed to provide care for such patients are not required to recognize the need to be medical doctors and either become expert in this type of evaluation and care or are required to refer to a provider that is expert, patients will continue to suffer.

The Early Twenty-First Century:
Diagnostic Validity Continues to Decline

Despite its stellar reputation and an array of bright people doing well-funded research, the department of psychiatry, where I now work, was in my view in 2000 clinically pretty much like many big academic psychiatric departments throughout the United States. From discussions with psychiatrists elsewhere and from consulting on patients from many parts of the country I have concluded that, if anything, the department was and is better than most. Its pattern of practice in diagnosing patients and in the use of psychiatric medications illustrates I believe present twenty-first-century U.S. psychiatry.

In the early 2000s, diagnoses in the department and almost everywhere else in the United States were made with only modest thought to the patient's symptoms beyond what is in the *DSM*, despite a rich literature and data about many behavioral features (termed psychopathology)[29] that are not mentioned in the *DSM* manual but that are critical to valid diagnosis. Consequently, many patients exhibit behavior not included in the manual and thus not recognized by their physicians. If a clinician doesn't know the different signs and symptoms of a disease the patient with that disease becomes incomprehensible. Thus, rather than identifying the specific illness, only the general category is recognized. Because of the lack of recognition, upward of a third of psychiatric patients end up being given the label NOS (Not Otherwise Specified). The term is the *DSM* version of "We aren't sure."

Overdiagnosis of schizophrenia was still occurring, but the department clinicians, like the rest of U.S. psychiatry, had no consensus on what that condition represented. Was schizophrenia an illness that can best be defined as a type of developmental disorder or was it a heterogeneous admixture of patients who shared a few clinical features but for whom there was no underlying coherence?[30] If the latter, then no longitudinal requirements for the diagnosis are needed and the *DSM* criteria are sufficient. If schizophrenia is considered a form of developmental disorder, then the patient's childhood behaviors and neuromotor functioning must also be considered. The mother's prenatal and delivery experiences become important diagnostic concerns. Early detection and intervention can be applied to reduce some of the long-term disabilities associated with the condition. These issues were rarely if ever considered. Every patient with the diagnosis of schizophrenia was treated similarly but not as if the treaters were being guided by the developmental view. They just prescribed the latest antipsychotic and hoped for the best. The year was 2000, but the diagnostic and treatment approaches were vintage 1965. To a significant degree the faculty was influenced by granting agencies that define schizophrenia from the *DSM* perspective as a distinct single disease process. This is akin to assuming mental retardation and dementia are single diseases.

Most new admissions to the university teaching inpatient psychiatry unit in the early 2000s received an antipsychotic to tranquilize rather than a more specific treatment. The behavioral changes that result from epilepsy, traumatic brain injury, migraine, and stroke were often unrecognized.

Catatonia was almost unknown to the faculty other than as a historical footnote, although studies indicated that they should have been seeing catatonia in 5–10% of their inpatients.[31] As psychiatrists in a major teaching medical center, they should have known better. Inpatients with catatonia frequently went unrecognized by the primary team psychiatrists. The team didn't know what to look for. The *DSM* offers a handful of catatonic features, but there are over 40, and the syndrome can emerge with several different patterns. If you don't recognize the catatonia, the patient's underlying condition may be missed and inappropriate treatments may be prescribed. Some catatonias become life-threatening. Missing catatonia can get the patient and the treaters into big trouble.

As I had previously written papers and co-authored a book about catatonia, I demonstrated the features to some of the younger faculty members and they too became interested in the condition. We were increasingly asked to evaluate patients to see if catatonia was present. Today the inpatient and consultation psychiatrists know a lot about catatonia. The rest of U.S. psychiatry has not caught up.

Like most psychiatrists in the United States in the early twenty-first century, many of the faculty I met thought that they had rarely if ever seen or never would see a patient with catatonia. The assumption was that the patient had to always be in a persistent frozen and mute state. This is not the case. Many patients with the condition move about and at times speak. When lecturing about catatonia to large groups of psychiatrists who work in hospital settings, I start off by asking the audience how many of them had seen 10 patients with catatonia in the past year. Of course, no one raises their hand. Even when I reduce the number to five no hands go up. At one patient, I might get a few hands in the air. At the end of the talk, after describing all the features of catatonia that are not mentioned in the *DSM* or in most modern psychiatric textbooks, I ask the same original question again of the audience and about half raise their hands.

The Early Twenty-First Century:
Clinical Psychopharmacology Declined

Although diagnosis in the department in the early 2000s was in my view old-fashioned, the prescribing of psychiatric medications was ultramodern but like the rest of the field, was in my opinion flawed. Several psychopharmacologists have lamented this decline in the quality of psychopharmacology practice in the United States. Residents learn simple algorithms and not the art and science of psychopharmacology. They learn this cookbook care from their supervisors.[32] Again, the department I work in illustrates the national problem.

Many of the psychiatrists in the department and thus most of the trainees often prescribed multiple psychiatric medications to each patient as if the data supported such widespread polypharmacy. They appeared to know but did not use the fundamentals of psychopharmacology in their dosing. Applying this information is necessary to determine how to properly manage a patient's medication. Seemingly ignoring the fundamentals, medication decisions were done haphazardly and often contrary to the pharmacology of the medications they used. Whenever a new drug came on the market it was quickly prescribed by the residents as if they had just discovered something finally better than sliced bread.

Proper psychopharmacological practice requires therapeutic flexibility, not cookbook adherence. It demands knowing not only what to do but also when to do it. In discussions over the past decade with psychiatric residents on what principles they are being taught on how to dose (e.g., number of times daily, time of the day), what doses to prescribe, when to increase doses, when to add an additional agent, and when to switch from one medication to another, they approach these important clinical decisions by trial and error. They don't use the principles of pharmacotherapy that relate to how the body deals with the drug from ingestion to distribution to excretion. They try something and wait for an unspecified number of days or weeks and then maybe try something else if the first effort proves wanting.

As an example, when the antipsychotic aripiprazol (Abilify) was introduced, residents immediately began prescribing it to their acute inpatients. To be effective for acute inpatients, however, medications need to have a fairly rapid onset. The more acutely ill the patient, the more there is the need for quick action. To resolve the patient's condition and maintain the response, the medication needs to reach equilibrium in the body so that what is ingested and eliminated balance out. With the balance, the drug's blood and body levels remain steady. This is called the steady-state. The steady-state is roughly four to five times the drug's elimination half-life. The elimination half-life means how long it takes for half a drug dose to be eliminated from the body. For aripiprazol, the half-life of an oral dose is between 75 and 94 hours. This half-life is much too long for an agent to be effectively useful acutely. The steady-state is about 14 days. Two weeks was twice the average hospital stay for the unit. Although aripiprazol is used less today for acutely ill adult inpatients, it is still commonly prescribed for adolescents. But when it was first marketed, the residents seemed totally unaware of the drug's long half-life and how it and other influences of the body on the drug shaped the drug's use. They were never trained to pre-scribe psychiatric medications by this method.

Older, well-established medications had been abandoned throughout the department in favor of newer, better promoted, and much more costly new agents. This was then true for most U.S. academic departments of psychiatry. It remains true a decade later. Only two or three of the faculty at that time prescribed the older tricyclic antidepressants (TCAs) despite the evidence that they work well and are safe (see Chapter 3). Some, per-haps, prescribed monoamine oxidase inhibitors (MAOI), another class of antidepressants used in the United States prior to the *DSM-III* when there was recognition that all depressions were not the same and that sufferers with different forms responded best to different agents. None of the 40 or so residents in the early 2000s, however, had ever begun a patient on an MAOI. A leading educator in the department said he never prescribed lith-ium because it was "a dangerous drug" and he discouraged residents from using it. It still remains the best medication for manic-depression and the most effective agent for enhancing the therapeutic effect of an antidepres-sant. It is also useful in the treatment of erratic mood states experienced by persons with traumatic brain injury. Very few of the other attending psy-chiatrists were prescribing lithium. They prescribed all the newest agents promoted as mood stabilizers.

As my colleagues and I began treating patients with the older estab-lished medications or we recommended them for patients who had not responded to other antidepressants, it was quickly apparent that many of the faculty did not know how to prescribe the older agents, although these medications were still widely used elsewhere in the world. For example, several psychiatrists with major roles in the department's train-ing programs did not know how to dose the TCA nortriptyline (once at night works best) and when to obtain blood levels of the agent needed to guide dosing. Most recently a psychiatrist, at our recommendation, reluc-tantly prescribed nortriptyline for a patient who had recovered from a depressive illness. The psychiatrist started with 10 mg daily and just left the patient on that dose for months and did not obtain any blood levels. A typical dose of nortriptyline is 75–125 mg daily. The patient relapsed. The faculty also did not appear to know that although lithium is often pre-scribed several times daily for inpatients to take advantage of the associ-ated mild sedative peeks of such dosing frequency, that for outpatients it is often better to prescribe it once daily at night with a snack so that the blood levels vary over the 24-hour period. The period of lower levels may provide the kidneys, where lithium is excreted, with a rest, reduc-ing the risk of the renal complications associated with long-term lithium treatment.[33]

The disconnection between the science of psychopharmacology and its practice at a major university medical center filled with the "best and the brightest" continues and is not unique. It is standard throughout the United States. A recent study, for example, assessed psychopharmacology practice among resident physicians at the University of Massachusetts Medical School.[34] The hospitals and clinics in which those residents train are also considered among the better ones in the nation. The study focused on the care of patients with depressive illness. Polypharmacy was common even though patients did not do better on more than one agent. The fundamentals of psychopharmacology were not evident in prescriptions or changes in dosing or in the agents prescribed. The study concluded that "Many patients did not receive an adequate monotherapy trial either by dose or duration." Residents, however, practice what they are taught. Their errors are the errors of their teachers.

The Early Twenty-First Century: Psychiatric Training Was Highjacked

Present day psychiatric diagnosis and treatments are problematic. Fixing the problems will be impossible as long as the substantial influence of pharmaceutical representatives on training remains. The reps at our medical center were ubiquitous until banned a few years ago. In the early 2000s the reps provided financial support for many department activities. The reps did not compete among each other as much as they blitzed the faculty and residents with promotional material and free samples to "try out." Their common goal was to encourage the physicians in the psychiatry department to prescribe as much as possible. The image they evoked was supermarket shelf space. If there are lots of cereal choices presented in a grand array more people are likely to buy cereal than if only a few choices are available. If the shelf of psychotropics is long and packed with choices, more prescriptions will be written. Every rep's company will make money.

I was asked to participate in a resident run seminar, "lunch and learn." A drug representative said he would pay for the lunches if he could first speak for 10 minutes to the resident group about his company's psychiatric drugs. Offering to feed residents almost always gets them to attend. Seeing nothing unsavory about allowing the drug rep to speak at what was supposed to be a teaching experience, the residency director quickly agreed despite studies that demonstrate that when drug reps provide new information to residents and other physicians they make "errors," and these misstatements commonly favor the drug they are promoting. As a residency director and a department chair I had never allowed drug representatives in teaching areas let alone classrooms and only permitted them to gather in designated public places in the hospital. Sure enough, within minutes of the sales pitch of the rep I had to stop and challenge him on a statement, *"Surely you didn't mean to say … ?"* The "errors" were clearly designed to mislead the residents to favor the rep's drug over competitors.[35]

The increased influence of the pharmaceutical industry upon physician training is one of the most pernicious changes in the past 40 years. In the 1960s, Merck pharmaceuticals gave *every* U.S. graduate MD a doctor's black bag, a stethoscope, an ophthalmoscope, an otoscope, a tuning fork, and a blood pressure cuff and meter (a sphygmomanometer). But after that bonanza, I don't recall any interactions with drug representatives during my training. Things have changed.

The profession's awareness of this evolved in the 1990s with the recognition that interactions between pharmaceutical representatives and trainees was common and that trainees received many gifts and meals. The more a trainee received, the less he or she thought there was undue influence.[36] A review of English language articles from 1966 to 2004 on the subject[37] found that contact was common and that the number and degree of contacts were associated with resident physician prescribing. The more the contacts, the more the resident was likely to prescribe the rep's drugs. The availability of samples was a critical factor. When a drug rep gives free samples of a new drug to a physician, the physician tends to give them to patients and then continues to prescribe them if they are found to be effective. The continued prescriptions of course are no longer free and almost always cost more than older agents that may work just as well. The process is like the playground drug pusher offering free samples to the kids until they are hooked. Then the charges quickly escalate.

Human nature being what it is, while the acceptance of gifts and favors, and the offering of free samples influences prescribing, trainees tend to believe that it is their peers that are influenced, not them.[38] The same influences impact medical students who have substantial contact with pharmaceutical representatives. These contacts can affect the attitudes of the students throughout their careers to favor the reps and what they do and say.[39] Capture them early and keep them forever is the goal, just like the tobacco industry's marketing to teens.

Despite efforts to curtail interactions between trainees and pharmaceutical reps at teaching medical centers, contact continues outside the centers at industry-sponsored lectures, drug lunches and dinners, and professional meetings.[40] *The New York Times* reports (Adam Liptak, Tuesday June 19, 2012) that there are over 90,000 pharmaceutical representatives in the United States making a median annual base salary of $70,000. This tidy sum does not count commissions based on the number of prescriptions written for the rep's drugs.

The industry provides a substantial amount of material to trainees in the guise of educational, "scientifically endorsed" information.[41] It also sponsors about half of the costs of continuing medical education (CME) programs in the United States. CME credits are required for relicensing, so *every* physician in the United States must obtain a substantial number of credits. In the state of Michigan, we need 150 classroom-like CME credits every 3 years to be relicensed. The industry estimates that for every dollar it invests in CME it recoups about $3.50 in increased sales. Many of the physicians attending the CME programs are teaching faculty, so if they are adversely influenced, their students will too.[42]

Trainees should be trained by their faculty not by drug representatives. Faculty should be updated by reading the scientific literature and by their peers, not by drug reps. The only solution is for the pharmaceutical industry to be excluded from the CME process if U.S. psychiatry is to ever become truly an evidenced-based specialty. As a resident, I learned more from my peers, the psychiatric literature, and my patients than from most of my professors. I still learn from my peers and from the patients I meet. One of the greatest advantages of working at a teaching medical center is that students of many disciplines and psychiatric residents ask a lot of questions. I constantly have to check "my facts." Sometimes it's a resident or a student that finds the solution to a question we think is relevant to the care of a patient but for which we had no satisfying answer.

2012

What makes present-day U.S. psychiatry mediocre is its failure to discard the past and embrace the future. Residents continue to be taught psychodynamic theory as if it were valid. They are exposed to other forms of talking therapies that they will most likely not personally do once in practice. Their thinking about patients is warped by this training focus, perpetuating the deadly mind–body dichotomy. Inappropriate treatments are used by nonmedical practitioners and are tolerated by those who should know better. What could be more foolish and destructive than Hollywood's version of what psychiatric illness is and what is needed to treat it? A recent *New York Times* TV review, for example, detailed that the actress Laura Dern was starring in an HBO series in which she plays a person having a "nervous breakdown" (whatever that means). Hollywood almost never gets psychiatric illness right, so Ms. Dern was, according to *The Times*, "screeching at coworkers in the office with mascara streaming down her cheeks." This behavior is good for an Emmy but only a gullible psychiatrist would believe the histrionics. Ms. Dern's character then goes for a *successful* "cure" in Hawaii by swimming with sea turtles. What about ground unicorn horn dissolved in a cup of chamomile? Will turtle soup replace the well-established therapeutic chicken noodle soup? The TV images depict psychiatry as nonmedical, and psychiatric disorder as existential crises not the brain diseases that afflict so many.

The danger of thinking of psychiatry as fundamentally a psychological field and not a medical specialty is demonstrated by the story of a patient described to me a few years ago. The patient was a middle-aged EuroAmerican man suffering from depressive illness. He was also in the midst of separating from his wife. The man's depression worsened and he was hospitalized for several days at a local hospital and was then discharged for further outpatient care. It is a sad fact that the risk of suicide for a patient is at its life-time highest during the few weeks following discharge from a psychiatric hospital where the hospitalization was for depression.[43] This last sentence is not a typo. The high risk is in part due to hospitals discharging patients prematurely because of health insurance company pressure and pressure from the hospital's administration overly driven by the bottom line. The patient is sick enough to get admitted but cannot be kept long enough to recover. It can take weeks to resolve a severe depression. So, the patient leaves the haven of the hospital still ill, and hope quickly fades. Another reason the suicide risk is so high following discharge is that psychiatrists aren't particularly good at caring for depressed patients. Studies of suicide detail that prior to hospitalization less than 20% of depressed patients receive adequate treatment of any kind. We would all hope that treatment for patients admitted for depression and suicide plans or attempts would then improve, but in fact nothing changes and upon discharge, again less than 20% of patients are found to be receiving adequate treatment of any kind. Psychiatrists are also not particularly good at suicide assessment. In a 5-year follow-up of 4800 psychiatric inpatients, of those thought to be at risk of suicide 30% did not make an attempt (false positives) whereas 44% of patients who did make an attempt were originally thought to be at low risk (false negatives). It's the false negatives that are deadly.[44]

So, the patient in this story was discharged still ill. His wife told him so and indicated that if anything he was worse than before the hospitalization and that he should go to an urgent care psychiatric clinic. He did so. The social worker who saw him and his psychiatrist supervisor recognized that the man was in a period of high risk. They probably also knew that over 90% of the persons who kill themselves in the United States annually are EuroAmerican males (suicide among poor persons and minorities is undoubtedly undercounted so that the real figure is probably 60–70% EuroAmerican men).[45] The social worker offered the man hospitalization, which he refused. But from his history and as he was described at the conference, he was a patient who should have been hospitalized as a life-saving effort, even against his well. They decided not to pursue that approach because they wanted to keep a *"good therapeutic alliance"* with the patient for future psychotherapy. They thought of him as a person who needed psychotherapy not as a patient with a terrible, life-threatening brain disease. So, they let him go. But after he left the clinic he went to his office and killed himself with the gun he had been keeping there for that purpose. In addition to the bullet that destroyed his brain, the idea that psychotherapy is the lynchpin for treating a brain disease certainly helped pull the trigger.

A suicidal patient with depression or psychosis, a patient in manic excitement or manic delirium, and a patient with malignant catatonia are the traditional psychiatric conditions that are by their nature acutely life-threatening. We need to make sure we get the diagnosis and treatment of patients in these states of illness right. The suicide of the patient above indicates we sometimes do not get it right. The following story, although anecdotal, illustrates how we have declined in this responsibility.

I was recently having a conversation with two of my previous trainees and faculty members from the 1980s and early 1990s. One is now a psychopharmacology researcher and the other is an assistant residency director in my old department. In our chat I related that over the past 12 years I had seen more than a few residents who had suffered through a patient of theirs committing suicide, often a suicide that could have been prevented. I never esperienced such a tragedy and asked my prior colleagues about this experience when they were residents and young faculty members, and the present experience of the residents in my old program. The researcher said that when he was administering ECT for over a decade, despite treating a wide range of severely ill patients, none killed themselves. The other previous resident of mine said that in his 4 years of training he knew of one patient who had killed himself and another who had made a severely injurious attempt. I then asked him how many of his present residents have had a patient commit suicide. He said, *"Almost all of them."* He attributed the startling increase to the aftermath of the three Middle East wars upon veterans and the tanking of the economy that has affected everyone. These events are undoubtedly factors. But he also said that today's psychiatric residents do not learn how to examine or evaluate patients. They don't learn the psychopathology needed to properly assess a patient. They don't know how to manage suicidal patients. The specialty examinations they now take to become certified as psychiatrists no longer require them to evaluate a live patient; they just respond to video tape vignettes. He bemoaned the lack of commitment of residents as they are now required by accreditation authorities to work only 80 hours over a 2-week period. He is also in private practice and gives his cell phone number to his patients and encourages them to call him if they need to. Those with any risk of suicide *must* call in regularly. He works much more than 40 hours weekly. On a Monday morning he was making his morning teaching inpatient rounds with residents and at nine o'clock one resident began looking at his watch. When asked about it, the resident said that he had been on call the night before and was required to leave at nine, despite having responsibility for some of the inpatients. He had only seen four patients over that night. My prior resident, covering his private practice that weekend, had covered 45 patients. Although a tired surgery resident is not a good idea, having psychiatry residents clock out like retail sales persons does not prepare them to care for patients at a level that will prevent suicide. If they don't learn the needed psychopathology to diagnose, they will miss the illness the patient has or the clinical factors needed to predict what treatments to offer and what strategies to employ to maximize the safety of their patients. A child psychiatry fellow in our department presented a young girl with manic-depression to the ECT team for consideration for treating the now depressed and potentially suicidal 16-year-old patient. The fellow, with at least 3 previous years of training in psychiatry and being supervised by a faculty member at a prestigious university medical center, was unable to tell us about the patient's menstrual history and any association it might have with her mood disturbance (it often does), whether she was pregnant or not (affecting what medications we could prescribe), whether she suffered from migraine (perhaps a cause of her problems and certainly a factor influencing treatment choices), or whether she experienced signs of perturbation in the brain's limbic system (indicating the type of depression and long-term prognosis), all important factors in the proper care of a person with manic-depression. Half of such patients make suicide attempts and 15–20% kill themselves.

U.S. psychiatry also pays lip service to science and the understanding that it is the human brain that generates all behavior above basic reflexes. A major psychiatric educator in our the department announced at a teaching planning meeting that he did not need to know anything about the brain to make psychiatric diagnoses and treat psychiatric patients. He relied on the *DSM* and official treatment algorithms. He had and has great influence on the training of medical students and residents, the next generation. His clinical point of view would be similar to a general physician who claimed he didn't need to know anything about human physiology or the functioning of our different organs as long as he had enough information to recognize syndromes and knew what medications were required. Who would want to go to a physician like that? But thousands of patients in the United States are treated by psychiatrists exactly like that.

As we have learned more and more about the brain and how it generates complex behaviors, U.S. psychiatry remains wedded to a diagnostic and treatment system over 60 years old: identify a few clinical features that match a diagnostic label in the *DSM* and then apply the treatments that are said to work for that category of patient. It is cookbook diagnosis and treatment. Without thought, labels are applied and drugs with significant side effects but with only modest efficacy are prescribed. Various brands of psychotherapy are offered with little consideration of what actually helps and which patients are best suited to a particular brand. This is twenty-first-century U.S. psychiatry. As a field we have in my view ignored the oath to first, do no harm.

CHAPTER 3

☙

Free of Injustice and Mischief

"Whatever houses I may visit, I will come for the benefit of the sick, remaining free of all intentional injustice, of all mischief..."

Old version of the Hippocratic Oath

"I will respect the hard-won scientific gains of those physicians in whose steps I walk, and gladly share such knowledge as is mine with those who are to follow...I will apply, for the benefit of the sick, all measures [that] are required, avoiding those twin traps of over-treatment and therapeutic nihilism."

Modern version of the Hippocratic Oath

The modern Hippocratic Oath urges physicians to base what we do on science, not dogma or ignorant good intentions. The most recent term for this inconsistently achieved goal is "evidence-based medicine." For most of the twentieth century, however, what constituted "evidence" was unsettled as U.S. psychiatry was embedded in a continuous struggle for the intellectual understanding of behavioral disorder. The combatants were the proponents of the medical model of psychiatry and the adherents to the psychodynamic worldview.[1]

MODELS OF PSYCHIATRIC DISORDER

The Medical Model

For more than 100 years medicine has been guided by the medical model paradigm. Its core construct is that disease results from processes adversely affecting the functioning of a body organ. The dysfunction is expressed in characteristic signs and symptoms that identify the organ, its tissue pathology, and ultimately, with the aid of laboratory tests, the etiology of the dysfunction. As the pathophysiological cascade becomes clearer, treatments become more specific.

The medical model is applied as a method of syndrome identification using a standardized evaluation of the patient's history and present health status. Laboratory testing is employed to verify a definitive pathology. This information is then applied to determine a medical diagnosis. Almost all the advances in medicine in the twentieth century were the results of applying the medical model to the study of disease and to the treatment of disease sufferers. In the twentieth century, medicine eradicated smallpox, controlled poliomyelitis, and developed treatments for metabolic (e.g., diabetes) and some heritable disorders (e.g., phenylketonuria).

The medical model of illness provides the understanding that among the many labels assigned to the behavioral problems that afflict humans, there exist brain disorders that are the result of and are delineated by the same principles as are diseases of other body organs. The model indicates that psychiatrists, as physicians, should focus their attention and efforts on sufferers of these brain disorders. Like other medical specialists, we have an important, yet limited role in the care of others.

The Psychodynamic Perspective

The psychodynamic perspective understands that most behavioral problems are the result of conflicts between the stresses and strains of daily life and unconscious forces internalized in childhood and adolescence. Although traditional psychoanalysts were physicians, they paid little attention to the general medical concerns of their patients and focused instead on metaphysical interpretations of behavior. Their rejection of the medical model of behavioral disease encouraged nonphysicians to pursue analytic training and to become psychotherapists. The proponents of the psychoanalytic perspective were willing to take on as a patient almost anyone with behavioral difficulties.

The psychoanalytic view of behavior is ubiquitous in the arts. Novels, dramatic plays, and TV and film dramas almost always relate the motivations of the characters portrayed to psychological, often unconscious, mechanisms. Most educated Westerners accept these motivations as valid, and so it is understandable that when a real-world person exhibits abnormal behavior the behavior is attributed to the same kinds of psychological mechanisms found in the arts. The evidence, however, is absent for the extension of the metaphysical interpretation of behavior to the behavioral signs and symptoms of the brain dysfunction that has been demonstrated for many psychiatric syndromes. Manic-depression, psychoses, and obsessive-compulsive disorders, for example, have all been shown to have substantial genetic components and to be associated with brain dysfunctions at several levels.[2]

Demons and Humors

Prior to the twentieth century and through much of Western history the interpretation of the causes of behavioral disorder fluctuated between religious dogma that accepted demonic possession and witchcraft as causal agents, and perturbations derived from various imbalances in the falsely conceptualized body "humors" of blood, phlegm, and black and yellow bile.[3] The humoral theory is no longer a focus of medicine, but religious dogma as an understanding of behavior remains with us in the continued worldwide persecution of homosexuals who have a biological variant and not a disease but who are nevertheless hounded for perceived violations of religious injunctions.[4] The occasional formal efforts by priests and evangelists to exorcise behaviorally disturbed persons is another example.

The attribution of disease to perturbed substances in the body prevailed in Europe for over a millennium. Too much of one or the other humor was assumed to be responsible for many conditions as well as the pattern of a person's personality traits. From this paradigm we get terms such as melancholia (too much black bile), plethoric and sanguine (too much blood), and phlegmatic (too much phlegm). Treatments were based on the perceived imbalance in the patient's humors. For example, the flush of fever indicated too much blood and so was treated with blood-letting. If this sounds bizarre, just imagine what a twenty-second-century reader will think of the Jungian idea of species' archetypes somehow embedded in our psyches, or the old Freudian notion of arrested psychosexual development in an anal stage contributing to obsessive-compulsive disorders (OCD). By then it will be fully accepted that OCD is associated with dysfunction in the brain's basal ganglia.[5]

Neuropsychiatry, the Medical Model Applied to Behavioral Syndromes

Demonic possession and imbalanced humors, however, are unifying theories of disease. From either perspective madness was considered singular. Psychiatry and neurology evolved together under these rubrics and for generations were much the same specialty. As the dogmas faded, awareness emerged in the late nineteenth century that the central nervous system and the peripheral nerves played key roles in the processes that led to behavioral syndromes. Neuroses were considered disorders of the nerves, while psychoses were viewed as brain diseases. This view of behavioral illness and the continuing overlap of psychiatry and neurology extended into the twentieth century in Europe. The overlap is illustrated by Hans Berger, a psychiatrist from Jena Germany. Berger demonstrated in 1924 that brain cells (neurons) worked by generating electrical potentials and that the sum of this activity could be measured with electrodes pasted to the scalp. He built the first electroencephalogram (EEG). At that time, both psychiatrists and neurologists cared for patients with epilepsy, and Berger and others made the associations between specific EEG patterns and the specific forms of epilepsy. These associations are widely recognized today.

In the latter part of the nineteenth century and the first quarter of the twentieth century about half of the patients in Western mental hospitals suffered from neurosyphilis. General paresis of the insane (GPI) was a neuropsychiatric disorder. When you see depictions of asylums of that era and you see disheveled screaming patients wandering about in dirty sheaths and exhibiting odd gaits and other abnormal movements, you are seeing versions of what GPI looked like. Julius Wagner-Jauregg, a psychiatrist from Vienna, cared for such patients and recognized that they often improved following a high fever from typhus or pneumonia. In 1917, he transfused a series of sufferers of GPI with malaria parasites and the associated fevers led to improvements in his patients. Penicillin had yet to be discovered as the treatment for syphilis, and so there was no adequate response to the devastating illness. Wagner-Jauregg was certainly over the top with his intervention; the "cures" he achieved, however, were considered miraculous, and in 1927 he was awarded the Nobel Prize for medicine. It usually takes many decades before accomplishment is recognized by the Nobel committee and their speed of action illustrates the dramatic results of malaria therapy and the dearth of effective treatments at that time. Today research institutions have multiple review procedures so that such a drastic intervention is unlikely to be applied.

Psychiatry and Neurology Divorce

In the nineteenth century psychiatry and neurology began to diverge. Some psychiatrists who did not accept the idea that "madness" emerged from brain disease were called "alienists." Neuropsychiatrists were similar to neurologists in their views.[6] The ascension of psychoanalysis in the 1920s and 1930s, however, ended the hope for any reconciliation between psychiatry and neurology. For decades afterward, the breakup also sidelined the idea that psychiatric disorders were reflections of brain dysfunction.

Wondering why some physicians choose neurology and others select psychiatry, a survey done years after the break-up assessed the attitudes and personalities of neurologists and psychiatrists and found that the greatest difference between the two groups was their response to ambiguity. Neurologists are not comfortable with lack of precision and tend to reject even the brain change findings associated with psychopathology because the anatomic locations are not as precise as what is found in stroke and the neuropathology is not as distinctive as is observed in Alzheimer's disease. Psychiatrists accept ambiguity better.[7] The metaphorical Freudian language also drove neurologists up the metaphoric wall. The Id, Freud's notion of our most primitive drives, cannot be measured or located. Defense mechanisms, putative psychic strategies for negotiating the supposed struggle between the Id and reality, are not reliably identified and have no predictive value.[8] In contrast, the rate of transmission of peripheral nerves can be measured. The chemicals expressed by the nerves that affect muscle can be determined in the laboratory. Brain cells can be visualized and their internal and membrane functions studied. Some types can be grown in a Petri dish. Neuronal intracellular structures can be seen and their protein components can be identified. These tangibles became the primary concern of neurologists. When an artery in the brain leaks or is plugged the damage to the surrounding brain tissue can be delineated. Injury to the brain is definable. Degenerative disease of the brain can be seen under the microscope. As these and other brain processes and pathophysiologies became known, neurologists developed some treatment strategies that were effective. Until the introduction of ECT in 1938, there was no psychiatric intervention that clearly worked.[9] Well-considered efforts to reunite the groups in the areas of behavioral neurology or neuropsychiatry have been minimally successful.[10]

New Treatments Emerged as Diagnostic Validity Declined

While diagnosis was the linchpin of clinical medicine and as other medical specialties made great strides in understanding disease and treating patients, for much of the twentieth century American psychiatry languished in Freudian dogma and Adolf Meyer's approach that rejected the value of identifying syndromes by shared clinical features.[11] The concepts of Freud, Meyer, and their followers, however, would not have been so widely accepted had there been a contemporary competing biological model of psychiatric illness or effective treatments for psychiatric disorders. Early twentieth century neuroscience technologies and laboratory procedures were primitive and no somatic treatment had yet been established. In his 1907 Presidential Address to the American Medico-Psychological Association, the beginnings of the American Psychiatric Association, C. G. Hill, not a diplomat but an honest man, noted that *"our therapeutics is simply a pile of rubbish."*[12]

Treatments with varying degrees of efficacy, however, began to be introduced a decade later. Malarial fever, used to treat central nervous system syphilis and its associated behavioral syndromes (1917), was for obvious reasons not a long-term winner. Its dramatic effectiveness and medical nature, however, initiated analytic-dominated psychiatry's drift away from neurology and the rest of medicine. Throughout the first half of the twentieth century, whenever a behavioral syndrome's etiology was established or a medical treatment for it was developed, U.S. psychiatry "outsourced" patients with the syndrome to others. Patients with central nervous system syphilis and those with epilepsy were abandoned to neurologists because the patients' defined "organic" illness made them unsuitable for analysis. Psychiatrists who continued to care for severely ill patients whose behavioral syndromes remained enigmas (dementia praecox/schizophrenia, manic-depression) were mostly relegated to large asylums and retreats. Mainstream psychiatry became psychoanalysis.

Somatic treatments for psychiatric disorder, however, continued to be introduced. Insulin coma was established in 1933. In this procedure, which remained in use until about 1970, 60 to 80 comas were induced in a sufferer with intravenous insulin to resolve psychoses of all types. Despite enthusiastic proponents, it was never scientifically validated and the dangers of such comas and their adverse effect on cognition were eventually recognized. Prefrontal leucotomy followed in 1935. This surgical procedure was often done crudely and could involve the disconnection of the frontal lobes from many other brain systems. It was overly intrusive, never curative, and produced more harm than good. Modern psychosurgery, by contrast, is refined, relatively safe, and established as helpful for several circumscribed conditions, particularly some forms of seizure disorder. Patients with unremitting OCD have also benefited from psychosurgery. Some patients with Parkinson's disease respond to a form of the procedure. Psychosurgery is also a research procedure in the treatment of patients with unremitting or repeatedly relapsing depressive illness.[13]

Convulsive therapy, introduced in 1934, began with inducing controlled seizures using camphor in oil as a cortical irritant. In 1938, electrical stimulation became the standard method (more on this later). Antipsychotic drugs and antidepressant agents were first introduced in the 1950s.

The initial success of the medical treatments in quickly and dramatically relieving the most severe psychiatric conditions, and the sustained success of psychopharmacology and electroconvulsive therapy (ECT), challenged the psychodynamic model and changed clinical psychiatric practice. Once again, attention was directed to the brain as central to psychiatric disorders.

The therapeutic optimism, however, was of short duration, as the illnesss categories of the early diagnostic manuals, the *DSMs* (*I* and *II*), were quickly recognized as poor guides for choosing which psychiatric medications would work best for which patients. Many psychopharmacologists in the 1950s and 1960s described their frustration with *DSM-II* criteria for the selection of treatments.[14] One influential report that assessed the studies of medication treatments of patients with depression could find no diagnostic formulation that predicted what medications were best to prescribe for a specific patient.[15] The *DSM-II* system and its World Health Organization counterpart, the International Classification of Disease (ICD-8), also had poor reliability. Groups of psychiatrists couldn't consistently agree on the diagnoses of patients. This was dramatically demonstrated in international studies in which U.S. psychiatrists, compared to their overseas counterparts, overdiagnosed schizophrenia by 50% or more while they underdiagnosed manic-depression.[16] By 1965, psychiatric diagnosis was a joke: *"You get two psychiatrists to examine a patient and they'll come up with three diagnoses."*

Psychiatric diagnosis was weakened further by the social and community psychiatry movement. This perspective emerged from the wedding of the psychoanalytic interpretation of behavior and the World War II experience that it was not cost effective for one psychiatrist to spend several hours weekly with each of a handful of well-off patients while hundreds needed treatment. The movement's guiding notion was to provide services to large populations, apply the psychodynamic understanding of the individual to these populations to explain "the why" of societal problems, and then address these problems by community-based interventions. Psychiatric illness was deemed the result of societal forces that acted adversely on the psyche rather than the result of individual brain diseases. Asylums were unlocked. Patient advocates challenged the legality of commitment and the involuntary application of treatments. In the United States, patients in state hospital facilities were encouraged to return to "the community" but many ended up in city alleys and side streets. Community mental health centers, clinics, and networks as well as "therapeutic communities" sprang up in metropolitan areas across the United States with the implicit promise that public health concerns, poverty, and other inequities would be substantially ameliorated. Recruitment of U.S. medical students into psychiatry was never higher than during the peak of the community psychiatry movement in the 1960s. Over 10% of U.S. medical school graduates joined the field as if they were enlisting in the Peace Corps.[17]

Ironically, with the subsequent ascendancy of psychopharmacology the allure of solving the world's problems via psychiatric intervention waned. Instead of social reformers tilting against injustice, psychiatrists came to look like other physicians, but not nearly as sexy. Medical students often consider psychiatric patients to be too chronic to be satisfying, ignoring the fact that many other specialties care for patients who suffer with chronic and recurring illness. Patients with cardiovascular disease are typically ill for extended periods with relapses. A large proportion of patients seen by internists are diabetic, another long-term condition. But unlike psychiatry, these specialties offer high-tech expensive procedures and laboratory tests that can define illness cascades and causes. Today, about 3–4% of U.S. medical school graduates join psychiatry residency programs. Many are women, so the cartoonists better come up with new images for psychiatrists.[18]

MISCHIEF EMERGES

By the late 1970s, many psychiatrists thought the worst was over. Although the field was still controlled by leaders who valued psychoanalysis, psychoanalytic theory and treatments were mostly discredited by the evidence (see Chapter 1). Medical treatments worked for many patients with behavioral syndromes. Knowledge of how the brain generates normal behavior was expanding. Changes in brain function that result in psychiatric symptoms were being delineated. The *DSM-II*, widely recognized as inadequate, was going to be replaced by a science-based psychiatric classification of behavioral syndromes.

Unfortunately, despite the hopes for a better psychiatric classification system, one of the Hippocratic Oath's concerns was soon confirmed. Mischief emerged as politics and money combined to end the optimism of the 1970s.

Mischief Shapes the Proposed New *DSM-III*

In response to the inadequate diagnostic system of *DSM-II*, alternative operationally defined diagnostic criteria were proposed by several research

groups. The success of these efforts in predicting associated clinical features, family illness patterns, and treatment outcomes encouraged the
American Psychiatric Association (APA) to initiate the process to reformu-
late the *DSM-II*.[19]

The leadership for that effort was entrusted to the department of psychiatry at Washington University in St. Louis and to Columbia University's
Psychiatric Institute. Washington University was a leader in hard-nosed data-
based approaches to diagnosis and treatment, and the department adhered to
the medical model of disease. The Columbia effort was assigned to their biometricians who knew how to create computer-ready structured clinical assessment packets that were to become the style for the new manual's format.

The Washington University group had previously published a listing of 16
psychiatric syndromes that had supporting validating data.[20] Washington
University proposed that the new *DSM* version, *DSM-III*, should be based on
that list and any other conditions for which validation could be established.
The first U.S. classification in 1918 offered 22 diagnostic conditions.[21]

Many hailed the idea. U.S. psychiatry was going to adopt an evidence-
based medical model diagnostic system. However, this was not to be. The
DSM-II listed 182 disorders, which if all the bells, whistles, and subtypes
were removed, boiled down to about 100 conditions, not 16. Many of the
DSM-II categories had no validity, such as multiple personality (e.g., *The
Three Faces of Eve*) and *folie à deux*, a situation in which one psychotic person
in a duo influences the partner to also be psychotic, like catching colds. Each
DSM category, however, had a professional constituency that made its living treating or studying patients with the label of their interest. Interfering
with a person's livelihood, even in the name of science, is risky. The members of the APA, the largest and richest of psychiatric professional organizations, fought back and told the APA trustees that if the Washington
University plan was accepted, they would not support the new classification
and would defeat it in the required membership vote for approval.

Exit Washington University.

DSM-III ultimately included 292 disorders.

Politics Trumps Science

The biometricians at Columbia took over the responsibility for developing *DSM-III*. They, however, had little clinical experience. At one point
in the conversion about the new classification, the leader of the process
asked me and my colleague, Dick Abrams, to meet with him at his house
in Westchester County, north of New York City. As we told him about the
forms of psychopathology we used in our diagnostic criteria, he entered

the information directly into the first desk-top computer I had ever seen. It was of a size that if it were your airplane carry-on, the cabin attendant would make you check it.

As the *DSM-III* taskforce chairman entered our definitions and descriptions, he often muttered to himself encouraging phrases such as *"Oh, that's complicated... This is too difficult for the average clinician... I don't think we'd be able to use that."* So, first science was rejected from the *DSM-III* process as being politically untenable, and then most of the discipline of psychopathology was found to be too hard to understand for the physicians who were supposed to be experts in that discipline. The "idiot's veto" prevailed, and the new *DSM-III* became a crude system formatted to offer a list of a few features for or against each diagnostic choice. The system was disparagingly called "The Chinese Menu," the name inspired by "specials" on the menus found in neighborhood Chinese restaurants of that era, as in "two from column A and one from column B."

The *DSM-III* draft became a political rather than a scientific document that was fashioned to appeal to the widest audience in order to ensure approval by the APA membership. At a conference reviewing the data for several of the proposed *DSM-III* categories, an investigator from Washington University presented his findings about the proposed criteria for "somatization disorder," the modern version of the psychodynamic image of hysteria. For each proposed criterion, he methodically reviewed study after study that demonstrated that the specific criterion was hogwash. At the end of this seeming destruction of the notion of somatization, the audience was quiet. Then the head of the committee in charge of hysteria rose. He was the chairman of psychiatry at a prestigious medical center and a well-known analyst. He said, *"Well, that was an impressive review and we appreciate your effort, but we are going to keep the criteria as formulated."* When a patient sticks to an idea that all the data indicate is false and rejects efforts by others to change his mind, the patient is said to be delusional. When a chairman of a prominent academic department who is well-connected with the psychiatric establishment sticks to a clearly false idea, the false idea is accepted and the data are tossed out.

Lacking a consensus theory of psychiatric illness, the formulation of all the *DSM* categories was left to the members of each workgroup committee assigned to a category. So there was a mood disorder workgroup, a psychotic disorder workgroup, and so on. Different workgroups relied on different sources, idiosyncratic personal clinical experiences, and different psychological and pharmacological notions. The workgroups also represented diverse constituencies, and the final proposal was designed for acceptance by advocacy groups (e.g., psychoanalytic and psychosomatic organizations), and by the "typical" psychiatric clinician in order to ensure passage of the proposed manual. Reading the memos and letters from that effort, and participating in several conferences that were convened to help craft the *DSM-III*, it was clear that the process was and is very much like congress writing legislation. The procedure is messy and the results are wanting. Instead of "earmarks" we have new never validated labels and distinctions such as shared psychotic disorder, identity disorder, schizophreniform disorder, bipolar I, II, III as separate diseases, and many other "bridges to nowhere."

Two additional experiences highlight the dysfunctional process in the crafting of a DSM. The first occurred in the process of designing *DSM-IV*. The *DSM-III* personality disorder section was widely considered not to reflect the substantial amount of quality research on personality traits and structure.[22] In the early 1990s, I attended a two and a half day conference during which data were presented from numerous behavioral genetic and personality assessment studies that examined thousands of normal persons and families, identical and fraternal twins reared together or apart, adoptees, and cross-fostered kids. The overwhelming conclusion from the conference was that personality traits were not as they were depicted in *DSM-III*.

In the manual, the personality disorders were formulated as categorical entities like the common cold where you have it or you don't. Subsequent *DSM* versions are no different. Traits, however, are dimensional and each personality trait is a continuum that has a low and a high expression and degrees of expression in-between. Although the *DSM* personality categories imply illness, deviant personality as established by personality research does not necessarily mean illness or underlying brain pathology. Most deviations in personality are analogous to height. Most persons are around average height, give or take a few inches or millimeters if preferred. Those who are significantly taller or shorter than the average are, by definition, deviant or abnormal. Most such persons, however, have no illness or pathological reason for their deviation. Multiple genes and growing up in either a highly nurturing or modestly deficient environment determines the adult height of most persons. Most professional basketball players are abnormal in height, but not from illness. "Short" people are also abnormal, but most of them have no illness-based explanation for their stature. Even the idea of "short" is relative. A five foot five adult male in the United States would be considered "short." In Southeast Asia, five foot five is the average height for an adult male. Individual variations in personality traits are like individual variations in height but are more complex.

However, some persons are abnormal in their height because of disease. Pituitary tumors releasing excessive growth hormone during childhood can result in gigantism.[23] Persons with an extra Y chromosome (XYY) are usually above the average height.[24] Persons with vitamin C and D deficiencies in childhood and its resulting rickets will often be below average height.[25] Dwarfism can result from a number of pathophysiologies including low levels of growth hormone during childhood.[26] These conditions reflect anatomic or physiological disorder and are not simply variations of nonpathological traits. They require medical diagnostic methods for identification. In like fashion, some abnormal personalities can also result from a pathophysiological process. Substantial personality change after age 30 should be considered due to disease until proven otherwise, because personality traits tend to fully mature by the end of the second decade of life and then change little after that. Traumatic brain injuries to the frontal and temporal areas of the brain are most often the cause of personality changes that substantially alter functioning.[27] Stroke, chronic seizure disorder, and some degenerative brain processes are also associated with abnormal personality change.[28] A recent admission to the inpatient service at our hospital had been ill for a number of years. A prominent feature of his condition was a significant change in his personality after age 30. None of his previous psychiatrists considered this notable. My colleague, however, immediately obtained brain imaging that revealed a large stroke in the man's right frontal lobe that helped explain his symptoms. In some instances, the pattern of personality change can predict its cause or the brain area that is involved. This is an example of why neuropsychiatry is a powerful tool in behavioral diagnosis. The *DSM* does not consider any of these complexities in personality diagnosis.

The personality research also found that personality traits were stable over time, not like the *DSM-III* labels that might come and go in the same person from year to year, as in some years patients meet *DSM* criteria whereas in other years they do not. The research found that different "doses" of expression on each trait were mostly independent of the other traits so that many patterns stable over a life-span were possible. The science-based image of personality formed a coherent structure.

From this perspective, personality disorder occurred when the "doses" of the different traits were at the extremes, far from the norm. These extremes represented strong tendencies to respond to a variety of situations in ways so different from the average response that such a person repeatedly will have difficulties with others, or in adhering to social norms. Extremes might result in a person being overly shy and thus an unhappy "loner" or overly aggressive and experiencing a life peppered with unnecessary arguments and fights. Other high-dose traits might be expressed as being inappropriately self-sacrificing or at the other end of the dimension, selfish. Impulsivity and risk taking, or fearfulness and having a tendency to be too careful in response, are high opposing doses of another dimension.

Each personality trait pattern, normal or abnormal, was found to be the result of an interaction of environmental impacts upon the neural expressions of numerous small genes similar to what has been found in diabetes, and not one large gene as seen in Huntington's disease. The environmental influences that accounted for individual differences, even among siblings, turned out to be little from growing up in the same family and mostly from the effects of nonshared experiences in the first decade or two of life such as going to different schools, having a head injury or not, using street drugs or not. It turns out that Tolstoy was correct when he wrote that *"Happy families are all alike; every unhappy family is unhappy in its own way."*[29] In other words, kids growing up in normal families are sharing an environment similar to other kids growing up in normal environments, and so their individual differences in their personality traits are more likely due to nonshared experiences. An abnormal family, "unhappy in its own way," is a nonshared experience and so that environment will substantially affect the personality deviations of the children in it. The interaction is not "nature versus nurture." The better way of thinking about it is, what does nurture do to what nature offers?

The conference attendees considering changes to the *DSM-III* were excited that they had a picture of personality and of personality disorder that was reliable and valid and based on solid science. The neurological networks underpinning trait behaviors were also roughly being worked out.

The last speaker of the conference was the chairman of the workgroups that were responsible for formulating the personality disorder section for the proposed *DSM-IV*. He stood on the podium and surveyed the several hundred conference participants. He praised them for their wonderful work. Then he announced that only a few small changes would be made in the *DSM-III* personality section so that the *DSM-IV* personality section would not be much different from its predecessor. It was as if the conference had never taken place and that the substantial research delineating personality had never been done.

Since that conference, although the image of personality has been continuously refined, the *DSM* version has remained mostly unchanged. *DSM-5* is said to be adding a dimensional criterion to its format but that still will not reflect the science of personality. Medical students and psychiatric residents learn only the *DSM* version and so have been left behind in their understanding of normal personality structure and how that understanding can be used in counseling patients to adopt healthier life styles, to better comply with needed treatments, and to cope with the slings and arrows life throws at all of us. These traits also help predict future drug and alcohol abuse and the likelihood of relapse.[30]

The second example of how the process of creating a *DSM* is more political and administrative than scientific occurred just a few years ago early in the process of the development of what will be *DSM-5*. My colleague, Max Fink, and I wrote a textbook about catatonia in which we marshaled all the evidence to that point.[31] The data showed that catatonia was a syndrome much like delirium. It had many causes and several presentations. Catatonia was common in acute treatment psychiatric settings; it was not exclusively linked to schizophrenia as all previous *DSMs* had required but was more likely to be a feature of manic-depression and other brain disorders. We showed that if properly identified and treated, almost all patients with catatonia should recover quickly. Our effort and subsequent papers stimulated additional research that continued to support our conclusions. We encouraged the *DSM-5* workgroup responsible for deciding the fate of catatonia to make it a separate category as that best reflected the data.[32] The workgroup members generally agreed with us, but then one member called me and reluctantly said that they could not follow the data in this case because *"all the numbers"* were taken. Could we find a number for catatonia?

The workgroup member was referring to the fact that each *DSM* diagnosis must have an official number for insurance and charting purposes, and there was "no room" for a separate catatonia category. Imagine the medical establishment denying the official recognition of a newly discovered viral disease because the International Classification of Disease was booked for the foreseeable future. It's easier to get a hotel room in New York City for New Year's Eve at the last minute than a new number in the *DSM*.

DSM-III saw the light of day in 1980. In 1987, a revision, *DSM-IIIR*, was required. It offered 292 diagnostic choices. In 1994, another version, *DSM-IV*, with 295 choices hit the bookshelves. A *DSM-IVTR* next appeared in 2000. *DSM-5* is due in 2013 and will offer over 300 choices. The Roman numeral was dropped. Too many revisions are anticipated and, after all, it isn't quite the cultural icon the Super Bowl is.

The explosion of diagnoses from the 22 recognized in 1918 or the 16 identified by the Washington University researchers in the 1970s to the present of over 300 is a fabrication of the political process. Every practitioner group will have its pet condition: the "earmarks" of psychiatry. The pharmaceutical industry adores the explosion of conditions, because as "medical diagnoses" the *DSM* categories provide the rationale for prescribing drugs. It is too much of a coincidence in my view that more than half of the workgroup members that made the decisions on what would be included in the *DSM-IVR* had undisclosed financial ties to the pharmaceutical industry. Among the workgroup members for mood disorder, 100% had industry associations. Eighty percent of the workgroup members for anxiety and eating disorders had such ties.[33]

The links of medical academics and physicians responsible for fundamental decisions about their field to the pharmaceutical industry, however, are not limited to psychiatry. *The New York Times* regularly exposes these connections and their influence upon important decisions about pharmaceuticals. An article in the November 3, 2011 issue (pp. B1 and B6), for example, detailed the existing conflicts of interests of members of the health guideline panels making recommendations about medications for hypertension, obesity, and cholesterol. Five of 17, 8 of 19, and 7 of 16 members, respectively, had conflicts of interest. *All* of these conflicts were among the academics.[34] They will be passing this ethical standard on to the next generation of physicians.

The association between industry and the framers of psychiatry's diagnostic system continues in the development of *DSM-5*. The *DSM-5* process also suffers from the same sociopolitical pressures as its predecessors. A recent series of articles in the *New York Times* details the struggles among workgroups, lobbyists for different psychiatric constituencies, and previous *DSM* chairmen. Putative disorders were proposed and then under pressure the workgroup "backed down." Science had little to do with any of it. Guidelines were weakened for identifying several conditions, raising concerns that the mental health system would be overwhelmed by persons meeting the new diagnostic criteria but who would not be ill.[35] Standards for acceptable reliability were also watered down so that the present field trials of the proposed system yielded results that were worse than what was experienced in previous versions, including *DSM-II*. The watering down will help the pharmaceutical industry because as more persons are identified as ill, the justification grows for increased numbers of prescriptions. Authors of several surveys report an increase in the average number of DSM work group members with industry ties from 57% for *DSM-IV* to 83% for *DSM-5*.[36]

The latest *DSM* will be required reading for trainees. Like its predecessors, it will be used worldwide in categorizing research samples and it will be the standard diagnostic system in grant applications. It will also be needed for its diagnostic labels and their respective numbers for billing purposes, and it will be the standard reference in legal proceedings involving a mental health concern. Like previous versions, it will be a best seller. The APA publishes the manual and makes a mint from the purchases of each version. Although the bible, Quotations from Chairman Mao, the Koran, and Harry Potter do better, the combined versions of the *DSM* have sold about two million copies. Since the Gideons put a Saint James version of the bible in almost every hotel and motel room in the United States, can the APA be far behind in adding *DSM*s? After all, according to a National Institute of Mental Health (NIMH) study based on the newer *DSM*s, half the U.S. population will experience a diagnosable psychiatric condition during their lifetimes.[37] A weary traveler could get a "two-for." Browse the *DSM* in the drawer to find out what ails him and then read the bible for solace.

THE INJUSTICE OF A CORRUPTING INFLUENCE: THE PHARMACEUTICAL INDUSTRY

Political infighting among the many factions comprising U.S. psychiatry has undermined the science of psychiatric diagnosis. Money, in turn, has corrupted U.S. clinical psychopharmacology. There never was an "Eden," but there now is a serpent in the psychiatric garden, and it has taken the form of the pharmaceutical industry. I've already detailed how the industry adversely influences training.

The Hippocratic Oath instructs us to treat with optimism but not to simply throw one treatment after another at the patient. William Osler, the first professor of medicine at Johns Hopkins, and through his writing and teaching the most influential physician in the United States at the turn of nineteenth to the twentieth centuries, pointed out that *"the young physician starts life with 20 drugs for each disease, and the old physician ends life with one drug for 20 diseases."* Experience has always taught the receptive physician that less is often more. This axiom, however, does not prevail in U.S. psychiatry today. When making rounds in consultation to other services at the university hospital we often encounter a patient who is inexplicably on many medications. Sometimes the list reaches double digits and often includes unnecessarily duplicated medications. Frequently the patient receives medications that are not needed at all. Multiple specialists see the same patient and each prescribes treatments for that patient as if practicing in a vacuum. When I am asked by a resident or medical student what behavioral syndrome I think the patient suffers from, I offer the technical diagnosis and then often add that the more fundamental diagnosis is *"too much physician."*

In U.S. psychiatric practice today, most physicians, young and old, academic and in private practice, act as if they had little of the experience Osler praised. Mega-polypharmacy is common. Osler has been called "the father of modern medicine," but he'd surely disown present day U.S. psychiatry. For the past 25 years, U.S. psychiatry has been subverted by the pharmaceutical industry. The subversion became apparent in the late 1980s at the APA annual meetings. Most of the week-long meeting that used to be devoted to scientific presentations or workshops that were designed to improve patient care or the understanding of the pathophysiology of a disease had been coopted by the industry to present infomercials about their drugs. Every lobby, corridor, and meeting area offered video information about a drug. Drug reps were everywhere (hunk-types for the women docs, sexy young women in tight suits for the men docs). The reps held meetings to "teach" physicians about the new drugs. They offered hospitality suites overflowing with free food and drink and sponsored dinners at expensive restaurants for the APA members. They arranged future junkets to fancy spas for the promise of prescribing a minimum number of doses of the drug being promoted. The main convention hall that used to be an area in which new technology and textbooks were to be found was now an extravaganza of giant amusement park-styled structures lauding the merits of this or that psychiatric drug. In a study of all exhibit booths of pharmaceutical companies at the 2002 APA convention, 16 major rules violations were found.[38] The change in the APA meetings from an effort to update the membership on scientific, clinical, and social issues that impacted psychiatrists to week-long infomercials for the pharmaceutical industry is a symptom of the broader subversion of the science and clinical practice of psychiatry.

Who Controls the Data Controls the Prescribing

When the first generation of psychotropic agents was being developed, the pharmaceutical industry scientists worked with academic psychopharmacologists to produce drugs that were effective. The goal was useful and safe agents. New drugs were tested by the academics who designed and ran the studies and analyzed and published the data. Industry provided the drugs and supported the research but was minimally intrusive.

Beginning in the 1980s, research that assessed the efficacy and safety of psychoactive drugs became mostly an industry affair as their patent protections were reinforced by the federal Bayh-Dole Act. The legislation also offered universities protection of their intellectual property so that the "academic" laboratory could do the basic science and then "sell" the products to industry. Both parties climbed into the same bed.

To ensure the investment, the pharmaceutical companies took over the bulk of the clinical trials that tested the new agents. Industry recruited physicians in multisite collaborative efforts. This strategy was necessary because the new generation of agents was weakly effective and so patient samples larger than what were studied in the older research were required to demonstrate clinical efficacy. Statistical significance was the needed currency to demonstrate efficacy, not the actual remission of illness, and so large samples were needed to provide adequate statistical "power." Each company designed and funded its studies so that there was no independent scientific review of the proposal before getting started as is required for projects that receive grants from sponsors without conflicts of interest.

The participating physicians were often paid by the number of subjects that they entered into the study plus overhead costs. The more quickly subjects can be recruited and the larger their numbers, the greater is the likelihood the clinical site will continue in the project and maintain its financial support from the company. The principal investigator at a site might also receive direct payment as a stipend of thousands of dollars to be a "consultant" to the company. Some prominent psychiatrists were offered company stock, no small benefit as the pharmaceutical industry has been one of the most profitable industries in the world for several decades. Contract payment for the work was often based on the submission of the completed schedule forms for each patient visit. Bonuses were paid for completion of all the patient's scheduled records. Thus, the investigators were encouraged through financial incentive to get as many subjects as possible into the study and to completion regardless of what was scientifically or ethically warranted. They were also encouraged to complete all the forms regardless of whether the subject was able to reliably provide all the needed information. In one review of 500 randomly selected clinical trials published in influential journals between 1981 and 2000, almost two-thirds were identified as industry connected.[39] Those studies were designed to develop the minimal definition of a compound's efficacy, safety, and tolerability in order to meet government licensing requirements. Only two positive studies are needed for FDA approval.[40]

The domination of therapeutic drug trials by the pharmaceutical industry has not changed substantially despite the conspicuous breast beating of journal editors and some leaders in the field. In October 2011, a promotional campaign was launched by Forest Pharmaceuticals for their newest antidepressant vilazodone (Vibryd).[41] The ads claimed that the agent worked well and cited two of its sponsored studies published in psychiatric journals as proof. The differences in depression rating scores between the placebo groups and the drug groups, however, although statistically significant, were clinically meaningless. A statistical difference between a new agent and placebo is not a sufficient standard of adequate efficacy. There are several antidepressants on the market with "proof" that they work but many clinicians recognize that these agents offer little benefit to patients.

Several decades ago my department was involved in a multisite company-sponsored study that assessed the usefulness of what was then the newest antipsychotic (Clozapine). The drug was being touted as the best advance for the treatment of schizophrenia since the introduction of chlorpromazine, the original antipsychotic agent. Our department had access to a neuropsychiatric hospital with over a thousand patients that potentially could fit the study's requirements. Because of the study's design, however, it took us over a year to recruit a dozen patients, and about eight patients completed the project. Imagine our surprise when another study site with access to under 100 beds, most of which were not likely to yield appropriate study protocol patients, completed 25 subjects in 6 months. Even comic book superheroes don't work that fast.

Like most clinical trials today, the study design of our project, medication dosages to be used, evaluation points, duration of the investigation, and the construction of the rating instruments were determined by the company. The data crunching in such efforts is typically done by the company and not by the investigators, whose roles, as was our experience, are often limited to the selection of subjects and the entry and follow-up assessments. The role of the company, so critical to the design and all other clinical evaluations, is rarely described in the methods section in the published reports. In one survey, only eight of 100 studies identified the role of the industry sponsors.[42]

Conflicts of Interest Are Common

Despite efforts to ensure better editor oversight of the reports in their journals and implementation of strict guidelines to limit conflicts of interest, the role of the company in controlling drug studies in psychiatry and in the publication of the results continues.[43] The field has deluded itself into believing that by disclosing the connections between the investigators and the company, the results can be accepted as legitimate. When a speaker (or writer) discloses some affiliation the audience tends to then trust what the speaker is going to opine. "After all," they think, "he did fess up to his association with 'the mob'." So now, following the list of the authors of a study, are the details of their affiliations with industry. Despite the hoopla, less than 1% of published medical articles adhere to the policy. The disclosures that are reported, however, commonly require more space than the statements about the authors' academic affiliations. There is also evidence that the presenters making the disclosures become even more biased in what they say as some adopt the attitude that the audience "has been warned."[44]

But if there is any financial connection between the author or speaker and the company, how can we accept their findings? Simply disclosing the relationship doesn't pass the smell test. Would you accept a judge in a legal suit against you who said, *"In the spirit of disclosure, I just want you to know that the person suing you is my business partner?"* Psychiatrists, however, are supposed to do just that in accepting the results of a medication efficacy and safety study by investigators with a long list of "partnerships" with pharmaceutical companies.

The subversion of U.S. clinical pharmacology by the pharmaceutical industry cannot be overemphasized. As additional examples, the 2001 published reports from both print and electronic issues of *The New England Journal of Medicine* and *The Journal of the American Medical Association* were analyzed for author conflict of interest and for industry sponsorship. The two publications are considered to be among the most prestigious of U.S. medical journals. Almost 40% of authors of drug treatment trials were identified as industry consultants, reinforcing the impression that there is an association between the acknowledged consulting relationships and positive reports of the efficacy of the medication marketed by the sponsor.[45] An examination of all published articles reporting the "cost effectiveness" of antidepressant drugs found that studies of selective serotonin reuptake inhibitors or SSRIs (e.g., Prozac) sponsored by the manufacturer more often favored their drug over the older tricyclic antidepressants or TCAs (e.g., Elavil) than did non-industry-sponsored studies.[46]

Even more disturbing is the finding that among the authors of the highly influential clinical practice guidelines published by psychiatric associations and required reading by residents, 81% had industry ties that include research funding and direct compensation as consultants or employees. Such a conflict-of-interest relationship is prohibited for government employees.[47] Clinical practice guidelines set a standard not only for practice but for training residents and medical students in what drugs to start with and what to do if the first choice doesn't work as hoped. The trainees are tested on the guidelines. They are expected to follow them in practice, and their futures depend on their getting the "right" guideline answers on their standardized national specialty and licensing examinations. But what is being taught are industry-formulated guidelines, not evidence-based psychopharmacology.

SHELL GAMES

The influence of the pharmaceutical industry over U.S. psychiatry, however, goes beyond controlling studies assessing drugs and paying the investigators. Company-sponsored studies are fatally flawed regardless of who is involved.

"Fixing" the Race

A resident who before joining our program worked for one of the big pharmaceutical companies told me, *"All our double-blind studies were biased."* A double-blind study is a design in which neither the subjects nor the investigators doing the assessments know whether a subject is getting the active drug or the placebo, or, if the study is comparing an old drug to a new one, which drug a patient is receiving. The resident told me that the old drug was commonly selected to be one with side-effects that are easily detected so that the assessors really "know" who was getting what. One party in the double-blind study was "peeking."

Testing Antidepressants: Subjects Aren't Ill or Representative of Clinical Practice

Depression is one of the most common of conditions and the health care costs of it are enormous. The pharmaceutical industry loves depression and there is no way to avoid an ad for an antidepressant if you watch commercial TV. The drugs that are pushed for the treatment of depression are promoted as if they work for all types of depression, but the more severely ill depressed patients, those with suicidal risk and those in a hospital, are rarely included in clinical trials of antidepressant drugs. Most participants are outpatients or have been recruited for the study by advertisements offering free care under research auspices or payment for participation. These modestly ill persons comprise the bulk of the data in the industry-supported studies that are the basis for application for licensing for the marketing of antidepressants. The equivalent situation would be testing a medication as a treatment for lung infections but mostly in persons with head colds as well as a few with viral or bacterial pneumonia. Most of the subjects will recover, especially those with head colds. With such "efficacy established" the drug can be marketed as if it were useful for patients with all lung infections, including bacterial pneumonia. Some investigators who utilize ads and payments as a recruitment method have reported that some volunteers are fraudulent and apply to multiple studies to obtain the fee for participation.[48]

Standards for subjects to meet the criteria for "illness" are minimized, facilitating the recruitment of the largest number of participants. The volunteers who are elderly or adolescent, who have complicating general medical illnesses, or who are too severely depressed to be likely to complete an outpatient trial are rejected. Suicidal, psychotic, manic-depressive, stuporous, or catatonic depressed patients are excluded. Depressed patients with alcoholism, drug abuse, and anxiety disorder are typically excluded. Melancholic patients are often too ill for a drug trial or are excluded when placebo is a design feature because patients with melancholia are known to have low placebo response rates. Industry wants subjects with high response rates (see below). The selection criteria ensure that the subjects in most therapeutic antidepressant drug trials are minimally ill and do not represent the bulk of patients with depressive illness seen in clinical practice. In one survey of 346 outpatients with major depression, only 14% would have been eligible for the typical treatment trial study.[49] Thus although the pharmaceutical industry claims that antidepressants work for all persons with depression, they have actually shown that if they work at all, it is for a select group of patients. U.S. psychiatrists either don't know this fact or have chosen to ignore it because they prescribe the same antidepressants to almost all patients with the diagnosis of depression.

Although industry avoids the more severely ill, it still wants the sample to appear severely ill. A few years ago several medical centers participated in a multisite study of a medical device for depression: transcranial magnetic stimulation (TMS). A magnet is placed over the left front of the patient's head and it delivers a weak electromagnetic wave that penetrates to the underlying cortex. Our medical center was one site and several of us were willing to assess subjects before and toward the end of the treatment trial. To be part of the team, we had to assess some patients together. We used a rating scale for depression that I had used hundreds of times over the years in many other studies. I knew the scale by heart. I also know how to assess for depression and no one has ever questioned my clinical abilities. In fact, I'm good at assessing patients for depressive illness. I co-authored a book about it. One of the other participants, a nurse, had a similar long experience with the scale. Nevertheless, of all the clinicians assessing the patients in our prestudy exercise, only she and I were rejected as assessors by the manufacturer. The reason given was that we scored the patients too low on the scale. The company wanted high scores so that the subjects would appear to be severely ill. Then almost any intervention over time would end with patients with lowered scores and the appearance of improvement. That the most experienced raters were also the raters producing the lowest ratings suggested to me that we had seen many more patients with the severest of illness and so did not provide the highest ratings for the patients in the prestudy trial as they were not severely ill.

I happened to pass the waiting area for the study when the first subject showed up. I chatted with her and could detect few signs of depression. She was animated and in good humor. Patients with depressive illness are *never* animated and in good humor. Later that day, I asked our study site coordinator what the subject's score was on the rating scale and I was told "24." On that scale, a score of 24 meant substantial depression that should be easily identified. The industry bias is to make the subject appear as ill as possible so that the new drug being tested looks more effective than it actually is.

Hiding the Data

It is now routine for the company to maintain and analyze the data from the multisite studies, often with little or no investigator input. When results do not meet expectations, and are deemed unsuitable for a government filing, the data are "sealed" and are not published or available for scrutiny. One of my colleagues, Max Fink, told me of his experience participating in a company-sponsored randomized controlled trial of hospitalized depressed patients assigned to the company's drug (Zoloft), an old antidepressant (imipramine), and to a placebo. The data were sealed and the investigators were not given access to the code indicating which patients in their site had received which medication. Without that code the investigators could not do their own independent analyses. The ostensible reason given was that the records were incomplete, but the investigators remained concerned that the company's decision was because the company's drug was not distinguishable from placebo, or that the old antidepressant was found to be superior.

Perhaps the most egregious example of hiding the data was the industry's response to the suspicion that the Prozac-like drugs, the SSRIs, were somehow associated with an increased risk of suicide in teenagers. Industry offered as its defense all the studies that were in their favor and at first denied that there were contrary studies. They marshaled well-known U.S. psychiatrists who received substantial industry support to challenge the idea of increased suicide risk. It took Great Britain to force the issue. The

British government informed the industry that any company not releasing all the data to British investigators for analysis would have their vending license denied, thus preventing them from doing business in the United Kingdom. The companies had no choice but to release the data they first said wasn't there, and the British analysis confirmed the association between the SSRIs and increased suicide risk in teens.[50] The association between SSRIs and increased suicide risk, however, continues to be challenged. A recent analysis of *all industry-sponsored trials* of an SSRI [fluoxetine (Prozac)] and an SNRI [venlafaxine (Effexor)] did not find an association.[51]

The discrepancy may be the results of the biases built into industry-sponsored studies and of differences in the severity of illness among samples. The more severely depressed patients may be those at increased risk for suicide when prescribed SSRIs. The association is not because these drugs excite some suicide center in the brain as there is none. A more likely explanation is that SSRIs tend to make patients jumpy and interfere with sleep. Persons with severe depressive illness are already jumpy, anxious, and suffer from sleep difficulties. They don't need more of the same. The SSRIs are, at best, also weak antidepressants. Most patients receiving them do not have a timely remission of their depression. So, imagine a severely depressed teenager, despondent and feeling little hope, who then receives a medication that is supposed to work well but instead doesn't relieve the depression and makes things worse. Teenagers are often impulsive, and as things go from bad to worse, suicide suddenly becomes a "way out" of a seemingly hopeless and worsening situation.

The sequestering of data unfavorable to the company is not limited to psychiatric treatments and the associated immorality is just as disturbing. *The New York Times* (November 4, 2011, p. B6) reported that Medtronic, the maker of a product used during spinal fusions to enhance bone growth, refrained from publishing data showing the true high risk for cancer among patients exposed to the drug. One medical journal cited in the article also concluded that "much of [the] earlier research, which Medtronic financed, failed to accurately characterize the risks posed" by their product.

Data favorable to a company's product, however, are always published. In a recent study, 37 of 74 FDA-registered studies that were associated with positive outcomes were published and one was not. Only three of the 36 negative studies were published.[52] Why not publish all the studies? Because when *all* the data from clinical trials submitted to the FDA for the licensing of four new-generation antidepressants were analyzed, there were no significant differences between the drugs and placebo except in the most severely ill patients.[53]

Consistent adherence to the spirit of the government requirement (U.S. Public Law 110–85; Food and Drug Administration Amendments Act of 2007, Title VIII, Section 801) to publish all relevant studies would be a good start, but that change would not be sufficient to maximize confidence in those studies, and companies can still "hide" data they deem to be not relevant.

Many reports are also "ghost-written" by the company's professional writers with the acquiescence of academic investigators as the lead authors. The reports are published in journals that receive substantial advertising support from the company. Such practices are more prevalent in the United States than they are in Great Britain. The difference accounts, in part, for the pattern that drug trials from the United States tend to favor the new agents such as Prozac (fluoxetine) and the even newer drugs such as Cymbalta (duloxetine) and Celexa (citalopram). The trend is likely to continue as the next "new" agents are introduced. Drug trials from other countries, in which the connections between academics and the pharmaceutical industry are limited, tend to favor the older medications (tricyclic antidepressants or TCAs such as nortriptyline), which are less expensive drugs as they no longer are under patent and thus are available in generic forms.

The Industry's Definition of What "Works" Is Accepted Leaving Many Patients Ill

The industry also sets the standard for what is meant for a drug to "work." Many academic psychiatrists have bought into this odd situation. It is equivalent to the auto industry setting the standard rather than the government for what is "good mileage." For example, the pharmaceutical industry and the investigators that they have recruited have convinced the field that an antidepressant drug works if it achieves a 50% reduction in rating scale scores, rather than remission. This is a weakened and clinically inadequate end-point that favors drugs with only modest efficacy. It leaves many subjects who are identified as "responders" still significantly ill.

In a review of randomized controlled clinical trials of antidepressants and the data filed with the FDA to license antidepressant drugs, a prominent researcher of depressive illness not associated with industry[54] found that the effects of new antidepressants differed only marginally from placebo. Another independent researcher[55] concluded that the *"pharmacologic effects of antidepressants are clinically negligible."* Even industry-sponsored studies provide minimal support for the new agents. In one such study of the use of any SSRI drug in 601 primary care patients, 62% were assessed as receiving adequate treatment, yet only 23% achieved remission and 46% were nonresponders.[56] Reviews of the clinical trial literature conclude that the decreased standards of response contribute to lingering illness and frequent relapses. The longer an episode of depression lasts, the more likely that patient will have future episodes of depression and the more likely these episodes will be increasingly resistant to treatment. The repeated prescription of one weak medication after another for months and years with only minimal relief creates chronicity. Remission should be the gold standard to judge efficacy.[57]

Padding the Efficacy Data Using the Placebo Effect

Another slight-of-hand is the manipulation of the placebo effect. Some patients in studies respond to the "sugar pill." The effect is good news for the industry because the magnitude of the placebo response in a medication trial correlates with the magnitude of the "therapeutic" effect of the medication being tested. In other words, the more patients in the study who respond to placebo, the better, as that means there will also be placebo responders in the group receiving the company's drug. The drug's effect will be padded. Studies with a large placebo effect show a larger medication effect than do studies with a small placebo effect. You might wonder how it helps the results if both the drug group and the placebo group have similar padding. The first part of the answer is that industry prefers studies without a placebo group, comparing instead their new drug to an old agent. When placebo cannot be avoided, the new drug group will express both the weak new drug effect and the placebo effect. The placebo group gets the effect of only the placebo. If the sample is large enough, the small difference between the two groups can be statistically significant. In reports and ads the company can then legally say, *"In clinical trials our drug was better than placebo...50% of patients responded to our drug"* or *"'ProSmile' has been shown to work in scientific clinical trials."* As the saying goes, *"There are lies, damn lies, and statistics."*

One review considered antidepressant treatment trials from 1985 through 1998 as well as FDA-reviewed but unpublished studies. The review involved over 9000 patients. Among the patients receiving placebo, there was a 30% drop in the average rating scale score, compared to a 42% drop among those receiving one of the new antidepressant drugs. Both groups were still full of ill patients as the drops in scores are not clinically impressive.[58] In such a large sample, however, the difference is statistically significant and the companies could claim that the drugs are effective. Remember, the industry self-declared standard was a 50% drop. Thus, they had to ignore their standard to claim efficacy using these data. It gets worse.

Patients who respond to placebo are similar to patients who respond to SSRI agents such as Prozac. Thus, the response rates of SSRIs are substantially inflated with placebo responders.[59] This effect becomes particularly important when patient recruitment is in response to advertisements, rather than from clinical samples. This common practice leads to the inclusion of subjects who are not clinically ill. In one study of persons identified as "depressed," further analysis revealed that only 35% with modest to low depression scores actually had a clinical depression, whereas 86% with high depression scores were defined as clinically depressed. Studies sponsored by the company need raters who rate high so the patients appear ill.[60]

The Quality of Antidepressant Studies Is Poor and the Efficacy of the Newer Agents Is Weak

To make matters more disturbing, the quality of the studies passed off as evidence of efficacy is poor. Because so many studies involve small samples that report a range of results, there is now a trend in the psychopharmacology literature to rely on studies that pool the data from many small reports into one big one in which the data can be better analyzed. These pooled studies are called meta-analyses. Of course, pooling bad small studies doesn't make for a good big one, but that's the trend.

One meta-analysis of published medication studies in major depression from 1980 to 2002 identified 100 other meta-analytic reviews of randomized controlled antidepressant trials, i.e., a pooling of studies of pooled data, like bundling mortgages in a hedge fund. Many of the identified studies were rejected for critical inadequacies in design, biased subject selection, and ill-defined outcome measures. Using a guideline measure of quality of each study, the average quality score for the 32 remaining publications was calculated to be about 50%, or *"barely acceptable."* The investigators concluded that the data were too flawed to provide clear recommendations about the efficacy of antidepressant drugs.[61] This analysis captured 20 years of studies of the medication treatment for depression. The data boil down to the fact that the drugs that psychiatric residents and young psychiatrists are required to use first to treat patients with depressive illness are not very good. The remission rate for the Prozac-like agents, the SSRIs, is 20–30% and another 20% of patients are said to modestly improve. The placebo remission rate in the same studies is 30–40%. Would anyone want to take an antibiotic that had only a 30% chance of curing the infection and whose result might be only slightly better than a bowl of chicken soup?

The latest class of drugs for depression is called serotonin and norepinephrine reuptake inhibitors (SNRIs). These agents affect two different neurotransmitter systems: serotonin and norepinephrine. The remission rates of SNRIs are about 40%. They are better than the narrower spectrum SSRIs, but no one wins a Kewpie doll. The oldest antidepressants, the TCAs, have remission rates of about 50–60%. In some studies in which serum drug levels were used to guide dosing rather than the milligrams of the pills that the patients took, rates of remission or improvement approached 70%. These rates, however, were achieved for patients with melancholic type depressions not for the hodgepodge that comprises samples of depressed patients in recent studies.[62]

Despite all the studies detailed above, an "expert" NIMH panel stated that *"The SSRIs are* **clearly** *the drug treatment of choice for* **all forms** *of depression in the United States* [**my stresses added**] ... *These drugs are approximately equivalent to each other and to TCAs in efficacy ... The SSRIs have a much more benign side effect profile than TCAs and, largely for this reason, have replaced TCAs as first line therapy"*[63] What do these panelists, many supported by industry, offer as their reasons for the recommendation?

Ill-Considered Reasons Offered by "Experts" for Favoring New Antidepressants

The oldest antidepressants are more deadly: One rationale given for the official preference for the newer antidepressant agents is that although a lethal dose of a TCA can be amassed by a patient who wishes to kill himself, it is more difficult for most patients to amass a lethal dose with an SSRI. This is true. But here's how to minimize the risk of such an overdose. First, if there is any doubt, hospitalize the patient. If hospitalization is not needed, don't prescribe large numbers of pills! Recruit a responsible family member or loved one to dole out the medication. During the first week or two, before the medication's effect will be noticed by the patient, call the patient almost daily. A 5-minute phone round chat is reassuring and demonstrates to the patient the physician's commitment and that the patient is not alone. See the patient weekly until the depression is well on its way to being resolved. Many medications that physicians prescribe are lethal when taken in overdose, but we don't avoid a blood thinner that may prevent strokes or chemotherapy to treat cancer because there are risks in doing so. Such agents can be prescribed correctly and the patient can be closely monitored. If a patient with depressive illness is imminently suicidal, forget about drug choice, that patient needs to be hospitalized. If the patient can control any suicidal impulses then the best and fastest treatment under some supervision is the safest approach. If patients are cared for, not just prescribed some pills, they will most often comply with what needs to be done. Family and friends can help. Suicide is fairly common in the United States with over 30,000 *recorded* deaths annually. Most of these could be avoided by prescribing treatments that work well and by following William Osler's admonition, *"The good physician treats the disease; the great physician treats the patient who has the disease."*

The newer agents work as well as the older agents: Another reason that is given by the establishment for favoring the newer antidepressants is that as they have about the same efficacy as the older agents and since they are "safer," why not use them first? Industry-sponsored studies are cited to support this contention,[64] but those studies are suspect. The assertion also takes advantage of the simplified *DSM* and its low threshold for determining illness, particularly depressive illness. The market has gotten artificially larger by the low threshold, and promotion has increased demand further. The notion that there is only one kind of depression supports the industry's mantra that SSRIs are the first choice for all patients with depression. Almost all studies that have examined samples of patients with the *DSM* diagnosis of depression find distinct groupings, not homogeneity.[65] Similar to its predecessors, however, *DSM-5* will not recognize this heterogeneity for depression, or for patients who receive any of its many diagnoses. Recruiting a large "mixed-bag" sample in a drug trial masks real differences in responses to different treatments. Different forms of depression respond differently to different treatments.

For example, patients with melancholia respond to ECT whereas persons with milder forms of depression mostly do not. If all depressions were the same, then the milder forms should respond best to the most powerful treatment, but they do not. The more severe form does. Patients with melancholia are also more likely to respond to TCAs than to SSRIs. Clinicians in other countries know this.[66] A meta-analysis of drug trials also found efficacy to dramatically favor TCAs for hospitalized depressed patients, but not for other groups.[67] Hospitalized depressed patients are also more likely to be melancholic.[68]

Another meta-analysis also found that TCAs were more effective than SSRIs in treating severely depressed and elderly patients.[69] This finding is contrary to the industry's promotion of its newest patent-protected agents. The industry would like us to believe that older patients should not be given TCAs because they cannot tolerate them and are prone to adverse cardiovascular side effects. But dropout rates from the two drug classes are similar, and there are no significant cardiovascular problems when the second-generation TCAs are properly prescribed.[70] Other industry-independent studies also find TCAs to be superior to SSRIs in the treatment of patients with severe depression.[71]

Patients with melancholia associated with a neurological or a general medical condition also seem to benefit best from a TCA. For example, a report comparing nortriptyline to fluoxetine (Prozac) in the treatment of depression in poststroke patients found nortriptyline to be superior. Success rates were 77% for nortriptyline, 14% for fluoxetine, and 31% for placebo. Fluoxetine was accompanied by unwanted and substantial weight loss (average 8% of body weight). The average age for these patients was in the mid-60s, but contrary to accepted ideas about tolerance, the dropout rate in the fluoxetine group was three times that of the nortriptyline group.[72]

The newer agents have fewer and less severe side effects: In addition to the straw man of suicide risk with TCAs, another reason given for recommending the newer agents rather than the older medications is that the side effects of the newer agents are less common and less disturbing than those of the older medications. This conclusion, however, is the result of another misrepresentation by the pharmaceutical industry as the poststroke report above suggests. The distortion derives from studies in which an SSRI is compared to a TCA. The TCA in all but a handful of the comparisons, however, was one of the original TCA agents that often causes dry mouth, and for some patients constipation, and difficulty urinating. These side effects are due to the anticholinergic properties of the first-generation TCAs. They can also elicit dizziness, sedation, and weight gain. Most SSRIs [paroxetine (Paxil) is an exception] have few anticholinergic properties. These side effect differences are the clues that can subvert the double-blind study. However, the second-generation TCAs (desipramine, nortriptyline) have about a third of the anticholinergic effect and so are better tolerated than the first-generation TCAs. They are rarely the comparison old drug, however, because they are well tolerated by most patients. It would be harder to distinguish them in a double-blind study. In a meta-analysis of 115 suitable studies comparing SSRIs and TCAs, only one study compared an SSRI to nortriptyline and only six to desipramine, both second-generation TCAs.[73] Another meta-analysis of 105 randomized, head-to-head comparison trials found that no study included nortriptyline and that the comparison drug was commonly given in low, often inadequate doses. The company's drug was given at its recommended dose.[74]

The blatancy of the manipulation of the antidepressant drug literature and the demonstrated weak efficacy of the newer agents, despite the manipulation of studies in their favor, have encouraged a growing challenge to the idea that the SSRIs are better tolerated and safer than TCAs.[75] Leaders in the field, however, some beholden to the pharmaceutical industry, continue to support the newer agents and essentially ignore the studies I have discussed. Teaching institutions also ignore or minimize these studies but continue to accept industry funding for drug trials and other activities.

Industry Manipulates the Prescription of Other Classes of Medications

The promotion of psychiatric drugs other than antidepressants also distorts the usefulness of these agents. For example, the September 21, 2005, editorial page of *The New York Times* concluded, "*A government-financed study has provided the strongest evidence yet that the system for approving and promoting drugs is badly out of whack.*" The study cited in *The Times* compared five drugs used to treat schizophrenia and found that "*most of the newest, most heavily prescribed drugs were no better than an older drug that is far cheaper. The nation is wasting billions of dollars on heavily marketed drugs that have never proved themselves in head-to-head competition against cheaper competitors.*"

The *New York Times* article was referring to the newer types of antipsychotic drugs classified by their effects on brain chemistry as "atypical" antipsychotics (e.g., Ziprexa or olanzapine, Seroquel or quetiapine, and Rispiridol/Consta or rispiridone). These agents are heavily marketed as safe, sleep-enhancing, and agitation-controlling agents. Academic psychiatrists gave paid endorsements along with their photographs that were included in the promotional literature. These powerful drugs are offered as helpful in the management of patients with Alzheimer's disease, and they are widely prescribed for it. But I see the adverse results of this practice daily with patients becoming cognitively worse, Parkinson-like, or thrown into a life-threatening malignant catatonia. As an example, in a study of over 400 outpatients with Alzheimer's disease who were also psychotic, agitated, or aggressive, patients were randomly assigned to receive one of the newer antipsychotics or a placebo. They were followed for 36 weeks and regularly assessed for their cognitive abilities. Overall, as expected for patients with Alzheimer's disease, they showed steady and significant declines over time in most cognitive areas. The decline, however, was more severe in the patients who were receiving an antipsychotic than among those given placebo.[76] Another *New York Times* article, this one on December 23, 2011, documents the indiscriminant and rampant prescription of antipsychotic and other psychotropic agents to institutionalized persons with developmental difficulties. These patients are particularly at risk for a severe form of drug-induced catatonia that can be lethal if not properly and rapidly treated. Most recently (April 12, 2012, p. B1) *The New York Times* reported that Johnson and Johnson, the manufacturer of the atypical antipsychotic rispiridone, was found guilty in a jury trial of concealing the dangers of the drug and its risks for weight gain and inducing diabetes, and of causing strokes in older patients. The court fined the company 1.2 billion dollars. Eli Lilly, Pfizer, and GlaxoSmithKline (GSK) have also been fined billions of dollars for their "criminal conduct." The last of these convictions involved a study in which the antidepressant paroxetine (Paxil) was reported to be effective in children with depressive illness. The study was ghost-written by the manufacturer and the data manipulated to fraudulently appear to show efficacy. Adverse drug-related events including suicides were hidden. The American College of Neuropsychopharmacology has distanced itself from GSK, a previous sponsor, and many of the organization's members have called for the front-men academic authors of the report to retract the study or face further censure (personal communication from several members).

Aided and Abetted by Academia: Unneeded Drug Combinations

Another pharmaceutical industry ploy is to convince clinicians to use many medications simultaneously (i.e., polypharmacy), claiming that two are better than one. This is consistently true only for donuts. Although two psychiatric medications will cost the patient more and make more profits for the industry, drug combinations will mostly increase the risk of side effects rather than remission rates. In most cases (there are important exceptions such as the enhancement of an antidepressant with lithium) a two psychiatric drug regimen is no better than a single drug approach. For example, a large longitudinal study of almost 2000 patients with manic-depression assessed quarterly for an average of 21 months while the patients received one or two atypical antipsychotics reported that those receiving two agents experienced more side effects (e.g., sedation, sexual dysfunction, constipation, tremor, dry mouth) and used the health service more, but did not experience greater improvement in their symptoms or functioning.[77]

In another study,[78] a randomized trial of 665 outpatients at six primary care and nine psychiatric care sites, patients who had at least moderately severe nonpsychotic chronic or recurrent depression were assessed for the effects of being treated with one or two of the newer antidepressants. Remission and response rates and most secondary outcomes (e.g., global functioning in life situations and personal and employment relationships) were not different among the one- or two-drug treatment groups or for any combination of agents. The remission rates ranged from about a third to 50% for the groups regardless of whether they were receiving one or two drugs. The two-drug groups, however, experienced more side effects. The only positive effect of two of the same drug class is to the bottom line of the industry.

And there is no free lunch in medicine. Every treatment has its "costs." For example, the SSRIs increase the risk of bleeding in persons prone to bleeds four-fold. I recently met an octogenarian with melancholia who had extensive bruising of his arms and legs. In essence, he was bleeding under his skin. He also had Parkinson's disease and so was prone to falls and poor balance that increased the likelihood that he would bump into things. He was taking a blood thinner for a heart arrhythmia, but the laboratory measures of that drug's effects did not predict such bruising. His psychiatric treatments, however, did. Prior to admission and then continuing in the hospital, he was prescribed sertraline (Zoloft), an antidepressant that can increase the risk for bleeding in someone prone to do so (such as a patient on a blood thinner). Sertraline is also an agent that has a side effect of muscle spasm and rigidity, so it is not an optimal choice for someone with Parkinson's disease. His outpatient psychiatrists seemed unaware of these associations. The inpatient team quickly recognized the problem and stopped the medication.

Present-day psychiatrists have been lulled into a state of false security about new medications and often do not adequately take into account the costs of treatment in terms of the risks to the patient other than what the pharmaceutical industry proclaims. The situation is similar to political TV ads during an election campaign. If ads for a candidate make frequent false claims for that candidate and against the opponent, a substantial proportion of voters will buy into the falsehoods.

The SSRIs can also lead to substantial weight loss, a problem in older stroke patients. They typically make a male's sex life "go south." There are also reports of permanent sexual dysfunction even after stopping these agents.[79] When medical students are presented with the hypothetical situation that they are depressed and have the choice of a drug with a TCA side effect profile or a drug with an SSRI or SNRI profile, they always pick the TCA. Who wouldn't trade a dry mouth for an active sex life? And following the Newtonian principle that *"It ain't over 'til it's over,"* among elderly men prescribed an SSRI, the most common complaint is the sexual side effect. SSRIs and even the SNRIs also mess up sleep and make patients jittery, which are both bad for persons with depressive illness. They also have been increasingly linked to birth defects, which is bad for pregnant women with depressive illness and their babies. The sleep and jitteriness have become such a problem that it is now routine to prescribe an SSRI or an SNRI with tranquilizing drugs such as Ativan (a benzodiazepine) and additional agents for sleep. Such agents aren't cheap; they are addicting, and they can elicit memory and other cognitive difficulties, particularly in the elderly; they increase the risk of falling. Worse, the industry and the psychiatrists that are financially supported by the pharmaceutical industry have convinced the field that the newer antipsychotic drugs are safe to use as sleeping agents and that these agents also enhance the antidepressant effect of the SSRIs and SNRIs. These agents, however, can cause permanent brain damage in the form of tardive dyskinesia (TD). The abnormal movements (the dyskinesia) usually occur after months or more of exposure rather than in the first several days or weeks of exposure as do most side effects and so justifies the word tardive in the term. The damage is to the brain's basal ganglia and TD is resistant to treatment and is often permanent. The basal ganglia are the same brain areas affected in Parkinson's disease and antipsychotic agents can induce a Parkinson's syndrome. The new agents are promoted as unlikely to do this but the evidence is against them, and I have seen many stiff and tremulous patients who were exposed to these drugs. Stopping the drug slowly resolves the Parkinson's syndrome that the manufacturer avers will not occur. Antipsychotic agents also put patients at risk for life-threatening malignant catatonia.

A recent large study from the United Kingdom tells the tale.[80] The authors investigated the association between antidepressant treatment and risk of several potential adverse outcomes in persons over age 65 with the diagnosis of depression. They examined risks by class of antidepressant, duration of use, and dose. The patients were being treated between 1996 and 2007 in 570 general practices in the United Kingdom that supplied data to a national primary care database. A 1-year follow-up was also done. Over 60,000 patients were included. Patients were compared for the times they were receiving a psychiatric drug with when they were drug free. There is no U.S. study like it. Risks were assessed for all-cause mortality, attempted suicide and self-harm, myocardial infarction, stroke or transient ischemic attack, falls, fractures, upper gastrointestinal bleeding, epilepsy and seizures, road traffic accidents, adverse drug reactions, and low blood sodium (associated with delirium and heart arrhythmia), all adjusted for a range of potential confounding factors. Of the over 1.3 million antidepressant prescriptions issued to these patients, 54.7% were for SSRIs and 31.6% were for TCA antidepressants, the two prominent classes. SSRIs were associated with the highest rates for falls and low blood sodium compared to the time when antidepressants were not being used. A group of other antidepressants (MAOIs, buproprion, SNRIs) was associated with the highest rates for all-cause mortality, attempted suicide and self harm, stroke and transient ischemic attack, fracture, and epilepsy and seizures, compared to the time when antidepressants were not being used. TCAs did not have a high risk for *any* of the bad outcomes. Significantly different associations also existed between the individual drugs for the same seven outcomes; the SNRIs were associated with the highest rates for some of these outcomes.

So, the strong official and semiofficial treatment recommendations and standardized test required answers that U.S. medical students, psychiatric residents, and physicians of all stripes should use SSRIs and SNRIs as first-line antidepressants for all depressed patients and that TCAs are too dangerous to use except as a last resort are just plain wrong. Although it is understandable that the pharmaceutical industry would promote this view to enhance their bottom line, it is not acceptable that so many physicians who took the Hippocratic Oath are willing to shill for the industry, knowingly or not. That these same physicians are teaching the next generation is a tragedy.

Physicians Are People Too, Despite Denying They Are Influenced by Marketing

Also, let us not forget the marketing of the drugs on TV and in magazines. Sufferers are always searching for hope and then a new medication appears in an advertisement. Sometimes the "new" medication is just a new version of the old one, but the chemical tweaking extends the patent while discouraging the use of the generic form no longer in vogue. With each reintroduction the price is higher and so are the profits. In surveys, doctors claim that they are not influenced by advertising. Are we to believe that an MD degree provides some immunity or that persons who become physicians have previously mutated to be impervious to what the rest of the planet succumbs to regularly? In fact, studies show that the influence of the promotions is really upon physicians seeing the ads rather than upon patients seeing the ads. Most patients are reluctant to rush to their doctor demanding the latest this or that, but the more ads that are seen by physicians the more prescriptions are written for the promoted agent. The number of prescriptions written by a physician is also substantially influenced by the number of drug rep visits to the office. Name recognition is helpful to political candidates and for pharmaceuticals.[81] Direct consumer advertising of prescription pharmaceuticals is banned in most countries.[82]

In informal discussions I've had with many psychiatrists, it appears that what many believe about the pros and cons of psychotropic medications reflects the promotional information they receive more than the literature they should be reading. Depakote overtook lithium carbonate as the leading mood-stabilizing drug in the 1990s, not because it is better at treating patients with manic-depression, but because it was marketed better. Data still favor the cheaper lithium, which has a clear long-term effect on reducing suicide rates. The long-term use of anticonvulsants may also reduce suicide risk, but the relationship is less clear.[83]

A Partial Solution

All the above indicates that the studies of the efficacy of psychotropic medications are substantially biased, but that the problem can be fixed by better, industry-independent research. To a degree this is true, but it is not the whole solution. Even reasonable studies do not always reflect clinical reality. I was one of the first U.S. clinicians to use lithium in a clinical rather than a research setting. That use occurred in 1970 when I was in the navy. I obtained the lithium through the Department of Defense several months before it was available to the general medical practitioner. Lithium was and is a great medication. Then, in the mid-1980s I was unable to see patients regularly other than in teaching situations. When I finally was able to do so again in the 1990s, carbamazepine (Tegretol), an anticonvulsant agent, had been introduced and was heavily promoted as an antimanic drug to be used for acutely ill hospitalized patients with mania. So, when I returned to seeing inpatients on a regular basis, I encouraged the prescription of carbamazepine for the acutely ill patients with mania. It took about 2 weeks for me to realize that the studies were wrong and that carbamazepine was not nearly as effective as lithium. That view is now mostly accepted.[84] Clinical experience can be biased but without it medicine is lost. As William Osler wrote, *"To study the phenomena of disease without books is to sail an uncharted sea, while to study books without patients is not to go to sea at all."*

CHAPTER 4

✧

For the Benefit of the Sick

"The term beneficence refers to actions that promote the wellbeing of others. In the medical context, this means taking actions that serve the best interests of patients...James Childress and Tom Beauchamp in Principle of Biomedical Ethics (1978) identify beneficence as one of the core values of health care ethics. Some scholars, such as Edmund Pellegrino argue that beneficence is the only fundamental principle of medical ethics."

Wikipedia 2011

"Cure sometimes, treat often, comfort always."

Hippocrates

BENEFICENCE: THE FUNDAMENTAL
IMPERATIVE OF MEDICINE

Twenty plus years ago, in response to a growing concern that physicians were not living up to their billing as good moral role models, medical schools throughout the country began to offer courses in medical ethics. I was asked to give one of the lectures at the school at which I was then a professor and chairman of the psychiatry department. Some people erroneously think that even outside the office psychiatrists have unique insights into human behavior, and that we are often profoundly thoughtful. From long experience in participating in committee meetings and attending dinner parties I can assure you this is not the case. Nevertheless, I was asked to do it.[1]

Offering several clinical examples, I tried to convince the 170 or so of our first year medical students that all the opining about ethics and what the law has to say about a physician's behavior was of minimal use to them. The only principle that they needed to know and adhere to was *beneficence*. I told them that regardless of their legal concerns about a clinical situation or their worries about their hospital's regulations and the tons of regulations of medical oversight organizations, they would be on the firmest ethical, moral, and ultimately legal ground if they did what was best for the patient. If they did not do what they knew they should do because of what they perceived the law or the regulation to be, they would end up not doing what was best for the patient and the outcome would be bad. I was never asked to give another lecture in that course, although the citation from Wikipedia at the beginning of this chapter is consistent with what I was trying to say. Here's one of the clinical examples I used:

A woman with manic-depressive illness relapsed into mania. At home, claiming that it was too hot, she walked about the house in only her panties in front of her husband, her adult sister who was living with her, and her teenage son and daughter. The family in prior crises had tried to meet with the woman's psychiatrist to discuss the patient's difficulties and what they might do to help, but the psychiatrist had refused, citing the patient's privacy. They tried again to speak with him but were again told that the psychiatrist would meet only with the patient. Keeping a patient's privacy is another important standard of good care but it can be broken when the patient is in danger or threatens others. It can also be taken to extremes as in this situation.

The patient, in an abnormal mood state, angrily refused to see the psychiatrist. Had there been adequate communication with the family, they might have been able to bring the patient to him or might have been able to speak with him so that he could have alerted the police. The patient's behavior and moods might have been enough for the police to consider her a danger to herself or to others and bring her and the family to an emergency room. This did not happen. So, in a severe mania, the patient decided to go for a drive.

Fearing she would get into an accident, her teenage daughter insisted on riding with her mother. Both were in seat belts with the daughter in the back. The mother angrily refused to permit anyone else to drive her. Irritability is a common mood in mania. The daughter later stated that at some point in the drive her mother was speeding and became "frozen" at the wheel. Catatonia is also a common feature of severe mania. There was a horrendous one-car accident. The mother was killed. The force of the crash was so great that the daughter's acceleration into her lap belt severed her spine and she became paraplegic.

One or two family conferences with the psychiatrist might have avoided this tragedy because if the psychiatrist had included the family in his evaluations and periodic assessments while also giving the patient the opportunity to have private chats, the family would have felt free to contact him to tell him about the patient's deterioration. Only the old psychodynamic model excludes the family from the assessment. The psychiatrists and social workers at most university hospital services have regular family meetings to assist their patients. Treaters need to know whether the patient's family will be allies in the care of the patient or whether they are so pathological that they will in some way harm the patient's recovery. They need to plan the patient's recovery and the maintenance of the recovery with the family. By not including the family and refusing to speak with them, the psychiatrist in this tragic story was not acting in the patient's best interest.

The family brought suit against the psychiatrist and I testified in their behalf stating that the best interest of every patient is for the physician to keep supportive family members involved. Whenever possible, the family should be an ally not the enemy. They most often are the long-distance eyes and ears of the physician. Beneficence should have trumped privacy. If it had, the patient might never have gotten so ill and would be alive, the daughter would likely not be paraplegic, and the psychiatrist would not have been sued.

We had a jury trial. And although I think I did a good job as their expert witness, the family lost their suit. The treating psychiatrist adhered to one set of ethical rules while I had a different perspective on those rules. The jury maintained that although the treating psychiatrist's quality of care was poor, it was not different from the practice patterns of other psychiatrists in the region and so did not meet the standard for malpractice, which requires a pattern of poor care inconsistent with community practices. This standard, in my view, violates the beneficence benchmark because it excuses bad patient care if everyone is also doing bad patient care.

CLINICAL DIAGNOSIS REQUIRES DISCIPLINED CURIOSITY

Some ethicists note that the principle of beneficence needs to be weighed against the principles of autonomy (respect for persons) and justice. It might be in the best physiological interest of the patient to do procedure A, but if the patient with adequate capacity to make a decision about his or her care rejects the procedure should we respect the patient's autonomy and right to refuse care or should we set aside autonomy and do the procedure anyway? Autonomy supports the right of the patient to refuse treatment

in many circumstances. Justice refers to the need to treat patients by a reasonable standard of fairness. How else should we treat them?

From my perspective, both autonomy and justice are subsumed by the
beneficence doctrine. If a patient doesn't want a treatment and has the
capacity to decide, it is probably in the patient's best interest (beneficence)
to honor his or her right to refuse. A few years ago I was asked to see a surgical patient who had refused a procedure. Without the procedure she was
likely to die in a year or so. With the procedure, she might live longer but
had a 50–50 chance of becoming further incapacitated. Her surgeons considered her suicidal for refusing their treatment and wanted a psychiatrist
to declare her so. Psychiatrists, by the way, can only determine a person's
capacity to perform or make judgements. Only a court can declare a person incompetent. But this patient was not depressed and not suicidal. Her
judgment was pretty good. She said that her life was already quite limited
and that she didn't want it to be limited further. She preferred to spend
what time she had left able to meaningfully interact with her family. It was
in her best interest to honor her decision, and we did. Beneficence required
us to support her autonomy.

My peeve is that if beneficence becomes the guiding principle of patient
management by incorporating all other ethical principles, then it requires
many psychiatrists, at least many U.S. psychiatrists, to change what they
do in the care of their patients. I've personally interacted and communicated with, consulted to, and ended up treating the patients of hundreds
of psychiatrists across the United States. It's not a random sample, but it
represents psychiatrists from academia and from the public and private
sectors from coast to coast. Many were not curious enough to find the "evidence" needed to practice better evidence-based medicine. They seemed
content to work by trial and error (mostly error) or to follow the unsophisticated algorisms that are now taught. Many were intellectually lazy. Here's
an example of zero curiosity.

While on sabbatical in 2000 at a prestigious medical center I went to
an outpatient conference in which the treatment team was reviewing their
clinic patients. One patient, a man said to have a personality disorder, was
getting into constant difficulties at work and with local agencies that were
so foolish that anyone hearing the saga would wonder about the man's
intelligence. In the discussion of his medications, it was mentioned that he
had severe acne. I then asked my only question; did they know how tall the
man was? What are the odds of a room full of professional care givers in
a teaching institution being asked what on the face of it is an off-the-wall
question by a stranger, and not responding with *"Why do you ask?"* Even an
"Are you nuts?" would have been better than what I got, which was, *"Don't*

know," followed by more discussion of other matters. The treatment team members were not curious. Had they asked, we might have had a conversation about some of the biological contributions to deviations in personality traits. Did the patient have a chromosomal aberration of XYY. Most males have an X and a Y chromosome. The extra Y can be a problem. Once incorrectly thought to be associated with criminality (Richard Speck the killer of the Chicago student nurses had XYY), XXY is associated with being a tall man with acne who also has a low IQ.[2] XYY is not the only consideration of these features, but it was a start. Professionals in an academic department should be interested in such a topic. That information might have led to IQ testing or other cognitive assessments of the patient, and those results might have altered the treatment plan for the patient. No such testing had been done. The case conference members would have been informed, they would have engaged in scholarly activities. They would have practiced beneficence. Research and learning begin by asking questions. So does diagnosis.

Thoughtful Bedside Diagnosis Replaced by Shotgun Tests

The process of clinical diagnosis is based on disciplined curiosity. Without the desire to gather the information needed to understand the implications of the patient's signs and symptoms an evaluation will be cursory at best. In psychiatry, such lazy and uncurious clinicians are abundant and settle for a few bits of information needed to provide a *DSM* label. In the 1960s and 1970s despite the inadequacies of the official psychiatric diagnostic system (*DSM-II*) many in the field learned how to evaluate patients by obtaining the detailed story of their lives and illnesses. Classic textbooks and monographs were studied for their rich descriptions of psychopathology, the signs and symptoms of behavioral illness. The *DSM* was an "afterthought." Such expertise is rare today and many U.S. psychiatrists know little psychopathology beyond what is sketched in the *DSM*. Most of the rest of medicine has the advantage of a slew of laboratory tests to aid in any bedside shortcomings in clinical diagnosis. Although they have in my view gone too far in relying on the tests rather than thinking, they have some safety net to counter the effects of sloth or lack of knowledge.

I have a psychoanalyst acquaintance who laments about the psychiatric residents' lack of thinking about their patients' symptoms. He of course wants them to consider the psychological or symbolic meaning of the patient's behaviors. I have a different viewpoint, but I lament with him on the residents' lack of interest in knowing the patient's "story" and then "the story" of the patient's illness. Regardless of the perspective, a clinician who lacks curiosity will end up more often than not doing a bad job. Beneficence requires healthy curiosity.

Beneficence Requires Courage

Adhering to the beneficence benchmark also requires courage. Neither every health care provider nor every heath care delivery system places the patient's best interests first. When a clinician challenges the system in support of the patient there is always the danger that the system will retaliate. Some physicians play it safe. Here's an example of a courageous physician who put her patient's interests above her own.

A number of years ago, at our department's affiliate VA hospital, we were treating an inpatient with a psychotic disorder. The patient developed a fever and began to deteriorate physiologically. The patient was often in restraints as he was periodically violent and he could not readily leave the unit. A second-year resident requested that a portable X-ray machine be brought to the unit. A short time after her request she received a phone call from the head of the radiology service who told her he did not want to send the portable machine because he was fearful that the other patients on the psychiatry unit would break it. Apparently in some quarters psychiatric patients are well known for destroying medical equipment. The resident became incensed, and told the head of radiology that her patient was extremely ill, needed an X-ray, could not be transported, and that she'd *"rather have a broken machine than a broken patient."* She got her X-ray and a letter of reprimand. The patient had pneumonia but recovered. His psychosis resolved and he walked out of the hospital. Most faculty members would not buck the head of a clinical service. For a resident to do so was extraordinary. Individual physicians can make a difference, particularly when their patient care is guided by beneficence.

ELECTROCONVULSIVE THERAPY AND BENEFICENCE

Doing our best for the patient with a behavioral syndrome begins with determining the brain implications of the patient's symptoms and then applying the best treatments for that situation. If the patient's difficulties derive from social or environmental problems other professionals can better and more cost effectively provide care. But before detailing some further examples of the neuropsychiatric approach, I need to discuss electroconvulsive therapy (ECT). I don't like the term "shock therapy" and so I don't use it. Nobody gets "shocked" in the procedure until they look at the bill.

Most people in the developed world, however, have heard of "shock treatment." Many have seen *One Flew Over the Cuckoo's Nest* with Jack Nickolson as a psychopath being punished by being "shocked" while awake, or *The Snake Pit* with a terrified Olivia de Havilland being dragged into a dungeon-like room for some unimaginable torture. Television repeatedly refers to ECT as barbaric. In a recently aired *Law and Order: Special Victims* episode ECT was depicted as a treatment being performed in a room with a picture window as if a reality TV show with the patient awake and then going into spasm from an electric shock. None of these images reflects the reality of ECT, but the bias remains.

For example, several decades ago our psychiatry department affiliated with a hospital in Chicago that primarily served an African-American community. We had planned to rotate students and residents through the hospital's inpatient program and clinic. The hospital's medical director, also a psychiatrist, and I discussed how we could further develop their clinical services and I mentioned setting up an ECT program. He was enthusiastic about the idea as he had administered ECT when a resident and considered it an important treatment, but he did not have the expertise to establish such a unit. We did. He said he would discuss the idea with the hospital's board and the community board involved in the hospital's management. Several weeks passed without any word about it. Finally, I met my colleague at a meeting and asked about the proposed ECT program. He looked at me sheepishly and said, *"I'm sorry. I tried and feel very badly about this, but the community members adamantly refuse to consider the idea."*

"How come?" I asked.

"Because," he said, *"there would be too much of an uproar if the community found out that Jewish white doctors* [the school had a history of admitting Jews when other medical schools would not] *were shooting electricity through the heads of black people."*

Although self-defeating and ignorent, the community's response reflected a long history of outgrageous treatment by U.S. medicine. The African-American experience with the U.S. medical establishment, mostly white for centuries, has been described as "medical apartheid." Studies indicate that African-Americans are less likely than EuroAmericans to receive adequate medical care of any kind, including ECT. The horror stories of clearly unethical experiments, such as the Tuskegee study of injecting African-Americans with syphilis to see the untreated course of the disease, also play a role in the reluctance of African-Americans to place their trust in EuroAmerican physicians. The difference in use of ECT among African-

Americans compared to EuroAmericans has been true for over 40 years. Some of the disparity is attributed to slightly less access, but most of the difference is from other reasons. In one of the largest surveys of psychiatric admissions across the country from 1993 to 2007[3] lack of adequate health insurance was found to be a significant factor. Poor rural southern African-Americans were particularly affected. Another major factor reducing the prescription of ECT was patients' negative attitudes toward ECT as seen in the above anecdote.

In contrast to the public image of ECT, and after years of treating patients suffering from mood disorders and patients with other severe behavioral syndromes, many of these patients also treated with ECT, participating in ECT research, and considering all the alternative treatments, I detailed in my medical advanced directives that if I had any one of those behavioral syndromes, that I did not want any of the other treatments commonly prescribed, I want ECT.

Why is my view of the treatment so different from what much of the public believes? Here are some of the facts.[4]

Increased Usage, Declining Training

ECT, which is the oldest continuous medical treatment in psychiatry, declined in use in the United States during the 1970s and 1980s. Since the late 1990s, however, its usage in the United States has increased as increasing numbers of patients with depressive illness have been identified as "treatment resistant." Of course, not responding fully to a caravan of clinical trials with weak antidepressants is more "treatment deprived" than treatment resistant. In 2000 the program I work in administered about 800 treatments annually. Today, about 2000 treatments are given yearly.

Although the indications for ECT are well defined and supported by the American Psychiatric Association and other professional groups and authorities, the likelihood of a patient who should be treated with ECT actually receiving the treatment has a lot to do with the medical facility to which the patient goes for help. Almost 90% of training hospitals offer ECT and about 60% of VA hospitals have an ECT program. Less than half of private hospitals in the United States have ECT programs and only one in five state mental hospitals provide ECT to their patients. If you live in the southern United States and are African-American you are less likely to receive ECT than are EuroAmerican patients and patients living elsewhere. Among the facilities that offer ECT, usage varies greatly. Medical centers with highly thought of psychiatry departments are most likely to have a robust program.[5]

Despite the increase in use, less than 10% of psychiatrists in the United States administer ECT, an important factor in the spotty access to the treatment. This in my view reflects the decline in U.S. psychiatry. U.S. psychiatric training programs no longer produce adequate numbers of graduate psychiatrists skilled in the procedure. In one survey,[6] 25% of responding programs offered no ECT experience to their residents. This is an accreditation violation, but the accreditation council has never placed a program on probation for not providing ECT training. On the other hand, if a program doesn't provide many hours of training in psychotherapy, the program will be slapped with a fine. In the same survey, about a third of the programs estimated that their typical resident participated in fewer than 10 treatments and another 25% estimated that their typical resident cared for less than five patients receiving ECT. Most programs devoted less than four lecture hours to ECT. At our program, typical residents participate in about 5–10 treatments *every time* they are assigned to ECT. Each second year resident participates in 10–15 such sessions and in their senior year they can take an ECT elective, providing a skill foundation for evaluating their patients for the need of ECT and for administering ECT. Why does the program provide this high level of training?

The True Image of ECT

ECT in the United States is typically administered in a special suite. Where I work ECT is administered for inpatients and outpatients in the university hospital's preop/postop recovery area. It is a typical brightly lit surgery-related recovery room with lots of nurses and doctors in scrubs doing their jobs. The outpatients, accompanied by a family member or other responsible adult, are first assessed in our outpatient assessment area by trained nurses that the patient and the family know and who know them. This area too is brightly lit. On holidays it is thematically decorated like most homes across the United States. The waiting room for family members is cozy, always has coffee, and sometimes has cookies. After they have received substantial behavioral, social, and cognitive assessments, and when the patients are ready, they are placed on stretchers and taken down to the preop/postop area.

In the preop area, the patient has an intravenous (IV) line started (the most uncomfortable part of the procedure). The ECT treating physician for the day greets the patient and may have a brief chat with a family member if present. The patient is then brought into the treatment room, is monitored for all vital signs using the same devices you see in hospital shows, and receives anesthesia (sometimes this can elicit a burning sensation at the IV site) and full muscle relaxation before the treatment. The patient is not awake for the stimulation and does not thrash about. At least one psychiatrist and an anesthesia specialist deliver treatments. Because our program is in a teaching hospital, we have two anesthesia nurse specialists, a psychiatrist, and a resident or a psychiatric technician in the treatment room throughout the 15-minute procedure. The recovery area anesthesiologist may also be present. The patient's breathing is maintained by the anesthesia specialist delivering pure oxygen through a nose and mouth mask. Intubation is rarely required.

The electrical stimulation is designed to induce a controlled grand mal brain seizure that is monitored by an electroencephalogram (EEG). The electricity used is modulated by devices that make it extremely efficient to treat. In the defibrillations (cardioversion) that we see on TV when someone yells "clear" and everyone dramatically jumps away to avoid electrical arching and getting a true shock, and the patient jerks, the energy used is much greater that that used for ECT. During an ECT procedure no one yells, no one jumps, and no one jerks. In ECT (neuroconversion) the electricity does the same thing to neurons that the electricity of defibrillation does to heart cells. All other efforts during a treatment are designed to keep the patient comfortable and to reduce the convulsive movements (the outward sign of the brain's electrical seizure) to one foot. We could also stop the seizure in that foot, but use its movements as another method for monitoring how the patient is doing.

After the seizure has ended (it typically lasts less than a minute and after 90–120 seconds we stop it with medication), the patient is breathing on his own, and vital signs are as expected, the patient is taken to one of the recovery bays next to the treatment room and is cared for by recovery room nurses who know about the patient and ECT. Anyone seeing this process would find it similar to minor outpatient surgery, but with no blood or pain. Family members often wait with the patient in the preop area before treatment. During the course of treatments the patient's outpatient and inpatient psychiatrists are kept informed about the patient's progress and participate in planning for management after the ECT course is completed. The basic set-up and procedures I just detailed are standard practice and if you went to a community or regional hospital anywhere in the United States and they did ECT, you should see what I have just described.

The remission rates among patients suffering from severe depressive illness are about 30–40% for antidepressants in 12 or so weeks (just a tad better than placebo), whereas for ECT given correctly remission rates are 70–90% on average in about 12 treatments (4–6 weeks).[7] The remission rates for ECT are often achieved in patients who have not responded to several courses of antidepressant medications and combinations of drugs. Some have been continuously ill for years. The most severely depressed patients who are psychotic or catatonic or are repeatedly trying to kill themselves respond most rapidly to ECT, and remission rates for these patients are over 90%. Medications for these patients often do more harm than good. ECT is equally effective for mania (although more treatments are usually required than for patients with depressive illness). It is also useful for patients with some non-mood disorder psychotic conditions. It is the definitive treatment for catatonia. Among severely ill suicidal patients it is life saving.

A few years ago, a patient was hospitalized for severe depression. Her history was that she was unable to work or care for her family, had isolated herself, was despondent, and was experiencing suicidal thoughts and impulses daily. She had made several previous suicide attempts. I was asked to see her for an ECT evaluation. When I asked her if she was still feeling suicidal now that she was in the hospital, she tearfully nodded, "Yes." When I asked her if she had a plan, she paused for several moments and again nodded, "Yes." She finally whispered that she had been saving pills from her various prescribed medications and was planning to overdose. When I asked her where the pills were, she paused again, cried, and said that she had sewn her stash into the lining of the coat that she had with her and that she was planning to take them all that night. With some relief, she turned over the pills and the next morning she had her first ECT. I went to visit her that afternoon to see how she was doing. She was not in her room but in the dining room finishing a snack. When she saw me she smiled warmly and then thanked me. She said, *"For the first time in six months I don't feel suicidal."* She went on to have a full recovery. Among suicidal patients with depressive illness, about a third are fully relieved of these deadly thoughts and impulses within a few treatments. Almost all are relieved of suicidal impulses by 12 treatments. Although the risk for suicide is at its highest for a patient with depressive illness during the few weeks following discharge from a psychiatric facility, it is almost unheard of for patients who received a course of ECT to kill themselves in that time frame.

During the course of ECT, which is typically administered two or three times weekly, many patients experience a temporary problem with memory (e.g., keeping track of recent events and conversations). Once ECT is concluded, however, that form of memory improves over the next several weeks and typically becomes better than before treatment as the illness that required ECT has resolved. Commonly, ECT-responsive conditions are associated with memory and concentration difficulties. Some patients receiving ECT also lose memories of events that occurred during the weeks before treatment started. This information loss is spotty but permanent. It is never widespread and does not involve future long-term information storage. Patients do not forget their lives, their biographic information, their skills, or their stores of knowledge. Personalities don't change. There is no brain damage. Those who say there is damage are either ignorant, have been misled, or are being purposely misleading. In a recent study of all the patients in the Veteran's Affairs system who received ECT between 1999 and 2010 there were no deaths. The authors estimated that any deaths would be associated with the risks of anesthesia and might be one per 78,000 treatments. That's safer than childbirth.[8] Although we treat medically and surgically severely ill patients, sometimes in one of the center's several intensive care units (ICUs), our long-standing ECT program has never experienced an ECT-related mortality.

There is no treatment in psychiatry that is safer or more effective for severe psychiatric disorder than ECT.

The "Wow" Patient

By the third month of my residency I had seen and treated many severely ill patients. Almost all received an antipsychotic and some also an antidepressant. Many did well, but there was never a response that led to a "wow." Then one morning I came to work and saw a woman in her late thirties sitting in the day room. She was hunched over a table staring into some unimaginable abyss. Her hospital clothes were rumpled and her hair disheveled. Her expression was of anguish. Her eyes were sunken into her skull. She did not spontaneously speak and when efforts were made to engage her, she at first seemed not to hear the examiner's questions, but after a long delay, she might slowly give a one or two word response. She never took her gaze from that abyss. She did not move from that table throughout the day and needed to be in diapers. Her only movement was with her right thumb, which repeatedly picked at the tip of her right index finger. The bone on the index finger was exposed, the flesh eroded by the thumb nail's continual gouging. She had been in this melancholic stupor for weeks and when I first saw her she was physically debilitated.

A month later she was discharged from the hospital. Her thumb was bandaged and would soon receive a skin graft. She was dressed in a neat brown suit. Her hair was carefully combed. She was animated and smiled as the staff wished her well. This was my first experience with a "wow." Her treatment was ECT. I was not then familiar with the concept of beneficence, but at that moment, watching her, almost unrecognizably well, I decided I wanted to get patients better like that. Other than ECT, the only other "wows" in my career have occurred by giving lithium to patients experiencing an acute mania, resolving catatonia, giving an anticonvulsant to patients with a seizure disorder, or doing no harm by letting patients recover through their body's natural homeostatic processes by stopping all their psychiatric medications.

The most important lesson I learned from the "wow" patient is that caring for patients should not mostly be based on what gives the physician the most fun or what is the easiest to accomplish. Enjoying work is good and to practice medicine essential, but most importantly what a physician does should first be based on what works best for the patient. In other specialties the rules are clearer than they are for psychiatry. Holistic and herbal medicine and homeopathic medicine are not accepted mainstream approaches in internal medicine and oncology. They are, however, tolerated in psychiatry as is any version of psychotherapy. Some psychiatrists in California are combining the potentially brain-damaging drug Ecstasy with psychotherapy (NY Times, Nov. 20, 2012 D1 and 6).

THE MOST DANGEROUS OF DOCTORS

Prescribing what works requires knowledge of what works. It's okay to not know. It's okay to start out not knowing what works. However, it is not okay to not know and do nothing about it when that ignorance affects a patient. The most dangerous of doctors is the physician who does not know what he or she does not know and even when that ignorance is revealed does nothing about it. I've run across a number of MDs like that.

Beneficence Requires Awareness of the Limits of Our Knowledge and the Willingness to Learn

The following patient's story refers to several psychiatrists who in my view did not know what they did not know. At least one psychiatrist also was not willing to learn. The patient was a teenage girl with autism who periodically became violent. She was a large person and had injured others. The violent episodes were sudden and unprovoked. At other times she experienced episodes of extreme excitement. In the midst of one of those episodes, psychiatrists not knowing the diagnostic implications of her behavior or the risks to her of certain medications gave her a powerful antipsychotic throwing her into a life-threatening malignant catatonia that required a transfer from the child and adolescent inpatient unit to the pediatric ICU. A physician not knowing is usually bad news for the patient.

When I first met the patient, she was still in the ICU with tubes running in and out of her body. Malignant catatonia is marked by fevers, rigidity, and several other features including unstable vital signs, muscle breakdown from the continuous contraction and posturing, and encephalopathy (a generalized brain metabolic dysfunction). If the condition is allowed to persist, muscle breakdown and the by-products of this can result in kidney failure. The muscle rigidity can compromise breathing, and from all the metabolic perturbations that occur, fatal heart arrhythmias may result. Sometimes the condition is referred to as neuroleptic malignant syndrome (NMS) as it is often associated with the patient receiving an antipsychotic medication. Neuroleptic is a fancy word for antipsychotic and has the specific meaning of tranquilizing without sedating. NMS, however, is associated with many other conditions and with some other medications, so the "neuroleptic" name seems inappropriate. The syndrome was also first described in 1928 before neuroleptics were even a gleam in a chemist's eye. The syndrome was originally given the name "lethal catatonia," as 50% or more sufferers died. The preferred term of malignant catatonia would be moot if it weren't for the fact that the syndrome responds best to treatments for catatonia.[9]

The medication of choice is lorazepam (Ativan), which is safe in such patients, even in very high doses, and leads to remission in 70% of patients with the syndrome. If lorazepam doesn't do the job, ECT typically resolves the condition in the remaining patients. In other words, there is no reason for a patient with malignant catatonia not to fully recover from the catatonia if the patient's condition is recognized early and appropriate treatments are administered in a timely fashion.[10]

As I watched the girl in her bed among all her tubes she also had episodes that reminded me of patients with frontal lobe epilepsy (e.g., bicycling of the legs). Frontal lobe seizures can be expressed as episodes of unprovoked aggression, bursts of excitement and hyperactivity, and episodic movement disorder that characterized this girl's story.[11] Epilepsy can also lead to catatonia as can strong antipsychotic medications. In fact, there are many, many causes of catatonia. The first task, however, was to resolve the girl's deadly catatonia. This was accomplished with ECT and she was able to go home.

Several members of the treatment team wanted to continue with her ECT once weekly to prevent any return of the catatonia. This is a common strategy as most patients with manic-depression or catatonia will relapse within the first year from any successful acutely applied treatment if not provided with effective maintenance treatment. Sometimes patients who recover with ECT are kept well with ECT, sometimes with medication, and sometimes with both forms of treatment. If a patient does well with an acute course of ECT, a maintenance ECT taper over several months to a year is often the most effective and safest way of keeping them well. The fact that patients successfully treated with ECT will relapse if not provided with some maintenance treatment does not mean the ECT didn't work. Resolving a serious heart attack and then needing to keep the patient indefinitely on heart medication doesn't mean the treatments that countered the heart attack didn't work. Other than infection, most diseases require repeated or continuous treatment.

In the girl's situation, ECT maintenance was begun and the catatonia did not return, but the episodes of violence did. The response to the violence from some of her treaters was to continue with the ECT in the hope of stopping those episodes. Although ECT has some anticonvulsant properties (counterintuitive, but true[12]), it was not effective in resolving the girl's aggression, which I attributed to frontal lobe epilepsy. I sent the other treaters papers on the subject that described frontal lobe seizures that fit our patient precisely. I detailed her episodes and presented them to the other treaters as clear examples of seizures. I gave them a neuroanatomic explanation for all her symptoms. But it took over a year before they finally gave up on ECT and agreed to treat her with an anticonvulsant.

Their change of mind, however, was not the result of learning about frontal lobe epilepsy. They simply finally faced the reality that ECT was not achieving their treatment goals. Even when the patient was no longer violent and was free of other features of her seizures, the other treaters acknowledged that I was correct about her not needing ECT any longer, but they still would not accept the diagnosis I offered.

Neurologists Don't Like Psychiatrists

Most psychiatrists know little about the brain and most neurologists know little about behavior. It would just be silly if not for the thousands of patients whose brain diseases are expressed by behavioral change and consequently suffer because of the professional lapses in information.

Although present day psychiatric researchers have focused upon neurochemicals and the brain structures believed to be most involved in the perturbations underlying behavioral syndromes, clinical psychiatric practice is hardly touched by the advances in neuroscience. In addition, psychiatry today has mostly abandoned the psychopathology skills needed for sophisticated diagnosis. Practice has devolved into applying a few rudimentary clinical features that are then matched to *DSM* descriptors, and treatments are then applied based on the several algorithms endorsed by this or that professional group. Occasionally a psychiatrist will obtain a computed tomography (CT) scan of the patient's brain, but rarely does that psychiatrist have a specific idea of what to look for, and certainly that psychiatrist can't "read" or make neurological sense of the scan and has little idea when magnetic resonance imaging (MRI) is the better tool to use. A psychiatrist asking for an EEG to assess a patient's brain waves is as common as "hen's teeth" despite the help it provides in clarifying whether a patient is delirious (diffuse brain dysfunction with some alteration in alertness), has an encephalopathy (diffuse brain dysfunction usually without alteration in arousal), or has a seizure disorder.

Neurologists typically reject the significance of abnormal EEGs among psychiatric patients unless the tracing is absolutely unequivocal. Many times I have been asked to see a patient, I make a neuropsychiatric diagnosis predicting where the lesion will be, I obtain an EEG that shows an abnormality in that *exact* location, and because the EEG wave form is not specific, the connection I offered between the behavior and the brain area associated with the EEG abnormality is dismissed by a neurologist. Many neurologists seem to have forgotten that deep brain lesions are rarely associated with specific EEG signs when a patient is awake. A localized finding in the predicted area may be all that is revealed. All night sleep EEGs are often more helpful, but sleep laboratories are commonly under the aegis of the hospital's neurology department and they scoff at psychiatrists asking for such a study unless it is to assess the patient for sleep apnea. They also seem to have forgotten that epilepsy is a clinical, not an EEG diagnosis, and that way back "when" they knew this. When Hans Berger developed his EEG machine, neurologists brought their patients with epilepsy to him to see what the tracings looked like. They had already made the clinical diagnoses. More recently, an epilepsy spectrum disorder has been described that is characterized by several of the mood, perceptual, motor, and cognitive features seen in patients with the *DSM* labels of psychosis not otherwise specified (NOS).[13]

When a psychiatrist tells a neurologist that a patient has a brain disease, the neurologist more often than not dismisses the idea. It is as if the neurologist says *"How dare you presume."* On the other hand, many neurologists have no compunctions about making psychiatric diagnoses, despite the psychiatrist insisting that the patient's behaviors indicate a different condition. From their perspective we know little about the brain or behavior. This is sadly often true, but some credit needs to be recognized.

A number of years ago a resident of mine came to me upset. She had a patient whom she thought had a seizure disorder. Her psychiatrist supervisor thought the patient had "conversion hysteria." The resident lobbied her supervisor until he relented and obtained a neurology consultation. The consulting neurologist, however, agreed with the conversion notion and refused to obtain an EEG. The resident wanted help.

Her patient was a young woman who was hospitalized for possible malingering to avoid work. The patient's difficulties were described as "nightmares" during which she was observed to jump out of bed, scream for a minute or so, and then return to sleep. She had no recollection of these nightly events. She had similar episodes during the day and these continued in the hospital. She would abruptly stop what she was doing, flex both her arms with clenched fists, start screaming, and then repeatedly say "It's okay, it's okay...." Her arms moved up and down symmetrically as if she were pounding a table. She looked tense, with clenched teeth and tension in her general musculature. She had several brief episodes daily, and these were followed by the desire to lie down and sleep. On one occasion she was incontinent of urine. She had no recollection of these events.

Seizure-induced behaviors are typically paroxysmal. They erupt, peak quickly, and then end. They are stereotypic and repetitive. This patient's abrupt cessation of an activity suddenly replaced by repetitive stereotypic movements of both arms and repetitive speech (the term is forced speech) are classic for frontal circuitry seizures. The desire to sleep is a typical postseizure response. The brain is worn out from the enormous metabolic effort. Not recalling the events during the seizure is also typical. Some patients have vague memories of their episodes as if snippets of dreams as they are not fully unconscious during a "partial" seizure.[14] The psychiatrist supervisor, however, was not willing to consider a seizure disorder in the differential diagnosis of this patient because he was not trained to do so and had little curiosity to learn more than was needed to get by. The neurologist's refusal to even investigate the source of the patient's difficulties implies arrogance as well as ignorance.

I had taught this resident to recognize seizure disorder and I agreed with her diagnosis in this patient. The behaviors were classic for partial complex epilepsy.[15] We devised a plan. The resident was going to obtain a blood test for a neurochemical (prolactin) that rises rapidly in many patients after a seizure. The prolactin peaks in about 20 minutes following the seizure and is cleared from the blood in another 5 minutes. The resident had only a small window for success, and so she stayed on her unit waiting for the patient to enter an episode. After about 20 minutes after an episode onset she was able to obtain the needed blood sample. The prolactin was four times the patient's baseline and confirmed the diagnosis of a seizure. Anticonvulsant treatment resolved the episodes. This is another example of how an individual physician can make a difference.

Perhaps the most egregious example of neurologists (it was a whole team of them) ignoring the advice of a psychiatrist (a bunch of them) about a patient with a behavioral syndrome involved a woman in her late thirties, the mother of three. She was hospitalized for a sudden behavioral change that was considered to be the result of an inflammation of the blood vessels in her brain (vasculitis). We evaluated her and concluded that her stupor (a sedated-seeming state) and other catatonic features were expressions of a severe depression. Because there was little physical examination or laboratory evidence of the conditions that could cause vasculitis, we recommended that she be treated with ECT for the stupor and catatonia and the depression. Even if she had vasculitis, the ECT would be effective and safe. Instead, the neurologists and immunologists scoffed and did a brain biopsy. Yes, that involves drilling a hole through the skull and taking out a piece of the brain. That piece did not indicate vascular changes that could explain the patient's behaviors.

The neurologists and immunologists immediately lost interest in the patient. We treated her with ECT, she fully recovered, and she returned home to her family. As far as I know, those neurologists and immunologists never acknowledged that they were wrong and that the psychiatric team was right. We would also hope that after that experience, the neurologists would on future occasions give the psychiatry consultants the benefit of the doubt, but the consultants still face the same attitudes today.

Asking for Help Is an Example of Beneficence

Although most psychiatrists don't know what they need to know about the brain and behavior, some know that they don't know and, following the principle of beneficence, they ask for help.

A colleague referred the following patient to me after trying several treatment courses of antidepressant medications without success. The patient was a middle-aged man, and my colleague didn't know whether the patient was depressed or was suffering from posttraumatic stress disorder (PTSD). There were many other diagnostic possibilities that might have afflicted a patient like this man, but his treater, like most U.S. psychiatrists, chose only from the *DSM*.

The patient's story was that the year before he had been in a fire that destroyed his home and all of his belongings. He was not burnt and suffered only minor smoke inhalation. Since that fire, however, he had no energy and no interest in his previous hobbies of playing the guitar and knitting. He was a prolific knitter, creating sweaters, scarves, mittens, and other items for family and friends; he won prizes for these efforts. Since the fire, however, he stopped his hobbies, and just sat around his daughter's house like, "a couch potato."

When I met him, he was mildly slow in movement and speech for his age and general health. He was cooperative, but subdued. He said that he was now a useless person and that he did not have much of a life. He said he slept too much. He denied having nightmares, did not ruminate about the fire, and had no "flashbacks" of the fire. He said that at the rate he was going, he'd just as soon be dead, but had no plan to kill himself. He said he stopped playing the guitar and knitting, because *"the notes and needle movements are no longer in my hands. I can't make the needles work smoothly."*

One of the many problems with the *DSM* is that it is worthless as a source of learning about psychopathology or anything but rudimentary diagnosis. With a patient like the man above, the *DSM* choices are limited. He did not have the *DSM* features of PTSD as he did not ruminate about the trauma, did not have nightmares about it, and had no flashbacks. He did meet *DSM* criteria for "major depressive disorder," but if you compare his image with those of some of the patients with depressive illness I've described, like the first "wow" patient, you'll recognize that his "depression" was different. He was apathetic and had reduced volition and energy. Melancholic depressive illness is typically characterized by apprehension and gloom. On the other hand, a neuropsychiatrist understands that all behavior reflects brain function, and so all behavior, even behavior not in the *DSM*, is grist for the diagnostic mill. In this patient, the grist was his loss of the ability to knit or play the guitar. This ability reflects motor memory and when he said the movements were no longer in his hands he was saying that he no longer had access to this memory. The programs for the motor sequences might still be there but the recall of them was damaged. This implicated a part of the brain known as the basal ganglia, the same structures involved in Parkinson's disease.[16]

Because the man was in a fire, I wondered whether carbon monoxide might have damaged his basal ganglia. I didn't know the answer, but I was not lazy, I was curious, and I knew that not knowing might not be in the patient's best interests. So, I looked it up. And sure enough carbon monoxide can adversely affect the basal ganglia, resulting in basal ganglia calcifications. A CT scan confirmed this. The condition in referred to as Fahr's syndrome. It's not in the *DSM*. Such a condition can elicit behavioral change that looks like a mild to modest depression; stimulants, not antidepressants, can ameliorate apathetic syndromes as they did for this patient.[17]

Both neurologists and psychiatrists minimize the ability of behavior to predict where in the brain the problem lies. This attitude results from decades of frustration in failed attempts to pinpoint the source of hallucinations, delusions, and other classic psychiatric phenomena. But these specialists have thrown out the proverbial baby with its bath water. Although the precision of the neurological location of psychopathology is not as refined as that for aphasia, one-sided paralysis, or the derangements of the nerves to the eyes and throat and mouth, there are patterns that can lead to conclusions that benefit patients. Every psychiatrist needs to know about these patterns, but few are taught the necessary neurology of psychopathology. Here's an example of how such information can help.

A number of years ago I was having lunch with a colleague in the hospital cafeteria. He was just about to launch an assault upon a substantial wedge of delicious looking cherry pie when he got a page to come to his inpatient unit because his patient, a woman in her sixties, was angrily shouting at the nurses accusing them of moving and hiding her bedroom. She had gone to the unit dining room, but could not find her way back to her bedroom. As she was convinced she had no illness (the term is denial of illness or anosagnosia), the only other explanation that came to her was that the room had somehow been hidden. My colleague called the unit nurse and said he'd be right up to give the patient an antipsychotic. But there still was that cherry pie spread in all its gooey redness across the dessert plate. Had you been there you would have seen the mental wheels turning: *"pie...patient...pie...patient."*

As my colleague was eating his pie (to be fair, with some haste), he told me this story. The patient was a pure right-handed person in previously good general medical health. She had no prior psychiatric history. But suddenly she stopped answering her phone a few days before. Her daughter, who spoke with her daily, became concerned and went to the mother's home. The mother refused to admit her daughter and yelled through the door that aliens from outer space were trying to control her mind by beaming rays into her house, forcing out her own thoughts. She did not want to open the door and be taken over by the rays, but she finally relented. Upon doing so, she, in horror, pointed to her daughter and said, *"You're one of them. You're not my daughter. You're an imposter."* Terrified, she said that the aliens had taken control of the neighborhood, had removed it to another location with all of her neighbors, and had replaced the houses and people with alien houses and alien neighbors.

Now in the hospital where she was admitted to psychiatry with the diagnosis of late onset schizophrenia, the mother was causing a disturbance because her room had been "hidden" by the nurses. Her general neurological examination on admission was unremarkable. Such examinations are inadequate for neuropsychiatric patients, but that's another chapter.

It is safe to say that if there were a thousand identical patients brought to a hospital, most would be considered "psychiatric" and "psychotic," admitted to a psychiatric inpatient unit, and given an antipsychotic with little or no work-up other than the standard admission blood tests. It is also safe to say that once labeled psychotic, almost always labeled psychotic; once given an antipsychotic drug, almost always given such a drug.

Listening to the patient's story, I recognized a familiar pattern of psychopathology. I asked my colleague not to give the patient an antipsychotic but to instead mildly sedate her if needed, or better still, have the staff redirect her attention when she got irritable. Going out on a limb I predicted that if he did as I suggested the patient would likely fully recover in a week or so with no other treatment. I also told him that if he obtained a CT scan he would see that the patient had suffered a small ischemic stroke in her right hemisphere where her parietal and temporal lobes meet. Most strokes result from a blockage of a blood vessel leading to damage of the surrounding brain tissue from lack of oxygen. The process is termed ischemia.

The "limb" I went out on was stronger than it first appears. The "big picture" for this patient was a woman in her sixties, in previous good health, who experienced a sudden, substantial, and abnormal behavioral change. The odds are that this picture spells "stroke." However, she did not have changes in the functioning of the nerves to her head and neck, termed cranial nerves. And she had no muscle paralysis or weakness. She had no signs of speech and language difficulties (aphasia). So, if she had a stroke, it was not in the usual places. Her behavioral changes, however, helped localize the problem. She had denial of illness (anosagnosia), disorientation to the spatial organization of the inpatient unit (topographic disorientation), and reduplicative paramnesia in misrecognizing her neighborhood and neighbors as replicas and not the real McCoy. She had Capgras syndrome as she misrecognized her daughter as an imposter. All of these features have been associated with right cerebral hemisphere lesions, particularly in right-handed persons like this patient. None of the features, however, is in the *DSM*. She also had experiences that some outside force was controlling her body and putting thoughts into her head. These features are termed experiences of control and alienation and have also been associated with right cerebral hemisphere damage. So, based on all that, I crawled out on the limb.[18]

To his enormous credit, my colleague, though skeptical, followed my advice and sure enough the patient had a wedge-shaped little stroke where I predicted it would be. Like real estate, for brain lesions, its location, location, location. So a little stoke in a critical area can elicit a lot of symptoms. Antipsychotics can worsen strokes as they can trigger a neuron cell suicide cascade making a small lesion larger and preventing the surrounding neural tissue from reorganizing to assume some of the functions from the damaged area.[19] By getting the correct diagnosis and properly managing the patient, we did no harm and beneficence ruled. Afterward we could also encourage the patient to reduce any risk factors for future strokes. But the key ingredients in this success story, besides cherry pie, were my learning neuropsychiatry and my colleague's recognition that he did not know neuropsychiatry. His commitment to do his best for his patient was paramount. There are not many neuropsychiatrists roaming about, but there are even fewer physicians like my colleague.

CHAPTER 5

☙

Peeves

"I don't have pet peeves; I have whole kennels of irritation."
Whoopi Goldberg

It is more important to know what sort of person has a disease than to know what sort of disease a person has.
Hippocrates

MORAL SHORTCOMINGS

The fundamental problem with U.S. psychiatry is U.S. psychiatrists. In my view our ethics have declined over the past several decades, and we have become a sorry lot. Every couple of months we learn about some well-known psychiatrist who was paid to endorse a new treatment that doesn't work or worse causes harm. Among the 394 U.S. physicians in 2010 who received over $100,000 from the pharmaceutical industry, 116 were psychiatrists, well out of proportion to the percentage of psychiatrists in medical practice.[1] As a consequence, the manipulation of research to benefit the pharmaceutical industry has become common.

In concert, fancy devices have been introduced with claims of wondrous benefits that do not materialize. Light-emitting boxes were supposed to prevent winter depressions, but the evidence for this claim is weak.[2] Vagal nerve stimulation (an implanted electronic pacer in the chest with electrodes attached to a nerve in the neck) was supposed to relieve treatment-resistant depressions. It offers no demonstrated benefit but costs the poor soul subjected to it about $20,000 out of pocket.[3] Transcranial magnetic stimulation (TMS), a ring-shaped magnet that delivers a magnetic pulse to the head, was going to replace electroconvulsant therapy (ECT). It has not and the evidence for it indicates it has at best a placebo effect.[4] Psychiatrists with financial interests in these proposed treatments were paid by the manufacturers to give supportive academic talks and publish supportive papers.[5]

The science was bad but the promotion was good. Just like the new antidepressant and antipsychotic drugs that have been introduced in the past three decades, the idea of the new treatments was to make money. That goal has been accomplished. The pharmaceutical industry is one of the most profitable in the world. In 2006, sales in the United States alone topped 289 billion. Profits have been maintained and are rising, even as profits in other industries have been flat or have fallen during the great recession. Between 1998 and 2006 the industry spent 855 million dollars on lobbying, more than any other industry.[6]

While making money is the American way, when treatments are equated to widgets, profits will trump efficacy and safety. Can you think of an industry in which that has not been the case? This was not always the situation in U.S. psychiatry. The early psychiatric drugs were developed with industry and psychopharmacologists cooperating toward the production of agents that were effective and reasonably safe when properly used. They succeeded, and the older antidepressants and antipsychotics are as good as or better than the new agents; and they are a lot less expensive. The cost to patients drops from 18% to 6% of their medical dollar when they switch from patented to generic medications.[7]

P. T. Barnum supposedly said, *"You can't cheat an honest man."* In many ways, the new psychiatric drugs and novel treatments are frauds. The evidence that they work is weak at best and is often distorted to the point of fabrication. In Chapter 3, I cited studies that show that the new antidepressants achieve remission at only slightly better rates than do a placebo. The widely prescribed anticonvulsant valproic acid (Depakote) outpaces lithium in prescriptions as a mood stabilizer, but it is not as effective.[8]

In the 1990s the American Psychiatric Association published the first guidelines for the treatment of patients with manic-depression (bipolar disorder). Clinicians, medical students, and psychiatric residents were encouraged to follow the guidelines. My colleagues and I were shocked to read that the recommended first-line mood stabilizer was a new anticonvulsant, lamotrigine (Lamictal). There were not many studies supporting the agent. It turned out that at the time of the publication of those guidelines a majority of supportive studies were funded by the manufacturer and were led by an investigator who was prominent on the panel of "experts" who wrote the guidelines. The recommendation did not pass the smell test. The first-line agent in the treatment of manic-depression remains lithium followed by valproic acid (Depakote). That the newer agents have been accepted, mostly based on promotion, speaks as much to the moral shortcomings of academic psychiatry and psychiatric leadership as it does to the makers of these products.

Over the past half-dozen years academic psychiatry has attempted to wean itself from the pharmaceutical industry milk-cow. Drug reps are restricted at most medical centers and direct payments to departmental activities have also been limited. Although these are good first steps, financial support to departments still occurs. Multisite clinical trials are still industry affairs. Well-known psychiatrists and experts on panels crafting treatment guidelines and new versions of the *DSM*, and speakers at continuing medical education and other educational efforts targeted to faculty supervisors, are still industry supported. As the National Institute of Mental Health (NIMH) and other funding sources have cut back, industry's dollars have had greater impact. Despite the financial pain that might ensue, I think the only solution is to end the direct relationships. No academic responsible for the training and mentoring of medical students, residents, and specialty training fellows should accept any industry money. They receive adequate financial support from their institutions. If industry wants their products tested, restricted grants can be given to the institution, which can then monitor the use of the funds for a small overhead fee as is done for other funding sources. No more industry-designed and analyzed research. No more sequestered data. No more industry-supported lectures. No more direct industry support of any kind. Then what experts say and do might still be occasionally incorrect, but they'll come to their conclusions without real or perceived taint.

COMMUNITY PSYCHIATRY'S OVERREACH

Biological Psychiatry Remains Marginalized

When biological psychiatry emerged in the late 1960s, the hope was that psychiatry would truly become a modern medical specialty. The biological psychiatry movement offered an alternative to the Freudian movement. However, the promises that neurochemical studies would reveal the brain disturbances in mental illness and that gene mapping would disclose the determinants of mental illness did not quickly emerge. Psychiatric diagnosis was too arbitrary to provide more than a rough estimate on what treatments would work best for specific patients, and research samples were heterogeneous, confounding the meaning of any identified biological perturbations of some patients. All that the research told us was that patients with any of the "big ticket" psychiatric disorders such as psychosis and manic-depression were biologically different in various domains from normal controls.

In addition, the NIMH and almost all academic psychiatry departments were still controlled by psychoanalysts. The established perspective of what ailed patients remained psychological not biochemical. Biological psychiatry was for years a marginalized division in many departments. In my training, if I wanted to learn about the biology of psychiatric disorders other than the use of psychiatric medications, I either had a discussion with one of my resident colleagues or I traveled across town to a small building off Fifth Avenue that housed the Division of Biological Psychiatry. The only clinical service the biological psychiatrists were permitted to run was the heroin addiction inpatient unit and methadone clinics. This exception was given because the division received large grants to study the heroin epidemic of the 1960s.[9]

Social and Community Psychiatry Ignores the Psychiatric Medical Model

In the 1960s U.S. psychiatry reached its apogee in popularity. More than one out of 10 graduates of U.S. medical schools entered the field with the hope of alleviating social ills by improving the mental health of the country.[10] This was the era of hippies, LSD enlightenment, paranoia about "anyone over thirty," and the folly of the Viet Nam War.[11] Persons in authority seemed crazy. Against this background the psychiatric establishment exhibited the height of hubris by implicitly promising that it was going to fix the ills of society by the application of psychodynamic and related psychosocial interventions to large groups of the U.S. population that would be funneled through comprehensive community mental health centers and outreach clinics. How could young idealistic newly minted physicians resist?

But psychodynamic interventions do not particularly help individuals, let alone populations, so the idea as envisioned was doomed. The most enthusiastic of the community psychiatrists turned to social psychology and social work efforts. By 1971, the focus was on delivery systems and not on what kind of psychiatry was going to be delivered. This absorption is reflected in the number of journal articles devoted to the topic. Of the 22 articles in the February 1965 issue of *The American Journal of Psychiatry* eight were devoted to social and community psychiatry. This proportion is typical of that era. The goal was to serve as many customers as possible. Patients became "clients." Psychiatrists became "mental health providers" lumped together with psychiatric social workers, nurses, and psychologists. It was as if we all had the same skills and training. Nonphysicians were put in charge of medical programs. Colleagues began to refer to "working with" a "client" rather than "caring for" a "patient." If you were a CPA I suppose the change in terminology was okay. But if the job is to diagnose and treat patients with brain dysfunction, the language reflects a degrading of that process.

Politicians and Administrators Are Put in Charge

Because the mental health care delivery system became paramount and not the care itself, academic psychiatry turned to politicians and administrators for leadership of academic departments. The chairman at the New York State University campus at Stony Brook, Stanley Yolles, was a prime example of this change.[12] From leading a recent expansion of the NIMH, his task at Stony Brook was to establish a public model of comprehensive mental health care and an academic program devoted to training psychiatrists that would serve in needy communities throughout the country. Stony Brook was uniquely suited for this experiment as in addition to the university's new medical school and campus, the surrounding communities included three large state mental hospitals, a swath of rural farmland hamlets, a Native American reservation, a mostly African-American urbanized slum, and several wealthy Long Island coastal communities.

Like most of his generation of psychiatric chairmen, Stanley Yolles knew little clinical psychiatry. From my conversations with him, I doubt that he ever took care of a patient after his residency requirements. He had no personal interest in psychology or biological psychiatry. He thought psychoanalysis was not effective for most persons. He had no personal interest in residents or students other than their passing their required examinations. In the late 1970s and 1980s when I had the opportunity to meet many of the chairmen of U.S. psychiatry departments, most were like Yolles. I was recruited to establish Stony Brook's first-ever residency program in psychiatry. Yolles, however, had minimal interest in the residency program's content other than the teaching of sex therapy and the use of video teaching aides. The combination was funny, but coincidental.

The Origins of Primary Care Psychiatry

Community psychiatry leaders developed comprehensive delivery systems. The type of care they endorsed had little to do with a commitment to a particular treatment approach or a favored understanding of the mechanisms underlying psychopathology. The effort, however, had a lot to do with volume. The more customers served the better. Thus, the new breed of chairmen favored group over individual therapies. They preferred large clinics rather than hospital-based psychiatry units with limited bed capacity. Because psychiatric medications could be prescribed to large numbers of patients and in the 1960s and 1970s at a cheaper rate than psychotherapies, they preferred medication clinics to any psychoanalytic model. They didn't care how the medications worked or where in the brain the patient's problem might lurk. Volume and cost were major motivators of their efforts. They encouraged less expensive nonphysicians to do the therapy. Psychiatry was less academic and medical and more social and political. The systems they established led to the devolution of U.S. psychiatry into a primary care type specialty (see Chapter 6).

Yolles, like others in the community psychiatry movement, did not believe that medical students needed to know much psychiatry beyond rudimentary diagnosis and psychopharmacology. When one of my colleagues and I establishd the department's clerkship in psychiatry for the third year medical students, Yolles was dissatisfied because *"You taught them too much psychiatry. Why do they have to know about biological psychiatry and ECT? They're not going to be psychiatrists?"* He assumed that eventually most psychiatric care in the United States would be delivered within community health care systems by nonpsychiatrists and that they would have no need for sophisticated constructs and a large database about psychiatry.

In one sense, Yolles was right. By the end of the 1970s the number of U.S. medical school graduates choosing the field had plummeted from over 10% to less than 3%. Why spend all that money and make all that effort in medical school and then go through another 4 years of training to end up "seeing clients" and doing what social workers do, but not doing it as well as they did?[13]

Yolles, however, was fundamentally wrong about medical students not needing to know a lot about psychiatry. Psychiatry then and now is a required clinical rotation for all U.S. medical students. Physicians from other countries immigrating to the United States must demonstrate training and competence in psychiatry to be fully licensed here. The obvious reason for this is that no matter what the physician's clinical practice, other than the pathologist surrounded by reagents and tissue samples in the laboratory or facing a queue of corpses in the morgue, every patient a physician encounters will have a living central nervous system doing its thing and generating behavior. A physician who does not have a reasonable grasp of human behavior, normal and abnormal, will not be a very good doctor. A less obvious reason and one covered in the next chapter, is that most patients with behavioral syndromes are first cared for by generalist physicians or other nonpsychiatric medical specialists. The more these physicians know about psychiatry, the better it will be for their patients.

In the 1970s and early 1980s U.S. medical schools were convinced that they wanted clinical chairmen who could manage departments not inspire them.[14] The medical schools wanted their chairmen to develop miniempires to support the community health care systems. The administrator psychiatric chairman model was applied nation-wide. Psychiatry departments expanded beyond other clinical programs. Local governments, states, and the NIMH threw money at psychiatry and its effort to fix the ills of modern life.[15]

As part of the empire building, the largest U.S. departments of psychiatry established research divisions whose mandate was to develop sizable amounts of government grant money and other funding sources. These divisions were separated from the clinical services and they focused on bench research that appeared to have little impact on patient care. The physical and administrative separation of the research divisions into institutes and centers with their own directors and the laboratory absorption of their research efforts created a fire wall between the researchers, often tenure track faculty, and the nontenured faculty clinicians who had to care for patients. Stony brook had lots of PhD neuroscientists but not enough MD clinicians to take care of patients and teach medical students and psychiatric residents. Clinical programs suffered in reduced resources. They were chronically understaffed. The same approach is applied in many departments today. My present department's psychiatric research efforts, for example, are primarily housed in a large newly constructed facility (dubbed a "center") that has more laboratory and other research space than it has clinical space to see a small number of outpatients. Many of the researchers are PhDs and not clinicians. The department's several endowed professorships are for heavily granted researchers. It takes several months for patients to get an appointment because there are not enough clinicians to see them. This research/clinical facility is 20 minutes away from the university hospital that provides the bulk of the department's psychiatric care. The clinicians in the hospital settings have little time for research. The geographic separation challenges research collaboration between the two groups.

Providing good care to patients and training the next generation of physicians are endeavors that are too important to be left to people who do not have a passionate commitment to such efforts. Being able to develop and deliver clinical services and to organize and administer a clinical training department are essential, but without a philosophical framework, the organization is meaningless and its products in my view will be mediocre.

The community psychiatry movement encouraged primary care psychiatry. The no-frills approach was cheaper to deliver and served more patients than either psychodynamic therapies or neuropsychiatric evaluation and treatments and their foci on getting to the bottom of a patient's problem. Those efforts take too long when volume and cost drive the system. Primary care psychiatry, like primary care general medicine, is not a clinical money maker. It is also not sexy. Medical students eventually lost interest in primary care psychiatry.

CHILD PSYCHIATRISTS

Although adult general psychiatry seemed hopelessly mired between a rather uninteresting approach of giving some medications and hoping for the best and an invalid metaphysical alternative, there was still optimism in the latter twentieth century about caring for patients during their formative years. Many of the established psychiatric syndromes are associated with preillness problems in childhood (e.g., cruelty to animals and fire setting are harbingers of antisocial personality),[16] and some illnesses emerge in childhood (e.g., social and other phobias).[17] Personality traits are not fully formed until the end of the second or even into the third decade of life, so interventions to modulate abnormal traits might have their greatest impact in early and not in later life. Devoting efforts to children and adolescents in the prevention and effective treatment of childhood behavioral disorders has been recognized for decades as a critically important endeavor. The hope was that early interventions might make a difference. With that hope, an increasing number of psychiatry residents turned to additional specialized training in child psychiatry.[18] In my view, however, child psychiatrists have only rarely met the challenges they face.

Psychoanalytic Theory and Psychoanalysts Dominated U.S. Child and Adolescent Psychiatry for Much of the Twentieth Century

For the first three-quarters of the twentieth century child psychiatry was dominated by Freudians. Anna Freud, Sigmund's daughter, was the movement's conceptual guru.[19] Play therapy replaced the couch. Mothers and fathers, however, were still the villains.

Psychiatric residents since the 1960s have been required to rotate through the child and adolescent services of their departments. It remains so today. In the 1960s and 1970s, the field focused on delivery systems and psychodynamic theory and therapies. I surveyed the online medical publication source, PubMed, by entering the prompt "child and adolescent psychiatry." It yielded 18,102 citations. I examined the titles for a clear characterization of each article's focus to identify articles related to psychotherapy, psychodynamic theory, social and community psychiatry, and biological psychiatry. For example, a clear characterization in the title would include a specific statement about intensive or group therapy, a Freudian or related psychodynamic theoretical concern, a delivery system challenge or social influences on behavior, a study of a drug, a brain process or anatomy, or a genotype related to behavior. I looked at articles published from 1963 through 1970 and found 126 that I could classify. Of these, 27 were devoted to psychotherapies, 30 to psychodynamic theory, 43 to social and community psychiatry issues, and 26 to biological psychiatry. There were 117 articles that could be clearly characterized from 2012 alone, reflecting the enormous expansion of the field since the 1970s. Of these, 13 were devoted to psychotherapies (mostly cognitive-behavioral types), only 5 were related to psychodynamic theory, 17 addressed social and community concerns, and 82 were biological. The biological articles were mostly devoted to the biology and medical treatment of children with attention deficit disorder or depression. The theoretical shift away from psychodynamic psychiatry has been dramatic.

My child psychiatry experience in the 1960s reflects the survey. All of my supervisors were psychoanalysts, specifically Freudian, and were mostly intolerant of alternative views of behavior. At the child clinics, I discovered that child psychiatrists do not use articles or pronouns when referring to family members. It's never his mother, her mother, or the mother. It's always, "Mom." "Mom" said this or "Mom" did that, never "the Mom" or "her mother." I have never discovered the source of this aberration of spoken English, which today is still universal among child psychiatrists.

The child clinic was at the city-run Metropolitan Hospital. The clinic was always jammed with kids and their mothers. In general pediatrics infected ears and throats were then the bread and butter of practice. In child psychiatry in the 1960s it was bed-wetting (enuresis) and other sleep difficulties, family problems, phobias, and "conduct disorders." The last was the *DSM* term for sociopath in training.

Because the patients coming to the hospital's emergency room and clinics were all poor, mostly uneducated, and mostly Hispanic or African-American, the all-white psychoanalytic attendings had reached the theoretical conclusion that the patients and their families were too psychologically primitive to receive the Freudian word. So, we prescribed some medications and offered lots of social services. In hindsight, these interventions were undoubtedly more effective than whatever the attendings would have otherwise done. I do not recall ever being taught about child development other than the Freudian psychosexual stages, except for one child psychiatrist who was enamored with Piaget.[20] There were never discussions about personality outside the analytic model. There were never discussions of the neurological causes of behavioral change. At that time, autism was considered the product of abnormal parenting, a false notion that further damaged those families.[21] Lauretta Bender, a famous child psychiatrist from Bellevue, gave one lecture in which she introduced us to her paper and pencil cognitive test, *The Bender-Gestalt*.[22] I found it useful in the assessment of visual-motor function, but the faculty never used it. The child psychoanalysts preferred to interpret their patients' cognition through "play therapy" and projective psychological tests. In the latter the patient looks at an ink blot or an ambiguous picture and talks about what he or she sees. Because of the ambiguities of the images, what is related is supposed to reveal the viewer's inner psychology.

Several years later I was developing my own department of psychiatry. I had hoped to build a child psychiatry division that focused on neural as well as childhood social development. Some of the child psychiatrists tried to follow this approach, but most of them in the Chicago region, like their colleagues around the country, remained psychoanalytic in perspective or treated patients from another psychotherapy model. A few behavior therapists offered systematic desensitization as a treatment for children with phobias, but the child psychiatrists and the child psychologists feuded more often than they collaborated. At the time, there was only a handful of child psychiatrists interested in children and adolescents with manic-depression or obsessive-compulsive disorder from a medical model perspective.

Twenty-First-Century U.S. Child and Adolescent Psychiatry: Social Work with Medications

U.S. child and adolescent psychiatry largely abandoning the Freudian model was progress, but like the rest of U.S. psychiatry, it too has failed to adopt a coherent replacement model from which to diagnose and treat patients. Although parents are no longer being routinely blamed for some metaphysical shortcoming or pathological parenting practices, child and adolescent psychiatry has devolved into a focus on *DSM* labels, cookbook psychopharmacology, and attention to the child's social environment.

Psychoanalysis has been marginalized, but psychic turmoil is still offered as an explanation for childhood phobias, cutting and other self-injurious behaviors, eating disorders, and social and school problems. Psychological interventions are widely applied for patients with these conditions and much of these therapies are delivered by psychologists, councilors, and social workers.[23]

Biological contributions to these behaviors have received substantial attention by researchers, but when a child or a teenager acts up, the tendency remains among child psychiatry clinicians to quickly attribute the behavioral disturbance to parent–child or other social factors. Although these conundrums of life are often one of the determinants of the child's or teen's difficulties, other processes may also be at work, but a search for these causes is rarely made. The young woman I discussed in Chapter 2 who had a brain vascular malformation that ruptured and killed her had been seen by adolescent psychiatrists and therapists for almost 4 years without any of them considering a brain source for the then teen's depressions. That happened in the late 1980s. Today, diagnoses commonly missed in childhood include mild autism and Asperger's syndrome, developmental speech, language, and learning disorders, mood disorders, stress disorder, tic disorder, stereotypic movement disorder, and brain tumor, the last few because the behavioral symptoms are attributed to a psychological not a neurological cause.[24]

Today, therapists of all stripes continue to provide the bulk of care to children and teenagers with behavioral difficulties. When other etiologies are considered, they tend to remain within the *DSM* framework. So, if the family or peer group is not felt to be the primary source of the problem, the usual suspects are rounded up.

Ill-Defined Attention Deficit Disorder

Attention deficit hyperactivity disorders (ADHD) are at the head of the list of suspects, and the popularity of this diagnosis explains the explosion of prescriptions of stimulants for children. Stimulant prescriptions for children in the United States has increased about four-fold in the past several decades while rising significantly more slowly in other industrialized countries where limits are placed on the promotion of medications.[25] Few children treated with these agents, however, are first systematically assessed to determine if their classroom difficulties reflect a dysfunction in brain processing that can benefit from stimulants. False-positive diagnosis of hyperactivity and attention deficit disorder is common.[26] Children with confirmed ADHD have both neuroanatomic and neuropsychological abnormalities indicating a developmental frontal lobe dysfunction. Those that benefit from stimulants have problems with sustaining attention, particularly when distracting stimuli are present. Their performance decays on continuous performance tasks under those circumstances. Children with true attention deficits have difficulties on such tests and their performance will improve with proper treatment. Repeated testing is needed, however, to monitor treatments.[27] Relying solely on teacher and parent ratings may capture whether there is a school or behavior problem, but these assessments will not identify the cause of the difficulty or whether the child will respond to medical intervention. Much of what occurs today in clinical child psychiatry practice is accomplished by trial and error.

The Swollen Concept of Childhood Mood Disorder

Another common consideration for the twenty-first-century child psychiatrist is mood disorder: depressions, mania, and mixed states with rapid mood swings and overlapping intense moods. From my professor in 1966 opining that there was no longer any entity such as manic-depression to the recognition in the 1970s and 1980s that it is a fairly common condition, manic-depression has morphed into bipolar disorder and bipolar disorder has expanded into subforms from I to IV. This dramatic increase in the frequency of the diagnosis has been encouraged by the escalating availability of medications purported to treat mood disorder. The diagnosis of bipolar disorder has increased 40-fold over the past 30 years, with many more children given the diagnosis. The increase in children and adolescents cannot be fully explained by better awareness, but the increase does parallel a dramatic increase in the prescription of medications for this patient age group.[28] The commercial introduction of lithium in the United States in 1970, the promotion of anticonvulsants as mood stabilizers in the 1980s and 1990s, and the more recent claims that the atypical antipsychotics also modulate moods have legitimized making a diagnosis of bipolar disorder even if the clinician is unsure of that diagnosis.[29] The thinking is: *"What's the harm?" "Let's try it out. "If it works, great, if not, we haven't lost anything."* The harm of course is that for many patients, manic-depression will not be the correct diagnosis and the treatments for it may mask what needs to be revealed if definitive treatment is to be prescribed. Rates of serious side effects (e.g., diabetes) have increased with the overusage of these medications. The problem is especially acute with the increase in the prescription of antipsychotic agents for the treatment of several nonpsychotic childhood conditions. Sometimes these agents can be life-threatening for the patient.

Catatonia is not always associated with mood disorder: Although catatonia is commonly observed in adult patients with mood disorder, among children and adolescents other conditions also need to be considered. A few years ago, for example, a teenage boy with a developmental disorder was referred for ECT. A month or so earlier he had lost most of his modest language functions, stopped eating unless prompted, and stopped dressing himself. He sat in the same fixed posture for several hours unless urged to move. The teenager had substantial developmental difficulties since birth, and had periods of what were identified as episodes of depression and others of aggression. Mood disorders often cooccur with developmental disorders and autism, so his pattern of features was not considered unusual. His "depressions" and aggressive episodes were taken at their *DSM* value without further evaluation.

Following an episode of excited aggression the teen was given an antipsychotic and he then slipped further into a catatonic state. There are several similar stories in this book. Child psychiatrists, like their adult counterparts, respond reflexively to severe behavioral disturbances in their patients by prescribing antipsychotic medication. I have seen many patients with autism or a variant of it who developed catatonia induced by the administration of an antipsychotic drug. These agents are overprescribed for this patient group as they are perceived to be reasonable sleep enhancers, reducers of agitation and aggression, and mood stabilizers. They are poor choices for all of these concerns, while simultaneously they are potentially hazardous in persons with autism because such patients are at risk for the motor side effects of this class of medications. These patients may develop catatonia even without exposure to medications and so are at greater risk for it than are other patients. The catatonia can be life threatening.

Naively assuming the boy had received a thorough evaluation as he was now being cared for at a prestigious university hospital, I recommended that he be treated with high doses of lorazepam (Atavan) and that if his catatonia was not quickly relieved, he have a course of ECT. The lorazepam had only a modest effect, and so we began ECT. In almost all instances, ECT will relieve catatonia with a few treatments. If the patient suffers from malignant catatonia (this teen did not), 12–25 treatments may be needed.[30] This patient's catatonia improved somewhat, but he still did not have a full remission and was often described as in and out of stupor during which he was less responsive than usual, as if about to doze.

Because he had not fully and quickly responded, the ECT team reviewed what had been done in the boy's evaluation and we discovered that he had not had an electroencephalogram (EEG) and that there was no indication in his records that he had been adequately assessed for a seizure disorder. The possibility that his catatonia might result from seizures was never seriously considered by two different sets of child psychiatrist evaluators.

Unfortunately, once ECT has begun the standard EEG may temporarily show elements of a seizure so this detection method would not have been as helpful as it might otherwise be. We recommended other EEG methods of detection, additional strategies for identifying a seizure, and a careful history, but these steps were not accomplished.[31] None of the boy's present child psychiatrists accepted the idea that the boy suffered from anything other than catatonia. Finally, on an ECT treatment day, I had the opportunity to have a conversation with the boy's father who was able to describe behaviors prior to the boy's episodes of depression and aggression that were consistent with a seizure disorder. No one had asked the father about these behaviors and so he had not thought to mention them. This is a common story in patients with a seizure disorder. *"Don't ask, don't tell"* was around in the world of epileptics long before the Clinton administration adopted it for the U.S. military in the hope of appeasing the religious right and up-tight military. So that morning, armed with the new information suggesting that the boy had a seizure disorder, I let the EEG we use to monitor treatments run for some time before treatment while the boy was lying quietly on his stretcher. He was in a stupor and I could place him in various postures. The boy's EEG was markedly different from the pretreatment or between treatments tracings of other patients. He was having a seizure *before* we had stimulated his brain.[32]

Following this revelation the boy did not receive a more extensive evaluation. He was not then treated for epilepsy. He remained unchanged for another 6 months, until one day he was hospitalized on a neurology service following several spontaneous grand mal seizures that required emergency care as his breathing was compromised. He survived those seizures, and following the evaluation that should have been accomplished a year earlier by his child psychiatrists, he was diagnosed and treated for epilepsy. His catatonia, aggressive excitements, and depressions ended.

Expanding manic-depression: Bipolar disorder "I" is the classic presentation of manic-depressive illness, which includes fully formed episodes of mania and depression interspersed with varying periods of relative normalcy. When symptomatic, most patients with this variety of mood disorder will suffer most of the time with depression. The episodes of this form of manic-depression can be severe and may be associated with psychosis (hallucinations and delusions) and catatonia. Many psychiatrists still do not understand these associations and so give such patients the label "schizoaffective disorder." The evidence, however, does not support schizoaffective disorder as a distinct disease, but it persists in the *DSM* and is employed by clinicians who can't make up their minds and don't fully appreciate the consequences of an unclear diagnosis. The mislabeling can lead to unwarranted prescription of antipsychotic agents rather than mood stabilizers, antidepressant medications, and ECT.[33]

When manic-depression emerges in childhood or in adolescence, rather than in adult life, the periods of illness may be less circumscribed and distinct than those seen in the adult-onset pattern. The periods of illness may be less severe in intensity, but they may last longer than episodes occurring in the adult-onset variation. Episodes of mania and depression in the young may also overlap, giving a picture of a mixed abnormal mood state or of a highly emotional person with brief but frequent mood swings. The pathophysiology of this type of manic-depression is the same as that for form "I," but the *DSM* has nevertheless provided the additional subforms.[34]

Because the sufferer of this early-onset form of mood disorder is rarely without social, school, and other difficulties, but is also less likely to experience an intense abnormal circumscribed mood state requiring hospitalization, the sufferer can be mistaken as having an attention deficit disorder or a personality disorder.[35] Young persons with this form of mood disorder will commonly have family and school difficulties and some sufferers in their swings of emotion may also abuse street drugs. Episodes of self-harm are common among such patients. The combination of mood swings, self-harm, and social and interpersonal uproar often triggers the diagnosis of borderline personality disorder. This is another *DSM* creation that is mostly given to female patients who have annoyed or frustrated their treaters. It is not politically correct to refer to the patient as *"a pain in the ass,"* but the borderline label makes that clear to all mental health care providers.[36]

The overlapping features of the childhood-onset form of manic-depression can make diagnosis hard. The response to this challenge is often unsophisticated labeling followed by reflexive treatment. There is little effort to figure it all out. The *DSM* label is given and several medications are prescribed. The patient is exposed to all the side effects of each agent and to the adverse interactions among the drugs, but there is little benefit from the use of so many pharmaceuticals. They are then sent for additional talking therapies specifically designed for "borderline" patients as if these patients all had the same fundamental problem.

The Overuse of Antipsychotic Agents

Child psychiatrists have also accepted the pharmaceutical industry's promotion of antipsychotic drugs as mood stabilizers, accounting for the explosion of prescriptions for aripiprazole (Abilify) in this patient age group. According to a U.S. FDA 2011 report for the two years ending in March

2011, about 9.7 million prescriptions for aripiprazole were dispensed at retail pharmacies in the United States during that period. Nineteen percent of the prescriptions were for children and adolescents. *Seventy-one thousand were for children 6 years of age or younger.* These numbers do not include the children in hospitals and other institutions who are also frequently prescribed the agent.[37] Aripiprazol is now the most prescribed antipsychotic for children and teens. It and similar drugs, however, put children at substantial risk for tardive dyskinesia. These drugs have been linked to metabolic changes that increase the risk of heart disease and diabetes. Antipsychotic medications are not true mood stabilizers; they are tranquilizers. Patients with manic-depression do not fully recover with these agents but they are at risk for side effects. Unlike lithium, they also do not reduce the risk of future episodes of illness.[38] I would restrict their use in prepubescent children.

The Discarding of the Older Classes of Antidepressants

The prevalence of depressive illness among children and adolescents is high. The depressions can be severe, may discourage any normal schooling, and can lead to suicide. Suicide is the third leading cause of death among U.S. teenagers.[39] Child psychiatrists, like their counterparts who care for adult patients, also do not consider in their diagnosing and patient care that the *DSM* version of depression defines heterogeneity, not a single disease entity. They tend to treat all kids with depression similarly. But they have placed themselves in a bind. They have accepted studies from the 1970s and 1980s reporting that tricyclic antidepressants (TCAs) are not effective for depression in children and that this class of antidepressants also has dangerous heart side effects in this age group. They explain the presumed lack of efficacy by envisioning a developmental lag in the maturation of the neurotransmitter system the TCAs are thought to alter in their antidepressant effect. The problem with this notion is that TCAs have been used safely for decades in children for the treatment of enuresis and sleep disorders.[40] There are no heart concerns for children with normal hearts.[41] And to be effective for patients with enuresis or sleep disorders, the TCAs must work on the same neurotransmitter systems said not to have yet developed in young patients with depressive illness. Also, in the old studies that concluded the TCAs do not work in young persons with depression, the investigators combined their patients as if all had the same illness. Looked at carefully, these studies suggest that the TCAs might work for young patients with the severe form of depression, i.e., melancholia.

The prescription of these agents can also be monitored by blood levels to maximize efficacy while minimizing side effects.

Melancholia can be clinically recognized in children and adolescents. Late evening serum measurements of the endogenous steroid cortisol can determine if, like adult patients with melancholia, young patients experiencing the syndrome are also in a limbic system storm and a heightened stress response state. The limbic system is a brain region that among several important functions generates emotions. It subserves the flight-or-fight mechanisms that can lead to panic or rage. Patients with melancholia often appear to be behaviorally and physiologically stuck in a fearful state. All-night sleep studies can reveal if the young patient, like others with melancholia, has the characteristic sleep disturbances associated with melancholia.[42] These assessments are rarely done.

Rejecting TCAs as a treatment option is particularly problematic in the treatment of children and adolescents with depression because of the concerns about an increased risk for suicide in this age group from exposure to selective serotonin reuptake inhibitors (SSRIs). There is also no randomized study in youngsters using the other class of antidepressants, monoamine oxidase inhibitors (MAOIs), even though this class of medications has been available since the 1950s. The only agents left are the serotonin and norepinephrine reuptake inhibitors (SNRIs), and if the patient does not quickly respond to these there are few other options. This is one reason why an increasing number of adolescents suffering from depressive illness are receiving ECT.[43]

Superficial Evaluations

I have the opportunity to see or hear about adolescents with psychiatric disorders. It is rare, however, that I learn about a child or teenager who previously was properly evaluated, diagnosed, and treated. Although the extensive psychological and psychoanalytic assessments of the past have been discarded, they have not been replaced by a neuroscience-based model or any other method to guide the clinician. The *DSM* is the only "game in town." The tertiary care center where I work attracts patients suffering from the most complex of situations. The complexities are too great a challenge for the average clinician. Perhaps out in the hinterlands unobserved child psychiatrists are practicing the best of care, not the worst, for the more typical patients. But even at centers where the knowledge and care should be outstanding, the practice of child psychiatry in my view falls short as often as it delivers.[44]

A frozen princess: A few years ago I was contacted by an academic child psychiatrist who was distraught. She had seen a young teenage girl who had seemed depressed and the child psychiatrist had prescribed an antipsychotic as a mood stabilizer. The girl was now in a neurology intensive care unit (ICU). We went to see the patient together as the child psychiatrist tearfully detailed the situation. She now knew that the prescription of the antipsychotic had been a mistake and was fearful that the girl might die. But she had no experience with malignant catatonia.

When we entered the patient's room, the fragile-looking girl was ensconced in a window seat. She was bent over, her face toward a pad of paper on her lap. In her raised right hand was a pen. She was frozen in place, and the nurse with her said that she had been in that posture for over a half hour. Saliva hung from the girl's lips. She was being fed by an intravenous (IV) tube in her left arm and a feeding tube from her nose into her stomach. She could speak only in a whisper and after a few words her speech fizzled into an indecipherable mumble followed by silence. I gave the girl some lorazepam in her IV. After a minute or two she slowly emerged from the posture. She raised her head, lowered her arm to the pad, and tried to finish the sentence she had started 30 minutes before. She weakly smiled at her nurse and at me.

The child psychiatrist was elated at the response and my telling her that the girl should fully recover if we prescribed large doses of the lorazepam, or even better if we gave her ECT. The ECT would work faster and would be definitive. The girl's father, however, would not consent to ECT because another child psychiatrist who had originally cared for the girl told him it would be dangerous because the girl had several cysts in her brain. This was another example of someone not knowing what they don't know. The cysts would have required us technically to do some things differently, but we and others have successfully and safely treated patients with depressive illness and incidental brain cysts with ECT. So, it was lorazepam or nothing. Fortunately, after several more weeks with increasing doses of lorazepam we were able to get the girl off all her tubes and back to her baseline. She walked out of the hospital and returned home and to school, but on large doses of lorazepam.[45] I don't know what the child psychiatrists back home did for her, but I do know that they never contacted us for guidance.

A boy possessed: Another patient outcome was not as good, but it again illustrates the lack of adequate evaluations done by many child psychiatrists. The patient was a young teenager with a diagnosis of "autistic spectrum disorder" who was hospitalized because of "increasing aggressive statements and a threatening attitude toward males." In the hospital he

"randomly jumped up and started yelling obscenities" at males. He needed
to be isolated from the males on the unit. Several antipsychotics were prescribed that were believed to modestly ameliorate his aggression, but he
developed a "dystonia." No details of these behaviors, including the dystonia (a prolonged muscle spasm), were provided. Lithium and lorazepam
(Atavan) were added to the mix of several antipsychotics, based on the
assumption that the boy might be manic. The antipsychotics were then
changed to aripiprazole.[46]

As the boy's behavior did not substantially change with any of his medication regimens, ECT was begun. The course of ECT provided no relief, and
so haloperidol (Haldol), an older antipsychotic, was restarted. This also had
a minimum effect. It was next opined that he might be using profanity
because of obsessive-compulsive disorder (OCD). Corprolalia, compulsive
cursing, can be a feature of OCD as well as Giles de la Tourette's syndrome,
a tic disorder that is comorbid with OCD.[47] A newer SSRI was therefore
added as this class of drugs can help patients with OCD.

The first SSRI marketed, clomipramine (Anafranil), was found to be
effective for OCD over 25 years ago.[48] It is no longer used with regularity,
although it still has the best efficacy among the medications prescribed
for patients with OCD. This is another example of promotion over evidence and the susceptibility of physicians to industry advertising and
drug rep activities. But, for this boy, as the first SSRI did not seem to
work, a second SSRI was added. The patient, however, developed tremors,
became restless, and was said to be "confused" from possible serotonin
toxicity. The combination of the two serotonin-enhancing antidepressants was thought to have dangerously increased his brain serotonin levels. The syndrome is similar to malignant catatonia and can be as deadly.[49]
The second SSRI dose was reduced, although all his medications should
have been stopped as he was now toxic. The bursts of profanity continued, however.

Chlorpromazine, the oldest antipsychotic, was added and a behavior
therapy plan was begun for his theorized OCD. After a brief amelioration
of his episodes of profanity, his symptoms all returned. This relapse was
interpreted as psychological "regression" and attributed to "fears of being
discharged." Sometimes Freud still influences twenty-first-century child
psychiatry.

So, after all the medication trials and ECT with the patient essentially
unchanged from his preadmission behavior, the onus was placed on him,
not his treaters or treatments, and he was given the psychological label of
"regression," i.e., returning to a more primitive Freudian psychosexual stage
of development to avoid some present conflict-evoking environmental

stress. He was sent to a long-term facility for the chronic mentally ill. I never heard what happened to him there.

Not systematically gathering the details of the patient's story, and the story of the patient's illness, haphazardly prescribing one medication or treatment after another, and irrationally piling drugs on top of one another are all standard practices among many twenty-first-century child psychiatrists. When thinking fails, medical practice is often reduced to prescribing anything and everything with the hope that something will work.[50] It rarely does in such circumstances.

But the real tragedy of the young boy was not that his treaters were practicing poorly. The real tragedy was that they were shown what his diagnosis was and were told what would be the better treatment for it. They also had laboratory evidence supporting the alternative diagnosis, but they paid no attention to that evidence.

As in most clinical circumstances, his treaters were shown the diagnosis by the patient. A careful history paints a picture of the illness. A thorough physical examination offers further details. The patient in front of a doctor who looks with educated eyes and asks the right questions is diagnostic gold. Here is what the patient showed his treaters.

The boy was an average-looking youngster of somewhat lower than normal intellect. In a casual conversation with him he was too literal in his understanding of what was being said. He occasionally inappropriately interrupted, and he rigidly focused on only a few topics. Without provocation, however, and in mid conversation, he would suddenly stand or if standing suddenly shift into a different pose. His face would flush. He then began loudly uttering a stream of profanity that clearly had a life of its own. It was as if he were possessed by some alien force. He looked directly at the person with whom he had been conversing. He looked enraged, clenching his fists and thrusting his torso and head forward. He minimally responded to interventions during these episodes, but he did turn his gaze to anyone else who spoke to him at that moment. The stream of profanity, however, never stopped. After a minute or so of uninterrupted loud cursing, he gradually quieted. He then sometimes lay down to sleep for a few minutes. Sometimes he removed his clothes before lying down.

In observing several of these episodes I told his treaters that the boy was suffering from a seizure disorder, and that anticonvulsants were the class of medications to be prescribed. A portable EEG showed abnormalities in both temporal lobes consistent with "focal neuronal dysfunction," but no long-term EEG assessments were accomplished and no other laboratory studies helpful in defining a seizure disorder were done. So rather than providing him with a twenty-first-century work-up and treatment, he received a mid-twentieth-century effort that did not work and was then sent to a public asylum, a nineteenth-century construct.

That child psychiatry has moved away from the psychoanalytic model is in my view progress. The problem, however, is that child and adolescent psychiatry hasn't replaced the Freudian perspective with another conceptual framework. It has devolved like general adult psychiatry into an atheoretical primary care effort. It has no method. The standards are the *DSM* and the simple algorithms similar to those that have been applied to adults with behavioral syndromes. This lack of method and reliance on the *DSM* need not be the case, however. Individual child and adolescent psychiatrists can make a difference. I've worked with several very good child and adolescent young physicians, but the critical mass is not yet there to change the field.

ANTIPSYCHIATRY GROUPS AND STATE LEGISLATURES

Great damage to U.S. psychiatry has resulted from the declining quality of care that relies on oversimplified diagnosis and cookbook treatment. Further erosion of the field results from the subversive relationship it has embraced with the pharmaceutical industry. Psychiatry in the United States is inundated with increasing numbers of weak-acting drugs haphazardly applied to diagnostic labels of dubious validity. These self-inflicted injuries, however, have been matched by the attacks on the field by antipsychiatry groups. No other branch of medicine has been ridiculed more or more legally restricted.

Past Abuses

Part of the motivation for the restrictions on psychiatric care in the United States derives from past abuses. The film *One Flew Over the Cuckoo's Nest* was filmed at Oregon State Hospital and portrayed some of the real dehumanizing effects of the large mental hospitals that dotted the United States at that time. Well-documented patient abuse, assaults by staff and other patients, and the lack of adequate hygiene at Oregon State led to an investigation that literally unearthed the remains of patients who even in death were abandoned by their families.[51] *Titicut Follies*, a 1967 American documentary film about the patient-inmates of Bridgewater State Hospital for the criminally insane, a Massachusetts Correctional Institution, outraged many by its portrayal of inmates holed up in unlit cells, only periodically washed as they were forced to strip naked publicly, being force fed, and being physically and verbally abused by the institution's staff. Private psychiatric hospitals also came under fire for unreasonable commitments and inadequate care.[52] The image of systematic political abuse under the guise of psychiatric treatment in the Soviet Union and in China (to this day) loomed over the American landscape galvanizing civil libertarians to action, encouraging the patient's right to refuse all psychiatric medications, and of course ECT.[53] Although many of the reforms were needed, legislating restrictions of present-day U.S. psychiatry and psychiatrists as if we care little for patient rights has done harm to the most severely ill patients the legislation is supposed to protect. If a patient is not a danger to himself or others, he has the legal right to refuse all treatment regardless of how psychotic he may be. There is little middle ground upon which psychiatrists can take a stand to treat the patient, even if their effort is likely to substantially benefit the patient.

The Attack on Psychiatry in General and ECT in Particular

Although civil libertarians have inserted themselves into the psychiatrist–patient relationship for good cause, other groups have not. The Scientologists lead these antipsychiatric efforts. The organization believes that humans are reincarnated alien souls ("thetans") that have lived on other planets before living on Earth. Scientologists consider psychiatry to be destructive and abusive and so it must be abolished. They consider that the psychiatric medications we prescribe are poisons to our alien souls. ECT is anathema to them and their various websites rail against it.[54] The Scientologists' anti-ECT propaganda is spearheaded by the public rants of celebrities such as Tom Cruise. These efforts have been combined with the Hollywood image of psychiatrists and of ECT that the public sees in movies and on TV to give a distorted image of the reality.

ECT is the battleground: The propaganda against ECT has been successful and despite the improvement in the ECT process and in ECT devices, the treatment method has been handicapped by the FDA, which caved under antipsychiatry pressures and required that ECT devices in the United States be limited in the energy that they can deliver. In the rest of the world, the same manufacturer can calibrate the devices to deliver twice the energy of that same device when it is used in the United States. What this means is that we often need to prescribe additional medications to ensure adequate treatments. For some patients, the treatment cannot be given effectively. Can you imagine the FDA mandating that defibrillators be reduced in their electrical charge because of false claims that the electricity damaged the heart?

Recently, the FDA caved again. This time it agreed to rule on whether ECT devices should remain classified in the highest risk category (class III) for medical equipment (e.g., defibrillators), although the devices work efficiently and no one gets electrocuted. When the ECT devices were originally classified they were also "grandfathered in" as not requiring supporting premarket approval data because ECT had and has such a long and safe track record. Reclassifying them in the less risky class II would be appropriate given their record. Leaving them in class III would also require substantial new testing that the two small U.S. manufacturers could not afford and that patients and their physicians could not tolerate, as during the testing period ECT would not be available for clinical use. Over 100,000 ECT treatments are given in the United States yearly.

Anti-ECT advocates successfully lobbied the FDA to reconsider the issue based on inaccurate claims that ECT permanently and adversely affects memory. The panel that addressed the concern ended up split. The psychiatrists and anesthesiologists on the panel were familiar with the literature and endorsed the devices being reclassified into class I or II (e.g., X-ray machines, wheelchairs). The neurologists, psychologists, and biostatisticians on the panel, none of whom was conversant with the ECT literature, wanted the devices left in class III, triggering the lethal premarketing testing. The data they cited were decades old. Although individual psychiatrists have protested the panel's action, no U.S. psychiatric group, and certainly not the American Psychiatric Association, has vigorously denounced the impending restrictions.[55]

Some State Legislatures Have Supported
the Antipsychiatry Movement

The antipsychiatry lobby has also influenced state legislatures. They have taken notice of the political and financial clout of antipsychiatry groups. Other than abortion, ECT is the only medical treatment specifically and directly limited by politicians. Here are some examples.

California: The California state legislature, well-known medical and fiscal experts, mandated that the state of California will require the agreement of at least three psychiatrists before proceeding with ECT. Two of the three must be independent of the psychiatric team wishing to treat the patient.

This requirement is designed to impede the process because it is not easy to find two psychiatrists not involved with the patient's care who are also experienced with the indications for ECT. Most U.S. psychiatry residency programs do not provide adequate ECT training. Some programs provide only an observational experience. In addition, because two of the three psychiatrists must be independent of the ECT team they must be recruited from separate facilities or practice groups. The delay in accomplishing the independent assessment is needlessly adverse.

The California code further restricts the use of ECT by requiring a consent process that includes overly detailed descriptions of side effects and a 24-hour waiting period after the side effects have been explained before the patient can sign consent. Only abortion has such restrictions. However, persons with severe depression are often so overwhelmed by their apprehension and uncertainties that by the next day many will need the consent process repeated, thus never reaching the 24-hour end point to legally permit treatment. The code goes on to stress that patients have the right to refuse treatment, which is a standard policy across the United States, but the code formulates this injunction as they *"have the right to refuse psychosurgery, electroconvulsive therapy, experimental and other hazardous procedures."* ECT is neither hazardous nor experimental. The restrictions are driven by an image of ECT as barbarous and of psychiatrists as unprincipled. Berkley, California passed a city ordinance that was subsequently overturned by the state Supreme Court that mandated that ECT could not be performed within the city's limits.[56]

Psychiatrists in California seemed cowed by the anti-ECT atmosphere. In 2011 two California psychiatrists came to our program for ECT training. One told me that at his *teaching* hospital their ECT device became inoperable in 2000 and the psychiatrists wanted to purchase a new one. The hospital's nonphysician head denied the purchase (about $15,000) until 2011. The psychiatrist was very upset by not having the ability to treat the most severely ill of his patients and felt that some had died because of the unavailability of the treatment. But there was no uproar. No hospital oversight entity got perturbed. No training accreditation agency cited the hospital for inadequate training. His colleague said that he had never administered ECT even though he graduated from a well thought of psychiatry residency program. If a residency doesn't offer intensive psychotherapy training, an intervention that most likely doesn't work and will certainly be used by only a small percentage of trainees after they graduate, the residency program will be placed on probation or disaccredited. On the other hand, if the program does not offer ECT, which does work and is often life-saving, the training program gets "a pass." This is one reason why less than 10% of U.S. psychiatrists know how to administer ECT. Most have never been trained to do it.[57]

Texas: In the state of Texas, it appears to be socially acceptable to execute teenagers for their transgressions. It is not acceptable according to that state's illustrious legislature to administer ECT to a teenager, even if the teen and the parents and their physicians think the procedure needs to be done.

A few years ago, we had a child and adolescent psychiatrist from Texas come to us for ECT retraining. She said she was disgusted with the limits the Texas legislature had put on ECT. She said a new department of psychiatry chair in Oklahoma wanted to establish an ECT program so that patients from Texas who needed the treatment could get it without having to travel across the country. After her retraining she was moving to Oklahoma to work in the new ECT program.

Also a few years ago, I had the opportunity to treat the youngest patient I have so far treated with ECT. The literature details safe and effective treatments for patients from the "tweens" to 100.[58] The young girl from Texas was 12 years old. I know the picture this last sentence evokes: a frail young girl, hovering psychiatrists, electrodes, and lightning bolts. The last is an image used by Scientologists in their anti-ECT campaigns. But visualize the same patient having her appendix removed, or undergoing cardiac surgery. Those endeavors also can be made to sound terrifying and ghoulish: a frail young girl, hovering surgeons in green masks, knives, and blood. But as I describe in Chapter 4, ECT is not as portrayed by Hollywood.

So, the girl from Texas had been suffering from manic-depressive illness since she was 8 years old and had been unable to attend school for over a year. Her treatments consisted of the new antipsychotics, her child psychiatrists accepting the pharmaceutical industry's promotion that these agents stabilize mood. They did not in her case. But what they did do was to give her a movement disorder, tardive dyskinesia (TD).

Some patients with TD also experience the cognitive difficulties associated with basal ganglia disease.[59] This young girl had a form of TD termed the Meige's syndrome. This is a combination of blepharospasm and oromandibular dystonia. Blepharospasm ranges from an increased rate of forceful blinking to uncontrollable squinting and the closing of the eyes particularly during speech (which she had). Eye damage can occur. The oromandibular symptoms range from difficulty opening the mouth (trismus), clenching or grinding of the teeth (bruxism), spasms of jaw opening, sideways deviation or protrusion of the jaw, lip tightening and pursing (the rabbit syndrome, which she had), drawing back (retraction) of the corners of the mouth, deviation or protrusion of the tongue, jaw pain, difficulties eating and drinking, and difficulties speaking (dysarthria). Her speaking difficulties were so severe that she sounded like a frog croaking and was difficult to understand.

Now imagine you are this girl. Your emotions seem to have a life of their own and you, like most sufferers of manic-depression, are mostly despondent and apprehensive. Despite being smart, you find the stresses of school tormenting. Then too boot, your doctors give you medication that makes it impossible for you to be with friends. You feel like a freak. Suicide suddenly becomes an option. Suicidal feelings are commonly not a desire to die as much as a desire to end the torment of the mood disorder as there seems no other way out. Imagine how the mother felt when she experienced her daughter's progression from bad to worse, went on line to learn that there were other medications better at mood stabilization, and that ECT was often more effective than the drugs. Put yourself in the mother's shoes when she was told her daughter could not even be considered for ECT in Texas for another 4 years.

Fortunately, among the committee members of child psychiatrists who formulated the guidelines for administering ECT to children and adolescents was one of my colleagues. The mother contacted her and then brought her daughter to our program for an evaluation. We agreed that the girl would benefit from ECT and she received 12 treatments. Her manic-depression remitted and we prescribed an accepted mood stabilizer for her. Most impressive was the effect of ECT on the girl's TD. She stopped squinting and shutting her eyes. She stopped pursing her lips and moving her jaw into odd angles. Her speech normalized fully. She left us, a fully normal, bright 12-year-old girl.

Michigan: Although California and Texas legislatures take the booby prizes, the Michigan legislature is not far behind in its restrictive mental health code. Without a guardian who has medical power-of-attorney and very specific advanced medical directives, if you live in Michigan and you have an incapacitating psychiatric disorder you are up the proverbial creek with no paddle. Your psychiatrists will be restricted in the treatments they can give you, unless you are in some life-threatening situation. Even then, the psychiatrist will have to be brave and put beneficence above all. Patients who are delusional and believe they are being poisoned or patients who are cognitively impaired are still expected to legally make decisions about their care. So, in the state of Michigan you may be delusional and believe that the garbage man is an extraterrestrial, but you are still expected to make decisions about the competence of your psychiatrist and the merits of the treatments he or she offers. The alternative is to have a judge guided by lawyers decide.

In Michigan, civil libertarians appear to have concluded that psychiatrists are members of the dark forces. It is as if the well-meaning advocates of the mentally ill are living in some unpleasant past or in a particularly odd neighborhood. They assume we will take advantage of our patients because our patients, defined as having a "mental illness," must by that definition have an altered capacity to understand and give informed consent to the treatments we offer. This is not just about ECT. The restrictions refer to *all* treatments offered by a psychiatrist.

First, it's unclear how different many psychiatric patients are from other patient groups in their ability to consent to treatment. To give informed consent the patient should have the *capacity to express a choice.* By this standard an unconscious patient or a patient in a catatonic state cannot give informed consent. These patients need a guardian or a court order for treatment unless they are in a life-threatening condition. In almost all cases, the only times such patients have been denied treatment has been when the patient is diagnosed with a psychiatric condition.

To give consent, the patient also needs to have the *capacity to understand* the treatment and its side effects. A patient with end-stage dementia, in a delirium, or who is substantially intellectually impaired cannot give informed consent. Most minors do not meet the standard. The patient needing *to appreciate the personal relevance* of the treatment is another consent requirement. So again, the above patients cannot provide informed consent. Finally, the patient must have *sufficient logical reasoning* to weigh the pros and cons of the treatment and be able to make a reasoned choice. The above patients fail this standard. The assumption is that until proven otherwise so do all psychiatric patients with psychosis, mania, and depression.[60]

In one representative study, however, patients with severe depressive illness met the standard if they were educated about the treatment.[61] Patients with depressive illness also met the standard to give informed consent when a support person (family member, other caregiver) was present.[62] Many patients with mania meet the standards, but not surprisingly some are more optimistic about the outcome than other patient groups.[63] Patients with psychosis may not meet the standards if their illness impairs their cognition. Hearing voices or being delusional (parts of the definition of psychosis) is not by themselves disqualifying.[64]

In an analysis of 99 studies, elderly, *nonpsychiatric* patients had diminished capacity in one or more of the four standards.[65] Older and non-college-educated patients scheduled for elective orthopedic surgery have difficulties understanding treatments and complications compared with younger well-educated patients.[66] Among another group of surgical patients, over 40% could not recall *any* potential complication described in the consent process.[67] Among almost 400 patients in the midst of an acute cardiac event, only 18% read the consent form and over half were assessed at below the standard to make a decision about their treatment.[68] The bottom line is that the data do not support the automatic singling out of psychiatric patients as being diminished in their capacity to provide informed consent. Yet the Michigan mental health code does exactly that.[69]

Michigan requires all treaters of any stripe to provide a written list of side effects and complications to the patient. If the treatment is "typically" used as a general medical intervention or is prescribed by a general medical physician or surgeon it comes under one code that does not require many hoops for treaters to jump through. If the intervention is typically used as a psychiatric treatment or is prescribed by a psychiatrist it comes under the mental health code, which applies additional restrictions, including the requirement of obtaining a court order if the patient balks at any intervention. In my experience this judicial process can take several weeks as the judges in Michigan don't seem to be in a rush.

A class of medications, beta-blockers, provides an example of the bias against psychiatry. Some of the better known beta-blockers are propranolol, metoprolol, atenolol, and labetalol. Beta-blockers have been around for decades. They reduce the effects of adrenalin and noradrenalin and are mostly prescribed in the treatment of patients with cardiac arrhythmias or hypertension. They also have some anticonvulsant properties and so are sometimes prescribed by neurologists as add-on medication for some patients with seizure disorder. Some physicians also prescribe these agents in high doses to modulate the irritability of patients who have suffered a traumatic brain injury. They can ameliorate some medication-induced tremors. They have been used to treat patients with anxiety, particularly public speaking phobia. If the doctor is not a psychiatrist these agents can be prescribed for any of these indications with little instruction and certainly no written list of side effects get provided. If a psychiatrist prescribes these same medications, in the same doses, for the same reasons, the intervention falls under the mental health code. If the psychiatrist does not fully adhere to the code he or she could theoretically be hit with a fine or jail time.

Because of the Michigan mental health code, I have seen psychiatrists shy away from treating patients who should have been vigorously treated and I have met patients whose treatments were delayed and their lives endangered because of the code. The best spin I can put on the efforts of civil libertarians to limit what U.S. psychiatrists are permitted to do is to evoke the aphorism, *"The road to hell is paved with good intentions."*

THE RAPACIOUS HEALTH INSURANCE INDUSTRY
AND THEIR MINIONS

Those Who Don't Care

Most everyone in the United States recognizes that the medical care system in the country if not broken, is bent. Those who don't care about this situation fall into several groups. The first group is libertarians who are often at or near the poverty line, who have no health insurance and don't want it because they can go to emergency rooms for assistance. By law they cannot be turned away. They think they are being independent and free of government, but the rest of society pays their bills through the U.S. treasury or with state funds. Such visits are many fold more expensive than is an office visit to a physician or clinic. Some inexpensive coverage and education about health care would save the country a bundle. As an example of the effect the libertarian position can have on health care, the republican-dominated Michigan legislature recently repealed the state's motorcycle helmet requirement as the mostly libertarian biker community considered it a government intrusion. Many states have repealed similar laws for similar reasons, despite the data that show that the helmets save lives and reduce catastrophic health care costs. The costs are mostly born by the rest of us. According to the Center for Disease Control, between 2008 and 2010 only 12% of the over 14,000 motorcycle-related deaths during that period were from the 20 states that had helmet laws, saving over 3 billion dollars in health care costs. In the health care world, libertarian notions cost a lot of money.

At the other end of the sociological spectrum of persons who care little about health insurance is the very rich who don't need health insurance as in a pinch they can always buy the hospital. A third group consists of ideological Darwinians like many in the U.S. congress who have gotten "their own" with a very good government-financed health insurance plan and so figure that those that do not have such a great plan brought the deficiency upon themselves and so don't deserve coverage.

Last, but certainly not least, is the health insurance industry and their supporters that know the industry is interested only in collecting the premiums while not delivering the benefits. An example of industry's attitude toward patient care occurred a few years ago when one of my responsibilities was evaluating patients who were said to have "treatment-resistant depression." The term implies that there was a lack of response despite two treatment trials of adequate length with different antidepressants in adequate doses. For the most part, however, these patients have treatment-deprived depression because they are almost never prescribed the older medications or ECT. Some patients I met had been so poorly evaluated that they weren't even suffering from depressive illness. Those that did have a depressive illness often had been ill for years, but had been inadequately treated.

The patient in this example was referred specifically to see if she was a candidate for ECT. I thought she would benefit from the treatment and sent my written recommendations back to the referring psychiatrist. A few weeks later I asked the ECT administrative assistant if the patient was going to start her course, but I was told that her insurance carrier had denied approval for the treatment. I said I would speak to the insurance doctor. His name was familiar. It turned out that he was the same psychiatrist who had referred the patient for the ECT evaluation. When I finally got him on the phone I asked about this obvious contradiction and he replied that as the insurance physician he was *"wearing a different hat."* I told him he was nuts. The patient finally received ECT and did well. But that psychiatrist's thinking was not unique to doctors who work for the insurance company. Knowing the situation and the need for treatment the psychiatrist in this story still denied coverage because that was "his job" as the insurance company physician. Benficence has little to do with the actions of health insurance providers.

Private insurance carriers practice bait and switch all the time. Up-front they are tough and limit coverage so that the number of hospital days, office visits, and procedures are restricted and co-pays exorbitant. Having to shell out 50% for a thousand dollar a day hospital room is not good coverage, even if they throw in meals and snacks. When the patient needs specific care, there can be further onerous requirements. I've seen debilitated older patients with severe depression denied hospital days seemingly offered in their coverage because *"those tests can be done while an outpatient."* Sure, the tests could be done at a clinic, but the patients were too ill and needed to be hospitalized. Some carriers will try to limit paying for ECT by restricting it to an inpatient procedure and then limiting hospital days. This maneuver prevents a full course of treatments or requires a schedule of treatments that is not best for the patient. If a patient is hospitalized because he tried to kill himself and we do a good job and he is no longer suicidal, some carriers will press for immediate discharge, regardless of the patient's other difficulties and the awareness that those next several weeks posthospitalization involve a period of high suicide risk. If the patient kills himself during those weeks the doctors or hospital might be sued, but the carrier will most likely not be targeted. I have colleagues who have told the carrier representative physician that should a patient commit suicide under such circumstances, they will encourage the family to sue the carrier and also the carrier's representative physician directly. The most reliable and reasonable insurance carrier we deal with is Medicare.[70]

The Bug-a-Boo of a Single-Party Payer

The recent political turmoil over health care has revealed the forces allied against adequate coverage such as Medicare. Those opposed to the Obama administration's health care plan have no other alternative other than more of the same. The folks yelling at meetings or ranting about socialized medicine are just the pawns of the powerbrokers who do not want to give up their insurance cash cow. Other than congress and nonmilitary federal employees who have their own plans, if you poll persons who have health care insurance coverage, the most satisfied will be those on Medicare. Besides being the most flexible and broad in choice it is also the most efficient health care coverage on the planet. Wheres 25% or so of the premiums of private carriers go to "overhead," only about 3% of Medicare premiums do. Medicare also has the best cost containment record in the U.S. health care market.[71] If the young as well as those over age 65 were eligible for Medicare, the system would be solvent for decades because those under 65 use the health care system much less than do older subscribers. Their premiums combined with less use would keep the system in the black. Some form of "Medicare for all" would be a good start at fixing the rocketing costs of providing health care in the United States. This approach is not "socialized medicine" as claimed by the insurance industry and its supporters. Socialized medicine means government agencies own the facilities and employ the staff. The VA hospital system is an example of socialized medicine. If you ever hear a conservative rail against the VA version of socialized medicine, you know they are wearing overcoats in hell.

Another argument against fixing the U.S. health care system is that it is the "best in the world" so don't alter it. But it is not the best in the industrialized world if you measure best by outcomes and cost. We may be fancier and more high tech, but here are some figures. According to the Washington Post blog (Ezra Klein Wonkblog March 4, 2012) costs for medications and procedures in the United States are higher in 22 of 23 major categories than costs in all the European countries. Among 191 countries studied in another survey,[72] the United States ranked 37th in the quality of care. Canada and its mostly publically funded system ranked 30th. Most of Western Europe is ahead of us on all outcome measures. Focusing on North America, the United States spends almost twice as much per capita on health care as does Canada ($7960 versus $4808) and 15% of its gross domestic product (GDP) to Canada's 10% of GDP on health care. In the Canadian government's commitment to universal health care it supports 70% of the costs with private insurers footing the bill for the remaining 30%. The U.S. government, however, finances 46% of health care. So when some idiot yells, *"Get government out of health care,"* that means getting rid of Medicare, Medicaid, the VA and active duty health care systems, and government employee health care (federal, state, and local). The government support, by the way, includes some of the folks in congress who rail against government involvement in health care. When those congressmen bellow to get rid of government involvement in heath care, they mean yours and mine, not theirs. On the other hand, despite paying less, Canadians experience lower infant mortality and longer life expectancy than persons in the United States. They have fewer new cancer cases and about the same survival rates as in the United States. There is almost no measure in which they don't do better, including patient satisfaction. The "long waits" myth is just that. I've had to wait weeks and months to get appointments in the United States. If you want an outpatient magnetic resonance imaging (MRI) in my town you'll likely get an appointment several weeks down the road and for one o'clock in the morning.

So, if our health care costs us more, and we are getting less bang for our bucks, why have we as a nation been unable to come up with a system that works and that applies to all of us? Unlike Europe and Canada, which essentially offer universal health care to their populations, the political and social systems in the United States have never been unified. We are a patchwork of many different constituencies, making a consistent and widely endorsed approach difficult. Powerful political and business forces take advantage of the diverse U.S. social landscape and advertise against a unified system regardless of its merits. Here's an example.

When the Clintons' were trying to fix the health care system in Mr. Clinton's first term, I was a department chairman and a member of our school's faculty executive committee. As the Clintons were proceeding, we and *all* the medical schools in the United States received a call from representatives of the American Medical Association (AMA). The AMA physicians said that they would like to meet with our senior faculty and deans to get "our views" on the Clinton plan. The AMA physicians also said that the meeting was "voluntary."

Now there are times when deans and senior faculty of universities act as if they are not the sharpest knives in the drawer, but my dean understood that when the AMA asked for a "voluntary" meeting what they meant was "do it or else." What the dean and all of us understood was that the AMA is part of what is referred to as The Liaison Committee on Medical Education

(LCME). The LCME is the nationally recognized accrediting authority for medical education programs leading to the MD degree conferred by all U.S. medical schools. The LCME is sponsored by the Association of American Medical Colleges and the American Medical Association. If the LCME doesn't like what your school is doing or not doing, it can shut you down. So, we had the "voluntary" meeting. We were told that most schools in the United States had a similar voluntary meeting.

In their request to come and visit, the AMA representatives stated that they wanted to get our opinions and those of other schools about the Clinton proposals so that the organization could formulate its view of the plan. We met in a large conference room. There were three of them and 20 or so of us. The meeting lasted about 2 hours. Other than the introductions and farewells, I don't recall any dean, chairman, or other senior faculty member having an opportunity to discuss the situation. The AMA representatives spent the bulk of the meeting telling us why the Clinton plan was flawed and why we should oppose it. They raised the health care system in Canada as a socialist monster at our border even though no serious proposal for the United States calls for government ownership of hospitals and clinics and providers becoming government employees. The goal in the United States has been universal coverage and for many, me included, a single party payer like Medicare fits the need best. The AMA representatives, however, had no interest in our views. The goal of their visit was to tell us what our views should be. The threat of an LCME unpleasant accreditation visit was implicit. Whatever our opinions, we should keep them to ourselves and let the adults take care of the Clintons. They did. The Clintons made it easy for them, but we saw no health care reform then and the effort for reform now is under siege.

The worst of health care coverage is for mental health. Despite congress passing the Mental Health Parity Act in 1996, which mandated that health insurance plans could not make annual or lifetime dollar coverage benefits for mental health any lower or more restrictive than such limits on other medical or surgical benefits, parity is worse today than before the bill passed. This is in part due to the insurance industry putting caps on days allowed in the hospital. Only about 10% of plans in the United States are reported to offer reasonable mental health parity. A recent report from a large community mental health system followed over 400 patients with "serious mental illnesses" for 2 years. Outcome measures were good, but the program had to be suspended because about 60% of the patients had no mental health insurance, not even Medicaid.[73]

The health insurance controversy is all about money. Patients are collateral damage. That authoritative forces in U.S. medicine, such as the AMA, have fought against adequate universal health care belies the notion that their officers took seriously any version of the Hippocratic Oath. The idea that they are fighting for practitioners is blatantly false. Health care providers in Canada are financially doing okay under a mostly federally funded health care system. Physicians there as in the United States mostly drive upscale vehicles and live better than most of their patients. The clinicians caring for patients are not the problem. Lawyers are also not the problem, although I do tell residents and medical students that under every patient's bed there lurks a personal injury lawyer. Legal costs account for about two cents of every health care dollar spent in the United States. Instead, the enormous cost of U.S. health care is the result of needless tests, the endless purchase of high-tech equipment, the overuse of high-priced pharmaceuticals, the ever more complex high-cost surgical procedures attempting to fix or replace every problematic body structure or organ, the desire to keep some people on full life support alive despite no chance of recovery, and the need to dispose of pieces of equipment that come into contact with the patient. Progress also carries a big price tag. I was told that the cost of going from a clearly inadequate and inefficient paper patient record system to mostly electronic records for our facility's health care system was over 60 million dollars. Six years later we are introducing a revised electronic system that many clinicians don't like for the tune of over 100 million dollars.

ACADEMIC PSYCHIATRISTS

Despite its destructive influence, the most profound problem with U.S. psychiatry is not the health insurance industry. It is also not the pharmaceutical industry. Both subvert patient care, but they are abetted by the field itself. The most profound problem with U.S. psychiatry remains U.S. psychiatrists. Those responsible for the training of medical students and residents are the most culpable. Among the many chairmen of psychiatry and the directors of their medical student and residency training programs that I have worked for and met over the past half century, many were the wrong persons for the job of training the next generation of psychiatrists. Some chairmen knew little about clinical psychiatry or had no passion for any perspective in our field. Some were more interested in building monuments to themselves in mortar and steel than in developing sound psychiatric physicians and so the graduates from their residency programs were mostly indistinguishable from the general practitioner in diagnosing psychiatric disorders and in prescribing treatments for psychiatric patients. The buildings, however, were nice.

Some chairmen were skilled laboratory scientists who paid scant attention to their department's training programs, leaving these efforts to others, often persons of different theoretical persuasions. It is still common for a chairman known for his expertise in genetics or neuropharmacology to have a training program known for its psychotherapy bent. For example, among the six medical schools in the Chicago area in the mid 1970s, other than me, the other psychiatry chairmen were skilled politicians and experienced administrators. They, however, knew little about biological psychiatry and psychopathology, and had only passive interests in the content of their department's training programs. They were satisfied as long as their departments made money from clinical billing or from grants, their medical students and residents passed their standardized national examinations, their residents became board certified, and the trainees at each level gave the department a good evaluation. The examination questions, by the way, are crafted by persons these chairmen recommend, so as long as they teach to the examinations all will be well. When that old guard in Chicago changed and several experienced researchers were appointed chairmen, the training programs hardly altered. The priorities of chairmen of psychiatry in the United States today are the same. Stanley Yolles' vision of American psychiatry providing extensive delivery systems is the model academic departments follow today in their training programs. The content of the program is of less importance and the educators remain committed to past paradigms.

If there were any doubts of what are the important concerns of psychiatric educators, a survey I did of published articles about psychiatric residency training should resolve them. A "psychiatry residency training" prompt of the U.S. National Library of Medicine's PubMed website generated 464 articles that began in 1950 with the bulk published since 1990. Fifty articles had titles that directly focused on psychotherapy teaching. Many others focused on the teaching of cultural, ethnic, and gender issues. Others were concerned with the mental health of psychiatric residents and suggested that the educators were worried about the emotional toll a psychiatry residency takes upon its trainees.

Ten articles in the survey addressed the decline in numbers of psychiatric resident graduates who become researchers. This decline will continue as long as departments maintain the separation of their high-tech NIMH-funded research from clinical research that needs to take place in the hospital services and clinics where residents spend most of their time. Residents will model themselves after the people who spend the most productive time with them. If these clinical faculty supervisors are not also engaged in research and can't encourage residents to join their efforts, most residents will think of research as a far removed esoteric endeavor in a laboratory only tenuously connected to the care of their patients. They will likely not incorporate the critical thinking needed for good research into their clinical thinking. They will continue to practice by trial and error and not by reasoned data-based decision making.

In the era of psychopharmacology and neuroscience, only seven articles in the survey were devoted to psychopharmacology training of psychiatry residents. One article title mentioned ECT. No article mentioned neuropsychiatry or neurology before 1995. After that, three did.

The dominance of articles about psychotherapy training may seem surprising until it is placed in the context of the mandate in 2001 from the accrediting body for U.S. residency training programs, the Residency Review Committee (RRC), that psychiatry residency training programs must demonstrate that their residents, also by demonstration, have competency in doing psychotherapy, psychodynamic therapy, as well as cognitive-behavior therapy. However, the amount of classroom, patient care, and supervision time required to meet this mandate is disproportionate to the efficacy of the required psychotherapies and the greater need to learn skills that should be unique to psychiatry. Psychologists, psychiatric social workers, and other nonphysician care givers can do psychotherapy and they receive extensive training in providing it, but psychiatrists must diagnose their patient's syndromes and then provide medical as well as pharmacotherapy care. Some will gain competency in administering ECT. There is not enough time in a residency to do it all. Often the graduate ends up master of nothing. Surveys of graduates indicate that their most common practice activity relates to psychopharmacology. Some do psychodynamic therapy and supportive therapy. Few do psychoanalysis. Almost none are neuropsychiatrists.[74] For much of academic psychiatry, it is as if time stopped 20 years ago.

MYTHS

Besides the epic legendary characters of many cultures and their sagas, the secondary definitions of myth are *"a popular belief or story that has been associated with a person, institution, or occurrence"* and *"a fiction or half-truth especially one that forms part of an ideology."*[75] By these definitions there are several myths surrounding psychiatry that shape the public's understanding of the field and the training of psychiatric practitioners.

Most Psychiatrists Are Psychoanalysts and Psychotherapists

Some of the myths I have already detailed. Most clinical psychiatrists are not psychoanalysts and most do not do much psychotherapy. Most psychotherapists in the United States are not physicians. Most brands of psychotherapy, particularly psychodynamic psychotherapy, don't work, particularly for melancholia, manic-depression, psychotic disorders, and severe anxiety disorders. The images of psychiatrists as psychoanalysts and therapists in the media are fictions and half-truths. If you were to shadow most private practice psychiatrists for a week, you'd see a physician doing what most office-based physicians do but without all the surrounding medical equipment and white coat. If you shadowed a psychiatric hospitalist for a week, you'd get the white coat. The consultation psychiatrists would be in and out of ICUs and patients' hospital rooms for much of each day. They would be interacting with other physicians and nurses, checking laboratory results, monitoring medications, and making recommendations for care. The psychiatrists caring for psychiatric inpatients would be making rounds, examining patients, ordering and checking laboratory results, and prescribing treatments. The unit would look like a medical unit without the fancy equipment. There would be spaces for patients to engage in activities, as most would be able to walk about. The unit would be better lit and cleaner than any of the other hospital spaces other than the ORs. Whether patients self-refer or are referred by a health care provider, patients should not expect what they have seen on screens large and small. As I discuss in the next chapter, what they will find is a physician who is very much in the mold of a primary care provider but with a limited repertoire that hopefully is backed up by the knowledge and skills needed to fix what ails the patient.

To increase the present poor odds of being cared for by a competent psychiatrist, my solution, detailed in the last chapter, is for psychiatry to become a neuropsychiatric specialty one practitioner at a time. Being a neuropsychiatrist, however, does not mean that the practitioner should not also be skilled in putting patients and their families at ease. A good physician needs to be able to "doctor" as well as diagnose and prescribe. It does mean, however, that we will better define the patient we can help. Most persons suffering from interpersonal, social, and employment difficulties will not benefit from neuropsychiatric intervention. We need to promise more, but to fewer people.

To accomplish the change, however, the substantial influence of psychodynamic psychiatry on training programs must be recognized and ended. Some think the influence no longer exists. They are wrong. The RRC mandates of competency in psychodynamic therapy, the attitudes of residents that psychodynamic theory and treatments are core aspects of present day psychiatry, and the focus of the psychiatry training literature attest to the continuing influence. Psychiatry's involvement with the psyche needs to end. Because of the effects of environmental impacts on the brain and behavior, psychiatrists need to be able to assess these impacts and recruit colleagues who are skilled in counseling and in providing social services and rehabilitation, but our training programs should not be required to produce general psychiatrists who are highly skilled in these interventions. Other providers are better trained to do this.

Psychiatric Diagnosis Today Is Better Than It Was before *DSM-III*

It is also a fiction that medical psychiatric diagnosis today is better than it was 40 years ago. The recent versions of the *DSM* may be more reliable than the earliest editions but they have no better and in many ways have worse validity. The problems with the *DSM* are detailed in several previous chapters as are the high diagnostic error rates of psychiatrists. This sad situation is further discussed in the next chapter. If the field can reinvent itself as neuropsychiatry with its more refined and valid diagnostic approach, the *DSM* will eventually catch up, although it will take several generations of new psychiatrists to accomplish the metamorphosis.

Psychiatric Treatments Today Are Better Than They Were before Prozac

Another fiction is that medical psychiatric treatments are better today than they were 40 years ago. The efficacy of ECT hasn't changed since its earliest years, although the procedure is much more benign and safe and the patients are kept more comfortable than 50 years ago. The newer antidepressant medications, mood stabilizers, and antipsychotic agents have no greater efficacy than the older agents. The second-generation TCAs and lithium still have the best efficacy data and side effect profile. Chapters 2 and 3 detail the data for this assertion and the malignant influence of the pharmaceutical industry on the prescribing of psychotropic agents. Psychiatrists accept the promotional fictions of industry and insist that unlike the rest of human kind we are not influenced by advertising. We are. The only solution in my view is to sever all direct connections between the industry and individual academics and practitioners. Then the myth that psychiatric practice is evidence-based could become a reality.

CHAPTER 6

✧

Extinction of U.S. Psychiatry
as We Know It

Survival of the Fit

"It may metaphorically be said that natural selection is daily and hourly scrutinizing, throughout the world, the slightest variations; rejecting those that are bad, preserving and adding up all that are good; silently and insensibly working, whenever and wherever opportunity offers, at the improvement of each organic being in relation to its organic and inorganic conditions of life. We see nothing of these slow changes in progress, until the hand of time has marked the lapse of ages..."

Charles Darwin, *Origin of Species*

Healing is a matter of time, but it is sometimes also a matter of opportunity.

Hippocrates

If clinical general psychiatry were a species, a good bet would be its extinction by 2100. Species occupy environmental niches. A species captures its ecological neighborhood because the individual members of that species have some advantage in that environment over individuals of other species. If the niche changes or another species evolves a better advantage, the original niche occupiers will be supplanted. If there are no other environmental spaces for the supplanted species, it will become extinct. That's the present situation for U.S. clinical psychiatry. Clinical psychiatry's niche is changing. Other care givers have evolved advantages to the present health care environment that psychiatrists do not have. And there is no other space for psychiatry to go. Consider history and the facts.

A RUDDERLESS SHIP

Present day U.S. psychiatry muddles along without a guiding principle. In contrast, as examples of the rest of medicine, infectious disease experts work within the framework that various organisms invade the human body and do harm. Oncologists diagnose and treat patients with the understanding that some cells in the body for a variety of reasons alter their genetic programming and inappropriately proliferate. U.S. psychiatry is no longer directed by any analogous model.

U.S. Psychiatry Has No Core Values

The brain gets only lip-service: In 1974 E. Fuller-Torry predicted *"The Death of Psychiatry."*[1] In his book he bemoaned psychiatry's history of rejecting the responsibility for caring for patients that had previously been the traditional responsibility of psychiatrists. Once the pathophysiology or etiology of a "psychiatric illness" was established, psychiatry abandoned patients suffering from that illness to others. Patients with general paresis of the insane (central nervous system syphilis), epilepsy, and dementia filled mental asylums in the nineteenth and first half of the twentieth century. Most such sufferers are now the primary responsibility of neurologists. It was a psychiatrist, however, who invented the electroencephalogram (EEG), now the iconic tool of the neurologist. Today, however, only a handful of psychiatrists in the country can make any sense of a patient's EEG. Most do not know when to order an evaluation and what pertinent clinical facts need to be conveyed to the EEG laboratory so that the proper assessments can be done. Different patterns of relationships among the standard scalp electrodes are sensitive to different brain regions and conditions. Correctly choosing which of these "montages" to use can make the difference between detecting an area of pathology or not. Most U.S. psychiatrists have no idea what an EEG montage is. EEG is utilized clinically by psychiatrists in about 10% of their patients, although studies also show that the procedure warrants more frequent use.[2]

Few psychiatrists can adequately evaluate the brain imaging studies of their patients and most never consider the need to obtain a computed tomography (CT) scan or a magnetic resonance imaging (MRI). Few even know when to order such laboratory assessments, what is the relevant clinical information that would be most helpful to the imaging technicians, and what to do with the information gathered from the studies.[3] I often run across a patient who needs brain imaging but has not been assessed with that technology. When imaging is obtained by a psychiatrist, there is rarely any consideration given to the purpose of the assessment (this information can alert the neuroradiologist) or whether to ask for a CT scan, better at detecting bone pathology and blood, or an MRI, five times as sensitive as a CT scan in detecting small but clinically significant lesions and brain white matter disease.[4]

Functional brain imaging that provides a metabolic picture of the brain processing information is an important tool in detecting the beginnings of a dementing process. Patients with Alzheimer's disease will typically show reduced metabolism bilaterally in the parietal and temporal lobes.[5] Persons with a frontal lobe dementing process will show frontal hypometabolism.[6] Persons who have experienced substantial weight loss (>25% of body weight) as seen in anorexia nervosa, starvation, and gastric restriction surgeries may have a metabolic pattern similar to that seen in patients with Alzheimer's disease.[7] Psychiatrists rarely order these assessments, although we regularly see patients who might benefit from functional imaging. The assessment helps in establishing a prognosis (more treatment resistant with the Alzheimer pattern), choice of treatment (patients with depression syndromes but different metabolic patterns respond to different interventions), and etiology (the identification of cause leading to more specific interventions and prevention).

Most psychiatrists know enough about epilepsy and dementia to pass their specialty certification examinations but not enough to care for patients suffering from these conditions. If you ask a psychiatrist to assess a patient's cognitive functioning to determine if the patient is becoming demented and if the dementia is Alzheimer's disease or frontal-temporal dementia, most will be at a loss. Most U.S. medical students are taught to administer a paper and pencil cognitive test and they know what a poor score is, but few can tell you what cognitive function each item of the test is assessing and which brain regions might be involved. Few medical students, residents, and their faculty supervisors can perform a bedside cognitive assessment other than the brief paper and pencil test. To illustrate how far we've fallen, Alzheimer, one of the most famous neuropathologists in history, accomplished his work while on the staffs of psychiatric clinics. His most important position was working in the Munich clinic directed by Emil Kraepelin, the most famous psychiatrist of his era. Kraepelin's construction of the notion of dementia praecox, later to be renamed schizophrenia, was based, in part, on Alzheimer's autopsies of the brains of Kraepelin's patients. Freud was initially trained as a neuropathologist.[8]

Ironically, given Freud's training, psychiatry's rejection of its neuropsychiatric past was largely influenced by the Freudian movement. Freud refocused psychiatric attention on the neuroses and the "worried well," relegating the responsibility for the care of the most severely dysfunctional patients to state mental hospitals. Medical schools followed this trend and lost interest in these public institutions and the most severely and chronically mentally afflicted. Although some state mental hospitals still exist, they are typically underfunded and understaffed, and the quality of the care that they provide is marginal.[9] As a resident, I was required to spend time at a state mental hospital. The experience was invaluable. Residents today have no such training obligation. Most have only a vague idea what persons with chronic mental illness look and act like.

Psychodynamic psychiatry is taught but rarely practiced: Since the 1980s, however, psychoanalytic psychiatry, like neuropsychiatry before it, also became marginalized in practice. Less than 5% of graduates from U.S. psychiatry residency programs develop a psychoanalytic practice. In a generation psychoanalysis has declined from the essence of psychiatric thinking and practice to a mostly classroom and residency training exercise. Psychoanalysis is time consuming. Health insurance carriers will not cover it other than as an office visit and will not pay for more than a dozen or so office visits per year. Psychoanalysis, often requiring several sessions weekly, rapidly uses up any insurance coverage.[10] It is affordable only to the financially well-off. As the evidence amassed that persons with the traditional "neuroses" [e.g., obsessive-compulsive disorder (OCD), panic disorder, and agoraphobia] had brain disorders, psychoanalysis, other than in Hollywood, was deemed not central to the understanding and treatment of such patients. The HBO Mafia don, Tony Soprano, spent years on inadequate doses of Prozac and in the analyst's office receiving substandard care during which his panic disorder was opined to result from his unresolved Oedipal conflicts. He should have put a contract out on the script writer for malpractice. Psychoanalytic influence remains, however, among an old guard that retains substantial control over residency training accreditation and specialization national tests.

The community psychiatry movement has been marginalized: The community psychiatry movement, once a drawing card for the recruitment of one out of ten U.S. medical school graduates into psychiatry, has stalled. Its hubris at promising to shape a better, mentally healthier society was eventually recognized for its overreach. Sounding better and more humane, community mental health systems, nevertheless, provided about the same mediocre care as delivered by the large state hospitals. Medical schools also distanced themselves from the community systems as they did from the state mental hospitals. The community systems are no longer abundantly funded by government at any level. Community psychiatry has become county-based, and community mental health systems now offer minimal care for the poor. Without mental health insurance parity and with Medicaid funding being further cut, county-wide community mental health systems will continue to devolve to below adequacy of care.

Thus, the three conceptual frameworks that dominated U.S. psychiatry since the latter part of the nineteenth century, neuropsychiatry, psychoanalysis, and the community psychiatry movement, are now marginalized. What has emerged to take their place is a primary care model of practice.

A SPECIALTY OFFERING NOTHING SPECIAL

The Primary Care Model

The primary care medical model was crafted to deliver modest, less expensive care to the largest number of patients. A primary care physician is usually the first medical practitioner contacted by a patient. The primary care physician commonly serves as the entry point for substantially all of the patient's medical and health care needs, and is not limited by problem origin, organ system, or diagnosis. Ideally, primary care physicians are also advocates for the patient in coordinating the use of the entire health care system to benefit the patient. These physicians need to be "jacks of all trades" so that they can diagnosis and treat common, uncomplicated medical conditions. If the situation is complex or treatments falter, the primary care physician is asked to refer the patient to the appropriate specialist. The specialist is expected to have more focused experience, greater knowledge, and better skills in the specialty area than the primary care physician. The fees for primary care are also less than those of specialists and so as most patients with common, uncomplicated conditions will recover without having to be referred to a specialist, the costs to society will be substantially less than if patients had *carte blanche* to go to any specialist they wished. *"Why pay more for the same results?"* is the economic philosophy behind favoring primary care.[11]

There is, however, another understanding of primary care that does not require the primary care physician to be the first contact. From this perspective, physicians who are not trained in the primary care specialties of family medicine, general internal medicine, or general pediatrics can provide patient care services that are usually delivered by primary care physicians. *"These physicians may focus on specific patient care needs related to prevention, health maintenance, acute care, chronic care or rehabilitation. These physicians, however, do not offer these services within the context of comprehensive, first contact and continuing care."*[12] Such a physician must be specifically trained to provide this service, and devotes the majority of practice to providing services to a defined population of patients. This type of practice is what most U.S. psychiatrists now provide.

The Primary Care Psychiatrist

Most often the generalist or primary care psychiatrist sees patients by referral, but this is a relationship determined by access. Primary care physicians offer easier access as do emergency rooms (ERs). Health insurance plans often require a patient to see the primary care physician first before any referral to a specialist will be approved for coverage. A rich person, of course, could without penalty self-refer to a psychiatrist.

The generalist psychiatrist sees adults of either gender. Persons below age 18 are typically seen by child and adolescent psychiatrists who have completed a 2-year fellowship after 3 years of general residency training. Child and adolescent fellowship graduates strive for nationally recognized certification in child and adolescent psychiatry.

Although the generalist psychiatrist will have patients over age 65, geriatric psychiatrists focus their attention on such patients, particularly those with complex clinical problems. Geriatric psychiatrists also obtain a 1-year or 2-year fellowship and certification in geriatric psychiatry. There are also certification specializations in substance abuse (alcohol and illicit drug use), forensic psychiatry (capacity, competency, and criminality), and psychosomatic medicine (consultation to general medical, surgical, and neurological colleagues). The term psychosomatic is a leftover from the Freudian heyday. There are also a few fellowships in neuropsychiatry and a national written examination toward subspecialty certification in neuropsychiatry. The test, however, is sponsored by the American Neuropsychiatric Association and not by the more established American Board of Psychiatry and Neurology, which provides certification for all general psychiatrists and neurologists and the other fellowships. Neuropsychiatry fellowships need the imprimatur of the American board to achieve reputational parity and a fair chance to compete with other fellowships for graduate trainees.

The distinctions of the fellowships are somewhat misleading. Patients rarely fall into neat categories. A person with manic-depression might very well abuse alcohol and use street drugs. During the height of a mania or intoxication such a person might run afoul of the law. A general adult psychiatrist, a psychiatrist specializing in the treatment of patients with mood disorder, and specialists in substance abuse and forensic psychiatry might all have something to contribute to such a patient's care. If in the heat of the moment the patient injured himself and needed surgery or suffered a heart attack, the psychosomatic psychiatrist as the psychiatric hospital consultant to other services would be called in. Most psychiatric hospitalists commonly treat patients with such complex difficulties.

For the most part, severely ill psychiatric patients of all stripes go to ERs for acute care and are hospitalized when needed. When in the psychiatric inpatient unit they often receive their care from a psychiatric hospitalist. Hospitalists in all specialties spend most, sometimes all of their clinical time working in a hospital setting. In contrast, most generalist psychiatrists confine their clinical efforts to outpatient clinics or to private office settings. They rarely work extensively in psychiatric ERs and have limited experience treating hospitalized patients. Of course the different clinical divisions fragment care, but in large medical centers that serve the most severely ill, knowledge, skills, and experience trump continuity. You don't want an operation from a surgeon who does the procedure only occasionally. You want the guy who regularly does many. The same is true for psychiatrists and the different treatments they provide. Sometimes, however, the boundaries are blurred in a group psychiatric practice where the functions of the outpatient, inpatient, consultant, and ER psychiatrist are shared. The quality of care, however, is almost always spotty in these group practices. No one is an expert in every aspect of care.

What the general adult and child psychiatrist does today, however, remains primarily an office practice, caring for a variety of modestly ill patients who see other psychiatrists when they become more severely ill or have complicating factors (e.g., alcohol or substance abuse). The typical adult general psychiatrist in fact takes care of the same psychiatric patients and uses the same treatments as does the nonpsychiatrist primary care physician.[13]

The similarity of present day psychiatric care in the United States to general medical primary care is also seen in the practice patterns of the two officially distinct medical domains.[14] Office visits are short, diagnosis is accomplished as quickly and with the least amount of information as possible, laboratory testing is minimal, ancillary staff do much of the time-consuming interventions, and follow-ups are far apart. When counseling or some form of psychotherapy is deemed needed, both the primary care physician and general adult psychiatrist usually refer to a nonphysician therapist. The big difference between the two types of physicians is that the primary care physician can and does treat many patients with general medical disorders, and the fees charged by the general medical primary care physician are less than those asked for by the general adult psychiatrist. One-stop "shopping" is a hallmark of primary care, and the costs are less. According to a 2011 survey of over 15,000 U.S. physicians spanning 22 specializations, psychiatrists on average earn between \$25,000 and \$50,000 more annually but see substantially fewer patients weekly than do primary care physicians. The primary care physician spends about 15 minutes per patient compared to 25 minutes per psychiatric visit.[15] The traditional psychoanalytic session lasted 50 minutes ("the 50-minute hour") and occurred three or five times weekly.

REDUCED HABITAT

Contrary to the statement at the beginning of this chapter that present-day clinical psychiatry is on its way to extinction are surveys that show that in the past several decades until recently the number of psychiatrists in the United States increased.[16] There are about 45,000 psychiatrists throughout the United States making it the fourth largest U.S. medical specialty. The increase in psychiatrists is particularly noticeable for child psychiatrists, who have experienced an almost 200% increase in numbers. This does not seem like extinction.

Most U.S. Psychiatrists Are Located in or Near Urban Centers

The distribution of psychiatrists reveals that the psychiatric habitat is not uniform. The largest numbers of psychiatrists are crowded into just a few states. New York, California, Massachusetts, Pennsylvania, and Texas account for 36% of U.S. psychiatrists. Many states seem to be woefully underserved. At last count, Wyoming and Idaho had only four child psychiatrists each. One of them gets hit by a buffalo, and then what do kids out there do?

The uneven distribution of psychiatrists results in uneven access. Because most health insurance plans require patients to first see a primary care physician before being referred to a specialist, patients in rural and low population areas not only first see a primary care physician for their initial psychiatric care, they are likely to continue to receive that care from the same physician rather than being referred to a psychiatrist who may be hundreds of miles away. To make the trip worthwhile, the psychiatrist will have to offer some skill and knowledge not common among primary care physicians. Most psychiatrists do not have such advantageous attributes.[17]

Urban areas in the Northeast, Mid-Atlantic States, and Texas, overpopulated with psychiatrists, are under the same health insurance requirements as are the regions that are psychiatrically underpopulated. Patients living in cities need to see a primary care physician first unless they pay out of pocket or go to a public hospital emergency room. Referral, of course, will be easy as in some metropolitan areas psychiatrists are more numerous than working public pay phones and taxis on a rainy evening. But if the patient seems to be "getting by," referral will not be forthcoming. How will all those urban psychiatrists survive?

Urban-Centered U.S. Psychiatrists Avoid the Poor

To survive, the overpopulation of urban psychiatrists might consider providing services in their city's poor neighborhoods. Inner city urban areas are psychiatrically underserved. But many citizens of the inner city are without insurance or receive Medicaid, and specialists have traditionally shied away from such patients. In the 1960s and 1970s, New York City supported 19 municipal hospitals. There are now 11 New York City hospitals. However, these institutions 40-plus years ago and for the most part now were staffed by trainees and their supervisors. The only private practice psychiatrists I ever saw while in training were the psychoanalysts who came by to supervise us in our intensive psychotherapy patients. To their credit, the New York City psychoanalysts donated the supervision time but they did not take care of patients at the hospital. When I moved to the Chicago area, I could not entice any private practice psychiatrist to volunteer supervision in our department. They all wanted to be paid at the going rate.

Psychiatrists in urban centers also rarely migrate to a rural habitat. The psychiatrist from mid-town Manhattan does not pull up stakes and heads for Gillette, Wyoming. So the overpopulation of urban psychiatrists is faced with even worse survival pressures than their rural counterparts. Primary care physicians initially see most "psychiatric" insured patients[18] and refer patients only if the clinical situation worsens. Primary care physicians are also more willing than psychiatrists to accept Medicaid patients and so care for more of the poor and minority groups.[19]

Not enough paying city patients and too many urban psychiatrists is the situation. These psychiatrists appear unable to expand their habitat to poor city areas or of migrating to places where psychiatrists are needed. They have never done so and some will not survive the economic stresses they face. Like their rural counterparts, most urban psychiatrists do not have the skills and a *qualitatively* different knowledge base that substantially separate them clinically from primary care physicians. Without meaningful advantages in the services they provide while still charging more, urban general adult psychiatrists will slowly disappear from the scene.

The Extinction Has Started

One reflection of the extinction process is seen in the recent cost-containment decision of Cedars Sinai Medical Center in Los Angeles to cut most of its psychiatric services. This large urban medical center is not alone. Although general hospitals such as Cedars Sinai still provide the bulk of inpatient psychiatric services and ambulatory and emergency psychiatric care in the United States, and as a group are the largest employers of psychiatrists (over 4000 psychiatrists), the peak of this segment of U.S. psychiatry was 1998 with about 54,000 beds. By 2002 the number had declined to 40,000 beds, a 25% drop. Teaching hospitals also have cut back. Over 500 general hospitals during the almost 15-year period ending in 2007 closed their inpatient psychiatric unit. Reimbursement was part of the problem with health insurance paying only 60% of the costs of maintaining such units.[20]

Another example of the contraction of U.S. psychiatry is seen in a study that examined trends in the supply, distribution, and demographics of psychiatry residents during the 1990s. The study examined data obtained from the American Medical Association's (AMA) Annual Survey of Graduate Medical Education (GME) Programs, the AMA GME directory, and the American Psychiatric Association's Graduate Medical Census. The surveyors found a significant decline in the number of psychiatric residents during the years studied. The median training program size also decreased. The authors worried whether the field could afford anymore residency downsizing in light of emerging evidence of a shortage of psychiatrists.[21] Should this trend continue there will be significantly fewer young psychiatrists entering the field by mid-century. Their place in the medical environment will be taken by generalists.

LITTLE ADVANTAGE AT A HIGHER COST

Not all parties in this conversation agree that psychiatrists have nothing unique to offer patients. A common opinion among psychiatrists is that on average they provide better psychiatric care than do primary care physicians. They site studies that support the view that specialists do better than generalists. For example, some studies that compare the knowledge base and quality of care provided by generalists versus specialists find that the specialists are more knowledgeable and provide better care within their specialization.[22] Other studies of the equality of care, however, find that preventive health care is generally better provided by primary care physicians. An analysis of elderly patients, for example, found that patients seeing generalists, as compared to patients seeing specialists, were more likely to receive influenza vaccination. In health promotion counseling, studies of self-reported behavior find that generalists were more likely than internal medicine specialists to counsel patients and to screen for breast cancer. Better preventive health care also saves health care dollars later on.[23]

Do the differences between specialists and generalists also directly apply to psychiatrists? What is the quality of care provided to patients with behavioral syndromes? Is this care for the most part good? Is there a substantial difference between the care provided by primary care physicians and psychiatrists? If there is a difference that favors psychiatrists, is that difference substantial enough to support the specialty? In other words, is psychiatry fit enough to survive?

U.S. Psychiatrists and Primary Care Physicians Provide Equivalent Care

I have already detailed my conclusion that U.S. psychiatrists as a group do not provide very good care. Many studies support this conclusion. For example, in a study of patients attending the clinics of two university medical centers, 180 patients with depressive illness who became suicidal had to be admitted to the associated university hospitals. University clinics and hospitals are thought to offer the best, often "cutting edge" care. In the 90 days before hospitalization, however, only 21% of the 180 patients were found to have received adequate antidepressant treatments. The researchers assessing the patients who were admitted to the two university hospitals also followed the patients after hospitalization. Despite the history of a suicide attempt and a hospitalization for the attempt, they found no improvement in treatments *despite additional suicide attempts.*[24]

The sad fact is that even when psychiatrists recognize the suicide risk of a patient there is no guarantee that the care they will provide will improve. Studies from other parts of the industrialized world also reveal poor care for psychiatric patients. For example, in a study of 43 patients with depressive illness who made a suicide attempt, 16% were found to have received adequate pharmacotherapy before their hospitalization compared to 17% after discharge. None received electroconvulsive therapy (ECT), although ECT is established as the most effective antidepressant for persons with severe depressive illness and the only acute treatment intervention that resolves suicidal pressures quickly.[25] In a study of persons with manic-depression who killed themselves, 74% were found to have been undertreated, even though 39% *communicated their intent*. Only 11% received adequate antidepressants, 32% were prescribed lithium, a terribly low figure for a sample of patients with manic-depression, and none received ECT.[26]

Poor treatment often follows poor diagnosis. There are numerous studies documenting frighteningly high error rates in the diagnosis of patients with psychiatric disorders. The reported error rates for not recognizing a dementia when present (false negatives) or for concluding a person is demented when the patient is not (false positives) range from 16% to 72%.[27]

Every medical student in the United States is instructed repeatedly to recognize delirium. They are also warned that they will likely not learn from this instruction and will miss delirium in patients or diagnose delirium when it is not present. Studies repeatedly find that physicians do not accurately diagnose delirium in from 50% to 95% of patients.[28]

Several years ago one of the hospital's consultation psychiatry physicians burst into my office, flopped down in one of the chairs, and began to curse. She had just come from the inpatient psychiatric unit were one of the other psychiatric attendings had insisted that a patient was delirious. The consultation psychiatrist thought the patient was catatonic and in a "benign stupor," a semi-dream-like state. *"I make my living diagnosing delirium,"* she yelled. *"That patient is not delirious, he's catatonic and IM lorazepam will prove it."* The inpatient psychiatrist had refused to consider the diagnosis of catatonia and would not try the medication challenge that might resolve the disagreement. After the extensive and fruitless evaluation of the patient for all possible causes of delirium, a new inpatient attending rotated onto the service. He immediately did the medication challenge, which was positive, and then successfully treated the patient who fully recovered. The consultation psychiatrist regularly bemoans the inability of physicians from other specialty services to recognize whether or not a patient is delirious.

Depression is another syndrome that is repeatedly discussed in medical school and in most nonsurgical residencies. Despite the emphasis on teaching about depression, about one out of four to almost half of depressive episodes are not recognized by physicians.[29] Here's an example of a psychiatrist mistaking a psychotic depression for delirium from my textbook with Max Fink on melancholia.[30]

A woman in her eighties with a history of recurrent melancholia was living with her daughter and enjoying life. For many years she had been taking a daily preparation combining an antipsychotic agent with an antidepressant. These combinations of two agents into one pill are generally a bad idea other than for the manufacturer's bottom line. The dosing is almost always imbalanced toward one or the other agent, so that to prescribe an adequate dose of one automatically overdoses the other. Adding insult to injury, the long-term exposure of a patient to an antipsychotic does not prevent depressions from emerging, but this chronic use does increase the risk for tardive dyskinesia. The combination had been prescribed because the patient had a history of depression and had previously received ECT and had done well. An antidepressant in an adequate dose over the years would likely have worked as well.

After all those years on the antipsychotic, the patient finally developed tardive dyskinesia (TD). TD can be incapacitating. I evaluated a patient suffering from TD whose upper body and neck were rigidly twisted into a corkscrew posture that moderated only when he was asleep. Another patient had many antipsychotic-induced abnormal movements, but the most problematic were spasms (dystonias) in his back forcing him to walk along walls to prevent him from falling backward. In the woman's case, she developed uncontrollable chewing mouth movements. Because of these, her prescription was changed to another antipsychotic–antidepressant combination now in two separate pills. The logic of this substitution and combination is beyond me. She became progressively depressed.

Her depression was a classic melancholia. She experienced a loss of interest and energy, loss of feelings of enjoyment (anhedonia), poor concentration, and feelings of hopelessness and worthlessness. She reported hearing God's and the Devil's voices, and of seeing the Devil and demons. The prescription was again changed, this time to another antidepressant. The second change, like the first, provided the patient with no relief. A fourth combination was prescribed, also with little benefit. This repeated switching to a different medication or combination is standard practice among U.S. psychiatrists and is encouraged by well-known but in my view flawed studies and treatment guidelines based on those studues.[31]

The patient either remained in bed or roamed about the house, appearing "confused." She unnecessarily changed her clothes frequently and took repeated showers. She wandered outside and stopped eating and drinking at the instruction of the voices. They "told" her that she was "evil." She threw away her credit card and jewelry, and lost substantial weight in several weeks. She began pinching herself and twisting her arms to punish herself. She said that she wanted to die.

The patient was hospitalized and received a cascade of overlapping prescriptions that had no benefit but led to further "confusion." She required tube feeding. She developed urinary retention, was catheterized, a urinary tract infection followed, and an antibiotic was given. Her blood sodium dropped adding to her cognitive difficulties. She developed left lower lobe pneumonia. The patient was then transferred to another hospital for further psychiatric and general medical care.

The above scenario is not rare in the United States. We treat patients from across the Midwest with similar stories. In every inpatient unit I have worked in patients, like this patient, were admitted regularly. The panicked prescribing of one combination of medications after another, sometimes several combinations at once, is all too common among U.S. psychiatrists. In this story, the patient's exposure to polypharmacy surely exacerbated the cognitive dysfunction associated with a psychotic depression. Her low sodium and pneumonia both are associated with cognitive dysfunction, particularly in older patients. So, her depression was not resolved and she developed a treatment-induced delirium. In American football when the offense is not doing well, the team punts. In medicine, when the physicians are not doing well, the patient is often transferred to another hospital. The hope is that the physicians in the second hospital will clean up the mess created by the physicians in the first hospital.

On admission to the second hospital the patient was observed to be agitated and disoriented and made little eye contact. Her speech was sparse. She mumbled "incoherently." When understood, she described hearing demonic voices and seeing frightening visions. Her most immediate symptoms were consistent with a delirium, but because of her earlier depressions, a history of successful ECT 30 years before, and the features of melancholia leading to the admission to the first hospital, a colleague and I evaluated her for ECT.

We found her to be emotionally restricted. She said she was evil and was being punished. She was stiff, postured, and exhibited other features of catatonia. She was not feverish as can happen with severe catatonia, but we attributed this lack of physiological response to her age. Older folks do not readily produce the chemical responses that elicit fever.[32] The patient's features were also consistent with melancholia, a psychotic depression. A neuroleptic malignant syndrome/malignant catatonia was also emerging. Her laboratory findings supported the diagnoses. We recommended ECT. ECT is the best treatment for psychotic depression and can achieve 90–95% remission rates within 12 treatments. It is the definitive treatment for catatonia. When a patient's catatonia takes the malignant form as was occurring in this patient, ECT is life saving.[33]

The patient's inpatient psychiatrist followed part of our advice and reluctantly discontinued the patient's medications. The patient continued, however, to have mild features of her pneumonia and low sodium, and remained "confused." These features led the psychiatrist to reject our diagnoses of melancholia with psychosis and catatonia. Instead, she concluded that the patient continued to have a delirium secondary to infection.

The patient's vital signs continued to fluctuate, a feature of malignant catatonia. She then suddenly began to scream about mid-chest pain and began hitting her chest. In the classic textbooks I was encouraged to read as a resident, this behavior was described as a common feature of psychotic melancholia. Residents and faculty today rarely read these classic books, and the inpatient psychiatrist was unaware of this feature, and concluded that the patient was experiencing a heart attack or a blood clot in her lungs. The psychiatrist transferred the patient to a critical care medical unit that found neither condition and sent the patient back to the psychiatry unit. A second episode of screaming and chest beating led to another transfer to critical care, but again nothing alarming was found and the patient was transferred back to psychiatry. These transfers and the ensuing substantial testing were a form of medical error, but they are not recorded as error. They also cost a bundle. With all the transferring back and forth, over a week had passed. We again recommended ECT trying to convince the patient's inpatient psychiatrist that all of the woman's behavioral symptoms could be attributed to severe depression and catatonia. The psychiatrist again rejected our conclusions and insisted that the patient had a metabolic delirium.

The patient's condition deteriorated. She remained bed-ridden, posturing and stiff, refusing food and drink. My colleague and I finally confronted the patient's inpatient psychiatrist and achieved the agreement that we would obtain an EEG and that if it was inconsistent with a delirium we would give the patient ECT. A bedside EEG was done and was read as normal and inconsistent with a delirium. Almost all delirious patients have an abnormal EEG. Over the next 2 weeks we gave the patient six ECT treatments. She had a full recovery. She was again animated, active but weak, eating and drinking, and gaining weight. She returned to her daughter's home where she continued to do well. The patient's inpatient psychiatrist never admitted error.

Diagnostic errors are also common for other severe psychiatric conditions. Half of the diagnoses of manic-depression are wrong. In some cases the patient has another condition such as the frontal lobe disinhibited syndrome. In many patients with manic-depression, the associated psychotic features are assumed to represent schizophrenia and the patient either receives that diagnosis or the meaningless schizoaffective label.[34] These errors are reminiscent of what I saw happening when I was a resident and then a young faculty member. That was 40 years ago.

In addition to not reaching the correct diagnosis in many patients, there is also a substantial delay before the patient's actual condition is recognized. From onset of symptoms to correct diagnosis is typically about 3 years for persons with depressive illness, 5 years or more for those with the several variations of manic-depression, 10 years or more for persons with complex forms of manic-depression, and 12 years for sufferers of obsessive-compulsive disorder.[35]

What all the above comes down to is that U.S. psychiatrists do not do a very good job in diagnosing and treating their patients. How does this compare with the psychiatric care offered by primary care physicians?

Psychiatrists versus Primary Care Physicians

In a large study of patients with the diagnosis of depression in the California Keiser health system, over 800 were followed. Most received their care from a generalist, and of these patients, only 20% received "appropriate" medication and only 17% received "appropriate" counseling based on the researchers' independent assessments.[36] Although not directly head-to-head, these figures are similar to those found in the two-university hospital study detailed above in which the patients were treated by psychiatrists. The psychiatrists at two different university medical centers and the primary care physicians at one of the largest health care systems in the country did equally poorly in their care of patients with depressive illness.

In one direct comparison,[37] patients with anxiety disorder were identified at 15 clinical sites. These patients were then assessed for the psychiatric care provided by either a primary care physician or by a psychiatrist. Almost half of the patients being treated by a primary care physician did not receive specific treatments, particularly pharmacotherapy. The most common reason for not receiving medication was that the patient "did not believe in taking medication for emotional problems," or that the primary care physician did not recommend such treatment. An increasing number of studies report that persons with the milder forms of depression or anxiety disorder do not respond to antidepressant medications and do better with cognitive-behavior therapy or counseling, so that not prescribing medication may have been the correct decision.[38] The patients in the study who were treated with medication tended to be more severely ill, often had a depression along with their anxiety, and were EuroAmerican. Compared to the psychiatrists, the primary care physicians prescribed similar medications and did so at similar doses. The overall care offered by the two types of treaters was found to be similar. Other studies also find that psychiatrists are less likely to treat minorities and older patients who are more likely to seek care from a primary care physician. The rest of their care, however, is similar to that provided by generalists.[39]

Additional studies focused on family physicians. Family physicians are basically primary care physicians, but they are trained to provide care for all family members. Strikingly, they find their method of psychiatric diagnosis to be more complex and thorough than what is expected from the *DSM* approach.[40] In one odd study of equivalent groups of depressed patients followed for over 4 months, *depressed patients undetected by their primary care physician did as well as depressed patients treated by a psychiatrist.* This suggests that the care provided by the psychiatrists was equivalent to doing nothing. Their care at best was a placebo. The study was done at a university medical center.[41]

In the late 1990s, a relative of mine living in another state developed a melancholic depression. He went to his primary care physician as required by his insurance carrier. The primary care physician immediately referred him to one of the system's psychiatrists. This psychiatrist prescribed a month's supply of a second-rate antidepressant and gave my relative an appointment in 4 weeks. No appointment a week later to make sure things were going well and no daily phone rounds to repeatedly reassure the patient. This level of effort in the treatment of persons with depressive illness is not uncommon, but is a formula for suicide. I insisted that my relative see another psychiatrist, and she did a better job of caring for him.

In the early 2000s, an acquaintance of mine also living in another state developed a severe depression. Normally an active, vibrant person, she was now housebound, lethargic, and despondent. I recommended that she seek care at her nearby university medical center and only from a psychiatrist who worked within the center's mood disorder clinic. This type of program should offer the top care possible.

The mood disorder psychiatrist initially prescribed an antidepressant that I would not have chosen for a patient with a melancholic depression, which is what my acquaintance had. The psychiatrist prescribed starting dose was at the low end of the therapeutic range and I hoped that he would know that most patients who respond to antidepressants do so at higher not lower doses. Alas, even after a month he did not increase the dose and of course my acquaintance was no better. I spoke to her family and encouraged them to lobby for a dose increase. This was finally accomplished, but we had to repeat the procedure a month later as there was no improvement and the psychiatrist did not independently increase the dose. Four months had now passed without results. I again encouraged the family to press for the psychiatrist to either switch medications or add a specific agent that might favorably interact with the medication he was prescribing. He chose the latter course and within 2 weeks my acquaintance's depression began to rapidly resolve. So, a psychiatrist at a prestigious medical center who superspecializes in mood disorders did not select the best choice medication to begin with and then did not know what to do with his medication choice when the patient did not quickly respond. That is the level of care offered by most of U.S. psychiatry as far as I can tell.

In studies of the pharmacological care of depressed patients offered by primary care physicians the quality is about the same as what is found in studies of the level of care provided by psychiatrists.[42] If there is a difference between the two groups of physicians, it is that primary care physicians are aware of their need to improve. They have developed training programs to do this,[43] including the outpatient management of the more seriously ill psychiatric patients who are suicidal[44] or who have manic-depression.[45] Unlike U.S. psychiatrists, primary care physicians as a group appear to know what they do not know. If my conclusion is correct that there is nothing in medicine more dangerous than a physician who does not know what he or she does not know, what are the implications when an entire specialty appears to be unaware that it often provides inadequate care? If the present trend continues, and psychiatry's competitors get better at the diagnosis and treatment of psychiatric patients, achieving parity in the quality of care, and they continue to do it for less U.S. health care dollars, why would anyone go to the general adult psychiatrist for outpatient care?

THE PROCESS OF EXTINCTION

The answer to the question at the end of the last section is that patients and insurance carriers will shun such a specialty and at some tipping point that specialty will all but disappear. Although seemingly not fully aware of the specialty's shortcomings, U.S. psychiatrists are well aware of the adverse effects of managed care on their practices[46] and lack of adequate mental health insurance coverage.[47] In surveys they, more so than primary care physicians, endorse statements that managed care reduces their income and that *clinical decisions in the best interests of their patients reduce income.* The conflict of interest of this attitude is obvious and shocking. These surveys and other studies indicate that primary care physicians are surviving managed care better than psychiatrists.

The process of extinction is underway and the psychiatric piece of the patient pie is getting smaller for psychiatrists while it is getting larger for other providers. An increasing number of the providers of health care are no longer physicians. U.S. medicine has now allowed health care workers other than physicians to deliver some primary care and psychiatric medical services. These clinicians include nurse practitioners, physician assistants, and some other health care providers (e.g., psyDs who are less rigorously trained than PhD psychologists, psychotherapy counselors with almost any degree, and psychiatric social workers). Originally conceived to counter the shortage of physicians in underserved areas, physician's assistants and nurse practitioners are now recruited because they are less expensive to the clinical facility that employs them than are physicians, and to the health insurance carrier that reimburses for their services.

Primary care physicians recognize that they are providing most of the initial care to patients with behavioral syndromes. They understand that in many cases they are providing care equivalent to that offered by psychiatrists. From treating patients with depressive illness and anxiety disorder, primary care physicians are beginning to focus attention on the care of patients with other forms of psychiatric illness. Some are now willing to treat patients with manic-depression, some of the most difficult patients to care for, and whose care should be provided by only the most skilled and experienced of physicians.[48] Primary care physicians are increasingly providing continuous treatment for patients with depressive illness. Some opine that it is preferable for a patient with depressive illness to be treated by a primary care physician rather than a psychiatrist because primary care physicians *"have better relationships"* with such patients than do psychiatrists as they also care for the patients' other illnesses and there is less stigmatization in a primary care setting.[49] A logical extension of this perspective is the increased acceptance among primary care physicians of responsibility for suicide-risk management.[50] Even psychiatrists have a tough time with this challenge.

The facts are that most psychiatric patients in the United States receive their initial care from nonpsychiatrists and many receive all their psychiatric care from nonpsychiatrists. Among primary care practices about 60%

of their patients are recognized as having anxiety disorder or depression.[51] As many as one of ten primary care patients receive a diagnosis of major depression.[52] In one representative U.S. study of the years 2001–2005, among persons with psychiatric diagnoses who received treatment, only 12% were treated by a psychiatrist. Sixteen percent were treated by a nonpsychiatrist mental health specialist, and 23% were treated by a general medical provider. An assessment of the quality of the treatments given found that 48% of patients treated by a psychiatrist received adequate care whereas 13% of those treated by others received adequate care.[53] Although the psychiatrists clearly did better, still more than half of the patients that they saw did not obtain adequate care.

A national survey of patients in the United States in 2009 with a diagnosis of depression found that almost two-thirds received their care from a generalist or family physician. Psychiatrists and therapists split the other third. As some patients were seen by more than one type of provider it was also found that 40% saw a psychologist or counselor, 18% saw a religious advisor, 11% saw a social worker, 7% saw an herbalist, and 6% saw a nurse.[54] Many more groups are cutting into the psychiatric patient pie, and when psychiatric patients go more frequently to herbalists than to nurses, you know something is amiss.

The decline in the size of psychiatry's "market share" began when social workers and psychologists recognized that they could provide psychotherapy as well as psychiatrists. The days of psychoanalytic dominance of the field were numbered not because psychiatrists suddenly saw that the Freudian emperor had no effective treatment clothes, but because insurance would not pay for the expensive version when they could get just as good or bad psychotherapy for less. A big slice of the patient pie was consumed by nonpsychiatrists. Then with the simplification of the *DSM* and the promotion of recipe-like psychopharmacology treatment algorithms, clinical psychologists opined that they could diagnose and treat just as well as could psychiatrists and they could do it for less money. They have been lobbying legislatures for licenses to prescribe medications.[55] Generalist physicians came to the same conclusion and as they have such licenses, they now prescribe more psychiatric medications then do psychiatrists.[56]

Unless patients with behavioral syndromes are in such dire straits that they go to an emergency room or are directly admitted to a psychiatric inpatient facility because of the severity of their condition, they will most likely receive care from someone other than a psychiatrist. Only if the clinical situation becomes extremely complicated or the patient does not respond to numerous treatment trials will a psychiatrist be consulted. But even a quick reading of the previous chapters shows that most psychiatrists are not up to the task of caring for the most severely ill psychiatric patients. They mostly do a mediocre job in diagnosing and caring for such patients.

In thinking back to all the inpatient units I've been associated with (six) and the patients who were admitted to them (thousands), the most important thing we did for many was to stop the irrational medications they were prescribed by psychiatrists. This experience was coast to coast and over a period of 45 years. Many times, the diagnosis the patient carried for years was wrong. Just as disturbing, the treatments prescribed were commonly incorrect for the diagnoses that were made. Whatever those physicians thought was wrong with those patients they did not know the proper treatments for the conditions they diagnosed. In northern Illinois there were four Veteran's Administration (VA) hospitals. Our school was affiliated with one and at the time it had the largest service for more chronically ill psychiatric patients. We often received transfers from the other three hospitals. Many of the transferred patients had been briefly admitted at the other facility, put on a bunch of medications, and then were shipped off to our VA. When I was making rounds with the residents we played a game. They would tell me the medications the newly transferred patient was prescribed at the other hospital and I'd guess which hospital had transferred the patient based on the number and combination of the psychiatric medications that had been prescribed. The patient's diagnosis was almost irrelevant as each hospital had its set package of drugs that were going to be prescribed come hell or high water. My prediction rate was pretty good. If the number of psychiatric medications was more than six, it was always one particular place.

In the early 1970s, when I was residency director at Stony Brook, I was lamenting about the requirements that we had to teach psychodynamic psychotherapies. One of the faculty, Joseph Wortus, who had been analyzed by a direct disciple of Freud, but who had eventually given up on psychoanalysis, was then the editor of the journal *Biological Psychiatry*. He told me not to worry. He predicted that the health insurance industry would eventually refuse to pay for psychoanalytic treatment recognizing that it was not cost-effective. He predicted that the third-party payers would further prefer nonphysicians as providers of any form of psychotherapy as their fees would be less than those demanded by psychiatrists. He was correct in both forecasts.

Today, talking therapies are mostly provided by nonpsychiatrists. Most patients receiving psychopharmacological therapies are being treated by nonpsychiatric physicians. Most patients with behavioral syndromes directly the result of brain damage and disease are being treated by neurologists and neuropsychologists. The number of psychiatric inpatient beds is shrinking. Natural selection still determines species fitness. Inflexible and inefficient organisms do not survive. This is also true for societies. U.S. psychiatry cannot survive the harsh judgment of such a process unless it adapts. In my view, that will mean becoming a specialty that offers skills and a knowledge base that psychiatry's competitors do not possess but that are essential for the proper care of patients with complex behavioral syndromes. Most present-day U.S. psychiatrists do not have such skills and knowledge. There still is a great need for the specialty of psychiatry, but unfortunately it is not the specialty that we now have.

CHAPTER 7

ᴄᴧᴐ

Back to the Future

The Once and Future King

"The reader will find no other definition of 'Psychiatry' in this book but the one given on the title-page: 'Clinical Treatise on Diseases of the Fore-Brain.' The historical term psychiatry, i.e. 'treatment of the soul,' implies more than we can accomplish, and transcends the bounds of accurate scientific investigation."

Theodor Meynert's 1885 textbook[1]

Life is short,[the]art [medicine] long, opportunity fleeting, experiment treacherous, judgment difficult.

Hippocrates

Theodor Meynert was one of the most influential European psychiatrists of the latter part of the nineteenth century. His textbook inspired several generations of physicians concerned for patients with behavioral syndromes. The title of his book and the quote above from its title page distill the essence of neuropsychiatry as I see it. Then and now, we cannot be physicians of the soul. Meynert did not dismiss the notion of soul or the need for its soothing. He simply said that such an effort was for others, not for psychiatrists. From Meynert's perspective, the soul could not be studied by applying the scientific method and so it had no valid place in psychiatric thinking. Had Freudian and other psychodynamic views of behavior been prominent during Meynert's era, he would also have rejected these constructs because they too are metaphysical. They have no reality in neuroanatomy, in neurophysiology, or in neurochemistry. They are philosophical ideas about why people behave the way we do. He would have also rejected the *DSM* system, as it ignores the brain as well as the wealth of psychopathology that Meynert recognized. In his view, psychiatrists were physicians who should focus their attentions on the brain and its behavioral expressions. He singled out the forebrain (primarily the frontal lobes and their subcortical circuitry) as the source of much psychopathology, but he would undoubtedly have broadened that perspective given our present understanding of behavioral neuroscience.

Meynert rejected a metaphysical approach to the diagnosis of patients with behavioral syndromes because the application of metaphysics to behavior cannot be measured scientifically and it does not predict the causes of those behaviors or an individual's future behavior. Whether the metaphysics is termed psychoanalysis or psychodynamics, these understandings of behavior are philosophical constructs. There are many biographies of well-known personages that offer a psychological understanding of their motivations and actions, but these claims are drawn from hindsight and exist in tautologies. I know of no biography or psychological evaluation that predicted what a well-known person would do later in life *before* the person did it. As far as I know, the best predictor of future behavior is past behavior. How a person has behaved in the past is how they are likely to behave in the future when in similar circumstances, unless they have suffered a brain injury or developed a brain disease.

A BRAINLESS DIAGNOSTIC SYSTEM

Meynert would have rejected the *DSM* as a meaningful diagnostic system because it is disconnected from the brain. It has no central guiding principle. It does not predict the sources of aberrant behavior or responses to treatment from any perspective that attempts to understand behavior. This sad fact is not surprising as the manual is a political not a scientific document.[2] Although it became increasingly clear in the last few decades of the twentieth century that the brain is the generator of behavior, the framers of the *DSM*, from version *III* to the present *IV*, tried to formulate an atheoretical document so as not to upset influential American Psychiatric Association (APA) constituencies that saw behavior through a psychodynamic or psychological lens. Disorders were described in superficial terminology and defined in neutral constructs so that psychiatrists of all theoretical persuasions would be willing to use the manual. The goal was to achieve a classification system of reasonable reliability without making too many waves. The results are unsatisfying to most clinicians.

The Sad Example of Schizophrenia

An example of the problem with much of the *DSM* is illustrated by its presentation of schizophrenia. To receive the diagnosis of schizophrenia a patient must exhibit any two of five features. If the patient experiences hearing voices and believes he is the king of Outer Mongolia but is not depressed and does not appear manic, the patient meets the *DSM* criteria for schizophrenia. Most psychiatrists can agree on this identification, and so achieve reliability. Reliability refers to precision. Using target practice as an analogy, good precision would mean the shooters all hit the target in about the same spot. In diagnostic terms, they mostly agree on the label each patient can be given. However, most clinicians also know that there are many pathophysiological processes that are associated with the pattern of symptoms I just described. Clinicians know that reliability or precision does not equate with the accuracy of the diagnosis on which physicians might agree. Accuracy is validity or the truth of the diagnosis. It is not enough to agree on the label, the label must reflect the patient's illness. In days of yore most physicians might agree that a patient was demonically possessed. They had good reliability, but poor validity. In the target practice analogy, if the shooters are very precise and they all hit the target about in the same spot, but if that spot is far from the bulls-eye, they have no accuracy. The effort has reliability but no validity. Without some understanding of the generators of the symptoms and the notion of what is the central nature of schizophrenia, the *DSM* diagnosis becomes a category without a disease. The criteria can be applied to achieve reliability, but the validity of the diagnosis is questionable.

The lack of a meaningful concept of schizophrenia (like almost all *DSM* categories) has substantially contributed to our lack of progress in identifying the causes and the underlying processes of the disorders of the patients in this category. Without a unifying concept, much of the research on schizophrenia has been based on the examination of heterogeneous samples. The diagnostic criteria are overly broad, and if there is no common agreement on what the condition represents, many patients with different conditions but with similar presenting symptoms will be accepted into studies. As a result of this heterogeneity, most findings about schizophrenia are nonspecific.

A review of the *world's research*[3] identified 77 assumptions about schizo-phrenia that have been reported to be "important" in understanding the condition. Only 23 of these were found to be consistently supported by the research. In other words, most things the field believes to be true about schizophrenia are not evidence-based. The evidence-supported 23 find-ings, however, did not delineate a disease. Among the review's findings were studies that determined, for example, that the annual incidence (new cases) and prevalence (new plus old cases) of schizophrenia vary five-fold across countries for no discernible reason other than diagnostic practice (i.e., indicating poor reliability). Although reports conclude that there is a substantial genetic component to the syndrome, genetic studies yield few positive results despite four decades of sophisticated effort.[4] The most accepted genetic finding from these investigations accounts for only 2% of the variance in individual differences in illness presentation.[5] To "account" for only 2% of why a syndrome differs from others does not contribute much to our understanding of the syndrome. The reviewers concluded that the heterogeneity in neurobiology, clinical manifestations, severity, course, and treatment response of schizophrenia is great. No single feature defines it and the *"boundaries between schizophrenia and other psychiatric disorders are indistinct."*

In other words, schizophrenia as presented in the *DSM* is a label without a unifying biological distinction.[6] Should most patients with hallucinations and delusions and without mood disorder or identifiable neurological dis-ease be labeled schizophrenic? Is schizophrenia a developmental disorder expressed early in life before the psychoses emerge as some researchers conclude or is it a disease afflicting any age group? Is a residual decline in function always present or can the illness remit? Is a 17-year-old unso-cial loner with longstanding problems of emotional expression, volition, and social and motor awkwardness suffering from the same illness as a 50-year-old person with adequate premorbid functioning, if both meet the cross-sectional criteria? A person with preserved personality and normal emotional expression but experiencing persistent auditory hallucinations and a person with catatonia and delusions of grandeur or disorganized speech both meet the criteria. Do they suffer from the same illness? Like the criteria for schizophrenia and depression, diagnostic criteria in the other *DSM* categories also guarantee sample heterogeneity. Here are two examples of patients with the same *DSM* label but who were clearly suffer-ing from different conditions.

Schizophrenia only in the morning: A number of years ago, one of my neu-ropsychiatry fellows saw a patient who was then in his late 20s. The patient had been having difficulties since a teenager. He was unable to work full-time but was able to perform menial tasks. Almost every morning as he awoke he experienced rapidly escalating anxiety until he was immobilized with fear. He stayed in bed. Then he began hallucinating. The voice he experienced was loud and persistent, perceived to be external in its source, and frightening. After several hours the voice abated. The patient was then able to get out of bed and become involved in limited activities. His life was so restricted that he had no friends and had never dated. He was lonely. On an examination in the late afternoon, he appeared to be a man of average to low intelligence, but otherwise normal. He had never experienced a depression or mania and had always been considered generally healthy. Throughout the decade of his psychiatric illness he had been diagnosed as schizophrenic and he indeed met *DSM* criteria for the syndrome.

What the *DSM* doesn't do is to put symptoms into context or patterns. Any of the required number of features in any order of emergence will do. So, there was never any consideration given to the following aspects of the patient's illness. The voices occurred upon awakening. They were time-linked or linked to the state of awakening. The voices were preceded by intense anxiety. After some time they abated and he was hallucination-free for the rest of the day. Schizophrenia has never been considered a condition that fluctuates during the course of the day in a diurnal pattern. The hallucination emerging after awakening following a brief period of panic is also different from classic descriptions. Many U.S. psychiatrists today do not know the classic descriptions because these features are no longer being taught. Based on our understanding of psychopathology, we concluded that the patient did not have schizophrenia despite meeting *DSM* criteria. We further assessed him for a seizure disorder, identified it, and successfully treated his "schizophrenia" with an anticonvulsant.[7]

In the 1980s I had a grant to study psychopathology and family illness patterns in patients with schizophrenia or manic-depression. As part of that effort, my colleagues and I reported that both schizophrenia and manic-depression were more common than expected in the first-degree relatives of both the patients with schizophrenia and those with manic-depression. First-degree relatives are parents, siblings, and children. They are your relatives with whom you share the most genes.

I presented our findings at a conference. After I had finished several other presenters accused me of overdiagnosing schizophrenia and stated that our schizophrenic patients must have been manic-depressive to explain why they had so many relatives with manic-depression. The irony for me was that in the 1970s I had been accused of the exact opposite, being too restrictive in my diagnosis of schizophrenia. However, several prominent researchers came to the defense of our data because they had visited the hospital in which we recruited our patients and they had personally examined the patients in our study. They vigorously stated that the patients we were diagnosing as schizophrenic were the real McCoy. Here's a description of one of the patients. He too met *DSM* criteria for schizophrenia, but he sure was different from the man who woke up to hallucinations. By the way, some genetic overlap between schizophrenia and manic-depression is now recognized.[8]

Hebephrenia, the original notion of schizophrenia: One patient the other investigators saw on their visit to our hospital was a 28-year-old man who had spent most of the previous decade in various hospitals and the last 3 years in ours. Throughout his life he had been emotionally aloof, but he had done well academically until age 17 when he stopped all of his activities other than eating. He was now a bloated version of his former self.

I recall that the visitors met the patient in an open hospital dayroom. The patient was sprawled in a chair away from the other patients. He was unclean and rank. Although he said he didn't mind talking to the visitors, he never made eye contact with them. He never smiled at them but occasionally he smiled knowingly to the space away from us. He responded slowly with an unvarying undertone of suspiciousness and hostility. He looked at his surroundings only from the corner of his eyes. His speech was fluent and he articulated well, but he never initiated conversation. His responses were mostly vacuous and he rarely used nouns, making it difficult to follow his train of thought. On occasion he stopped addressing the visitors and mumbled to one side as if he were conversing with someone. On these occasions he would laugh. It was an eerie sound without warmth. He said that he was hearing several persons other than us talking to him. He smirked when we said we did not also hear them. He said he could feel them push and poke him to gain his attention. He said the TV often communicated to him even when it was off. He said he had no plans for the future and inanely laughed at the idea. He had no interest in leaving the hospital. We all thought that he suffered from the original idea of schizophrenia, hebephrenia.[9]

The advantage of seeing the *DSM* as flawed and its categories as heterogeneous can be seen from the two patients who met the *DSM* criteria for schizophrenia. From the *DSM* perspective, both would be prescribed an antipsychotic and perhaps some efforts at socialization would be made. But from a neuropsychiatric perspective, the patient with the seizure disorder would have benefited from early detection and specific treatment for epilepsy allowing him to have a more productive life. We were able to control his seizures but we could not give him back his lost years. The patient we saw as suffering from hebephrenia had been ill for years. But the early identification of his illness might have led to vigorous rehabilitation as a tertiary prevention to minimize his dysfunction and chronicity, and not just treatment with an antipsychotic.

The APA and the creators of the *DSM* have lost the forest for the trees that they have planted. The purpose of a diagnostic system is to achieve more than uniformity of language. It must identify homogeneous group-ings of patients so that the best treatments for them can be prescribed and common pathophysiologies identified so that treatments can become more specific, etiologies determined, and prevention strategies formulated. The *DSM* provides none of this. Identifying more clinically homogeneous patient groups is the best first research step in trying to understand their conditions.

AN ALTERNATIVE DIAGNOSTIC APPROACH

To make sense of the behavioral syndromes that afflict humanity, the clini-cian needs to know the relationships between the brain and behavior and the wide range of the signs and symptoms of brain disease. Many of the patients I have described are examples of the merit of this neuropsychiatric approach. Other examples follow.

The Harbinger of Alzheimer's Disease

On October 28, 1980 Ronald Reagan and President Jimmy Carter held the first of their two televised debates in the presidential campaign. My wife and I watched. As the debate progressed, I became increasingly uncomfort-able as I noticed Mr. Reagan's difficulties finding words and logical slippages in his train of thought. At times he appeared as "the deer in the headlights" waiting for some thought to express itself that wasn't emerging. At times, his mind seemed blank.

I don't make diagnoses over the TV, and what I observed were brief lapses in cognition, but halfway through the debate, I turned to my wife and said, *"I think he's becoming demented, no one is going to vote for him."* The next morning at work, my neuropsychiatry fellow rushed in and before any of the usual social greetings, blurted, *"Did you see the debate last night? He's becoming demented. No one will vote for him."*

About 23 years later I was making rounds with our psychiatry consulta-tion team. We had just seen a man who both I and the consultation team attending thought was demented. Outside the man's hospital room, I was discussing the patient's symptoms and cognitive difficulties and was telling the residents and students about how indicators of Alzheimer's disease can sometimes be identified years before the sufferer becomes clinically demented. As I started to reference the Reagan–Carter debate, the consultation psychiatrist, the only other member of the department who defined himself as a neuropsychiatrist, interrupted me and said, *"Yes, Reagan showed signs of Alzheimer's disease in the first debate, but he reconstituted in the second."* The stress of the first debate had taxed Mr. Reagan's cognition revealing his difficulties. He was more comfortable in the second debate, and therefore did better.

This anecdote is not trivial. Three independent observers skilled in neuropsychiatry without elaborate testing recognized the behavioral harbingers of dementia in a man a decade before his physicians were willing to make the diagnosis of Alzheimer's disease. That the man we recognized as suffering from the onset of a terrible degenerative brain disease went on to be a two-term president of the United States has profound implications. None of us thought after that debate that Mr. Reagan would be elected. Surely, we thought, most viewers would see his difficulties and if they were not able to put a name to them, they would at least have been worried about his capacity to fully function in office. We were correct about the diagnosis. We were good at what we did, but we were lousy prognosticators of elections.

After Mr. Reagan was officially diagnosed (several years after he left office), his previous White House physicians insisted that there was no indication of Mr. Reagan's difficulties while in office. In my view these statements were disingenuous and self-serving, or signs of incompetence. To test my disbelief I created a clinical anecdote that I used in classes for second year medical students in their course on clinical neuropsychiatry and behavioral sciences. The details I compiled were from news reports of Mr. Reagan's behaviors plus the observations from his presidential debate. The students invariably reached the conclusion that the nameless patient in the vignette was suffering from the very early stages of a degenerative brain disease and that most likely it was Alzheimer's dementia. Here's the vignette.

A teaching vignette: A 68-year-old man, the CEO of a large corporation, is known for his management style of not being involved in the details of the company. He does, however, make major decisions about the opportunities and difficulties the corporation faces, and the company flourishes. He is also known for not recognizing some of his middle managers and some of his best customers and business rivals. One of his aides is assigned to be with him during meetings to quietly tell him the identities of the people he is meeting. He is also known for supporting some of his decisions based on events that in fact had not taken place but were parts of movies that he had seen and that he had incorporated into his own biographic memories. At a stockholders meeting he appears tentative, has some difficulties finding words, and on occasion loses his train of thought before recovering.

Many of the behaviors detailed in the news reports of Mr. Reagan were regarded as quirky, or at worst a lack of interest in working hard. He was an actor after all. But one reason the students were able to consider the behaviors in the vignette as potentially ominous was that they had previously learned that Alzheimer's disease is a long process that may take years before the decline is recognizable as dementia.[10]

Dementia is a syndrome defined by extensive and substantial cognitive decline with prominent memory difficulties. The definition requires this decline to be without alterations in arousal and consciousness, although these changes can at times occur. When a patient suffers from diffuse cognitive difficulties and alterations in arousal, the diagnosis of delirium is made.

The predementia phase of Alzheimer's disease is referred to as MCI or mild cognitive impairment.[11] The individual and close family members often are aware that the sufferer is having some difficulties, but as most such persons are generally functioning adequately and are over age 65, the difficulties are attributed to "senior moments" or fatigue. If systematically tested, however, these persons perform below age-adjusted norms. Once they are identified, between 10% and 15% of persons with MCI continue to deteriorate into clinical dementia each year thereafter. For some, the MCI may span several decades before the patient is diagnosed as being demented. Unfortunately, most U.S. psychiatrists who see patients over age 65 do not know or use this information in the assessment of their patients even though previous depression is a risk factor for Alzheimer's disease.[12] Early detection and intervention can lead to some amelioration in the decline and in better patient and family planning for how best to respond to the decline.

So, how were the three neuropsychiatrists able to recognize the signs of dementia in Ronald Reagan over a decade before he received the diagnosis? It was not magical and we were not "Super Docs." We just applied the principles of diagnosis and the database that neuropsychiatrists rely upon daily in the care of their patients. This approach has substantial predictive clinical value. So, what exactly is a neuropsychiatrist? What are the principles that guide neuropsychiatrists? And, when applied, how do these principles affect patient care?

A NEUROPSYCHIATRIST DEFINED

There is a short answer to the question: "what exactly is a neuropsychiatrist?" A neuropsychiatrist is a psychiatrist or a neurologist who applies the principles of neuropsychiatry to the diagnosis and care of patients with behavioral syndromes. The answer is similar to the answer to the question: what makes a writer or a painter? If you seriously write or paint almost daily, then you are a writer or a painter. Like most other endeavors, there will be a range of competence in the writing and painting, but those who seriously do, are.

There are several overlapping groupings of physicians who refer to themselves as neuropsychiatrists. There are a small number of U.S. fellowships in neuropsychiatry. Physicians from these programs are usually graduates of a psychiatry residency. They then obtain further postresidency training experience in neuropsychiatry where they gain skills at integrating neurology and psychiatry. They then practice what they have learned. These neuropsychiatrists typically work in departments of psychiatry or have psychiatric private practices and care for patients with a wide variety of behavioral syndromes, some traditionally classified as psychiatric and others as neurological. They rightfully call themselves neuropsychiatrists.

There are even fewer opportunities for physicians becoming neuropsychiatrists by obtaining residency training in both psychiatry and neurology. This pathway may take up to 6 years, but unlike the neuropsychiatry fellows, these physicians can take their specialty boards in both medical fields. "Double-boarded" physicians are rare birds. They are also faced with the lack of communication between most psychiatry and neurology departments, so if they are to become neuropsychiatrists they need to self-integrate their training. As a reflection of this challenge, among these double-boarded practitioners, those who think of themselves primarily as neurologists sometimes refer to themselves as "behavioral neurologists." Those who think of themselves mostly as psychiatrists refer to themselves as neuropsychiatrists. Regardless of the self-image, most of the practitioners with the two pedigrees focus attention on patients with dementia, stroke, epilepsy, traumatic brain injury, or movement disorder, rather than the typical high-ticket psychiatric syndromes of mood disorder and psychosis. Double-boarded neuropsychiatrists commonly will superspecialize and focus on patients with only one of the more traditional conditions of neurology.

Then there are people like me. I am self-taught. That means I know a lot about a number of neurological topics, but these subjects were self-selected and so there are other areas of neuroscience that I should have learned but that I did not. A systematic approach to mastering a field is usually better than ad lib learning. However, when I began the learning process, there were no neuropsychiatry fellowships, no opportunities of dual training in neurology and psychiatry, and only a few opportunities to learn from a handful of like-minded biological psychiatrists and PhD neuropsychologists. The neuropsychiatry fellowships emerged in the 1980s and 1990s. They are nowhere near the critical mass needed to influence U.S. psychiatry.

My version of neuropsychiatry encompasses all the classic psychiatric syndromes such as psychosis, mania, depression, catatonia, obsessive-compulsive disorder, anxiety disorders, and more, plus the behavioral syndromes associated with conditions that psychiatrists over the twentieth century have mostly ceded to neurologists. These include dementia, stroke, epilepsy, traumatic brain injury, and movement disorder. What's the difference between the classic psychiatric syndromes and the behavioral syndromes associated with the classic neurological conditions? From my viewpoint, there is no fundamental difference. These syndromes all represent brain disease or dysfunction.

The basic science of neuropsychiatry from any of the above perspectives is neuropsychology. This discipline focuses upon the relationships between brain anatomy, neural functions, cognition, and behavior.[13] Neuropsychologists work in assessing patients with cognitive impairments associated with traditional neurological (e.g., traumatic brain injury, stroke) and psychiatric (e.g., depressive illness, psychosis) conditions. Their assessments help establish diagnosis, prognosis, and the shaping of treatments. Neuropsychologists also participate in rehabilitation programs for patients with traumatic brain injury, stroke, and degenerative brain diseases. Neuropsychologists also provide the basic research in our understanding of how the brain works on a macrolevel. Cognitive neuroscience is basic science neuropsychology.

THE PRINCIPLES OF NEUROPSYCHIATRY

The Mind Is Brain

The principles of neuropsychiatry from my perspective are easy to state, but for many difficult to accept. The most important is the most challenging. *The brain is the organ of the mind.* From this consideration, the mind is a short-hand term for what the brain is doing within our awareness. The mind is a metaphor rather than a biological entity. This is not semantics.

How a physician thinks of the brain–mind notion shapes diagnosis. I've detailed two patients who died because the physicians involved considered the mind as somehow different from the brain and thus believed that it required a different kind of assessment than what should be done to assess brain functioning.

Throughout our lives our healthy brains are functioning 24/7. They maintain our chemical and fluid balances (homeostasis), breathing, somatosensory processing, and much more. Unless our attention is specifically drawn to these functions, they occur out of our awareness and even then much occurs of which we have no subjective experience.[14] If I ask you to focus your attention on your rear-end and its relationship to the surface on which you are sitting (a necessary assumption for the exercise), you are suddenly aware of it and in some detail. Your somatosensory system was always aware of it but you were focused on other things. Throughout the day your brain is processing information of which you have no awareness or only marginal subjective experience. The brain process doesn't change with the refocus. It is not transformed from a biological brain process to a nonbiological mental process because of the refocus.

All "Mental" Experience Is in Reality Brain Processes

Brain processes that we commonly subjectively experience are traditionally termed "mental," but they are no less biological than the brain functions that occur out of our awareness. All such processes are neurophysiological and are subserved by process-specific neural structures.[15]

Language: Hearing someone speaking to you, responding in the same language, reading, and thinking words (even internal speech and your conversations with yourself) involve specific networks of neurons located in the left cerebral hemisphere in about 98% of humans. When a part of the language network is damaged, forms of aphasia or other language-related deficits emerge.[16]

Forms of memory: Much of working memory, the ability to briefly "hold" a small piece of information so it can be processed, is subserved by frontal lobe circuits. Working memory permits you to "remember" a phone number you are told until you can dial it. If the number is striking, such as 22-FLUSH for the plumber, you might easily transfer that information from your working to your long-term memory. If the information is more complex, you may have to rehearse the information to store it. Working memory is a necessary step to long-term storage and retrieval and it has several subsets that relate to the sensory modality in which the information is received.[17]

Many neuropsychiatric conditions adversely affect working memory and other aspects of memory and cognitive functioning. For example, working memory is perturbed when a person is in the depths of melancholia. Sufferers of this type of depressive illness have difficulties learning new information. This cognitive difficulty normalizes with recovery.[18]

Biographical memory is your life as you remember it. Declarative memory is information you have learned, such as the 50 U.S. states and their capitals, and this information you can recall, thus "declaring" that memory. Working memory also helps us bring up from storage information on which we need to "work." In Alzheimer's disease, the storage sites are directly affected. In frontal dementia, working memory is affected first. The stored information is still there but its availability is diminished. The difference between these two types of memory decline can be assessed, aiding in diagnosis.[19]

The different memory domains are subserved by different but overlapping neural networks.[20] Verbal and nonverbal declarative memory domains are also subserved by different neural structures. Verbal memory mostly involves left (dominant) hemisphere structures whereas nonverbal memory mostly involves right (nondominant) hemisphere structures. The dominant/nondominant terms, however, are misleading. One hemisphere doesn't control the other. The terms are vestiges from the era in which neurologists knew a bit about the language functions of the left hemisphere and called it "dominant" for language-related functions. They knew little about what the right hemisphere does, and so dubbed it "nondominant," which really meant "details to follow."

Implicit memory is memory that cannot be "declared"; it must be demonstrated.[21] If you can drive your car safely from one place to another that fact implies you have functioning memory of the rules of the road and how to drive a car. The memory is implied rather than stated or declared as in reciting a poem. The patient in Chapter 4 who lost the ability to knit and play the guitar suffered the loss of a form of implicit memory termed procedural memory. What could be more "mental" than learning how to play a musical instrument, reading music, playing on a guitar and singing a song, talking about the times you have played for others, and conversing with friends about music? Yet all these "mental" acts are supported by different brain structures and neural networks and when one or another of these structures or networks is damaged or diseased the sufferer exhibits features of that damage or disease that can delineate the general, if not the specific, location of the problem.

Function leads to location; location leads to cause: The location of the problematic brain area may also help in determining the cause of the difficulty.

Just as different geological areas are susceptible to different natural disasters, e.g., flooding in low lands near a river and forest fires in mountains, different areas of the brain are susceptible to different neuropathological disasters, e.g., herpes virus has an affinity for the temporal lobes; aneurysms are more common in the brain's anterior blood vessels near the base of the brain.[22] An area of the brain referred to as the retrosplenial system is located in the parietal lobes just behind the corpus callosum, a connecting bridge of nerve fibers between the two cerebral hemispheres. When viewed from the side the corpus callosum looks like the back end of a parenthesis ("close parenthesis") taking a nap. The downward back part of the curve is called the splenium. The region just behind it is therefore retrosplenial. The retrosplenial system stores "spatial maps," and when it is damaged or diseased, as in Alzheimer's disease, the sufferer loses the ability to learn spatial directions and forgets previously familiar routes.[23] The woman patient in Chapter 4 whose doctor was eating cherry pie while she was unable to recall the route from the dining room to her bedroom had a stroke that temporarily affected part of this system. Fortunately her brain was able to reorganize around the stroke area and regain much of that function. Had she been simply given her most likely *DSM* label of psychosis not otherwise specified (NOS), she would have received an antipsychotic that might have interfered with that reorganization.

A few years ago, I was asked to see a man in his mid-50s to ascertain if he was demented and if so, was he suffering from Alzheimer's disease. He had been in decline for a half-dozen years. The referring psychiatrist, a group of trainees, and I met the man in his hospital room. After the preliminary social greeting exchanges, which he did appropriately, I suggested that as we were a large group we move to a patient area room, "the room with the piano," at the other end of the inpatient unit. The route was circuitous and the man had just been admitted the night before. I asked him to lead us and he did so flawlessly. In doing so, he demonstrated adequate working memory, alertness, adequate spoken and receptive language, and that his retrosplenial system was capable of forming new maps and storing them. Patients with Alzheimer's dementia of several years duration will have difficulties in this domain. This is one reason why in nursing homes pictures of each patient are placed outside their rooms so that if they lose the "map" of the unit they may be able to recognize themselves and by extension their room. The patient leading us to the room with the piano also walked normally. Patients with early-onset Alzheimer's disease (i.e., onset in the 50s rather than the 70s or 80s) often experience increased muscle tension that alters their gait.

So, even before we all sat down to fully evaluate the patient, I was able to tell the referring psychiatrist that the man did not suffer from Alzheimer's disease. The pattern of his adequate functioning was not consistent with that diagnosis. Psychiatrists focus on symptoms, reflections of what is not working. Neuropsychiatry requires the focus to also include what is right with the patient. That tells us as much about the patient's brain functioning as do his symptoms. It turned out the patient in this story was in the early stages of primary frontal lobe atrophy, which has different implications for the patient and his family than if he had been suffering from Alzheimer's disease, which has a familial form.[24]

Emotion: The mind-as-brain construct also extends to our emotional life. The expression of an emotion consists of the subjective experience and the motor manifestations of that experience in tone of voice, posture, and facial expression that communicate to others the emotion that is being experienced. Some patients with brain damage to their nonlanguage frontal areas can still experience the emotion subjectively but cannot produce its motor expressions. They appear emotionally flat. One patient had to add profanity to the end of her comments to her family so they would know she was feeling a strong negative emotion. The term for this clinical feature is motor aprosodia. Other patients I have met who suffered strokes in their right frontal areas appeared so bland and avolitional that they were misdiagnosed as depressed. Needless antidepressant treatments followed.

The motor expression and subjective experience of an emotion are brain processes that are subserved by structures and networks that differ in part from those that recognize and make sense of the emotional expressions of others. If a patient cannot recognize the emotional states of others, he is said to have receptive aprosodia.[25] Patients in the later stages of Alzheimer's disease suffer from deterioration in these brain areas, misinterpret the emotional expressions of others as anxiety or anger, and become anxious and fearful in response. Behavioral strategies can minimize the miscommunication. For example, speaking clearly and softly in the voice's lower register while maintaining a relaxed posture can put patients at ease.

What all the above relationships come down to is that all thought, all so-called mental activity, no matter how poetic or philosophical, all ideas no matter how complex or lofty, all feelings and memories no matter how romantic or traumatic are products of our brains working. There is nothing else going on, but that is quite enough. This fundamental principle is the neuropsychiatric equivalent to evolution by natural selection as the fundamental principle of the origin of species. All else depends on it. There is no modern biology that is not based on evolution by natural selection.

There is no effective neuropsychiatric endeavor that is not based on the recognition that whatever the patient is doing and subjectively experiencing reflects the patient's brain doing something. Accepting the principle permits Ronald Reagan's missteps during his first debate with Jimmy Carter to be recognized as the harbingers of a terrible brain disease. It allows the patient from Chapter 4 who suffered through a fire to be seen as having frontal lobe apathy and procedural memory problems and not a stress disorder. He benefited from the correct understanding of his difficulties. Many of the patients described throughout this book were affected for their good or for ill by whether or not their behavioral change was recognized as reflecting a change in their brain function. The man in Chapter 2 with left-sided numbness died because the principle was not applied to his symptoms. The young woman, also in Chapter 2, who had a vascular malformation growing in her brain for years might be alive and well today had the principle not been violated. *Other than a few psychiatric residency programs and the handful of neuropsychiatry fellowships, almost none of what I have just detailed is taught to U.S. medical students and young physicians learning to be psychiatrists.*

The Main Function of the Human Brain Is to Generate Behavior

Once the fundamental idea is accepted that there is no mind, only brain, it becomes clearer that *the main function of the human brain is the generation of complex nonstereotypic behavior.* The complexity of human behavior is not obvious when we read the news of politicians acting like monkeys, but even they do more than the stereotypic behaviors characteristic of many species. We humans can alter our behavior as we experience the world about us. Even though other primates appear to have behaviors similar to ours in their expression of emotion, communications, and social interactions, our behaviors are at least more elaborate if not more functional than theirs.[26] We speak more elaborately. We write and read. We construct intricate tools and create objects for pleasure and philosophic inspiration. Our proclivities design and establish customs. All of this is brain-derived.

The fact that our brains are constructed mostly for the generation of these complex nonstereotypic behaviors is recognized when the brains of different species are compared.[27] Most animal species on our planet (e.g., Mayflies, ants, worms) have little or no brains. Yet these creatures maintain their physiological balance, move about, acquire nutrients, escape danger, and protect themselves. They find mates and procreate. Ants build elaborate living quarters and have a complex social order, raise their young, and forage for food. Some ant species go on the warpath. Some ant species are farmers growing fungi for their kids. They and most invertebrates do all the basic behaviors without brains or just nubs of neural tissue. Birds do all their complex behaviors with bird brains. The bird brain is similar to our brain stems and mid brain structures plus a rudimentary cortex and cerebellum. Canines in the wild live in small-group social orders, hunt in coordinated packs, and when trained hunt with humans. They fetch, play Frisbee, and can do elaborate circus tricks. Their brain is only slightly larger than that of birds. Primates, particularly apes, have many individual and social behaviors that are prototypes of ours. Their cerebral hemispheres and cerebellum are bigger than those of canines, but are relatively smaller than ours. They also do all the basics. The human brain, in contrast, is substantially proportionally larger and more elaborate than the brains of these other creatures and with more complex microarchitecture. The difference is mostly in the cerebral hemispheres, particularly in the frontal and parietal lobes, and in the cerebellar neocortices.[28] These regions are the largest parts of our brains and they are clearly not needed for the basics. As far as anyone has been able to ascertain, the primary anatomic differences from other vertebrates to primates to humans is to generate nonstereotypic behavior. Among humans, the behavior is species-specific, extremely complex, and yet remarkably malleable. The ability has permitted us to survive as a species.

The evolution of the human brain is notable beyond the increase in the size and organization of the cerebral hemispheres and the cerebellar neocortex. Older structures that function in other species continue those functions in humans but these older structures have also acquired additional roles as they interact with the further evolved human-specific structures. For example, the basal ganglia, located deep in the forebrain, help regulate movement in many species. There is little evidence that the left and right groupings of the basal ganglia have different functions in these other species. In humans, however, they do. The left grouping in humans has acquired language functions and is involved in conversational speech. When the basal ganglia are damaged, speech becomes halting and word finding becomes more difficult. Depression-like syndromes may emerge. In studies of patients who have been designated as having "treatment-resistant depression" about 10% are not suffering from depressive illness but from damage to their brain that produces symptoms that overlap those of depressive illness. The patient who suffered from carbon monoxide poisoning that mostly affected his basal ganglia is an example of such a patient.[29]

The Most Common Expression of
Brain Disease Is Behavioral Change

The additional human-specific functions that have evolved for many of the brain's older structures, the continuation of the basic behavioral functions of these structures, and the expansion of the cerebral hemispheres and cerebellar neocortex as generators of our most complex and wide-ranging behaviors mean that *most of the mass of the human brain is devoted to behavioral generation*. This translates clinically to mean that *behavior change is the most common expression of brain disease*. Popular science and movies and TV have alerted the public to some of the classic features of stroke such as one-sided paralysis and the speech loss and dysfunction of the aphasias. What is not well recognized is that most pathological processes in the brain do not elicit paralysis, the common aphasias, or the classic reflexes that fill neurology textbooks. These pathological brain processes most often elicit changes in behavior and cognition. Understanding this and using it clinically are the basis of the neuropsychiatry I believe U.S. psychiatry must adopt to survive.

Two patients immediately come to mind whose brain disease revealed itself from behavioral change and not from "neurological symptoms." The first was a 33-year-old woman who was experiencing a depression-like syndrome for about 6 months. Antidepressant medications had no effect on her symptoms, which were marked by reduced volition and apathy. She slept excessively and gained weight despite saying that she had no appetite. Without relief, she became demoralized and thought she was a "hopeless case" and would "be better off dead." A general medical examination found her in "good health." A standard neurological examination also found her to be "without neurological disease." Unfortunately, the standard neurological examination performed by most psychiatric evaluators assesses the structures found in the bird brain. I rarely see a psychiatric evaluation that comments on the functioning of a patient's different cerebral hemisphere lobes or their cerebellar cognitive functions. So this patient was not adequately examined and was diagnosed as having "major depressive disorder." A neuropsychiatric examination, however, found that she had poor motor regulatory functioning that was worse in her preferred right hand (indicating left frontal problems), and deficits in her abilities to make decisions, switch cognitive sets, generate words and ideas, and make plans (more indicators of left frontal problems). These findings along with her significant behavioral change indicated structural brain disease. A magnetic resonance imaging (MRI) revealed a large but operable tumor filling much of her left frontal lobe.[30]

The second patient was a middle-aged man who began to experience auditory hallucinations and delusions of being poisoned. He was angry at the voices and became irritable with his family. He was psychiatrically hospitalized and both the general medical and standard neurological examinations reported him to be "in good general health." The neuropsychiatric examination, however, found him to be unshaven on the left side of his face only. When asked about this, he said he was letting his sideburns grow. When challenged that the right sideburn was shaved much shorter than the left, he became angry. He refused to look in a mirror. On a test of copying a house with a fence and tree on each side, he omitted the objects on the left of the house. This and his odd grooming were recognized as examples of left spatial neglect and were indicative of a right parietal lobe lesion. He also was unable to copy geometric shapes. Poor visual-motor coordination, an intact function that is required in the copying of shapes, is another example of right-sided brain dysfunction. His denial of illness was also consistent with a right parietal lobe problem. A computed tomography (CT) scan revealed a subdural hematoma (a blood clot under the fibrous covering of the brain) over his right parietal lobe. Once it was removed surgically and he was recovered from his "psychosis," we learned that while in his home office it was his habit to lean back in his desk chair and that one day he lost his balance and the chair tilted too far back so that the man hit his head on the corner of a wall bookshelf incurring the subdural bleed.[31]

The Human Brain: Overlapping But Also Distinct Functional Networks

To be a neuropsychiatrist requires practicing from the perspective I have described. To do it well, also requires an understanding of how the brain works on a macrolevel. Over the past 40 years, neuroscientists have clarified the macrounderstanding that the human brain is composed of functional brain systems or networks. There is now popular awareness that the two cerebral hemispheres are involved in different functions. In 98% of us, the left hemisphere is organized for most language tasks whereas the right hemisphere is better at nonverbal visual-spatial processing. I was able to recognize the location of the stroke in the "Cherry Pie" lady in Chapter 4 based on this understanding and the relationship of different forms of psychopathology to the different hemispheric functions.

But the brain is more complicated than a simple left or right. There are a number of functional brain networks and each has its signature signs and symptoms. Each network is composed of components that also have their signature signs and symptoms. The networks also neuroanatomically overlap. Knowing and recognizing the signature signs and symptoms and their associated psychopathology are the hallmarks of neuropsychiatric diagnosis. The different brain functional networks also have different vulnerabilities (e.g., head trauma often affects the frontal lobes). Knowing the vulnerabilities also helps with syndromal diagnosis and also in establishing the cause of the patient's condition.[32]

Awareness of the different networks and what they do aids in distinguishing patients with different forms of depressive illness and in prescribing the most efficacious treatments for these patients. Patients with melancholic depression can be understood as being in a limbic "storm." The limbic system is an evolutionarily old part of the human brain, although it does both old (engages in flight or fight under stressful or dangerous circumstances) and new things (decodes language). It's name means border, and it looks like a concentric series of arcs (amygdala and hippocampus; fornex) and deeper structures (septum, thalamus) underlying the lower border of the cerebral cortex. Patients with melancholia have many features associated with perturbations in the limbic system such as emotional dysregulation and disruption in sleep cycles, appetite, and libido. They experience memory and perceptual distortions. No amount of talking will relieve sufferers from this form of depressive illness. They do best with electroconvulsive therapy (ECT), tricyclic antidepressants (TCAs), and lithium as an enhancing agent.[33] Patients with nonmelancholic, characterlogical depressions are not in a limbic storm but have temperament traits that under stress are associated with maladaptive pessimism and other nonspecific features of depression such as low self-esteem. These patients do not respond to ECT, TCAs, or for that matter to any antidepressants. They do better with cognitive interventions.[34] U.S. psychiatry pays little attention to these differences, and endorses the idea that all depressions are the same condition differing only in severity and thus all patients with a depression should be treated basically alike.

Trying to figure out the brain implications of a patient's behaviors as a step in diagnosing persons who are classified as having a psychiatric disorder seems at first novel. But this is the typical diagnostic approach to diseases in other organs of the body. The gastrointestinal (GI) tract is a good analogy. The overall function of the GI tract is to ingest and assimilate nutrients and eliminate waste. When the system is diseased there are almost always sufficient signs and symptoms of dysfunctional input, assimilation, or output to alert the physician that the patient has a GI problem. Many pathophysiological processes and causes affect the GI system. But the GI system, like the brain, is composed of components that have different functions that support the GI tract's overall function. These components have their own signature signs and symptoms permitting the GI dysfunction to be localized to the liver, or esophagus, or large bowel as specific examples. Different diseases affect the different components. Thus a more refined diagnosis is possible and a more specific etiology can often be determined. This process of disease identification can be applied to the brain and its behavioral syndromes as long as the brain is treated as a body organ and not as a metaphysical mind.

All Behavior, Normal and Abnormal, Is Grist for the Diagnostic Mill

Once the above brain–behavior relationships are understood and accepted, the practice of clinical psychiatry is fundamentally and dramatically altered. It reveals that *all behavior, normal, deviant, and pathological, is an expression of brain function.* Thus, *all behavior becomes diagnostically relevant.* Knowing the brain–behavior relationships delineates which functional brain networks are working well and which are not. From the pattern syndromes emerge. From the syndromes a differential diagnostic list can be formulated. The choices on the list can be further assessed and the most likely choice can be selected. The selection leads to the most specific treatments we presently have available. The *DSM* becomes clinically irrelevant except as a source for labels and numbers required by regulatory agencies and insurance companies. The extension of the *DSM*, the mental status examination, a term used to denote what clinicians are supposed to do when assessing the behavior of psychiatric patients, becomes a meaningless phrase. There is no "mental." The process should be entitled "the behavioral examination of the brain."

The choice of what to call an examination at first seems superficial. It is not. Along with the term "mental status examination," comes the baggage of the *DSM* superficial and often vague terminology that U.S. psychiatry has accepted. U.S. psychiatry has also rejected neurology's terms for some of the same brain functions that psychiatrists are still required to assess. Psychiatrists and neurologists, for example, describe a patient's language functioning totally differently from one another: same patient, same utterances, but different terms. The neurologist's goal is to determine if there is a localized brain lesion that explains any language difficulty the patient may exhibit. From that effort may come the determination of the etiology of the patient's difficulty. To this end, the neurologist's descriptors of language are reasonably precise and focus on structural elements of language as well as its content. Thus the neurologist considers the patient's speech spontaneity, fluency, articulation, word usage, and syntax. Naming, recognizing, reading, and writing are also assessed in the good neurologist's evaluation of a patient's language.[35] The good neurologist wants to get to the bottom of the problem.

Ironically, when U.S. psychiatric thinking was dominated by psychodynamic theory, the goal of the psychiatrist's interactions with the patient was also to get to the bottom of the problem. The problem was assumed to be a psychic perturbation. The task was to discover the perturbation through the patient's behaviors. Every behavioral detail was important to consider. Once psychiatry devolved into a primary care specialty, however, the underlying problem was no longer as relevant. It is now important to establish the *DSM* diagnosis as quickly as possible and then apply the related treatment formula. *DSM* terminology is the diagnostic currency. If the patient's symptoms match a few *DSM* features, that becomes the bottom of the problem. The present-day U.S. psychiatrist's assessment of a patient's language functioning, for example, is limited to terms such as "disorganized" and "confused." These terms have no syndrome, disease, or neuroanatomic specificity. They are merely terms that satisfy some criteria in the *DSM*.

THE BIOPSYCHOSOCIAL REGRESSION

The Brain Is Ignored

As more and more psychiatrists practiced within the *DSM* system and spent most of their time prescribing medications, the leaders in the field looked longingly in the rearview psychodynamic mirror and mandated that psychiatric evaluations become "formulations" harkening back to the psychoanalytic model. To further mold their thinking, resident physicians are now required to produce a "formulation" not just a diagnosis. The formulation is termed "biopsychosocial." At first glance the idea of this amalgam looks good. Wouldn't we all want our physicians to know about our social situations and inner turmoil as well as our illness? The problem with it, however, is that it muddies the water and diverts the attention of the psychiatric physician away from what should be the main clinical issue when a patient experiences a substantial and adverse behavioral change. What has happened to that patient's brain needs to be the initial focus.

Unfortunately, the "bio" part of the phrase really has to do with the *DSM* diagnosis, and that has no direct bearing on what may have happened to the patient's brain. Although general medical and neurological disorder is supposed to be part of the "bio," that assessment is typically minimal for these important concerns. The "psycho" part of the phrase has to do with the putative psychodynamics or psychology of the situation. Again, the brain is ignored and there are disciplines other than psychiatry that better train their care givers at therapy. In addition, they provide their care for less cost. The "social" part of the biopsychosocial phrase relates to the patient's family, home, job, and related concerns. This area of the patient's life is extremely important. Stressful situations at home can precipitate illnesses of all kinds and can trigger relapses among psychiatric patients. Although important, concentrating on the patient's social and interpersonal environment does not directly address the brain problem that the patient may be having. Also, when these concerns require the most knowledgeable and skilled interventions, psychiatric social workers are commonly given that responsibility. They deal with the patient's social concerns better than do most psychiatrists and they are trained to deliver supportive psychotherapies; they provide both for less cost than do psychiatrists.

The Birdbrain Neurological Examination Is Adopted

At a teaching hospital, trainees commonly write the findings of their patient evaluations in a series of standard sections in the chart or electronic record. In the past decade I have read many of these history and physicals or "H and Ps." As mandated, they all contain a large biopsychosocial section. The records rarely, however, contain an adequate neurological examination and what neurological assessment is done is typically focused on the neural structures found in a bird's brain. Most cognitive functioning related to the human cerebral cortex is not mentioned. Fine motor skills and motor regulation are not assessed. A stick figure graphing the patient's reflexes is the most that is offered, but whether your knee jerks or not when hit by a reflex hammer will bear little relevance to most behavioral conditions.

The evaluations also rarely contain a neuropsychiatric assessment and a search for behaviors that signal specific brain problems. The records might mention that the patient had a head injury, but details are lacking and the sequella of the head injury are almost never mentioned. For example, different brain injuries occur depending on whether the patient's head is moving into the impact as in a fall or whether the patient's head is stationary and receives the impact as in a mugging.[36] Most sport fans are now aware of the long-term consequences of sports-related concussions. U.S. psychiatry must have missed that news because if a patient received such an injury, the presence or absence of the possible consequences of a concussion is rarely mentioned. Patients with postconcussion syndrome can be misdiagnosed as suffering from a depression or anxiety disorder and thus not properly treated for the lingering physiological effects of the head injury. For some patients, the fatigue, dizziness, headache, anxiety, and depressive features of the head injury can become chronic.[37]

An evaluation for seizures is rarely done. Those seizure evaluations that are offered are typically inadequate. A single waking electroencephalogram (EEG), the best to hope for in an evaluation by most U.S. psychiatrists, is insufficient to capture seizures in about 20% of patients with seizure disorder. Seizure disorder is associated with episodes of psychosis that can be mistaken for schizophrenia, leading to the wrong treatments for the patient.[38]

The Devil May Be in the Details, but the Details Are Often Missing

I occasionally see outpatients for a second or third opinion. Like patients in the 1920s and 1930s, most of these referred patients do not receive general medical and neurological examinations as part of their psychiatric evaluations. The psychiatrists that see them assume that some other physician has considered these domains, but if there is no evidence to that effect, the psychiatrist rarely performs these evaluations or makes sure that they are accomplished *before* seeing the patient, permitting a differential diagnosis.

In many evaluations, even the details of alcohol abuse and street drug use are not considered other than from a social perspective. The amounts, frequency of use, and health consequences of the use are rarely reviewed. The evaluations are less detailed and helpful than what residents had to do 45 years ago. The low level of detail is what is done at most teaching hospital centers in the United States. On rounds at another medical facility a few years ago, the residents insisted that the patient we were about to meet was not an alcoholic despite a history that would encourage any internist to examine the man's liver. The residents insisted that the patient had only one drink daily. The residents, however, did not know what was in that one drink or its size. We entered the room and there before us was a middle-aged man who looked like every skid-row alcoholic depicted on TV or in the movies, but he did indeed swear that he only had one drink daily. It was vodka, no ice. I asked him to stop me when my hands were as far apart as the size of the one glass. The distance he endorsed indicated a 36-ounce container. Psychiatric residents today are not trained to get this degree of detail, even though it can, as in this patient's situation, be confirming of a diagnosis. They are not trained to pay attention to the patient's image. There are no images in the *DSM*, so they ignored the man's appearance, which would have been a dead give-away to any TV watcher.

Here's another example of why the present level of practice is inadequate and how applying neuropsychiatric principles and getting the details are necessary.

A woman in her sixties living in a nursing home had an extended history of manic-depression, but had been well for some time. Over a week, however, she exhibited a substantial behavioral change. She was uncharacteristically irritable and became agitated. She was unable to sleep and was said to be "disorganized" in her speech (the *DSM* term) and "confused" (another *DSM* term). She was said to not know the date or where she was. A recurrence of mania was diagnosed.

It is not unreasonable to consider that a patient's change in health status is related to the patient's long-standing recurrent condition. Thus, it was a distinct possibility that the patient had relapsed into mania. Psychiatric disorder, however, does not protect a patient from other diseases. And it is a sad fact that patients with a psychiatric disorder who then have a substantial behavioral change are commonly considered to have psychiatrically relapsed rather than to have experienced a different problem, regardless of the evidence to that effect. Most medical students are taught this potential misstep and how to avoid it, and many medical school graduates (i.e., MDs) make the mistake anyway. One of the major causes of such a mistake is applying the imprecise *DSM* terminology and not considering the need to get to the bottom of the problem.

So, given the conclusion that the patient had relapsed into another mania, she was sent to an inpatient psychiatric facility. I met her there. Unlike the psychiatrist at the nursing home, I examined her from a neuropsychiatric perspective. This approach was not applied because I had some sudden insight about the patient. I applied it because that is what I do. I found the patient's speech, which had been described only as "disorganized" and "confused," to be spontaneous and fluent, with no dysarthria, meaning normal articulation. She, however, was often paraphasic. For example, she called a pen an "ink thing" and a wristwatch a "timer." She exhibited several agrammatisms as some of her utterances made little sense, like double-talk. She used the incorrect sounds to form some words resulting in neologisms (i.e., new words). She could repeat simple phrases, but at times she was nonsequitive in her conversational responses. She had naming problems and was circumloculatory, i.e., giving round about explanations or the function of an object rather than specifically naming the object. She did not have circumstantial speech or flight-of-ideas that are typical of mania.[39] Her speech, however, was typical for a form of aphasia termed transcortical sensory aphasia. Given the suddenness of her behavioral change I concluded that she had not had a relapse of mania but had suffered a stroke. Brain imaging documented the clinical diagnosis.

Fortunately for this patient, her stroke was not due to a brain hemorrhage. This type of stroke occurs about 20% of the time. Her stroke was ischemic, the result of a blockage or spasm in a brain blood vessel. Because much of her symptoms resolved spontaneously over the next week, she had technically suffered from a RIND, reversible ischemic neurological disorder.[40]

The big deal about this patient's story, however, is that many such vascular events do not spontaneously resolve and can lead to permanent and substantial disability if not treated within a few hours of the beginning of the event. Patients do best when the blood clot that causes the ischemia is dissolved within 90 minutes. Because this patient's stroke was missed she never had the opportunity to have her stroke addressed acutely. Fortunately she recovered and was not permanently impaired. But as long as the mental status is the psychiatric examination, other such patients will not be as lucky.

NEUROPSYCHIATRY MARGINALIZED

Given the widely recognized inadequacies of the *DSM* system and the ineffectiveness of the treatment algorithms U.S. psychiatrists are encouraged to use, contrasted with the patients who have benefited from a neuropsychiatric approach, it seems extraordinary that neuropsychiatry is not what most U.S. psychiatrists practice. So, what happened to marginalize it?

Freudians and Psychiatry Rejected the Medical Model

Before the Freudian revolution, a primitive version of modern neuropsychiatry was the full scope of the discipline of psychiatry. Psychiatrists and neurologists often cared for patients with similar disorders. Freud had training as a neuropathologist with Meynert in Vienna and spent a fellowship year in Paris with that city's most famous neurologist, Jean-Martin Charcot.

A significant distinction between psychiatrists and neurologists in the second half of the nineteenth century, however, was turf and focus. Psychiatrists mostly practiced within the growing number of large asylums located outside of urban centers. Patients with syphilis-related behavioral syndromes, epilepsy, and what became recognized as manic-depression were their primary concerns. Their interventions gravitated to custodial care and rehabilitation. Neurologists kept to the cities and cared for patients with traumatic brain injuries, stroke, and muscle-related and peripheral nerve disorders. The last gives us the term "neurosis" and patients with these conditions (e.g., anxiety disorders, "hysteria") were also treated by neurologists. They searched for medical treatments for their patients. The breech widened when the two groups fought over control of the asylums. Neurologists argued that "insanity" was a neurological condition best treated by neurological means. But as they had no treatments to offer, psychiatrists maintained control of the "mentally ill."[41]

The final split between neurology and psychiatry may have been inevitable, but Freud certainly hastened the rupture as psychiatrists increasingly embraced psychoanalytic concepts and terminology. Psychiatrists accepted metaphysics as their framework for understanding behavior whereas neurologists focused their attention on the brain. This fundamental difference in the appreciation of human behavior has shaped the two medical specialties and continues to keep them at arms lengths of each other. Ironically, many psychiatrists left the asylums and the most severely ill of patients anyway, and embraced the neuroses as psychological phenomena.

Although neurologists continued to consider behavioral disorders from the medical model perspectice,[42] U.S. psychiatrists adopted the Freudian metaphysical model. We put patients on couches and let them free-associate. Wearing a doctor's coat and carrying a stethoscope were taboo. At the medical center I work at now, psychiatrists are the only physicians who see acutely ill patients but who do not routinely carry stethoscopes and reflex hammers. Many of us rely on someone else actually examining the patient from that perspective. As a resident over 45 years ago, medical examinations by psychiatrists were also shunned because touching patients was given symbolic significance that might elicit psychic trauma. We had medical students do the "PG-13"-rated general medical history and physical. If a patient had an illness that affected the body between the naval and the upper thigh, the patient was on his own. That body territory was taboo to psychiatric concern other than from a psychodynamic perspective. The injunction was, always ask about the patient's sex life, but never about bowel movements, unless you were a child psychiatrist. Child psychiatrists wanted to know about fecal retention and bed-wetting as reflections of parental–child psychic difficulties. The only "test" that was acceptable was the unreliable and never validated Rorschach ink blots.[43] Patients who didn't recover within a few weeks were sent to state hospitals. There, they languished in those monuments to despair. Many never left Manhattan State, the New York State mental hospital I rotated through as a resident. The long stays were more the result of poor diagnosis and care rather than treatment-resistant disease. If patients were EuroAmerican, rich, and not as severely ill, they were advised to sign into one of the prestigious psychoanalytic clinics dotting the United States. They might spend years in the Menninger Clinic in Topeka, Kansas[44] or the Austin Riggs Institute in Stockbridge, Massachusetts, shrines to Freud, where patients are still exposed to various brands of psychotherapy.

On my first day as a psychiatric resident, one of the inpatients went into heart failure. I had just finished my year-long rotating internship at Lenox Hill Hospital in New York City and so I had treated a number of patients with acute cardiac problems. No one else on the psychiatry service seemed to know what to do, so I stabilized and treated the patient until he was transferred to the medical service several hours later. I would have passed muster on ER. There was no such thing as a critical care or intensive care unit in those days. I was "it" that late afternoon. I recall feeling pretty good about my skills in treating that patient.

A few years later, in its myopia, U.S. psychiatry eliminated the medical internship as a prerequisite for joining a psychiatry residency. Today, graduates of U.S. medical schools can go directly into a psychiatric residency. In the first year of these residencies, they gain 4 months of general medical experience and 2 months of neurology. These experiences are not a sufficient foundation to provide acute general medical care to psychiatric patients. Although psychiatric residents know a lot, because they typically work in medical centers with specialists literally around every corner and more types of ICUs than all of New York City had when I was taking care of that patient on our psychiatry unit, psychiatric residents today don't have to have that capability. Others will do what they cannot. What skills they do have when they enter psychiatry will quickly erode. By the time I finished my residency 3 years after I saved that inpatient's life, I would not have been prepared to save another person's life who had suffered an acute cardiac event. Most psychiatrists are in the same boat. Continued training in how to respond to acute medical problems should be required of all psychiatrists who see patients.

Perhaps psychiatry's stepping away from medicine explains to some extent why plays, novels, and movies offered the psychoanalyst version of U.S. psychiatry to the public. It's the only psychiatry that most creative people experienced. In the play and movie *Harvey*, Jimmy Stuart is committed to an Austin Riggs-like psychoanalytic institute for befriending a large magical rabbit. In the movie version of *Arsenic and Old Lace* Cary

Grant commits his brother, who believes he is Teddy Roosevelt, to a psychotherapy center for life. The heroine in *Splendor in the Grass* is analyzed for over a year in a Menninger-like complex for her depressive illness. When medical psychiatric treatments were finally developed, beginning with convulsive therapy in 1936 and then psychotropic medications beginning in 1954, practitioners of these methods either also became analysts or they were marginalized.

After two wars with Germany, that country's psychiatric tradition was suspect in the United States. Psychiatric diagnosis and classification were demonized as "Germanic" and those psychiatrists interested in the medical model were denounced as having fascist proclivities. Several of my professors referred to the German psychiatrist Emil Kraepelin, one of the creators of the modern psychiatric classification system, as "a Nazi" because Kraepelin considered dementia praecox and manic-depression to have substantial genetic components and the Nazi had all sorts of notions about genes and psychiatric disorder. It took the field almost a century to catch up to Kraepelin and now the idea that many behavioral syndromes are associated with a genetic component is generally accepted.

Biological Psychiatry: A Microchemical Approach to Macrofunctioning Brain Networks

The identification of neurotransmitter systems and neuroendocrine substances, beginning in the 1960s, and the development of related pharmaceuticals to ameliorate the severest behavioral syndromes offered psychiatry an opportunity to embrace the medical model and to consider psychiatric disorders as brain dysfunctions.[45] Had the medical model been adapted, it would have been a conceptual sea-change for psychiatry. However, this approach was not accepted. Biological psychiatry focused on the neurochemical brain and microbrain structures. Its universe was the synaptic junction, the tiny space between two communicating neurons. It offered no explanation for why people sometimes do strange things other than "You have a chemical imbalance."

Psychodynamics also remained the center of training and thus the existential heart of the field because academic departments were controlled by analysts. In the 1960s all psychiatric residents were expected to provide dynamic psychotherapy to acutely ill hospitalized patients. Some academics were enamored with John Rosen's "Direct Analysis." In this odd perspective the patient's delusions were to be endorsed by the therapist and then together the therapist and patient would logically pursue a way out of the delusion.[46] Patient's of course got worse, but in that era any notion proposed by a well-known analyst was accepted as legitimate. No scientific proof was needed. How else can we explain the patient abuse inflicted by primal scream therapy that "returned the patient to the uterus" and then a birth simulation via a non-Olympic size swimming pool, or psychodrama in which the "director" led the patient "actors" through cathartic scenes that would have been the envy of Eugene O'Neal? In 2012, psychiatric residents in our program are required to trek from their patient care clinics and hospital to the local psychoanalytic institute for supervision of their intensive-treatment psychodynamic patients. The analogy in an internal medicine residency would be learning how to administer poultices (a concocted paste applied to the skin) and blood-letting to normalize the perturbed bodily humors of their patients.

However, to give lip service to the emerging knowledge of neurochemistry and psychopharmacology, department divisions were established in the 1960s and 1970s for researchers interested in biological psychiatry. There was no training mandate to learn this perspective other than to know how to use psychiatric medications to treat patients with depression or psychosis. Mania was not recognized in most of the United States in the 1960s. When my colleagues and I published a series of papers demonstrating that mania was not uncommon and could be readily identified and treated, I was approached by several members from the prestigious department of psychiatry at Washington University in St. Louis who wanted to know where we had learned about manic-depression. They thought they were the only group in the United States that recognized the syndrome.

Other than depression and psychosis, all other psychiatric syndromes were considered by many of the leading figures in U.S. psychiatry of that era to be behavioral reflections of underlying psychic perturbations that required psychodynamic interventions. Male homosexuality was a pet analytic interest.[47] Freud wasn't interested in female homosexuality, so neither were the analysts who adopted Freudian perspectives. One notion of male homosexuality was that it resulted from the impact of a boy growing up with a domineering mother and a weak father. The idea was that the boy would psychically recognize that the mother had metaphysically castrated the father and would also castrate him if he acted masculine. The best psychic strategy was to shun female genitalia, which had "teeth," and identify with the aggressor mother. One of my professors was a leading exponent of another psychodynamic conclusion that opined that male homosexuality resulted from an unresolved Oedipal complex. To avoid the jealous father castrating him (by one theory or the other his genitalia were in danger), the boy changes his sexual orientation proclaiming no interest in sleeping with his mother and thus defuses the father's rage.

Homosexuality was removed as a medical diagnosis from the *DSM* in the 1970s. It was no longer to be considered a disease. The change was championed by, among others, Alfred Freedman, the chairman of my department of psychiatry while I was a resident and young faculty member. The APA membership that voted for the removal, however, did so for sociopolitical reasons rather than because of the scientific evidence or any established principle of disease classification. The science, mostly established since the change, supports the removal of homosexuality as a disease. The APA, however, in the removal, referred to homosexuality as a "life-style choice" rather than what science tells us is a human biologically determined variant.[48] The use of the touchy-feely term has had unexpected consequences as the religious right has locked onto the idea of choice and therefore has concluded that homosexuals could have a heterosexual orientation if they wished. That is nonsense. Psychiatry did, however, have a choice of deciding what is or is not a disease based on science not politics. In my lifetime it has mostly chosen politics.

Biological psychiatry started out as a medical adjunct and potential alternative to metaphysical psychiatry. But even at its peak, biological psychiatry as practiced in the United States was never interested in the brain from a macrolevel, until recently. It focused on the functional communication structures between neurons and the neurochemicals that inhabit these synaptic systems. Biological psychiatry themes were neurochemistry and psychopharmacology and not functioning brain networks and behavior. The official diagnostic system of psychiatric patients was never influenced by biological psychiatry. Biological psychiatry encouraged further research into the biology of psychiatric syndromes, but it was irrelevant to the formulation of psychiatric classification. Other than the few guidelines it offered in the use of psychiatric medications, biological psychiatry's impact on clinical practice was providing some rationale for using medical treatments for patients suffering from psychiatric disorder. Everyday clinical psychopharmacology, however, was accomplished by following the rules of pharmacology not neuropsychiatry.

The Decline of Skilled Clinical Psychopharmacology Further Limits Biological Psychiatry

By the 1980s, however, the rules of clinical psychopharmacology were only superficially taught and psychiatric clinicians followed simplistic algorithms. I routinely ask residents and medical students about how to dose and prescribe psychiatric medications. Over the past decade I can't recall any resident who routinely followed the pharmacology rules I was taught as a resident and that still apply. Several writers have severely criticized the present cookbook approach.[49]

Within two decades of its emergence biological psychiatry devolved into a pharmaceutical industry-manipulated prescription practice that relies on the atheoretical *DSM*. Treatment reverted to symptom-based, rather than illness-based prescription. If the patient reports hearing voices, an antipsychotic is prescribed. If the patient reports feeling sad, an antidepressant is required. If the patient cannot sleep, a sleep aid is ordered. If the patient reports feeling anxious, an antianxiety agent is prescribed. If all these symptoms are endorsed by the patient, all four classes of drugs will be utilized even if the different symptoms derive from the same illness that could be treated with one agent. Target symptom-based treatment guarantees inappropriate polypharmacy. Its efficacy is poor whereas side effect risks are substantial.[50]

As biological psychiatry devolved into a restricted form of primary care medicine, neuropsychiatry became further marginalized because the *DSM-III* rejected the medical model as a classification schema. Too many "disorders" would have been expunged as invalid. Political, not scientific, considerations stymied the proposal to base the highly anticipated *DSM-III* on the medical model.[51] The *DSM-III* version that was finally approved in 1980 was designed to be more reliable than its predecessors but uncommitted to any conceptual paradigm, thus making it acceptable to the diverse APA constituencies (e.g., see *DSM-III*, pp. 1–14).

The atheoretical *DSM* system avoids complexity and reduces diagnostic criteria to short lists of brief descriptors to formulate a diagnosis. The clinician asks a few questions based on the list and once the patient endorses the required number of features that match one of the lists, that's what the patient is said to have. The present generation of psychiatrists accepts this method as the diagnostic standard in their education because that is what their supervisors accept. The trainees are not taught to recognize classic syndromes nor the heterogeneity in the major diagnostic categories.[52]

BACK TO THE FUTURE

Knowledge about Functional Brain Networks and Their Signature Behaviors Is Not Taught or Applied to Psychiatric Clinical Care

To care for patients with complex behavioral syndromes requires clinical skills to identify the diagnostic, neurological, and neurophysiological implications of a broad range of psychopathology. Such knowledge is not available within the *DSM*. The application of the medical model to behavioral syndromes also requires an understanding of functional brain networks and their signature behaviors. This information is almost never taught in psychiatric residencies and when there is a seminar series devoted to these brain networks and their signature behaviors, there is never a critical mass of faculty that knows about the topic to permit trainees to use the information in their day-to-day care of patients. Previous chapters detail patients whose illnesses were identified by recognizing the diagnostic and neurological meaning of Capgras syndrome, spatial neglect, psychosensory features, catatonia, and loss of procedural memory, among others. None of these features are mentioned in the *DSM*. Many other patients could be added to this list whose correct diagnosis and effective treatment hinged on recognizing the illness implications of their experiences. A young woman I met as a resident who was a few days postpartum and who became panic-stricken because she suddenly saw objects in her hospital room becoming larger and then smaller as if she were seeing the world through a repeatedly shifting camera zoom lens was experiencing seizures. She recovered with anticonvulsant treatment.[53] A young man who was arrested by the police for running about the streets on all fours growling like a wolf and trying to bite people was catatonic. He recovered with ECT.[54] These patients' features are also not mentioned in the *DSM*.

Behavioral syndromes that are established in the neurological literature are not represented in the *DSM*. Not having the syndromal image to compare to patients elicits incorrect diagnoses or the meaningless "not otherwise specified (NOS)" label. Most *DSM* categories offer this option when the clinician thinks the patient may fit into a large category but does not know what illness within that category the patient has. So, we have "psychosis, NOS," "Mood disorder, NOS," and so on. It's analogous to your physician telling you that you probably have an infection, but she doesn't know what kind or really what to do about it.

Examples of well-established behavioral syndromes not in the *DSM* are numerous. Not considering these syndromes can lead to misdiagnosis. Frontal lobe apathetic and disinhibited syndromes give, respectively, a false impression of depression and mania and the needless prescription of antidepressants and mood stabilizers. Frontal lobe and temporal lobe seizures may evoke a psychotic disorder label and incorrectly elicit the prescription of multiple classes of psychiatric medications or ECT.[55] Classic psychopathological syndromes (e.g., catatonia, melancholia, and hebephrenia) are inadequately detailed, leading to misdiagnosis and inappropriate treatment. The prevalence of diagnostic errors in psychiatric practice is widespread.[56]

Several previous chapters describe a number of teenagers who were incorrectly diagnosed and who did not receive optimal treatment. Their classic features of frontal lobe seizures were unrecognized because their psychiatrists were not taught to recognize these features. The patient in Chapter 4 who was exposed to carbon monoxide is an example of another frontal lobe syndrome that was not recognized because his treaters were unaware that such a syndrome existed.

Psychopathology beyond the *DSM* Is Not Taught or Familiar to Many Practicing Psychiatrists

To successfully use the medical model in psychiatric diagnosis also requires examination skills beyond what is taught from the superficial *DSM* perspective. In that perspective, all behavioral syndromes said to afflict humans are considered as listed in the manual and all the signs and symptoms needed to diagnose all the syndromes are presented. There is implicitly no need for further knowledge about psychopathology. Both premises are patently false. For example, in addition to not including the various neurological conditions that present with substantial behavioral change, most of the various forms of psychopathology are not mentioned in the manual. Psychiatric residents will need to look elsewhere if they are to learn this information.[57]

Surveys of psychiatry residency training programs reveal that classical psychopathology, other than as minimal phenomena cited in the *DSM* framework, is not widely or extensively taught in postgraduate training programs in the United States.[58] Commentators have repeatedly cautioned clinicians against the reliance for diagnosis on *DSM* criteria other than as a tool to assign the required label and number identification for charting, statistical, and reimbursement purposes.[59] But without applying *DSM* diagnoses, residents cannot graduate from their training programs, residency graduates cannot pass their specialty boards, and clinicians cannot be reimbursed for services. The *DSM* must be used despite all the evidence that it is not a very good diagnostic system.

Several U.S. psychiatrists recognize the decline in psychiatric skills of diagnosis and treatment. Among these critics, Nancy Andreasen, professor of psychiatry at The University of Iowa, and former chief editor of *The American Journal of Psychiatry*, the American Psychiatric Association's official peer-reviewed medical journal, attributes the blame to the simplistic *DSM* and associated treatment algorithms.[60]

Department chairmen and their residency directors could have accepted the *DSM* as a necessary documentation tool while still teaching adequate psychopathology, but they have not done this. I don't think the majority of the leaders of academic departments of psychiatry recognize the shortcomings. They have accepted the *DSM* and the treatment algorithms and do not require teaching of diagnosis and medical management beyond this level other than for psychotherapy. The accrediting body of U.S. residency programs has mandated that programs provide extensive training in psychodynamic psychotherapy but barely mentions neuropsychiatry.[61] Most psychiatric residents accept the psychotherapy teaching mandate as an essential part of their training.[62] They do not clamor for more neuropsychiatry. They have little idea what it is. In a survey of the numerous psychiatric residents in New York City, a staggering 57% of the respondents said that they were personally receiving treatment in psychotherapy or psychoanalysis and that for them, *taking a psychotropic medication was a stigma to be avoided.*[63] These figures indicate a vortex of ignorance centers in area code 212. Either residency directors there are recruiting the behaviorally walking wounded or they are creating so much angst among their trainees that treatment is felt necessary. That their residents also believe that taking a psychiatric medication is stigmatizing is depressing. That attitude will inhibit their appropriate prescribing of medications for their patients and it will be sensed by their patients leading to reduced compliance.

Unfortunately, the only thing that seems to matter to department leaders is that their residents pass the required standardized national tests and then pass their board certification examinations. These are the validators of what they do. The examinations, however, are written by these same department leaders or their designees, the champions of the *DSM*, and the creators of the cookbook psychopharmacology algorithms residents are required to learn and use. The tautology is obvious. Residents are taught mediocre psychiatry and then the same teachers craft "independent" examinations to ensure that mediocre psychiatry is learned. If most of the residents pass the tests and obtain certification, the teaching is considered to have been successful. The patient care standard, however, remains mediocre.

"Green Shoots"

Some clinical faculty members, however, recognize the limitations of standard U.S. training because these clinicians are challenged daily by patients whose psychopathology goes beyond the *DSM* and who also exhibit behaviors reflective of specific brain dysfunction. These clinical faculty crave this information and when they have an opportunity to learn about these topics, they take advantage of it and use the information in their care of patients. But a few clinical junior faculty members trying to apply neuropsychiatric principles and sophisticated psychopathology to psychiatric diagnosis are not a sufficient force to change their departments' attitudes, let alone their specialty's value system.

A few neuropsychiatrists in the United States have tried to assist, and have criticized the field for not training psychiatry residents in neuropsychiatry. Efforts to address this training shortcoming have focused on encouraging greater emphasis on neurology experiences[64] and on offering additional subspecialty training (e.g., geriatric psychiatry) for interested residents. The present requirement is 2 months of neurology experience in the first postgraduate year without additional training in movement, cognitive, and seizure disorders. These are common problem areas among hospitalized psychiatric patients and many geriatric patients. Trainees receive no practical training in brain imaging and EEG. They know the hospital procedures for ordering such tests, but they do not know the many indications for the tests or how to interpret the meaning of the results obtained. They leave all that to neurologists.[65] Subspecialty training is also unlikely to substantially change the diagnostic paradigm used by trainees because subspecialty core competencies differ minimally from those of general psychiatric residency programs; they all rely on the *DSM* system (e.g., see the on-line proposed competencies for geriatric and psychosomatic fellowships). Proposals for fellowships in behavioral neurology and neuropsychiatry are directed at the "willing few," so most psychiatric residents learn little about these overlapping views of behavioral syndromes.[66]

Additional alternatives to the present training program model have been offered. Integration of neurology and psychiatry[67] or merging psychiatry, neurology, and neuropsychology[68] into a single specialty of neuropsychiatry has been proposed. Joint fellowships in behavioral neurology and neuropsychiatry are described (e.g., see the proposed curriculum in the *Journal of Neuropsychiatry and Clinical Neuroscience*, 2006). But although these proposals emphasize the need to understand the common neuropsychiatric conditions (e.g., dementia, seizure disorder), they do not address how the neuropsychiatric practitioner is to function within the *DSM* system or how neuropsychiatry will be integrated into clinical practice.[69]

As long as the *DSM* is the accepted diagnostic paradigm, it will be taught and used, guaranteeing another generation of psychiatrists with no more skills at diagnosis and patient care than other providers whose services can be obtained for less cost. How long will it take before the more expensive services of clinical psychiatrists are completely rejected in the marketplace? Is it not likely that the profession of clinical psychiatry will fade as has psychoanalysis or be degraded to the status of a nonmedical profession? By the end of the twenty-first century the discipline of general clinical psychiatry is likely to disappear as we know it. Whether a marginalized discipline of neuropsychiatry can take the place of the present version of U.S. psychiatry will depend on the profession embracing the medical model of diagnosis as its core methodology.

Summing Up

The future of psychiatry is unclear and psychiatry trainees are somewhat aware of this and are rightly concerned. From that angst, I was asked to write an essay for the residents in my old department. I was asked to write something "inspiring." I was to accomplish this in 250 words for their brief newsletter. I told them, however, that inspiration would be hard to achieve because I had bad news as well as good news.

I gave them the bad news first. I described how psychiatry is in the doldrums. That the *DSM*, although a good money maker for the APA, is a diagnostically unhelpful document and other than those working on version five, I know of no expert on psychiatric diagnosis who thinks it should be used for other than its labels and numbers so that cloistered librarians, bean-counting administrators, and miserly insurers don't have fits. And, of course, trainees need to know it to pass tests. I told them that the argument that it provides a "common language" is baloney. Gibberish spoken by all is still gibberish. I went on that even worse than the *DSM*, once the patient is given one of its labels, they were being taught to then apply cookbook treatment algorithms as if making a pie. The system is so easy that psychologists lobby to prescribe medications and about 85% of psychiatric patients in the United States receive treatment from nonpsychiatrists. Who needs us, I asked, when others can do the same mediocre job for less cost? The trend is for the field to disappear.

Had I had room, I would have offered the story of the following patient that encompasses so much of what is wrong with U.S. psychiatry today.

The patient was in her fifties when I met her. She had an extensive psychiatric history with many hospitalizations. She was once again hospitalized, this time for a severe depression. On previous admissions and on the admission during which I met her, she was given the following discharge psychiatric diagnoses: major depressive disorder (recurrent, severe, with

psychotic features), schizophrenia (paranoid type), conversion disorder with psychogenic blindness, and borderline personality disorder. If
there ever was an example of nonsense this combination of diagnoses is
it. Schizophrenics do not have emotional ups and downs and lead stormy
lives as required to be labeled "borderline." Although schizophrenics may
experience a depressive-like syndrome early in the course of their illness,
they do not experience psychotic depressions later in life. These conditions
are considered to result from different pathophysiologies, but none of her
treaters over the years wondered about this paradox or tried to make sense
of it. One rule of diagnosis that works well, however, is the rule of parsi-
mony. The rule encourages the effort to find the fewest number of explanations for the patient's difficulties because if that number can be reduced to
one, treatments are likely to be easier and more effective. In this situation,
I tried unsuccessfully to convince her inpatient psychiatrist that the single
explanation was manic-depression.

Because I have a bias against the conversion diagnosis, I asked if I might
examine the patient and was grudgingly given permission. The details
the patient provided me solidified my view that she suffered from manic-
depression. Her "paranoid schizophrenia" episodes were misdiagnosed
manias, a common error in the field my colleagues and I reported in the
1970s. Her "borderline personality" was the emotional breakthroughs of
poorly treated manic-depression. Manic-depressives most often suffer from
the depression phase of the illness and her recent psychotic depression was
consistent with that finding. During her depressions she also experienced
the racing thoughts and irritability associated with the depressive phase
of manic-depression. Her diagnosis and treatments were as bad as those I
had seen four decades ago. For years she had suffered from an illness that
explained most of her difficulties, yet she was never treated for it.[70] She was
also given the "borderline" label, which is the somewhat polite term psychiatric care givers employ to let each other know that they think the patient
is unpleasant. Borderline personality is nonsense made official.[71]

But, it gets worse. The patient was an obese woman who wore sunglasses
and walked about the inpatient unit using a visually impaired person's red-
tipped white cane. I watched her eat lunch and she was clearly impaired.
She said that she saw shadows and could make out outlines of objects but
nothing more. She said her visual experience was like "being in a darkened
room." This visual problem was interpreted by *all* her previous treaters as a
conversion disorder of psychogenic blindness. Now to diagnose any condition as "psychogenic" the examiner is supposed to rule out pathology that
might explain the "psychic" symptoms. In this patient's case, other than a

visual examination performed years before (on which they could find no eye pathology), *no other assessment was done.*

I also learned from the patient that she had suffered a serious closed-head injury 20 years earlier *before* her visual problems began. Shortly after that injury she said she was told that she had a seizure disorder. Also since the injury, she experienced migraines. These headaches were now occurring weekly, with occasional periods of daily incapacitating headaches. Sure enough, in her records she was listed as having a history of a traumatic brain injury, a seizure diagnosis, and migraine. An MRI several years before was reported to show diffuse loss of brain volume. *No one paid any attention to this information.* When I suggested that her erratic mood states could be a combination of manic-depression and the results of a brain injury, the conclusion was rejected by her treaters.[72] When I pointed out that migraines are associated with visual difficulties that present exactly like those the patient was experiencing, that the visual problems could last for hours or days after a headache, and that with frequent migraines the visual problems could overlap or become constant, this conclusion was also dismissed.[73] When I had a neuroophthalmologist examine her and he found deficits in the perception of visual frequency that are commonly problematic with migraine, nothing was done about it.[74] The patient was treated as if she were the villain in the story. It was her fault she had the mood swings. It was her fault that her "psyche" was perturbed. It was her fault that she didn't do as her physicians demanded and "give up" her conversion. She was discharged with the same ridiculous diagnoses that she had been receiving for over a decade, somewhat better from her depression that was triggered by a family crisis, but no better off in the long run. This is U.S. psychiatry today and is clearly bad news.

After I summarized the bad news for the residents in my little essay, I then gave them my "good news." Had I had room, I would have started out by telling them about the following patient. This patient's difficulties illustrate that despite the flaws and limits in the care of persons with behavioral syndromes, being knowledgeable in the fields of psychopathology and neuropsychiatry and employing the medical model of disease to psychiatric patients can lead to a "happy ending."

This patient was in her forties when the consultation psychiatry team first met her. She was hospitalized on the neurology service because she had experienced a rapid and substantial "behavioral change." Other than stating that she was "confused, very emotional, and perseverating on unexpressed guilt-ridden thoughts," the only other description of her behavior was that she could no longer care for herself and "was very slow and disorganized in her activities of daily living." Six months before this hospitalization she was admitted for similar vaguely described behavioral problems, and with the concurrence of a psychiatric consultant who saw her on that admission, she was said to have a frontal lobe dementia. That psychiatrist did not believe that the patient was suffering from "a primary psychiatric disorder." This means that he believed that her behavior was the result of a specific neurological pathophysiological process and not just a *DSM* syndrome.

When "the story" of the patient's illness is so vague and the treaters are not prepared to get the story, the only avenue left is to order a zillion dollars worth of laboratory tests in the hope that one of the tests will provide the answer that most likely could have been obtained by a careful history and behavioral examination. This patient also had a history of autoimmune hepatitis[75] that had recently exacerbated as her liver function had somewhat declined, so trying to link the behavior to her known illness was in itself reasonable. For that exacerbation, she had received a large steroid dose, and steroids are a known trigger of abnormal mood states and delirium.[76]

The tests that were done assessed a wide range of disorders from infection and infestation to other autoimmune conditions to stroke to metabolic disorders and vitamin deficiencies and degenerative brain disease. All the tests, including two EEGs that were read as normal, were unhelpful other than the fact that the indicators of her autoimmune hepatitis were now within normal limits making that condition an unlikely explanation of her present problem. An MRI, however, showed her to have cerebellar atrophy. But other than this being the likely cause of some gait difficulties (the need to walk with a wide-base and the inability to walk heel to toe), it was also not believed to explain her present state. The remainder of the traditional neurological examination revealed no other dysfunctions. She did, however, do poorly on a paper and pencil test of cognition (price about two bucks at your local supermarket) and from this evidence of cognitive decline and her behavior, the neurologists concluded that she was experiencing a "hepatic encephalopathy, steroid psychosis, and a rapidly progressive dementia." What dementia she was said to be experiencing was not opined. Dementia, however, is not a definitive diagnosis. It is a condition that requires a more specific diagnosis because it has many causes, some of them treatable. Medical students learn this, but some physicians forget it.

Because the patient was thought to be suffering from a steroid-induced psychosis, the psychiatry service was again consulted. One of our consultation psychiatrists saw the patient, elicited several signs of catatonia, and then asked me to see the patient.

We met the patient in her hospital room. She was sitting on her bed staring blankly at empty space. Her hygiene was at best fair, she was somewhat disheveled, and was dressed in sweatpants and two hospital gowns. Her responses were markedly delayed and she had difficulty focusing on the simplest of tasks. She looked like a person who was dazed, but she was not on sedating medications and had not just awakened. This is an image of a patient in a benign stupor and it is a classic sign of catatonia. A person in such a state will perform in the dementia range on cognitive tests.

The patient had many other features of catatonia that were observable. For example, she remained in positions for prolonged periods but her limbs could be manipulated. She resisted these manipulations with equal force to the effort to move her, a form of catatonic negativism. I elicited automatic obedience as despite instructions to the contrary she obeyed my touch as if magnetic. When I moved her arm in several circles and then stopped, she continued the movement until restrained. Her speech was slow, whispered, and toward the end of an utterance it trailed off into an incomprehensible mumble, another classic sign of catatonia.

Sitting to the side of such patients rather than directly facing them, and then whispering so as not to inhibit then from speaking, sometimes avoids catatonic negativism. When a patient doesn't respond to a care giver, the tendency is to get in their face and speak louder, but such a strategy will freeze a patient with catatonia. Perhaps because of this approach, she was able to tell us that she was greatly distressed. She became more interactive and quietly cried. She said she was despondent and feared that she had done "bad" things in the past and was not being "good" to her family. She was also fearful that she was in danger and that she was going to be imprisoned.[77]

We concluded that the patient was suffering from a psychotic depression with catatonia and that although the steroids may have made her condition worse it was not the cause of her depressive illness. We considered the cerebellar atrophy to be unrelated to her present state. She had likely been descending into her melancholia for some time rather than the abrupt image the neurologists saw. Her husband confirmed this with the consultation psychiatrist. His wife had been irritable for months before the recent hospitalizations became necessary and they had been in marriage counseling because of it. She also had a family history of mood disorder. Knowledge of psychopathology and neuropsychiatry merged to permit our conclusions. Getting the patient's story and the story of her illness was also critical.We treated this patient with ECT and after a short course, all her symptoms resolved. No more "encephalopathy," no more "rapidly progressive dementia," and no more "steroid psychosis." She went home to her family happy and resumed her life.

The best part of this story is that I am being called less and less by the consultation psychiatrists. Learning psychopathology and neuropsychiatry is not reserved for the elite few. Any psychiatrist who recognizes the shortcomings of our field and who is willing to put in the effort to be better than the field can learn the information and acquire the skills to care for patients similar to those I've described in this recollection.

I ended my essay for the residents with the following. "You have free will. You will not be jailed, exiled, or condemned for practicing better than the average psychiatrist. In fact, if you learn the databases and skills of neuropsychiatry and apply these in a caring thoughtful manner, admittedly harder than the *DSM* alternative, you will be admired by your peers and your patients, and you will prosper. It's your choice. Don't you want to be proud of the person in the mirror?" The same question goes for all the psychiatrists in the United States now teaching medical students and residents and also caring for patients.

Evolution by natural selection impacts individuals. If enough individual members of a species have a selective advantage over individuals of another species that occupy the same environmental niche increasing numbers of the individuals with the selective advantage will survive and procreate producing other individuals with that advantage. Ultimately the species with the individuals with the advantage will survive and perhaps supplant the less advantaged competitor species.

Psychiatrists who practice no better than generalist physicians have no advantage. They are also hampered by the disadvantage of being more expensive to maintain. They are being supplanted and with them the specialty. U.S. psychiatry as presently practiced will most likely disappear from the health care environment. Neuropsychiatry, however, offers a clear advantage. Every neuropsychiatrist I know has thrived. Those who went into academic medicine have done well and are highly regarded as clinicians and as teachers. The first of these that I helped train began their neuropsychiatric careers in the 1970s. The latest began his career 2 years ago. Those that have entered private practice fill up their clinical time quickly. An early graduate of my residency program in Illinois went to practice on his own in southern Wisconsin. As is typical for physicians new to a practice, most of the early referrals he received consisted of the most difficult patients of others who had done their best for the patients and were now looking to give the new guy on the block a shot. One of these patients struck my residency graduate as having a classic psychosensory seizure disorder and not just a treatment-resistant mood disorder. He ordered an EEG and asked the EEG laboratory to specifically target the temporal lobes in their assessment. A few days later, my graduate received a call from one of the hospital's neurologists, who asked, *"How did you know?"* My graduate told him that he was taught to look at behavior from that perspective. By the end of his first year he needed to take on a partner as his referrals arrived in droves. His story is not unique. The many patients in this book attest to the need for the neuropsychiatry perspective and when a neuropsychiatrist is available, his or her expertise is highly valued. Several of my present colleagues have adopted this perspective and are the kind of younger psychiatrists who could save the specialty.

What is needed, however, is more of us. The field, like most institutional organisms, is static and is unlikely to change, but individuals can change and make a difference. The resident who insisted that the chief of radiology send his portable X-ray machine to her unit to help assess her patient and the resident who bucked her supervisor and the consulting neurologist and sat on her unit waiting for her patient to have an episode so she could obtain a serum prolactin level to document her patient's seizures are examples of how individuals can make a big difference. All the patients our consultation and ECT teams help when other services have given up are further proof that individuals can change the field. We have gotten seemingly "hopeless" patients better. Some who eventually walked out of the hospital having recovered literally had their hospice papers on their bedstands. Several of the consultation psychiatrists refer to these individuals as our "Lazarus" patients. If psychiatry is also to rise from the dead, survive, and flourish, we will need more physicians such as these consultants and their counterparts elsewhere. With enough of them, the tipping point can be reached and the inadequate psychiatry of the present can be supplanted by the neuropsychiatry of the future.

NOTES

INTRODUCTION

1. There are several medical traditions. Ancient and recent Hindu medical tradition is voluminous, developed independently from the Greek, and reached many similar conclusions. Older writings understood psychiatric disorders from a metaphysical perspective. Arabian medicine offers familiar descriptions of several psychiatric syndromes.

    Western thoughts about behavioral illness and its treatments were formalized by Greek physicians who detailed familiar images of epilepsy, mania, melancholia, paranoia, hysteria, alcohol-related and toxic states, and dementia. Some considered psychiatric disease to originate in the head. The great Roman physician (of Greek origin) *Galen* (130–200 CE) also considered behavioral conditions to reflect brain disorder. Classifications of behavioral syndromes followed his formulations until the mid-nineteenth century, with perturbations in pulse and fever the main guidelines for separating syndromes. Epilepsies were well delineated. Melancholia was an established disorder and was understood to include episodes of mania. Catatonic stupor was reported. A user-friendly history of psychiatry is Shorter (2005).

2. William Osler (1849–1919) was a Canadian physician who immigrated to the United States and became one of the founding professors at Johns Hopkins Hospital. He was the hospital's first Professor of Medicine and founder of the Medical Service. Osler created the first residency program for specialty training of physicians, and he was the first in the United States to bring medical students out of the lecture hall for bedside clinical training. He has been called the "Father of modern medicine." Many of the guidelines to practice advanced in this book reflect Osler's writings and several are quoted.

3. The versions of the Hippocratic Oath detailed in the introduction come from, where else? Wikipedia.

CHAPTER 1: THE ORIGINS OF INDIGNATION

1. Righteous indignation or righteous anger is a term that derives from the Christian notion of anger being sinful. However, because some acts are so terrible, to respond to them with anger in moderation is warranted. Jesus' anger at various inequities is the model for righteous anger. The moderation part is what's hard.

2. The medical school was again purchased, this time by a Jewish Orthodox school, Touro College, a countrywide organization with about 19,000 students. See *New York Times* article, March 5, 2012, by Richard Perez-Pena.

3. Medical students would never be permitted to do today what I was required to do as a student. Residents are also closely supervised. Hospitals pay close attention to this supervision and require a confirming statement on the record by the supervising attending so insurance will pay the fee and the accreditation agencies won't have hissy fits.
4. Motor abnormalities are common among patients with behavioral syndromes (Fink and Taylor, 2003).
5. Louis "Jolly" West was Chief of Psychiatry at Lackland Air Force Base in San Antonio, Texas. He studied U.S. pilots and veterans who had been tortured and brainwashed as prisoners in the Korean War. Because of his interest in brainwashing, he served as an expert witness in the Patty Hearst kidnapping case. In 1962, he studied the phenomenon of *musth*, a period of extremely high testosterone levels in male elephants, by administering LSD to a bull elephant at the Lincoln Park Zoo in Oklahoma City. The elephant died. At age 29, West was appointed professor and head of the Department of Psychiatry, Neurology and Bio-behavioral Sciences at the University of Oklahoma School of Medicine, making him the youngest person to have held a chairmanship in psychiatry in the United States. In 1969 he was appointed head of the department and director of the Neuropsychiatry Institute at UCLA.
6. The pneumoencephalogram was introduced in 1919. It caused discomfort and its resolution was coarse by today's imaging standards. It was replaced by CT imaging in 1971 and by MRI in the early 1980s (Hoeffner *et al.*, 2012).
7. Halstead and Wepman, 1949; Fiskov and Goldstein, 1974.
8. The evidence against the efficacy of psychoanalysis was marshaled by several behavior therapists. Their work was extremely influential in the development of biological psychiatrists and neuropsychiatrists. See Eysenk and Rachman, 1965; Wolpe and Lazarus, 1966.
9. Wilkinson, 1986.
10. Anonymous, 1984. The British National Health Service still reimburses for other psychotherapies but at low rates. It favors cognitive-behavior therapy over psychodynamic forms, indicates that the main indications for these interventions are personality and stress disorders, and encourages patients interested in those services to seek treatment from private providers (NHS choices website 2012).
11. Marshall *et al.*, 1996.
12. Gray, 2002.
13. Leichsenring, 2005; Leichsenring *et al.*, 2006.
14. Mullen, 1989.
15. To secure medical officers for the Department of Defense on a more equitable basis, Congress, in September 1950, passed public law 779, the so-called "Doctor Draft Law." This act, in essence, removed physicians and related professional persons from the general manpower pool, and established them as a separate pool of "special registrants." The law was crafted by Dr. Frank Berry, the Assistant Secretary of Defense (Health and Medical), and was then named for him (Council on National Security; Berry Plan History).
16. Normal pressure hydrocephaly is characterized by ataxia (unsteadiness of gait), urinary incontinence, and substantial cognitive or behavioral changes. It is relieved by a surgical shunt from the brain ventricles into the blood venus system (Price and Tucker, 1977; Siedlecki, 2008).
17. The book is the *Comprehensive Textbook of Psychiatry*. It is now in its 10th edition. The first edition was created in the Department of Psychiatry at New York

Medical College in 1968 when I was a resident. The first editors were Alfred Freedman (my chairman) and Harold Kaplan (my residency director). Everyone knew, however, that Harold Kaplan's wife, Edith, did most of the editing. She also taught psychopharmacology to us. Kaplan and Benjamin Sadock (our group therapy guru) somehow acquired the textbook from Freedman and took themselves and it to New York University. When Kaplan died, Sadock's wife assumed the co-editor spot. I have never liked the book. It has always been filled with the standard "party line."

18. The Viet Nam War, lasting 11 years, was the longest war in U.S. history, depending on how we count the years of the present Afghan war. The Viet Nam War was never declared by congress. However, 3.4 million Americans served in the Southeast Asia theater, and 2.5 served in South Viet Nam.
19. The literature on the brain-damaging effects of hallucinogens in rodents and in developing brains is substantial. Similar studies in adult humans are less common and the results are less dramatic but indicative of permanent dysfunction. See Grant and Judd, 1976; Grant *et al.*, 1978; Strassman, 1984; Miller, 1985; O'Malley *et al.*, 1992; Nestor *et al.*, 2008; Gouzoulis-Mayfrank and Daumann, 2009.
20. Wolfensberger, 1958, Watson, 1965; Simpson and Vega, 1971.
21. Ruddle and Bradshaw, 1982; Hart *et al.*, 1986.
22. Helzer *et al.*, 1987; Brewin *et al.*, 2012.
23. Gurvits *et al.*, 2006.
24. Toward the end of his life Freud conceded that psychoanalysis was less of an effective treatment and more of a self-exploration process. The Michigan Psychoanalytic Institute in Ann Arbor lists 37 members, only 13 of whom are MDs, consistent with the loss of relevance of psychoanalysis nationally to the practice of psychiatry other than as a teaching requirement in psychiatric residency programs. University of Michigan psychiatric residents must go there for supervision and some take electives there.

Behavior therapy was the first systematic challenge to psychoanalysis. This intervention derives from learning theories and classic conditioning paradigms developed by Ivan Pavlov and championed by B. F. Skinner. Early proponents of behavior therapy were Joseph Wolpe and Hans Eysenk. In the 1960s they marshaled the evidence demonstrating that psychoanalysis was no better than a waiting list experience for the treatment for phobias and other "neurotic" disorders. Based on reward or no reward (not punishment), Skinner's ideas were adapted in the residential treatment of persons with developmental disorders (termed token economies). Combining relaxation techniques with imagined and then actual incremental exposure to feared objects and situations, systematic desensitization was used to successfully treat phobias, panic disorder, and, to a lesser extent, obsessive-compulsive disorders.

Cognitive behavior therapy (CBT), developed by Albert Ellis and Aaron Beck, was introduced to treat depression. It employs problem-solving collaboration between the therapist and patient focusing on dysfunctional emotions, behaviors, and cognitions through goal-oriented systematically applied procedures. As with all treatments, the quality of its application varies and its proponents' claims of its usefulness in treating a wide range of conditions go beyond the treatment's capacity. It does little for the severe forms of melancholia and manic-depression (Taylor and Fink, 2006). There are now variations of CBT said to help persons with personality disorder, substance abuse, and eating disorder.

Interpersonal psychotherapy (IT) is a time-limited, highly structured intervention (it uses a stepwise manual) designed to improve interpersonal skills among persons with difficulties in that area of life. Because almost every psychiatric disorder is associated with interpersonal difficulties at some point during the course of the illness, IT has been applied to a variety of nonpsychotic patient groups. It was developed by Gerald Klerman and Myrna Weismann in the 1970s. Its proponents insist that it works for problems of living that result from personality disorder or psychiatric illness, but it does not directly treat such conditions.

25. Alexandra Luria was a famous Russian neuropsychologist whose work was seminal in understanding the cognitive and behavioral functions of various brain networks. His *Working Brain* should be required reading for all psychiatric residents. See Luria, 1976.

CHAPTER 2: FIRST DO NO HARM

1. A tube from the outside of the throat into the windpipe permitting the suctioning of secretions in the patient's airway and to permit the attachment of a respirator. No patient I suctioned that night was on a respirator.
2. Psychologists in several states have repeatedly, but as yet unsuccessfully, lobbied legislatures to permit their licensing to prescribe medications (Pies, 2010).

Several colleagues of mine were denied positions, including myself. One of my professors was denied a position as a department chair because of his biological perspective.

3. A classic textbook on denial of illness, distortion of one's body image, and loss of awareness of one's body is McDonald Critchley's wonderful 1953 monograph on the parietal lobes. Delusions of one's body rotting away or of being dead is also termed *Cotard syndrome* and is a feature of psychotic depression. See Critchley, 1953.
4. Vinik, 2003; Duncan, 1996.
5. Migraine is associated with many somatosensory and perceptual symptoms. Over the course of the illness, headaches may become less burdensome while the other features recur undiminished leading to many clinicians mistaking these features for hysteria or even psychosis. For the association between migraine and astasia abasia, see Kuhn *et al.*, 1997.
6. Dubois, 1905.
7. Pollmann *et al.*, 2004.
8. Venna and Sabin, 1992.
9. The human brain is best considered a collection of functional neural networks or systems. These groupings of anatomic structures function together to express the wide repertoire of human behavior. Each system has its characteristic functions and behavioral expressions. Each network is composed of component parts some of which also have characteristic behavioral expressions. These associations permit the identification and localization of brain lesions based on behavioral and other features.

Some networks and component parts are connected by groups of axon bridges, fasciculi, and commissures. The largest of these bridges, the corpus callosum, connects the two cerebral hemispheres helping them coordinate their different functions. When one of these bridges is damaged, usually by a stroke, it may disconnect systems or components within a system resulting in a very specific pattern of dysfunction. These patterns are termed "disconnection syndromes."

For example, damage to the posterior corpus callosum and the left posterior parietal lobe can disconnect the visual system in the occipital lobe from the language decoding system in the temporal and parietal lobes, eliciting a syndrome of alexia without agraphia. The patient can write (no agraphia) but cannot read what he has written (alexia). See Mulroy *et al.*, 2011.

10. One of the functional brain systems outlined in note 9 is composed of five frontal lobe circuits in each frontal lobe that originate from specific frontal cortical areas and project to circuit-dedicated nuclei in the basal ganglia, then to circuit-dedicated nuclei in the thalamus, and then back to the cortical area of origin. When diseased, these circuits are associated with circuit-specific frontal lobe syndromes. The cerebellum and its partner below it, the pons, are connected to the frontal circuits through the thalamus. Disease in the cerebellum can therefore be associated with frontal lobe syndromes. Some investigators refer to a "cerebellar cognitive affective syndrome" (Verhoeven *et al.*, 2012). Frontal brain areas function as the brain's CEO. Thus, the term "executive functioning" is used to describe "frontal lobe functions" (Alexander *et al.*, 1990; Chow and Cummings, 1999; Allen *et al.*, 2005).

11. Despite all the high-tech machinery now used in medicine, nothing as yet has replaced a careful history and physical examination for identifying the causes of the patient's difficulties. Cerebellar dysfunction is associated with highly specific signs and symptoms that are readily revealed on examination. The woman in the conference exhibited ataxia of her head, trunk, and limbs (unsteadiness of movement), intention tremor (shaking when doing a task but not at rest), dysdiodocokinesia (unable to perform rapid alternating movements), nystagmus (fluttering of the pupils), dysarthria (distorted word articulation), and past-pointing or dysmetria (overshooting a target object when asked to touch it). A fourth-year medical student will not graduate if he or she cannot demonstrate how to examine a patient for these features. Most U.S. psychiatrists therefore once could. Some cannot now, and most make no effort to do so.

12. Executive function is also easily tested at the bedside. See Taylor and Atre Vaidya, 2009, Chapter 13.

13. See the discussion in Taylor and Fink, 2006, pp. 22–23.

14. Postictal catalepsy (immobility often with rigidity) and stupor (a half-asleep state) are well-established sequela of some seizures. Physicians unaware of these conditions can mistakenly believe that the patient is being uncooperative, malingering, or hysteric. That the neurologists of a prestigious U.S. academic department missed this syndrome illustrates the profound bias they attach to all things "psychiatric."

15. See Piper and Merskey, 2004; Pehlivanturk and Unal, 2002; Moene *et al.*, 2000; Devinsky *et al.*, 1989.

16. Gould *et al.*, 1986.

17. Krem, 2004.

18. Factor *et al.*, 1995; Stone *et al.*, 2004; Taylor and Fink, 2006.

19. Aybek *et al.*, 2008; Ellenstein *et al.*, 2011.

20. For a detailed discussion of the history of psychiatric diagnosis see Taylor and Vaidya, 2009, Chapter 2.

21. Chlorpromazine (Thorazine) was introduced in 1954 as an antipsychotic. Its chemical class, phenothiazines, had been developed in the 1930s for the treatment of GI parasites. Chlorpromazine was hailed as the miracle treatment for schizophrenia, and indeed many long-term hospitalized patients with psychosis

who received the medication were able to return to their communities. A careful reading of the original paper, however, indicates that most of the patients in the first reported series were not schizophrenic but rather suffered from manic-depression, a much more treatment-responsive condition. Being lucky often trumps being right. With all the promotions for new antipsychotics, chlorpromazine has fallen out of favor, but it still works as well as it ever did. For historical discussions of the evolution and then decline of U.S. psychopharmacology, see Ban *et al*, 2002; Healy, 2002; Shorter, 1997.

22. See Taylor *et al.*, 1974; Abrams *et al.*, 1974.

23. The *DSM* does not recognize melancholia as a separate form of depressive illness. My colleague Max Fink and I marshaled the evidence for melancholia as a distinct depressive illness requiring specific treatments in our textbook on melancholia (Taylor and Fink, 2006). Many other psychiatrists share our perspective. See Parker *et al.*, 2010.

24. Sierles *et al.*, 1986.

25. Seltzer, 1994; Sarbin, 1995.

26. McHugh, 2005. For a discussion of the changes in who is counted as being depressed, see Taylor and Fink, 2006. For a full discussion of the problems with the *DSM* see Taylor and Atre Vaidya, 2009.

27. Gartlehner *et al.*, 2011.

28. Despite several laboratory aids and EEG assessments, epilepsy remains a diagnosis identified clinically. Knowing the phases of a seizure process and the behavioral expressions of each phase is essential in this quest. See Taylor, 1999, Chapter 10, pp. 298–324.

29. The creators of the *DSM* applied the "idiot's veto" in its design of a short list of features for each condition that they deemed sufficient to diagnose patients with behavioral syndromes. In the process they ignored many neurological conditions that present with behavioral change and the enormous range of psychopathology that must be considered to correctly diagnosis patients. Most U.S. psychiatrists are unaware of many of these phenomena. See Taylor and Atre Vaidya, 2009.

30. Findings from many studies using a variety of methods have converged to delineate an image of schizophrenia more in keeping with its original description as "hebephrenia" (Taylor *et al.*, 2010). This condition has an emergence similar to a developmental disorder with early childhood motor, cognitive, emotional, and socialization deviations. The onset of the characteristic psychosis is commonly in the late teens, recurrence is common, and general functioning is chronically reduced even when the striking features of hallucinations and delusions are no longer present. Risk factors include a family history of depression and psychosis, the heavy use of cannabis in adolescence, labor and delivery difficulties associated with poor oxygenation of the fetus and newborn (anoxia), and maternal starvation or exposure to an influenza virus during pregnancy. Low-dose antipsychotic treatment helps resolve the psychoses, but the model indicates that the best response to the illness is better prenatal care and childhood rehabilitation programs once the early, prepsychotic features begin to emerge (Taylor, 1999, Chapter 9, pp. 271–277).

31. Fink and Taylor, 2003.

32. Glick *et al.*, 2009.

33. Once-daily lithium dosing at night is well-tolerated (Abraham *et al.*, 1992). Some studies fail to find a clear renal advantage to single rather than multiple daily doses (Abraham *et al.*, 1995), although others do (Hetmar *et al.*, 1991).

34. Glezer *et al.*, 2009.
35. Sierles *et al.*, 2005; Austad *et al.*, 2011.
36. Hodges, 1995.
37. Zipkin and Steinman, 2005.
38. Wang and Adelman, 2009.
39. Sierles *et al.*, 2005; Austad *et al.*, 2011.
40. Brodkey, 2005.
41. Dubosky, 2005.
42. Brody, 2009.
43. Large *et al.*, 2011; Ruengorn *et al.*, 2011.
44. Maris, 2002. Of the many studies demonstrating the poor quality of care received by sufferers of depressive illness, see Oquendo *et al.*, 1999, 2002.
45. See the NIMH website: www.nimh.nih.gov. In the United States, suicide rates have slightly increased over the past decade despite efforts at educating the public and mental health providers. But the providers repeat their errors. In the United States, there are over 34,000 reported deaths annually by suicide, with an estimate of 11 attempts for every death. It is the tenth leading cause of death in the United States and rates are rising worldwide. The highest rates in the United States are among Native Americans and EuroAmericans. Males are four times as likely to kill themselves as are women because of the lethality of their efforts. Among teenagers, it is the third leading cause of death. The most dire combination of factors determining risk are a patient experiencing an agitated anxious depression, being male, heavy alcohol consumption, having a painful chronic general medical condition, and having access to firearms.

CHAPTER 3: FREE OF INJUSTICE AND MISCHIEF
1. For further discussion of the medical model see Fink and Taylor, 2008a, 2008b.
2. Kupfer *et al.*, 2011; de Castro-Manglano *et al.*, 2011; Felling and Singer, 2011; Perez-Costas *et al.*, 2010; Jindal and Keshavan, 2008; Westenberg *et al.*, 2007.
3. The history of psychiatry and psychiatric diagnosis presented here is fleshed out in Taylor and Atre Vaidya, 2009, Chapter 2, and Shorter, 2005.
4. Given the energy expended in the public discourse about the nature of sexual orientation, it is a testament to the timidity of academic behavioral medicine that there has not been more research on human sexual orientation, specifically homosexuality. There is as much research devoted to homosexuality of sheep as there is to humans. Homosexuality is not an exclusive human condition and over 30 species have been identified with variations in sexual orientation. Because of the availability and ease of study many investigations involve fruit flies (Yamamoto, 2007). Because of the money involved in the U.S. sheep industry, rams have been extensively studied to understand why so many prefer other rams to ewes (Roselli and Stormshak, 2009). The biological studies in humans have mostly been in males continuing the sexism of the Freudian movement's interest in homosexuality. The research that has been accomplished, however, is substantial enough and consistent. Homosexuality is a biological variation whose determination is primarily influenced by genetic and intrauterine processes (Savic *et al.*, 2010; Bao and Swaab, 2011).
5. Maia *et al.*, 2008; van den Heuvel *et al.*, 2010.
6. Perez-Rincon, 2011; Pearce, 2012.
7. Reynolds and Trimble, 1989.

8. A recent Greek study reports that they found the assessment of ego defense mechanisms reliable (Hyphantis *et al.*, 2011). Another study, however, found that even after extensive course instruction, second year psychiatric residents could achieve only 82% correct answers on a test in which they had to define and recognize defense mechanisms (Beresford, 2005). There are no studies that assess the reliability and validity of the ego defense mechanism concept as would be required for a putative fundamental concept of human behavior.

9. Convulsive therapy induced with the cortical irritant camphor in oil was sporadically used to treat patients by twelfth-century Arab physicians and by some eighteenth-century Scottish alienists (an old term for psychiatrist). Ladislas Meduna, a Hungarian psychiatrist, reintroduced the treatment in a systematic manner in 1936. His results were dramatic. Camphor, however, is not a reliable method for safely introducing controlled therapeutic seizures. Cerletti and Beni, two Italian psychiatrists, developed the first device for inducing therapeutic seizures electrically in 1938 (Shorter and Healy, 2007).

10. Northoff, 2008; Yudofsky and Hales, 2012.

11. Sanders, 2011.

12. Hill, 1907.

13. Mashour *et al.*, 2005.

14. Healy, 2002; Ban *et al.*, 2002.

15. Nelson and Charney, 1981.

16. Sandifer *et al.*, 1969; Spitzer and Fleiss, 1974.

17. Sierles and Taylor, 1995.

18. About 50% of U.S. medical students today are women. In my 1965 graduating class there were four women. One of them had the highest grades over the 4 years of school.

19. Taylor and Abrams, 1975; Taylor *et al.*, 1975; Abrams and Taylor, 1983; Kendler *et al.*, 2010.

20. Feighner *et al.*, 1972; Woodruff *et al.*, 1974.

21. *Statistical Manual for the Use of Institutions for the Insane*, American Medico-Psychological Association, 1918.

22. For studies of genetic influences on trait behavior see Caspi, *et al.*, 2005 and Roberts *et al.*, 2006. The complexity of the image is subtle (Clark, 2005; Cloninger *et al.*, 1993; Svrakic *et al.*, 1993).

    Males and females have the same basic "floor plan," and personality traits are normally distributed in both genders. Women, however, tend to score higher on traits that measure cooperativeness and the tendency to maintain behaviors that elicit external reward. See Cloninger, 1991. For a detailed discussion of normal and abnormal personality see Taylor and Atre Vaidya, 2009, Chapters 14 and 15; Caspi *et al.*, 2005; Clark, 2005; Roberts *et al.*, 2006.

23. Daughaday, 1992.

24. Pitcher, 1975.

25. Klingseisen and Jackson, 2011; LaFranchi, 2011.

26. Wilson, 2000.

27. Brooks, 1988; Yeates *et al.*, 2008.

28. Hermann and Riel, 1981; Sørensen *et al.*, 1989; Blumer, 1999.

29. Tolstoy, 1965, p. 3.

30. Cloninger *et al.*, 1988; Muller *et al.*, 2008.

31. Fink and Taylor, 2003.

32. Taylor and Fink, 2003.

33. Cosgrove *et al.*, 2006.
34. A more recent front page *New York Times* article details fees by drug makers to physicians of all stripes (Robert Pear, *NYT*, January 17, 2012).
35. A *New York Times* article, Wednesday May 9, 2012, pp. A11–12 (Benedict Carey), details the flip-flop of the panels. A *New York Times* article, Saturday May 12, 2012, p. A11 (Ian Urbana), describes the weakening of the diagnostic guidelines. Ironically, a severe critic of the proposed lowering of the requirements for several diagnostic entities is Alan Frances, who led the development of *DSM-IV*, which also added invalidated categories and lowered the standards for diagnosis. Dr. Frances also offered an opinion piece in *The Times* (Saturday May 12, 2012, p. A19).
36. Brauser, 2012; Spitzer *et al.*, 2012.
37. Kessler *et al.*, 2005; The Pios Medicine Editors, 2012.
38. Lurie *et al.*, 2005.
39. Buchkowsky and Jewesson, 2004.
40. Healy, 2004; Healy and Sheenan, 2001; Healy and Thase, 2003; Angell, 2004; Medawar and Hardon, 2004.
41. Drug companies like to give names to their agents that contain the letters V, X, or Z. Marketing studies have found that physicians and patients alike tend to consider drugs with these letters in their name as more potent than those without these letters. I have no idea whether this also applies in Eastern European countries where these letters are commonly used. Maybe in that part of the world, vowels are perceived as potent.
42. Gross *et al.*, 2003.
43. Vandenbroucke, 2002.
44. Friedman and Richter, 2004; Loewenstein *et al.*, 2012.
45. Krimsky, 2001.
46. Baker *et al.*, 2003.
47. Choudhry *et al.*, 2002.
48. Brody *et al.*, 2011.
49. Zimmerman *et al.*, 2002.
50. Geddes *et al.*, 2000.
51. Gibbons *et al.*, 2012.
52. Turner *et al.*, 2008.
53. Kirsch *et al.*, 2008.
54. Parker, 2004.
55. Kirsch *et al.*, 2002.
56. Corey-Lisle *et al.*, 2004.
57. Keller, 2004.
58. Khan *et al.*, 2003.
59. Ackerman *et al.*, 1997.
60. Cox *et al.*, 2001.
61. Hemels *et al.*, 2004.
62. Taylor and Fink, 2006, Chapters 10 and 11.
63. Tamminga *et al.*, 2002.
64. Pande and Sayler, 1993; Hirschfeld, 1999.
65. See Taylor and Fink, 2006; Parker *et al.*, 2010. Many of the *DSM* categories fail to capture biological realities. The categories are heterogeneous and patients in these groupings do not respond to similar treatments as predicted. Psychiatric practitioners have lost track of this fact, facilitating the "cookbook" treatments guidelines designed by academics who should know better.

66. Parker *et al.*, 1999.
67. Anderson, 2000.
68. Danish University Antidepressant Group, 1986, 1990, 1993, 1999.
69. Anderson and Tomenson, 1994.
70. Akhondzadeh *et al.*, 2003.
71. Dunner and Dunbar, 1992; Perry, 1996; Schatzberg, 1998; Danish University Antidepressant Group, 1986; Nelson *et al.*, 1999; Hildebrandt *et al.*, 2003; Roose *et al.*, 1994. Many of the independent studies comparing antidepressants and other psychotropic medications were done before 2000. Multicenter medication trials are expensive to accomplish and the NIMH doesn't fund small drug trials. The pharmaceutical industry thus had funded almost all of the recent psychotropic trials in the United States. As in poker, the guy with the most money can sometimes buy the pot even if he doesn't have the best hand.
72. Robinson *et al.*, 2000.
73. Anderson, 2000.
74. Freemantle *et al.*, 2000.
75. Healy 1997, 2004; Angell, 2004; Medawar and Hardon, 2004.
76. Vigen *et al.*, 2011.
77. Brooks *et al.*, 2011.
78. Rush *et al.*, 2011.
79. Csoka *et al.*, 2008.
80. Coupland *et al.*, 2011.
81. Sandergaard *et al.*, 2009.
82. Parnes *et al.*, 2009; Gilbody *et al.*, 2005.
83. Yerevanian *et al.*, 2003; Smith *et al.*, 2009; Tondo and Baldessatini, 2009.
84. The studies continue to indicate that carbamazepine works as well as lithium in the treatment of patients with mania (Ceron-Litvoc *et al.*, 2009). Almost all the clinicians I know who treat such patients still prefer lithium or valproic acid.

CHAPTER 4: FOR THE BENEFIT OF THE SICK

1. Medical ethics is not a disembodied topic. It is best taught by example at the bedside. Every patient has something to teach us about medical ethics. A wonderful book on the subject is Ottosson and Fink's *Ethics in Electroconvulsive Therapy* (2004). Their presentation of patients whose clinical situation involved ECT should be considered the "means" to the "end" of showing the reader what medical ethics is really all about.
2. Pitcher, 1975; Stocholm *et al.*, 2012.
3. For references to past and present abuse of African-Americans by the U.S. healthcare system see Gamble, 1997; Golub *et al.*, 2011. For the use of ECT among African-American patients see Case *et al.*, 2012.
4. The literature on the efficacy and safety of ECT spans over 70 years. The American Psychiatric Association has published reports from two task forces that thoroughly reviewed the treatment. There are several textbooks that also detail the procedure. See Maixner and Taylor, 2008; Fink, 2009; Ottosson and Fink, 2004; Abrams, 2001; American Psychiatric Association, 2001; Coffey, 1993. Also see Petrides *et al.*, 2001; Birkenhager *et al.*, 2003; and Birkenhager *et al.*, 2005 documenting how older patients with psychotic depression do best with ECT. Max Fink has also written a small book for patients and families (Fink, 1999). For a history of ECT, see Shorter and Healy, 2007.
5. McCall, 1989; Thompson *et al.*, 1994.

6. Dinwiddie and Spitz, 2010.
7. Petrides *et al.*, 2001; Husain *et al.*, 2004; Kellner *et al.*, 2006. The remission figures I cite are all for what is termed bilateral ECT. In this procedure, the stimulus paddles are placed on each temporal area toward the front of the head. Sometimes this is referred to as frontotemporal placement. In unilateral ECT the left frontotemporal electrode is moved away from that area and its verbal memory functions and is placed just to the right of the top (vertex) of the head. Almost all unilateral ECT is right-sided because 98% of people have language organized in their left cerebral hemispheres. Other treatment paddle placements have not caught on.
8. Watts *et al.*, 2011.
9. Fink and Taylor, 2003.
10. Ibid.
11. Frontal lobe seizures present with a variety of clinical pictures (Riggio, 2009; Elmi *et al.*, 2011). Frontal lobe seizures are common among persons with autistic spectrum disorder (Yasuhara, 2010).
12. About 60–70% of patients who undergo ECT experience an increase in the threshold at which they will have a seizure. Their seizure threshold rises. In laboratory animal studies seizure thresholds can be lowered by daily, brief subconvulsive electrical stimulations to the head leading to the animal eventually experiencing spontaneous seizures as if epileptic. The process is termed kindling. However, if the laboratory equivalent of ECT is administered before the daily subconvulsive electrical stimulations are begun, the animal's seizure threshold does not fall and the animal will not develop spontaneous seizures. ECT is antikindling. It is a very effective treatment for patients with epilepsy who have associated depressions or psychoses. It can be used to break the continuous seizures of a patient in status epilepticus (Maixner and Taylor, 2008).
13. Seizure disorder resulting from an excitatory focus deep within the frontal lobes is difficult to identify. The clinical picture can be misleading because during a frontal lobe seizure the patient may appear to be alert and responsive to others. The laboratory tests that assist in the diagnosis may not be helpful because the usual EEG cannot pick up the epileptic focus deep in the brain and the neurochemical flags of a seizure (e.g., an elevated serum prolactin level about 20 minutes postseizure) may not be present (Bagla and Skidmore, 2011; Braakman *et al.*, 2011; Beleza and Pinho, 2011). For epilepsy spectrum disorder, see Hines *et al.*, 1995.
14. Taylor, 1999, pp. 298–324.
15. Chen *et al.*, 2005.
16. Grigsby and Hartlaub, 1994; Gabrieli, 1998.
17. Tagariello *et al.*, 2009; Hardy, 2009; Bonelli and Cummings, 2007; Levy and Czernecki, 2006.
18. Hirstein, 2010; Devinsky, 2008; Feinberg and Roane, 2005; Ellis, 1994.
    Capgras syndrome is a delusion of misidentification in which the sufferer is convinced that familiar persons are impostors. I once helped treat a patient with the syndrome who stabbed his wife and dog because he thought they were impostors who were going to kill him. The dog died. The wife survived. We treated the husband and he recovered. Fregoli syndrome is similar to Capgras but in this case the patient believes unfamiliar persons are well-known to him or are celebrities (Mojtabai, 1994). I had a patient in the navy who was convinced that another patient was Charlton Heston the actor and a second patient, also a man, was Marilyn Monroe.

19. When brain cells are injured and repair is unsuccessful they need to be pruned. One of the mechanisms for this is termed programmed cell death or apotheosis. The programmed part of the construct is that the process is genetically influenced. At birth there are many more neurons than are needed at full maturation, which doesn't fully occur until about age 30. The "extra" cells serve several functions during fetal development, but toward the end of gestation and in infancy many of these cells are pruned beginning with the process of programmed death. Some programmed cell death is disease-induced because many diseases alter genes (Fuchs and Steller, 2011; Guo et al., 2011; Walter and Ron, 2011).

CHAPTER 5: PEEVES

1. Thomas Insel lecture at the 2010 Neuroethics Society Meeting, posted on Neuroethics at the Core, the blog of The National Core for Neuroethics.

2. Light therapy was introduced as an adjunct treatment for patients who experience low-grade depressive episodes during the winter months when there is a markedly reduced amount of daylight. The patient sits near a light box that is about the size of a modest flat screen TV but that is positioned vertically not horizontally. The light of between 5000 and 10,000 candles is left on for 30–45 minutes daily in the morning. The patient does not look directly into the bright screen. The effect of the effort is modest and is unlikely to benefit patients with melancholia (Lahmeyer, 1991; Eastman et al., 1998).

3. Vagal nerve stimulation (VNS) involves a procedure similar to the insertion of a cardiac pacemaker. A deck-of-cards size stimulator is placed in the chest wall under the skin and electrodes are run to the left vagus nerve in the neck. VNS was developed as an adjunct treatment for patients with seizure disorder. It was applied to patients with depression based on the observation that patients with seizure disorder and depression experienced some antidepressant effects from the nerve stimulation. The procedure does not work for patients with depressive illness (Noe et al., 2011; Martin and Martín-Sánchez, 2012).

4. Transcranial magnetic stimulation (TMS) of one or both frontal areas of the head delivers a magnetic pulse that penetrates the skull and stimulates the underlying frontal cortex. The early evidence for TMS is tainted as in the United States the studies of it have been controlled by the manufacturer. Other studies indicate it has about the same effect as the newer antidepressant drugs. This means that at best it has a weak antidepressant effect. Most likely, if it does have benefit it will be for patients with low-grade, nonmelancholic, nonpsychotic depression (Gross et al., 2007; Schutter, 2009). Unlike VNS, some health insurance companies will reimburse for TMS.

    Deep brain stimulation (DBS) is another effort at neuromodulation. This is a neurosurgical procedure in which electrodes are placed in a specific area deep in the brain (the anterior cingulate gyrus). The electrodes are attached by wires to a stimulator placed in the chest wall. The DBS studies are impressive and the patients who respond appear to have had severe depressive illness. The number of patients involved, however, is small, and the long-term effects of the procedure are not yet understood. It remains experimental (Kennedy et al., 2011; Lozano et al., 2012).

5. In 2011 alone there were eight articles in the New York Times reporting undue pharmaceutical industry influence on medical care and the approval of drugs. As examples, see Anahad O'Connor, March 9, 2011; Duff Wilson, March 29, 2011; NY Times February 15, 2011.

6. Wikipedia, 2011; IMS, 2007; public integrity, 2007; Moynihan, 2003; Healy, 2006.
7. Consumer Reports, 2011; Mark *et al.*, 2012.
8. Lithium remains the gold standard for mood stabilization. It is also the best augmenting agent of antidepressants (Cooper *et al.*, 2011). It has an additional advantage over anticonvulsants and antipsychotics as it reduces suicide risk. Among patients with mood disorder who are able to stay on lithium therapy for a year or more, suicide rates are substantially reduced. No other medication clearly has this effect (Müller-Oerlinghausen *et al.*, 1992; Bocchetta *et al.*, 1998; Leon *et al.*, 2012).
9. In the 1960s there was a heroin epidemic in New York City. At that time, it was estimated that across the United States there were one million heroin addicts and that 500,000 were in the city. Max Fink and other members of the division of biological psychiatry in our department were able to obtain numerous grants to study the problem and its possible solutions. To that end, Metropolitan Hospital provided a 25-bed inpatient service and clinic space for the study and treatment of persons with heroin addiction. Some residents were required to rotate on that service to provide general medical and psychiatric coverage. Most of the patients were sociopaths (Saviano *et al.*, 1971).
10. Sierles and Taylor, 1995.
11. In her wonderful book, *The March of Folly*, Barbara Tuchman (Tuchman, 1984) showed how governments that knew better did foolish things that led to a disaster. She defined folly as follows: a government is repeatedly told that what it is planning will end terribly badly. The government doesn't change its policy despite these warnings, information that clearly supports the warnings, and the prediction of disaster and responses to its initial actions that further confirm the impending debacle unless the government ceases the policy. The government continues on its course and thus the "folly." As examples, she presents Troy and the wooden horse, the renaissance popes provocation of the Protestant session, the British loss of its American colonies, and the U.S. engagement in Viet Nam. For a detailed history of the Viet Nam War that should convince most readers in the first 25 pages that the war was folly, see Karnow, 1983.
12. Yolles directed the NIMH from 1964 to 1970. He was dismissed from his position in a dispute over the decriminalization of illicit drugs, which he favored.
13. Sierles and Taylor, 1995.
14. Mandell, 1974; Brent, 1992.
15. Leaf *et al.*, 1985; Windle *et al.*, 1987; Liptzin *et al.*, 2007.
16. Hellman and Blackman, 1966; Miller, 2001; Becker *et al.*, 2004.
17. Kessler *et al.*, 2010; Dalrymple and Zimmerman, 2011.
18. Scully and Wilk, 2003.
19. Anna Freud, born in 1895, was Sigmund's youngest child. She had no higher education and received most of her schooling from her father and his colleagues. They both fled the Nazis in 1938 and settled in England. She established the field of child psychoanalysis. Her most influential work was *The Ego and the Defense Mechanisms*. She died in 1982 (*About.com Psychology*).
20. Jean Piaget was a Swiss developmental psychologist and philosopher who died in 1980. His ideas had an enormous influence on child development theories and approaches to early childhood education. His focus was on cognitive development and he proposed three phases of it: preoperational from ages 2 to 7, concrete operational from ages 7 to 11, and formal from ages 11 to 16 and into

adulthood. Piaget was not a scientist and his contribution was more in encouraging others to examine childhood cognitive and behavioral development than in defining that development. The child psychiatrists during my training thought of him as superficial as he did not incorporate Freudian notions into his schema.

21. The destructiveness of the nonscientific psychoanalytic approach to behavioral syndromes is poignantly illustrated by a psychiatrist father who writes about his autistic son and how the father's theories about pathological parenting as the cause of autism adversely affected his life (Kysar, 1968).
22. Lauretta Bender was a child psychiatrist who accomplished most of her work at Bellevue Medical Center in New York City. Although influenced by psychoanalysis, she was also a neuropsychiatrist and was interested in the cognitive functioning of children, particularly those with autism, The Bender–Gestalt is a paper and pencil test requiring the taker to copy a set of shapes. It assesses visual-motor coordination and constructional ability, mostly nondominant hemisphere functions (*The Papers of Lauretta Bender*, Brooklyn College Library online).
23. See Hall and Place, 2010, and Gregory and Mustata, 2012 for cutting; Williamson, 1998, Levine, 2012, and Loeb *et al.*, 2012 for eating disorders; Davis *et al.*, 2011 for anxiety and phobia; Diamond and Josephson, 2005 for conduct disorders.
24. Edgeworth *et al.*, 1996; Burger and Lang, 1998; Freeman *et al.*, 2010.
25. Safer, 2000; Gu *et al.*, 2010. The number of prescriptions for stimulants has increased dramatically for adults as well as for children (Castle *et al.*, 2007).
26. Chilakamarri *et al.*, 2011.
27. Bledsoe *et al.*, 2011; Hale *et al.*, 2011. Computerized and other standardized methods of assessing attention and working memory have refined the evaluation of children with the diagnosis of ADHD (Wehmeier *et al.*, 2011).
28. Van Meter *et al.*, 2011, document the increase in the bipolar diagnosis as have Holtmann *et al.*, 2008. The dramatic increase in the prescription of medications promoted to be effective in the treatment of patients with mood disorder is documented by Moreno *et al.*, 2007.
29. Anda *et al.*, 2007; Verdoux *et al.*, 2010.
30. Fink and Taylor, 2003; Taylor and Fink, 2003.
31. Continuous EEG monitoring by telemetry, all-night sleep studies, and obtaining a serum prolactin level 20 minutes after a suspicious event are some of the steps to be taken (Taylor, 1999, pp. 298–324; Sandstrom and Anschel, 2006).
32. Most lay persons know something about epilepsy. A movie about Julius Caesar typically depicts him having a grand mal seizure. But there are many forms of seizures and unless the physician painstakingly gathers the clues to detect them they can go unnoticed. The patient knows something is "wrong," but cannot put the experience into words. The examiner must know the experiences and describe them for the patient. Among psychiatric patients, epilepsy is common and the type most likely to be missed is partial complex epilepsy. In this form of seizure, the patient may have only a modest change in arousal or responsiveness and the behaviors elicited by the seizure may be mundane (Taylor, 1999, pp. 298–324).
33. Schizoaffective disorder is an invention, but a persistent one. It was first created in 1933 in an attempt to reconcile the reality of patients with mania or depression also exhibiting psychotic features that were believed to be exclusive to schizophrenia, and the Kraepelinian dichotomy that manic-depression and schizophrenia are clearly distinct conditions. It survives because in clinical practice patients exhibit "mixed" symptom pictures and psychiatrists are not well trained to respond to this challenge. The data, however, do not support

schizoaffective disorder as a homogeneous syndrome with a distinct pathophysiology (Heckers, 2009; Jäger *et al.*, 2011).

I treat patients diagnosed as schizoaffective for severe manic-depression
because the evidence leans that way and because it is always preferable when
confronted with diagnostic choices to diagnose the patient as having the illness
with the best prognosis and for which we have the best treatments.

34. Kraepelin first delineated the manic-depressive construct, although various
notions of a mood disorder with abnormal highs and lows had been recognized
for centuries. In the late 1960s manic-depression was divided into bipolar and
unipolar mood disorders. Bipolar disorder was the old manic-depression concept
whereas unipolar disorder was said to be genetically different with patients experiencing only recurrent depression. Beginning in the 1980s the long-recognized
variability in presentations of manic-depression was codified into subtypes. They
have no biological or treatment meaning but the subtypes grow (Taylor and Fink,
2006, pp. 15–44).

35. Samples of patients diagnosed as having borderline personality disorder (BPD)
commonly exhibit substantial heterogeneity indicating that the label does not
identify a single condition (Isaac, 1992; Asnaani *et al.*, 2007; Chilakamarri *et al.*,
2011). Persons who meet the criteria for BPD also meet the criteria for other personality disorders revealing one of the major problems with the *DSM* personality
section construct. People have one personality normal or abnormal, not several
(Barrachina *et al.*, 2011). Persons with the BPD diagnosis also have substantial
comorbidity with anxiety and mood disorders, which explains much of the core
feature of the BPD construct of emotional instability (Zanarini *et al.*, 1998).

36. The entire *DSM* personality disorder section is inconsistent with the wealth of
literature delineating the trait patterns that define personality and personality individual differences (Asnaani *et al.*, 2007; Skodol *et al.*, 2002; Nurnberg
et al., 1991).

37. Department of Health and Human Services, Food and Drug Administration,
Office of Surveillance and Epidemiology website.

38. Findling *et al.*, 2012; Pringsheim *et al.*, 2011; Maayan and Correll, 2011.

39. Pelkonen and Marttunen, 2003.

40. The use of TCAs in children and adolescents with depression has been discouraged because of safety fears and the understanding that this class of drugs is not
effective for the treatment of depressive illness in children (Papanikolaou *et al.*,
2006). Reviews and studies of safety, however, do not find that TCAs differ from
other antidepressants (Schneeweiss *et al.*, 2010). The studies that the FDA used
to recommend SSRIs and SNRIs over TCAs amount to six randomized controlled
studies (Cheung *et al.*, 2006). A review of the literature found that most antidepressants, including TCAs, have weak antidepressant effects in children and
adolescents (Tsapakis *et al.*, 2008).

41. In 24 studies involving 720 children and adolescents receiving a TCA the cardiovascular changes were found to be similar to those seen in adults and were
characterized as "uncertain" and "minor" (Wilens *et al.*, 1996).

42. Analyses of TCAs in children and adolescents find that the benefit is similar to
placebo (Papanikolaou *et al.*, 2006). But analyses comparing various antidepressants, including TCAs, find none of them to be of great benefit (Tsapakis *et al.*,
2008). These findings regarding TCAs are mostly based on studies done in the
1980s. The finding that TCAs are similar to placebo in children with depression
may be misleading because these studies also report that the TCA drug blood

levels might have been too low. Also, about 30% of the patients responded and these seem to be patients with melancholia (Puig-Antich *et al.*, 1987). For a discussion of the biology of melancholia and its expression in children and adolescents see Taylor and Fink, 2006.

43. Christopher, 2003.
44. The quality of psychiatric care of children in the United States is poor and in many health provider systems minimal standards are not being followed (Zima *et al.*, 2010; Stevens *et al.*, 2011).
45. In the 1930s catatonia could be temporarily relieved with high-dose barbiturates that induced deep sleep. As patients awakened, they were dramatically improved, but the improvement did not last. In the 1970s and 1980s, sodium amybarbitol was used to test for catatonia and the likely benefit of prescribing ECT for the patient. Today we use lorazepam. As a test for catatonia, lorazepam is best administered intravenously in half milligram doses every 5–10 minutes. Two to three milligrams may be needed to determine the result. Patients who respond to the challenge are then prescribed lorazepam as their medication treatment. Effective doses range from 8 to 32 mg daily. For the 70% or so catatonic patients who fully respond to lorazepam monotherapy, lorazepam is maintained for several months and then, if all goes well, tapered over another several months to avoid relapse. If a catatonic patient fails the challenge or does not adequately respond to the lorazepam treatment trial, ECT is the definitive treatment for the syndrome (Fink and Taylor, 2003).
46. Pringsheim *et al.*, 2011; Maayan and Correll, 2011.
47. There is a substantial overlap between OCD and Giles de la Tourette syndrome, particularly among patients whose symptoms develop in childhood (Ferrão *et al.*, 2009; Martino *et al.*, 2009).
48. SSRIs are the class of psychotropic drugs preferred for the medical treatment of patients with obsessive-compulsive disorder (OCD) (Kaplan and Hollander, 2003; Marazziti *et al.*, 2012). The original SSRI, however, was the tricyclic agent clomipramine (Marshall, 1971). Then and now, OCD can be a devastating illness. Clomipramine was at first considered a "miracle" drug but it was not available in the United States. Patients went to Canada to obtain it. It has fallen out of use mostly because of the marketing of other SSRI agents. In higher doses with blood level monitoring, it is still the best medical treatment for OCD.
49. The serotonin syndrome is clinically similar to malignant catatonia or the neuroleptic malignant syndrome as it is sometimes called. All three variations of what appears to be the same common final pathway condition can be relieved with lorazepam or ECT (Fink, 1996).
50. See the discussion of polypharmacy in Chapters 2 and 3.
51. Lazarus, 2009.
52. Trachtenberg, 1992.
53. Clayton, 1987; Cichon, 1992; van Voren, 2010.
54. Websites are scattered throughout the internet. They rarely rant under the Scientology imprimatur.
55. ECT devices have been around since 1938. Since then, there have been several substantial changes in their delivery of the electrical charge, not the least of which is the change from sine-wave devices (the same as the current from the wall socket) to those that deliver brief pulses of current. Brief pulses are more efficient at inducing a seizure and they do it with less energy. They also induce less of the temporary ECT cognitive side effects. Mostly because of its old public

image, ECT devices were classified in the Class III, most risky, category and in the United States they were limited in the charge they could deliver. The category also includes internal pacemakers and defibrillators, and is defined as having "a potential unreasonable risk of illness or injury" (Levin, 2010; Goodman, 2011; Kellner *et al.*, 2012).

56. See Title 9 of the California mental health code.
57. Whitcomb, 1988; Kramer, 1985.
58. In 1986 an NIMH survey estimated that annually 36,558 persons in the United States received ECT. In 1976 the NIMH figure was 58,667. In the same year, the APA reported that annually in the United States, 88,604 persons received ECT. Medicare reports that ECT treatments for the years 2001, 2002, and 2003 averaged 15,000 patients annually (Rosenbach *et al.*, 1997).
59. Wade *et al.*, 1987.
60. Rudnick, 2002.
61. Lapid *et al.*, 2004.
62. Teng *et al.*, 2012.
63. Misra *et al.*, 2008a, 2008b.
64. Palmer *et al.*, 2005.
65. Sugarman *et al.*, 1998.
66. Crepeau *et al.*, 2011.
67. Sahin *et al.*, 2010.
68. Williams *et al.*, 2003.
69. www.michigan.gov/documents/mentalhealthcode.
70. For a similar opinion, see Editorial, December 18, 2011, *New York Times*.
71. Medicare operates with 3% overhead, nonprofit insurance 16% overhead, and private (for-profit) insurance 26% overhead.
72. Comparison of the health care systems in Canada and the United States, Wikipedia, 2011; Kaiser Family Foundation: Snapshots: health care costs, United States and selected OECD countries, 2011; Health care in the United States, Wikipedia.
73. Druss *et al.*, 2011.
74. Althoff and Waterman, 2011; Petersen *et al.*, 2007.
75. Free online dictionary by Farlex.

CHAPTER 6: EXTINCTION OF U.S. PSYCHIATRY AS WE KNOW IT: SURVIVAL OF THE FIT

1. Fuller-Torry, 1974.
2. In addition to helping verify the clinical diagnosis of seizure disorder, an EEG study is helpful in the evaluation for delirium (other than for alcohol withdrawal, the pattern is diffuse slowing, commonly high-amplitude), encephalopathy (diffuse slowing with abnormal wave forms), and localized lesions [seizure foci, injury (Sidhu *et al.*, 2009; Jelic and Kowalski, 2009; Bagla and Skidmore, 2011; Brigo, 2011)]. All-night sleep studies are essential in the identification of the various sleep disorders and in the detection of nighttime seizures (Soldatos and Paparrigopoulos, 2005; Reading, 2007; Husain and Sinha, 2011).
3. See Fenton and Standage, 1993; Leuchter *et al.*, 1993; and Hughes, 1996, for EEG use among U.S. psychiatrists. There are no clear figures on the frequency of use of brain imaging in psychiatric diagnosis. On our inpatient service imaging is now commonly obtained for geriatric patients with behavioral syndromes and patients with suspected coarse brain disease. Patients with psychiatric diagnoses

referred to the medical center often have not had brain imaging even if the need was obvious (e.g., recent head injury).

4. Capote, 2009; Masdeu, 2011.
5. Beckett *et al.*, 2010.
6. Bozoki and Farooq, 2009; Seeley, 2009.
7. Delvenne *et al.*, 1997; Jáuregui-Lobera, 2011.
8. Maurer and Maurer, 2003.
9. The closing of state mental hospitals was also the result of the introduction of psychotropic medications beginning in 1954. For the first time patients were able to be discharged in large numbers from these institutions. Although many of these patients did well, for many others their discharge from the state hospital represented a shift in care rather than a return to a productive life. Nursing and half-way houses accommodated some. Many more ended up in the streets and alleys of U.S. cities (Greenblatt and Glazier, 1975).
10. Sturm and Ringle, 2003.
11. Institute of Medicine, 1996; Turner and Laine, 2001.
12. Weisberg *et al.*, 2007; Primary Care essay, Wikipedia, 2011.
13. Weisberg *et al.*, 2007.
14. Pingitore *et al.*, 2001; Weisberg *et al.*, 2007; Tamburrino *et al.*, 2011.
15. *MedScape* survey, 2011.
16. Scully and Wilk, 2003.
17. Pingitore *et al.*, 2001; Weisberg *et al.*, 2007; Tamburrino *et al.*, 2011; Wun *et al.*, 2011; Katerndahl *et al.*, 2011.
18. Wun *et al.*, 2011.
19. Pingitore *et al.*, 2001.
20. Cedars Sinai closing its psychiatric inpatient services was reported on the *MedScape* website in February 2012, "Should Psychiatrists be Worried?" and discussed by Jeffery Lieberman, Chairman of the Department of Psychiatry at Columbia College of Physicians and Surgeons in New York City. The statistics on the trends for U.S. psychiatric inpatient services are found in Liptzin *et al.*, 2007.
21. Nyapati and Rao, 2003.
22. Turner *et al.*, 1992; Fendrick *et al.*, 1996; Majumdar *et al.*, 2001.
23. Lewis *et al.*, 1991; Rosenblatt *et al.*, 1998.
24. Oquendo *et al.*, 1999, 2002.
25. Suominen *et al.*, 1998.
26. Isometsa *et al.*, 1994.
27. McDaniel *et al.*, 1993; Swigart *et al.*, 2008.
28. Kishi *et al.*, 2007; Swigart *et al.*, 2008.
29. Rothschild *et al.*, 2008.
30. Taylor and Fink, 2006.
31. Rush *et al.*, 2006; remission rates in this elaborate and widely cited as a successful treatment study ranged from 17% to 28%.
32. Fever is elicited by substances termed pyrogens. Some pyrogens are introduced into the body with the infectious agent. Present in the cell wall of some bacteria, some exogenous pyrogens can cause dangerous fevers. When under attack, the body defends itself. In this defensive cascade endogenous pyrogens are released. These substances, a type of cytokine, are produced by cells that help clean up the debris from the battle. The cytokines from these cleaners (phagocyte cells) increase the thermoregulatory set-point in the part of the brain termed the

hypothalamus. The immunological response to infection and stress declines with age. This is both good news and bad news. The good news is that in some circumstances a super immunological response does more damage than the infection itself. This is one reason why in the worldwide influenza pandemic of 1918–1920, older children and young adults had higher death rates than older persons. The bad news is that we need the immunological response to fight infections and so older persons are more likely to die directly from infection than are healthy younger adults (Dinarello and Wolff, 1982).

33. Fink and Taylor, 2003.
34. Hirschfeld, 2007.
35. Kishi *et al.*, 2007; Rothschild *et al.*, 2008.
36. Young *et al.*, 2001.
37. Weisberg *et al.*, 2007.
38. Wijeratne and Sachdev, 2008,
39. Prigitore *et al.*, 2011.
40. Schumann *et al.*, 2012; Katerndahl *et al.*, 2011.
41. Coyne *et al.*, 1997.
42. Tamburrino *et al.*, 2011.
43. Murrihy and Byrne, 2005; Berardi *et al.*, 2005.
44. McDowell *et al.*, 2011.
45. Dubovsky *et al.*, 2011; Rouillon *et al.*, 2011.
46. Sturm and Ringel, 2003.
47. Druss *et al.*, 2011.
48. Rouillion *et al.*, 2011; Dubovsky *et al.*, 2011.
49. Wun *et al.*, 2011.
50. McDowell *et al.*, 2011.
51. Stein *et al.*, 1995.
52. Halaris, 2011.
53. Wang *et al.*, 2005.
54. Alliance for Mental Health Reform, 2009 national survey on drug use and health: mental health; findings on line.
55. Pies, *Psychiatric Times,* May 27, 2010.
56. Pincus *et al.*, 1998; Vuorilehto *et al.*, 2009.

CHAPTER 7: BACK TO THE FUTURE: THE ONCE AND FUTURE KING

1. Meynert's grand opus, *Clinical Disorders of the Forebrain* (1884), has been reproduced and translated from the original German into English (Meynert, 2010).
2. Kirk and Kutchens, 2008.
3. Tandon *et al.*, 2008.
4. Psychiatric GWAS Consortium Coordinating Committee, 2009.
5. Fanous and Kendler, 2008.
6. Emil Kraepelin constructed the idea of dementia praecox in the last decade of the nineteenth century. He accomplished this by relying heavily on the constructs of catatonia and hebephrenia (Fink *et al.*, 2010), and then conflating other conditions into these syndromes based on an imaginative Aristotelian idea of mental domains and what he believed were similar outcomes among his collection of conditions. The logic, neuroscience, and nosology were flawed. For the next 100 years psychiatry has been trying unsuccessfully to fix the problem. Bleuler changed the name from dementia praecox to schizophrenia, but this rose still smells fishy. The present *DSM* version has no conceptual framework so that

anyone who meets the skimpy criteria can receive the diagnosis. When the foundations of a building are rotted, putting up new siding or even a new roof will not keep the building from eventually falling over (Taylor et al., 2010).

7. Sleep and epilepsy have been linked for decades and EEG studies assessing for a seizure disorder hope to capture the patient dozing in the EEG laboratory. Whenever psychopathology occurs around sleep, seizure disorder must be considered. If the clinicians' only source of information about psychopathology is the *DSM* these care givers will misdiagnose many patients.

8. Karege et al., 2010; Keshavan et al., 2011; Williams et al., 2011.

9. The construct of schizophrenia expanded exponentially over the twentieth century. The original idea was that it was a chronic psychotic disorder that emerged in the teens or early adult life. Emotional expression and its subjective experience were impaired as was thinking and conversational speech. Delusions and hallucinations became prominent. After a time the young person appeared almost demented. This image of hebephrenia was delineated by Karl Kahlbaum and his student Edvard Hecker. Emil Kraepelin incorporated hebephrenia, catatonia, and other conditions into his version, dementia praecox. Eugen Bleuler expanded the notion as schizophrenia. Others then added constructs such as schizophreniform and schizoaffective disorder. Between further expansions based on psychoanalytic theory and then the low bar for the diagnosis established with the *DSM-III*, the present population of patients receiving the diagnosis is unrecognizable from the original (Fink et al., 2010; Taylor et al., 2010).

10. The predementia phase of mild cognitive impairment is well documented and applies to several conditions in addition to Alzheimer's disease (Luck et al., 2010). One of the most famous studies that demonstrated that the cognitive hints of future dementia can be detected decades before the clinical diagnosis is made is "The Nun's Study." Cloistered nuns lead lives that are much more structured and controlled than are experienced by others and so they are not exposed to many of the factors that can impact disease such as cigarette smoking and heavy drinking. They are a unique population to study over decades. In one aspect in the series of studies of such nuns, personal statements they made upon entering their convent were correlated with brain autopsy findings decades later. Those whose personal statements were simple and uninteresting and lacking metaphor and detail were much more likely to develop dementia decades later. This finding, supported by other studies, has given rise to the idea of brain reserve. The more you have of it the more you can lose before you do not function well. Starting out with 60 cards in your "deck" is better than the typical 52 (Michel et al., 2009; Wilson et al., 2010)

11. Levey et al., 2006; Maioli et al., 2007; Luck et al., 2010; Rosenberg et al., 2012.

12. Geerlings et al., 2008.

13. Luria, 1976, 1980; Whitshaw and Kolb, 2008; Heilman and Valenstein, 2011.

14. Carter et al., 2009.

15. Luria, 1980; Goldberg, 2009.

16. Cerebral lateralization of cognitive functions is established but more complicated than simply language functions on the left in most persons and visual-spatial functions on the right. The popular idea of right brain-left brain learning is fiction. It sells books, however. To learn how the two hemispheres differ and how their functions can be measured to help in clinical diagnosis, see Lezak, 1995; Heilman and Valenstein, 2011.

17. Karlsgodt et al., 2011; Harkin and Kessler, 2011; Olivers et al., 2011.

18. Gohier *et al.*, 2009; Marazziti *et al.*, 2010.
19. Huntley and Howard, 2010.
20. Squire and Wixted, 2011; Robertson, 2012.
21. Dew and Cabeza, 2011.
22. Herpes simplex encephalitis is not uncommon and can be devastating to brain function. The limbic system is commonly affected early and in addition to testing for viral DNA in the spinal fluid a brain MRI can show temporal lobe swelling (Lee *et al.*, 2001; Whitley, 2006). Brain aneurysms are often found in the anterior blood vessels at the base of the brain [Lall *et al.*, 2009; Li *et al.*, 2011(in Chinese)].
23. Epstein, 2008; Vann *et al.*, 2009.
24. Brickell *et al.*, 2006; Bertram and Tanzi, 2012; Rahman *et al.*, 2012.
25. Just as lexical language can be roughly divided into motor and receptive domains that help in the identification of strokes and injury to the dominant cerebral hemisphere, the emotional expression of speech and the recognition of the emotional expression of others are important functions that can be assessed in helping delineate strokes and injury in the nondominant cerebral hemisphere (Blake, 2007; Ross and Monnot, 2008, 2011).
26. Lodwick *et al.*, 2004; Pusey *et al.*, 2007.
27. Butler and Cotterill, 2006; Pollen and Hofmann, 2008; Dechmann and Safi, 2009; Zilles *et al.*, 2011; Blazek *et al.*, 2011.
28. Whiting and Barton, 2003; MacLeod, 2012; Sherwood *et al.*, 2012.
29. The basal ganglia influence verbal fluency. In conversational speech they "hold" what is to be said until other brain language systems "check" what is to be uttered for its accuracy. When the "okay" is given, the basal ganglia release the motor program for the string of speech sounds that lets people know how clever you are (Kotz *et al.*, 2009). Basal ganglia dysfunction is also associated with language dysfunction in persons with developmental disorder and in other conditions (Watkins, 2011). Thirty to fifty percent of persons with basal ganglia disease such as Parkinson's disease and Huntington's chorea also experience depressive-like syndromes. Often the depressive syndrome precedes the motor features so the mood syndrome is not a "psychological" response to the motor disease but derives from the same pathological process. When both motor and mood features are present they do not correlate in severity. Thus the worse motor disabilities are not necessarily associated with the worse depressions, although the worse depressions will exacerbate the motor features (Rosenblatt, 2007; Blonder and Slevin, 2011; Chase, 2011; Weintraub and Burn, 2011). Other conditions, notably obsessive-compulsive disorder, are also associated with basal ganglia disease (van Duijn *et al.*, 2007). Because cognitive difficulties are also seen in persons with basal ganglia disease, I refer to these structures as the 3M Company of the brain. They are associated with motor, mood, and memory difficulties.
30. Disease that affects the dominant frontal lobe circuits is often associated with apathy and depressive-like syndromes. Executive cognitive function deficits and motor dysregulation are also common features (Bonelli and Cummings, 2007).
31. Critchley, 1953.
32. Abu-Akel and Shamay-Tsoory, 2011; Corbetta and Shulman, 2011; Rosazza and Minati, 2011; Wun *et al.*, 2011.
33. Taylor and Fink, 2006, Chapters 8 and 11.
34. Sherrill and Kovacs, 2002.
35. Benson, 1975, 1979.

36. Cantu, 1992; Meythaler *et al.*, 2001; Al-Sarraj *et al.*, 2012.
37. Ryan and Warden, 2003; King and Kirwilliam, 2011; Silverberg and Iverson, 2011.
38. Adachi *et al.*, 2000; Roy *et al.*, 2003.
39. Circumstantial speech is speech that is filled with unnecessary details and asides. Patients with mania typically experience rapid thoughts and lots of associations and these emerge in their speech. The patient with circumstantial speech, however, eventually gets to the point. When the associations and thoughts overwhelm the patient, speech runs on and on with interwoven themes and asides and never gets to the point. This type of speech is termed flight-of-ideas. When the patient with mania enters the most severe form of mania, delirious mania, speech disintegrates into fragments and the patient is said to speak in word salad (Taylor and Atre Vaidya, 2009).
40. There are two types of "strokes," hemorrhagic and ischemic. Both are neurological emergencies and must be managed within minutes to hours for the patient to recover. Hemorrhagic stroke is most dangerous. The blockage in ischemic stroke can be reopened with medication introduced into the vessels, but if the patient has a hemorrhagic stroke and this procedure is applied the bleed will worsen and the risk of the patient dying increases. So, as soon as a stroke is suspected, a CT scan is done to detect any bleeding. If the stroke is found to be ischemic and there are no other contraindications, the blockage is directly addressed. Transient ischemic attacks, or TIAs, are stroke-like events that occur when a blood vessel goes into spasm. To be considered a TIA, symptoms must last less than 24 hours. If symptoms last more than 24 hours but less than 2 weeks, a RIND is diagnosed. Symptoms lasting longer than 2 weeks are defined as a stroke. These symptoms can also resolve but recovery may take months and is often incomplete (Andrade *et al.*, 2012; Taussky *et al.*, 2011; Jaffer *et al.*, 2011).
41. Butler *et al.*, 2009.
42. Reynolds and Trimble, 1989; Hofmann, 2005.
43. Wood and Lilienfeld, 1999; Meyer and Archer, 2001; Hunsley and Bailey, 2001.
44. Karl Menninger founded the clinic. His first book, *The Human Mind* (1930), was a bestseller, introducing the American public to psychoanalysis. Menninger served as Chief of the Army Medical Corps' Psychiatric Division during World War II. Under his leadership, the Army reduced losses in personnel due to psychological impairment. In 1945, he was promoted to brigadier general. After the war, he led a national revolution to reform state sanitariums. The Menninger clinic still operates and its website boasts of famous patients. Brett Farve, the ex-pro-football quarterback, is listed.
45. Shorter, 1997, 2009.
46. Zinkin, 1953.
47. Bieber, 1962.
48. See note 4, Chapter 3.
49. Cowen, 2011.
50. Bostic and Rho, 2006; Meeks *et al.*, 2011; Cowen, 2011.
51. Shorter, 2009.
52. Fink and Taylor, 2003; Taylor and Fink, 2006; Taylor and Atre Vaidya, 2009.
53. Persons with limbic system disease, particularly within the temporal lobes, experience a wide range of illusions, hallucinations, and perceptual distortions. Patients with epilepsy, manic-depression, and some migraines are examples of patients with limbic disease that is associated with these features. Experiencing

the world as if viewing it through a shifting zoom lens leads to seeing objects getting smaller and then larger, like Alice in Wonderland. Dysmegalopsia is the perceived change in the size of objects. Dysmorphopsia is the perceived change in the shape of objects (Atre Vaidya *et al.*, 1994).

54. Lycanthropy is the delusional belief that you are a werewolf. Although that content is likely linked to Eastern European culture, the belief that a person is a dangerous animal, like the patient in the vignette, is seen in many cultures. It is most often a feature of melancholia with psychosis. Other catatonic features will also be present. The man who ran about the streets biting people went into a mute and immobile posture following admission. Later, while I was examining him, he suddenly roared and jumped to his feet. I raised my hands defensively and touched his outstretched hands and he froze to the touch, remaining in that posture until I moved him back to his bed (Fink and Taylor, 2003; Grover *et al.*, 2010; Bou Khalil *et al.*, 2012).

55. Several distinct frontal lobe syndromes have been delineated and related to specific prefrontal cortex-subcortical circuits (Duffy and Campbell, 1994; Mega and Cummings, 1994; Levy and Dubois, 2006).

56. Wakefield *et al.*, 2010.

57. Taylor and Atre Vaidya, 2009.

58. Vaidya and Taylor, 2005.

59. Bertelsen, 1999; Andreasen, 2007.

60. Andreasen, 2007.

61. Yager *et al.*, 2005.

62. Zisook *et al.*, 2011.

63. Fogel *et al.*, 2006.

64. Selwa *et al.*, 2006.

65. Duffy and Camlin, 1995.

66. Green *et al.*, 1995; Arcinegas and Kaufer, 2006; Vaishnavi *et al.*, 2009.

67. Yudofsky and Hales, 2002.

68. Cunningham *et al.*, 2006; Northoff, 2008; Lee *et al.*, 2008.

69. Roffman *et al.*, 2006.

70. Taylor and Atre Vaidya, 2009, Chapter 9.

71. Borderline personality is not a biological entity. Its name is an anachronism as it refers to the person with the label being on the border of psychosis, but who is not psychotic. That is equivalent to the idea of borderline pregnancy. Studies of the validity of borderline personality commonly find the category to be heterogeneous (Nurnberg *et al.*, 1991; Morey and Zanarini, 2000; Bondurant *et al.*, 2004; Paris, 2005).

72. Stratton and Gregory, 1994; Arciniegas and Topkoff, 2000; Silver *et al.*, 2009.

73. Visual impairment in sufferers of migraine is so well documented that for the treaters of this patient not to even consider her visual acuity problems as migraine-related is astonishing (Grosberg *et al.*, 2005; Schott, 2007; McKendrick and Sampson, 2009; Braunitzer *et al.*, 2010; Shams and Plant, 2011).

74. Migraine is a common condition among psychiatric patients. It is also associated with perceptual and mood disturbances that can be misunderstood as psychosis or mood disorder. A migraine can exacerbate depression. Migraine is comorbid with seizure disorder as migraine and epilepsy cooccur in the same individuals and the same families (Taylor and Atre Vaidya, 2009, Chapter 11).

75. Autoimmune hepatitis is a disease of unknown etiology mainly affecting females. Its hallmark is ongoing hepatic inflammation. It is a chronic condition, but it

is associated with periods of exacerbation that may end in liver failure. Some patients respond to corticosteroids and other to immunosuppressive treatment (Mieli-Vergani and Vergani, 2011).

76. Couturier *et al.*, 2001; Sirois, 2003.
77. For details of catatonic features and how to examine for catatonia see Fink and Taylor, 2003.

REFERENCES

Abraham G, Delva N, Waldron J, *et al.*: Lithium treatment: A comparison of once- and twice-daily dosing. *Acta Psychiatr Scand* 1992; 85: 65–69.

Abraham G, Waldron J, Lawson JS: Are the renal effects of lithium modified by frequency of administration? *Acta Psychiatr Scand* 1995; 92: 115–118.

Abrams R: *Electroconvulsive Therapy*, 4th ed. New York, Oxford University Press, 2001.

Abrams R, Taylor MA: The genetics of schizophrenia: A reassessment using modern criteria. *Am J Psychiatry* 1983; 140: 171–175.

Abrams R, Taylor MA, Gaztanaga P: Manic-depressive illness and paranoid schizophrenia. A phenomenologic, family history, and treatment-response study. *Arch Gen Psychiatry* 1974; 31: 640–642.

Abu-Akel A, Shamay-Tsoory S: Neuroanatomical and neurochemical bases of theory of mind. *Neuropsychologia* 2011; 49: 2971–2984.

Ackerman DL, Greenland S, Bystritsky A, *et al.*: Characteristics of fluoxetine versus placebo responders in a randomized trial of geriatric depression. *Psychopharmacol Bull* 1997; 33: 707–714.

Adachi N, Onuma T, Nishiwaki S, *et al.*: Inter-ictal and post-ictal psychoses in frontal lobe epilepsy: A retrospective comparison with psychoses in temporal lobe epilepsy. *Seizure* 2000; 9: 328–335.

Akhondzadeh S, Faraji H, Sadeghi M, *et al.*: Double-blind comparison of fluoxetine and nortriptyline in the treatment of moderate to severe major depression. *J Clin Pharm Ther* 2003; 28: 379–384.

Alexander GE, Crutcher MD, De Long MR: Basal ganglia-thalamocortical circuits: Parallel substrates for motor, oculomotor, "prefrontal," and "limbic" functions. In Ulyings HMB, Van Eden CG, De Bruin JPC, *et al.* (Eds.), *The Prefrontal Cortex, Its Structure, Function, and Pathology in Brain Research*, Vol. 85. Amsterdam, Elsevier, 1990, pp. 119–146.

Allen G, McColl R, Barnard H, *et al.*: Magnetic resonance imaging of cerebellar-prefrontal and cerebellar-parietal functional connectivity. *Neuroimage* 2005; 28: 39–48.

Al-Sarraj S, Fegan-Earl A, Ugbade A, *et al.*: Focal traumatic brain stem injury is a rare type of head injury resulting from assault: A forensic neuropathology study. *J Forensic Leg Med* 2012; 19: 144–151.

Althoff RR, Waterman GS: Commentary: Psychiatric training for physicians: A call to modernize. *Acad Med* 2011; 86: 285–287.

American Psychiatric Association: *Task Force Report (Weiner RD): Practice of Electroconvulsive Therapy: Recommendations for Treatment, Training, and Privileging*. Washington, DC, American Psychiatric Association, 2001.

Anda RF, Brown DW, Felitti VJ, *et al.*: Adverse childhood experiences and prescribed psychotropic medications in adults. *Am J Prev Med* 2007; 32: 389–394.

Anderson IM: Selective serotonin reuptake inhibitors versus tricyclic antidepressants: A meta-analysis of efficacy and tolerability. *J Affect Disord* 2000; 58: 19–36.

Anderson IM, Tomenson BM: The efficacy of selective serotonin re-uptake inhibitors in depression: A meta-analysis of studies against tricyclic antidepressants. *J Psychopharmacol* 1994; 8: 238–249.

Andrade SE, Harrold LR, Tjia J, *et al.*: A systematic review of validated methods for identifying cerebrovascular accident or transient ischemic attack using administrative data. *Pharmacoepidemiol Drug Saf* 2012; 21 (Suppl 1): 100–128.

Andreasen NC: DSM and the death of phenomenology in America, an example of unintended consequences. *Schizophr Bull* 2007; 33: 108–112.

Angell M: *The Truth About the Drug Companies: How They Deceive Us and What to Do About It.* New York, Random House, 2004.

Anonymous: Psychotherapy: Effective treatment or expensive placebo? [editorial] *Lancet* 1984; 1: 83–84.

Arciniegas DB, Kaufer DI: Joint Advisory Committee on Subspecialty Certification of the American Neuropsychiatric Association; Society for Behavioral and Cognitive Neurology: Core Curriculum for training in behavioral neurology and neuropsychiatry. *J Neuropsychiatry Clin Neurosci* 2006; 18: 6–13.

Arciniegas DB, Topkoff J: The neuropsychiatry of pathologic affect: An approach to evaluation and treatment. *Semin Clin Neuropsychiatry* 2000; 5: 290–306.

Asnaani A, Chelminski I, Young D, *et al.*: Heterogeneity of borderline personality disorder: Do the number of criteria met make a difference? *J Pers Disord* 2007; 21: 615–625.

Atre Vaidya N, Taylor MA, Jampala VC, *et al.*: Psychosensory features in mood disorder: A preliminary report. *Compr Psychiatry* 1994; 35: 286–289.

Atre Vaidya NA, Taylor MA: *Psychiatry Rounds: Practical Solutions to Clinical Challenges.* Miami, FL, MedMaster, 2004.

Austad KE, Avorn J, Kesselheim AS: Medical students' exposure to and attitudes about the pharmaceutical industry: A systematic review. *PLosMed* 2011; 8: e1001037.

Aybek S, Kanaan RA, David AS: The neuropsychiatry of conversion disorder. *Curr Opin Psychiatry* 2008; 21: 275–280.

Bagla R, Skidmore CT: Frontal lobe seizures. *Neurologist* 2011; 17: 125–135.

Baker CB, Johnsrud MT, Crismon ML, *et al.*: Quantitative analysis of sponsorship bias in economic studies of antidepressants. *Br J Psychiatry* 2003; 183: 498–506.

Ban TA, Healy D, Shorter E: *The Rise of Psychopharmacology and the Story of CINP.* Budapest, Animula Publishing, 2002.

Bao AM, Swaab DF: Sexual differentiation of the human brain: Relation to gender identity, sexual orientation and neuropsychiatric disorders. *Front Neuroendocrinol* 2011; 32: 214–226.

Barrachina J, Pascual JC, Ferrer M, *et al.*: Axis II comorbidity in borderline personality disorder is influenced by sex, age, and clinical severity. *Compr Psychiatry* 2011; 52: 725–730.

Becker KD, Stuewig J, Herrera VM, *et al.*: A study of firesetting and animal cruelty in children: Family influences and adolescent outcomes. *J Am Acad Adolesc Psychiatry* 2004; 43: 905–912.

Beckett LA, Harvey DJ, Gamst A, *et al.*: Alzheimer's disease neuroimaging initiative: The Alzheimer's Disease Neuroimaging Initiative: Annual change in biomarkers and clinical outcomes. *Alzheimers Dement* 2010; 6: 257–264.

Beleza P, Pinho J: Frontal lobe epilepsy. *J Clin Neurosci* 2011; 18: 593–600.

Benson DF: Disorders of verbal expression. In Benson DF, Blumer D (Eds.), *Psychiatric Aspects of Neurologic Disease*, Vol. I. New York, Grune & Stratton, 1975, pp. 121–136.

Benson DF: *Aphasia, Alexia, Agraphia: Clinical Neurology and Neurosurgery Monograph*. Edinburgh, Churchill Livingstone, 1979.

Berardi D, Menchetti M, Cevenini N, et al.: Increased recognition of depression in primary care. Comparison between primary-care physician and ICD-10 diagnosis of depression *Psychother Psychosom* 2005; 74: 225–230.

Beresford TP: Learning to recognize ego defense mechanisms: Results of a structured teaching experience for psychiatric residents. *Acad Psychiatry* 2005; 29: 474–478.

Bertelsen A: Reflections on the clinical utility of the ICD-10 and DSM-IV classifications and their diagnostic criteria. *Aust N Z J Psychiatry* 1999; 33: 166–173.

Bertram L, Tanzi RE: The genetics of Alzheimer's disease. *Prog Mol Biol Transl Sci* 2012; 107: 79–100.

Bieber I: *Homosexuality: A Psychoanalytic Study of Male Homosexuals*. New York, Basic Books, 1962.

Birkenhager TK, Pluijms EM, Lucius SA: ECT response in delusional versus non-delusional depressed patients. *J Affect Disord* 2003; 74: 191–195.

Birkenhager TK, van den Broek WW, Multer PG, et al.: One-year outcome of psychotic depression after successful electroconvulsive therapy. *J ECT* 2005; 21: 221–226.

Blake ML: Perspectives on treatment for communication deficits associated with right hemisphere brain damage. *Am J Speech Lang Pathol* 2007; 16: 331–342.

Blazek V, Brùzek J, Casanova MF: Plausible mechanisms for brain structural and size changes in human evolution. *Coll Antropol* 2011; 35: 949–955.

Bledsoe JC, Semrud-Clikeman M, Pliszka SR: Anatomical and neuropsychological correlates of the cerebellum in children with attention-deficit/hyperactivity disorder—combined type. *J Am Acad Child Adolesc Psychiatry* 2011; 50: 593–601.

Blonder LX, Slevin JT: Emotional dysfunction in Parkinson's disease. *Behav Neurol* 2011; 24: 201–217.

Blumer D: Evidence supporting the temporal lobe epilepsy personality syndrome. *Neurology* 1999; 53 (5 Suppl 2): S9–S12.

Bocchetta A, Ardau R, Burrai C, et al.: Suicidal behavior on and off lithium prophylaxis in a group of patients with prior suicide attempts. *J Clin Psychopharmacol* 1998; 18: 384–389.

Bondurant H, Greenfield B, Tse SM: Construct validity of the adolescent borderline personality disorder: A review. *Can Child Adolesc Psychiatr Rev* 2004; 13: 53–57.

Bonelli RM, Cummings JL: Frontal-subcortical circuitry and behavior *Dialogues Clin Neurosci* 2007; 9: 141–151.

Bostic JQ, Rho Y: Target-symptom psychopharmacology: Between the forest and the trees. *Child Adolesc Psychiatr Clin N Am* 2006; 15: 289–302.

Bou Khalil R, Dahdah P, Richa S, et al.: Lycanthropy as a culture-bound syndrome: A case report and review of the literature. *J Psychiatr Pract* 2012; 18: 51–54.

Bozoki AC, Farooq MU: Frontotemporal lobar degeneration insights from neuropsychology and neuroimaging. *Int Rev Neurobiol* 2009; 84: 185–213.

Braakman HM, Vaessen MJ, Hofman PA, et al.: Cognitive and behavioral complications of frontal lobe epilepsy in children: A review of the literature. *Epilepsia* 2011; 52: 849–856.

Braunitzer G, Rokszin A, Kober J, et al.: Is the development of visual contrast sensitivity impaired in children with migraine? An exploratory study. *Cephalalgia* 2010; 30: 991–995.

Brauser D: DSM-5 field trials generate mixed results. *Medscape News* May 6, 2012.

Brent RL: The changing roles and responsibilities of chairmen in clinical academic departments: The transition from autocracy. *Pediatrics* 1992; 90: 50–57.

Brewin CR, Andrews B, Hejdenberg J, *et al.*: Objective predictors of delayed-onset post-traumatic stress disorder occurring after military discharge. *Psychol Med* 2012; 21: 1–8.

Brickell KL, Steinbart EJ, Rumbaugh M, *et al.*: Early-onset Alzheimer disease in families with late-onset Alzheimer disease: A potential important subtype of familial Alzheimer disease. *Arch Neurol* 2006; 63: 1307–1311.

Brigo F: An evidence-based approach to proper diagnostic use of the electroencephalogram for suspected seizures. *Epilepsy Behav* 2011; 21: 219–222.

Brodkey AC: The role of the pharmaceutical industry in teaching psychopharmacology: A growing problem. *Acad Psychiatry* 2005; 29: 222–229.

Brody B, Leon AC, Kocsis JH: Antidepressant clinical trials and subject recruitment: Just who are symptomatic volunteers? *Am J Psychiatry* 2011; 168: 1245–1247.

Brody H: Pharmaceutical industry financial support for medical education: Benefit, or undue influence? *J Law Med Ethics* 2009; 37: 451–460.

Brooks JO, Goldberg JF, Ketter TA, *et al.*: Safety and tolerability associated with second-generation antipsychotic polytherapy in bipolar disorder: Findings from the Systematic Treatment Enhancement Program for Bipolar Disorder. *J Clin Psychiatry* 2011; 72: 240–247.

Brooks N: Personality change after severe head injury. *Acta Neurochir Suppl (Wien)* 1988; 44: 59–64.

Buchkowsky SS, Jewesson PJ: Industry sponsorship and authorship of clinical trials over 20 years. *Ann Pharmacother* 2004; 38: 579–585.

Burger FL, Lang CM: Diagnoses commonly missed in childhood, long-term outcome and implications for treatment. *Psychiatr Clin N Am* 1998; 21: 927–940.

Butler AB, Cotterill RM: Mammalian and avian neuroanatomy and the question of consciousness in birds. *Biol Bull* 2006; 211: 106–127.

Butler MA, Corboy JR, Filley CM: How the conflict between American psychiatry and neurology delayed the appreciation of cognitive dysfunction in multiple sclerosis. *Neuropsychol Rev* 2009; 19: 399–410.

Cantu RC: Cerebral concussion in sport. Management and prevention. *Sports Med* 1992; 14: 64–74.

Capote HA: Neuroimaging in psychiatry. *Neurol Clin* 2009; 27: 237–249.

Carter R, Aldridge S, Page M, *et al.*: *The Human Brain Book*. London, UK, DK Adult, Har/DVdr, 2009.

Case BG, Bertollo DN, Laska EM, *et al.*: Racial differences in the availability and use of electroconvulsive therapy for recurrent major depression. *J Affect Disord* 2012; 136: 359–366.

Caspi A, Roberts BW, Shiner RL: Personality development, stability and change. *Annu Rev Psychol* 2005; 56: 453–484.

Castle L, Aubert RE, Verbrugge RR, *et al.*: Trends in medication treatment for ADHD. *J Atten Disord* 2007; 10: 335–342.

Ceron-Litvoc D, Soares BG, Geddes J, *et al.*: Comparison of carbamazepine and lithium in treatment of bipolar disorder: A systematic review of randomized controlled trials. *Hum Psychopharmacol* 2009; 24: 19–28.

Chase TN: Apathy in neuropsychiatric disease: Diagnosis, pathophysiology, and treatment. *Neurotox Res* 2011; 19: 266–278.

Chen DK, So YT, Fisher RS: Therapeutics and technology assessment subcommittee of the American Academy of Neurology. *Neurology* 2005; 65: 668–675.

Cheung AH, Emslie GJ, Mayes TL: The use of antidepressants to treat depression in children and adolescents. *CMAJ* 2006; 174: 193–200.

Chilakamarri JK, Filkowski MM, Ghaemi SN: Misdiagnosis of bipolar disorder in children and adolescents: A comparison with ADHD and major depressive disorder. *Ann Clin Psychiatry* 2011; 23: 25–29.

Choudhry NK, Stelfox HT, Detsky AS: Relationships between authors of clinical practice guidelines and the pharmaceutical industry. *JAMA* 2002; 287: 612–617.

Chow TW, Cummings JL: Frontal-subcortical circuits. In Miller BL, Cummings JL (Eds.), *The Human Frontal Lobes*. New York, The Guilford Press, 1999, pp. 3–26.

Christopher EJ: Electroconvulsive therapy in the medically ill. *Curr Psychiatry Rep* 2003; 5: 225–230.

Cichon DE: The right to "just say no": A history and analysis of the right to refuse antipsychotic drugs. *LA Law Rev* 1992; 53: 283–426.

Clark LA: Stability and change in personality pathology: Revelations of three longitudinal studies. *J Personal Disord* 2005; 19: 524–532.

Clayton EW: From Rogers to Rivers: The rights of the mentally ill to refuse medication. *Am J Law Med* 1987; 13: 7–52.

Cloninger CR: Brain networks underlying personality development. In Carroll BJ, Barett JE (Eds.), *Psychopathology and the Brain*. American Psychopathological Association Series, New York, Raven Press, 1991, pp. 183–208.

Cloninger CR, Sigvardsson S, Bohman M: Childhood personality predicts alcohol abuse in young adults. *Alcohol Clin Exp Res* 1988; 12: 494–505.

Cloninger CR, Svrakic DM, Przybeck TR: A psychobiological model of temperament and character. *Arch Gen Psychiatry* 1993; 50: 975–990.

Coffey CE (Ed.): *The Clinical Science of Electroconvulsive Therapy*. Washington, DC, American Psychiatric Press, Inc., 1993.

Consumer Reports Best Buy Drugs: Many common generics beat brand names. *Consum Rep* 2011; 76: 24–27.

Cooper C, Katona C, Lyketsos K, *et al.*: Systematic review of treatments for refractory depression in older people. *Am J Psychiatry* 2011; 168: 681–688.

Corbetta M, Shulman GL: Spatial neglect and attention networks. *Annu Rev Neurosci* 2011; 34: 569–599.

Corey-Lisle PK, Nash R, Stang P, *et al.*: Response, partial response, and nonresponse in primary care treatment of depression. *Arch Intern Med* 2004; 164: 1197–1204.

Cosgrove I, Krimsky S, Vijaraghavan M, *et al.*: Financial ties between DSM-IV panel members and the pharmaceutical industry. *Psychother Psychosom* 2006; 75: 154–160.

Coupland C, Dhiman P, Morriss R, *et al.*: Antidepressant use and risk of adverse outcomes in older people: Population based cohort study. *BMJ* 2011; 2: 343:d4551. doi: 10.1136/bmj.d4551.

Couturier J, Steele M, Hussey L, *et al.*: Steroid-induced mania in an adolescent: Risk factors and management. *Can J Clin Pharmacol* 2001; 8: 109–112.

Cowen PJ: Has psychopharmacology got a future? *Br J Psychiatry* 2011; 198: 333–335.

Cox BJ, Enns MW, Larsen DK: The continuity of depression symptoms: Use of cluster analysis for profile identification in patient and student samples. *J Affect Disord* 2001; 65: 67–73.

Coyne JC, Klinkman MS, Gallo SM, *et al.*: Short-term outcomes of detected and unde-tected depressed primary care patients and depressed psychiatric patients. *Gen Hosp Psychiatry* 1997; 19: 333–343.

Crepeau AE, McKinney BI, Fox-Ryvicker M, *et al.*: Prospective evaluation of patient comprehension of informed consent. *J Bone Joint Surg Am* 2011; 93: e114: 1–7.

Critchley M: *The Parietal Lobes*. New York, Hafner, 1953.

Csoka A, Bahrick A, Mehtonen O-P: Persistent sexual dysfunction after discontinua-tion of selective serotonin reuptake inhibitors *J Sexual Med* 2008; 5: 227–233.

Cunningham MG, Goldstein M, Katz D, *et al.*: Coalescence of psychiatry, neurology, and neuropsychology: From theory to practice. *Harv Rev Psychiatry* 2006; 14: 127–140.

Dalrymple KL, Zimmerman M: Age of onset of social anxiety disorder in depressed outpatients. *J Anxiety Disord* 2011; 25: 131–137.

Danish University Antidepressant Group: Citalopram: Clinical effect profile in com-parison with clomipramine: A controlled multicenter study. *Psychopharmacology (Berl)* 1986; 90: 131–138.

Danish University Antidepressant Group: Paroxetine: A selective serotonin reuptake inhibitor showing better tolerance, but weaker antidepressant effect than clo-mipramine in a controlled multicenter study. *J Affect Disord* 1990; 18: 289–299.

Danish University Antidepressant Group: Moclobemide: A reversible MAO-A-inhibitor showing weaker antidepressant effect than clomipramine in a controlled multi-center study. *J Affect Disord* 1993; 28: 105–116.

Danish University Antidepressant Group: Clomipramine dose-effect study in patients with depression: Clinical end points and pharmacokinetics. *Clin Pharmacol Ther* 1999; 66: 152–165.

Daughaday WH: Pituitary gigantism. *Endocrinol Metab Clin North Am* 1992; 21: 633–647.

Davis TE 3rd, May A, Whiting SE: Evidence-based treatment of anxiety and phobia in children and adolescents: Current status and effects on the emotional response. *Clin Psychol Rev* 2011; 31: 592–602.

de Castro-Manglano P, Mechelli A, Soutullo C, *et al.*: Structural brain abnormalities in first-episode psychosis: Differences between affective psychoses and schizophre-nia and relationship to clinical outcome. *Bipolar Disord* 2011 13: 545–555.

Dechmann DK, Safi K: Comparative studies of brain evolution: A critical insight from the Chiroptera. *Biol Rev Camb Philos Soc* 2009; 84: 161–172.

Delvenne V, Goldman S, Biver F, *et al.*: Brain hypometabolism of glucose in low-weight depressed patients and in anorectic patients: A consequence of starvation? *J Affect Disord* 1997; 44: 69–77.

Devinsky O: Behavioral neurology. The neurology of Capgras syndrome. *Rev Neurol Dis* 2008; 5: 97–100.

Devinsky O, Putman F, Grafman J, *et al.*: Dissociative states and epilepsy. *Neurology* 1989; 39: 835–840.

Dew IT, Cabaza R: The porous boundaries between explicit and implicit memory: Behavioral and neural evidence. *Ann NY Acad Sci* 2011; 1224: 174–190.

Diamond G, Josephson A: Family-based treatment research: A 10-year update. *J Am Acad Child Adolesc Psychiatry* 2005; 44: 872–887.

Dinarello CA, Wolff SM: Molecular basis of fever in humans. *Am J Med* 1982; 72: 799–819.

Dinwiddie SH, Spitz D: Resident education in electroconvulsive therapy. *J ECT* 2010; 26: 310–316.

Drug Lobby Second to None: How the pharmaceutical industry gets its way in Washington. publicintegrity.org. 2005–07–07. http://www.publicintegrity.org/rx/report.aspx?aid=723. Retrieved 2007–05–23.

Druss BG, von Esenwein SA, Compton MT, *et al.*: Budget impact and sustainability of medical care management for persons with serious mental illness *Am J Psychiatry* 2011; 168: 1171–1178.

Dubois P: *The Psychic Treatment of Nervous Disorders, The Psychoneuroses and Their Moral Treatment.* Jelliffe SE and White WA (trans). New York, Funk and Wagnalls Co., 1905.

Dubovsky SL: Who is teaching psychopharmacology? Who should be teaching psychopharmacology? *Acad Psychiatry* 2005; 29: 155–161.

Dubovsky SL, Leonard K, Griswold K, *et al.*: Bipolar disorder is common in depressed primary care patients. *Postgrad Med* 2011; 123: 129–133.

Duffy JD, Camlin H: Neuropsychiatric training in American psychiatric residency training programs. *J Neuropsychiatry Clin Neurosci* 1995; 7: 290–294.

Duffy JD, Campbell JJ 3rd: The regional prefrontal syndromes: A theoretical and clinical overview. *J Neuropsychiatry Clin Neurosci* 1994; 6: 379–387.

Duncan ME: Pregnancy and leprosy neuropathy. *Indian J Lepr* 1996; 68: 23–34.

Dunner DL, Dunbar GC: Optimal dose regimen for paroxetine. *J Clin Psychiatry* 1992; 53 (Suppl): 21–26.

Eastman CI, Young MA, Fogg LF, *et al.*: Bright light treatment of winter depression: A placebo-controlled trial. *Arch Gen Psychiatry* 1998; 55: 883–889.

Edgeworth J, Bullock P, Bailey A, *et al.*: Why are brain tumors still being missed? *Arch Dis Child* 1996; 74: 148–151.

Ellenstein A, Kranick SM, Hallett M: An update on psychogenic movement disorders. *Curr Neurol Neurosci Rep* 2011; 11: 396–403.

Ellis HD: The role of the right hemisphere in the Capgras delusion. *Psychopathology* 1994; 27: 177–185.

Elmi H, Kilincaslan A, Ozturk M, *et al.*: A case with hyperkinetic frontal lobe epilepsy presenting as a psychiatric disturbance. *Turk J Pediatr* 2011; 53: 574–578.

Epstein RA: Parahippocampal and retrosplenial contributions to human spatial navigation. *Trends Cogn Sci* 2008; 12: 388–396.

Eysenk HJ, Rachman S: *The Causes and Cures of Neuroses: An Introduction to Modern Behavior Therapy.* San Diego, CA, RR Knapp, 1965.

Factor SA, Podskalny GD, Molho ES: Psychogenic movement disorders: Frequency, clinical profile, and characteristics. *J Neurol Neurosurg Psychiatry* 1995; 59: 406–412.

Fanous AH, Kendler KS: Genetics of clinical features and subtypes of schizophrenia: A review of the recent literature. *Curr Psychiatry Rep* 2008; 10: 164–170.

Feighner JP, Robins E, Guze SB, *et al.*: Diagnostic criteria for use in psychiatric research. *Arch Gen Psychiatry* 1972; 26: 57–63.

Feinberg TE, Roane DM: Delusional misidentification. *Psychiatr Clin North Am* 2005; 28: 665–683.

Felling RJ, Singer HS: Neurobiology of Tourette syndrome: Current status and need for further investigation. *J Neurosci* 2011; 31:12387–12395.

Fendrick A, Hirth R, Chernew M: Differences between generalist and specialist physicians regarding Helicobacter pylori and peptic ulcer disease *Am J Gastroenterol* 1996; 91: 1544–1548.

Fenton GW, Standage K: Clinical electroencephalography in a psychiatric service. *Can J Psychiatry* 1993; 38: 333–338.

Ferrão YA, Miguel E, Stein DJ: Tourette's syndrome, trichotillomania, and obsessive-compulsive disorder: How closely are they related? *Psychiatry Res* 2009; 170: 32–42.

Filskov SB, Goldstein SG: Diagnostic validity of the Halstead-Reitan neuropsychological battery. *J Consult Clin Psychol* 1974; 42: 382–388.

Findling RL, Youngstrom EA, McNamara NK, *et al*.: Double-blind, randomized, placebo-controlled long-term maintenance study of aripiprazole in children with bipolar disorder. *J Clin Psychiatry* 2012; 73: 57–63.

Fink M: Toxic serotonin syndrome or neuroleptic malignant syndrome? *Pharmacopsychiatry* 1996; 29: 159–161.

Fink M: *Electroshock: Healing Mental Illness*. New York, Oxford University Press, 1999.

Fink M: *Electroconvulsive Therapy: A Guide for Professionals and Their Patients*. New York, Oxford University Press, 2009.

Fink M, Shorter E, Taylor MA: Catatonia is not schizophrenia: Kraepelin's error and the need to recognize catatonia as an independent syndrome in medical nomenclature. *Schiz Bull* 2010; 36: 314–320.

Fink M, Taylor MA: *Catatonia: A Clinician's Guide*. Cambridge, UK, Cambridge University Press, 2003.

Fink M, Taylor MA: The medical evidence-based model for psychiatric syndromes: Return to the classical paradigm. *Acta Psychiatric Scand* 2008; 117: 81–84.

Fink M, Taylor MA: Issues for DSM-IV: The medical diagnostic model. *Am J Psychiatry* 2008; 165: 799.

Fogel SP, Sneed JR, Roose SP: Survey of psychiatric treatment among psychiatric residents in Manhattan: Evidence of stigma. *J Clin Psychiatry* 2006; 67: 1591–1598.

Freeman RD, Soltanifar A, Baer S: Stereotypic movement disorder: Easily missed. *Dev Med Child Neurol* 2010; 52: 733–738.

Freemantle N, Anderson IM, Young P: Predictive value of pharmacological activity for the relative efficacy of antidepressant drugs. Meta-regression analysis. *Br J Psychiatry* 2000; 177: 292–302.

Friedman LS, Richter ED: Relationship between conflicts of interest and research results. *J Gen Intern Med* 2004; 19: 51–56.

Fuchs Y, Steller H: Programmed cell death in animal development and disease. *Cell* 2011; 147: 742–758.

Fuller Torrey E: *The Death of Psychiatry*. Radnor, PA, Chilton Book Co., 1974.

Gabrieli JD: Cognitive neuroscience of human memory. *Annu Rev Psychol* 1998; 49: 87–115.

Gamble VN: Under the shadow of Tuskegee: African Americans and health care. *Am J Public Health* 1997; 87: 1773–1778.

Gartlehner G, Hansen RA, Morgan LC, *et al*.: Second-generation antidepressants in the pharmacologic treatment of adult depression: An update of the 2007 comparative effectiveness review [internet]. AHRQ Comparative Effectiveness Reviews report no. 12-EHC012-EF, 2011.

Geddes J, Freemantle N, Mason J, *et al*.: SSRIs versus other antidepressants for depressive disorder. *Cochrane Database Syst Rev* 2000; 2: CD001851.

Geerlings MI, den Heijer T, Koudstaal PJ, *et al*.: History of depression, depressive symptoms, and medial temporal lobe atrophy and the risk of Alzheimer's disease. *Neurology* 2008; 70: 1258–1264.

Gibbons RD, Brown CH, Hur K, *et al*.: Suicidal thoughts and behavior with antidepressant treatment: Reanalysis of the randomized placebo-controlled studies of fluoxetine and venlafaxine. *Arch Gen Psychiatry* 2012; online February 6, 2012.

Gilbody S, Wilson P, Watt I: Benefits and harms of direct to consumer advertising: A systematic review. *Qual Saf Health Care* 2005; 14: 246–250.

Glezer A, Byatt N, Cook R Jr, *et al.*: Polypharmacy prevalence rates in the treatment of unipolar depression in an outpatient clinic. *J Affect Disord* 2009; 117: 18–23.

Glick ID, Balon RJ, Balon J, *et al.*: Teaching pearls from the lost art of psychopharmacology. *J Psychiatr Pract* 2009; 15: 423–426.

Gohier B, Ferracci L, Surguladze SA, *et al.*: Cognitive inhibition and working memory in unipolar depression. *J Affect Disord* 2009; 116: 100–105.

Goldberg E: *The New Executive Brain: Frontal Lobes in a Complex World.* New York, Oxford University Press, 2009.

Golub M, Calman N, Ruddock C, *et al.*: A community mobilizes to end medical apartheid. *Prog Commun Health Partnersh* 2011; 5: 317–325.

Goodman WK: Perspective: Electroconvulsive therapy in the spotlight. *N Engl J Med* 2011; 364: 1785–1787.

Gould R, Miller BL, Goldberg MA, *et al.*: The validity of hysterical signs and symptoms. *J Nerv Ment Dis* 1986; 174: 593–597.

Gouzoulis-Mayfrank E, Daumann J: Neurotoxicity of drugs of abuse—the case of methylenedioxyamphetamines (MDMA, ecstasy), and amphetamines. *Dialogues Clin Neurosci* 2009; 11: 305–317.

Grant I, Judd LL: Neuropsychological and EEG disturbances in polydrug users. *Am J Psychiatry* 1976; 133: 1039–1042.

Grant I, Mohns L, Miller M, *et al.*: A neuropsychological study of polydrug users. *Arch Gen Psychiatry* 1978; 33: 973–978.

Gray SH: Evidence-based psychotherapeutics. *J Am Acad Psychoanal* 2002; 30: 3–16.

Green RC, Benjamin S, Cummings JL: Fellowship programs in behavioral neurology. *Neurology* 1995; 45: 412–415.

Greenblatt M, Glazier E: The phasing out of mental hospitals in the United States. *Am J Psychiatry* 1975; 132: 1135–1140.

Gregory RJ, Mustata GT: Magical thinking in narratives of adolescent cutters. *J Adolesc* 2012; 35: 1045–1051.

Grigsby J, Hartlaub GH: Procedural learning and the development and stability of character. *Percept Mot Skills* 1994; 79: 355–370.

Grosberg BM, Solomon S, Lipton RB: Retinal migraine. *Curr Pain Headache Rep* 2005; 9: 268–271.

Gross CP, Gupta AR, Krumholz HM: Disclosure of financial competing interests in randomized controlled trials: Cross sectional review. *BMJ* 2003; 326: 526–527.

Gross M, Nakamura L, Pascual-Leone A, *et al.*: Has repetitive transcranial magnetic stimulation (rTMS) treatment for depression improved? A systematic review and meta-analysis comparing the recent vs. the earlier rTMS studies. *Acta Psychiatr Scand* 2007; 116: 165–173.

Grover S, Shah R, Ghosh A: Electroconvulsive therapy for lycanthropy and Cotard syndrome: A case report. *J ECT* 2010; 26: 280–281.

Gu Q, Dillon CF, Burt VL: Prescription drug use continues to increase: U.S. prescription drug data for 2007–2008. *NCHS Data Brief* 2010.

Guo MF, Yu JZ, Ma CG: Mechanisms related to neuron injury and death in cerebral hypoxic ischaemia. *Folia Neuropathol* 2011; 49: 78–87.

Gurvits TV, Metzger LJ, Lasko NB, *et al*: Subtle neurologic compromise as a vulnerability factor for combat-related posttraumatic stress disorder: Results of a twin study. *Arch Gen Psychiatry* 2006; 63: 571–576.

Halaris A: A primary care focus on the diagnosis and treatment of major depressive disorder in adults. *J Psychiatr Pract* 2011; 17: 340–350.

Hale JB, Reddy LA, Semrud-Clikeman M, *et al.*: Executive impairment determines ADHD medication response: Implications for academic achievement. *J Learn Disabil* 2011; 44: 196–212.

Hall B, Place M: Cutting to cope—a modern adolescent phenomenon. *Child Care Health Dev* 2010; 36: 623–629.

Halstead WC, Wepman JM: The Halstead-Wepman aphasia screening test. *J Speech Disord* 1949; 14: 9–15.

Hardy SE: Methylphenidate for the treatment of depressive symptoms, including fatigue and apathy, in medically ill older adults and terminally ill adults. *Am J Geriatr Pharmacother* 2009; 7: 34–59.

Harkin B, Kessler K: The role of working memory in compulsive checking and OCD: A systematic classification of 58 experimental findings. *Clin Psychol Rev* 2011; 3: 1004–1021.

Hart S, Smith CM, Swash M: Assessing intellectual deterioration. *Br J Clin Psychol* 1986; 25 (Pt 2): 119–124.

Healy D: *The Anti-Depressant Era*. Cambridge, MA, Harvard University Press, 1997.

Healy D: *The Creation of Psychopharmacology*. Cambridge, MA, Harvard University Press, 2002.

Healy D: *Let Them Eat Prozac: The Unhealthy Relationship Between the Pharmaceutical Industry and Depression*. New York, New York University Press, 2004.

Healy D: The latest mania: Selling bipolar disorder *PLoS Med* 2006; 3: e185.

Healy D, Sheehan DV: Have drug companies hyped social anxiety disorder to increase sales? *West J Med* 2001; 175: 364–365.

Healy D, Thase ME: Is academic psychiatry for sale? *Br J Psychiatry* 2003; 182: 388–390.

Heckers S: Is schizoaffective disorder a useful diagnosis? *Curr Psychiatry Rep* 2009; 11: 332–337.

Heilman KM, Valenstein KM (Eds.): *Clinical Neuropsychology*, 5th ed. New York, Oxford University Press, 2011.

Hellman DS, Blackman N: Enuresis, firesetting and cruelty to animals: A triad predictive of adult crime. *Am J Psychiatry* 1966; 122: 1431–1435.

Helzer JE, Robins LN, McEvoy L: Post-traumatic stress disorder in the general population. Findings of the epidemiologic catchment area survey. *N Engl J Med* 1987; 317: 1630–1634.

Hemels ME, Vicente C, Sadri H, *et al.*: Quality assessment of meta-analysis of RCTs of pharmacotherapy in major depressive disorder. *Curr Med Res Opin* 2004; 20: 477–484.

Hermann BP, Riel P: Interictal personality and behavioral traits in temporal lobe and generalized epilepsy. *Cortex* 1981; 17: 125–128.

Hetmar O, Povlsen UJ, Ladefoged J, *et al.*: Lithium: Long-term effects on the kidney. A prospective follow-up study ten years after kidney biopsy. *Br J Psychiatry* 1991; 158: 53–58.

Hildebrandt MG, Steyerberg EW, Stage KB, *et al.*, The Danish University Antidepressant Group: Are gender differences important for the clinical effects of antidepressants? *Am J Psychiatry* 2003; 160: 1643–1650.

Hill CG: How can we best advance the study of psychiatry? *Am J Psychiatry* 1907; 64: 1–8.

Hines ME, Kubu CS, Roberts RJ, et al.: Characteristics and mechanisms of epilepsy spectrum disorder: An explanatory model. Appl Neuropsychol 1995; 2: 1–6.

Hirschfeld RM: Efficacy of SSRIs and newer antidepressants in severe depression: Comparison with TCAs. J Clin Psychiatry 1999; 60: 326–335.

Hirschfeld RM: Screening for bipolar disorder. Am J Manag Care 2007; 13 (7 Suppl): S164–S169.

Hirstein W: The misidentification syndromes as mindreading disorders. Cogn Neuropsychiatry 2010; 15: 233–260.

Hodges B: Interactions with the pharmaceutical industry: Experiences and attitudes of psychiatry residents, interns and clerks. CMAJ 1995; 153: 553–559.

Hoeffner EG, Mukherji SK, Srinivasan A, et al.: Neuroradiology back to the future: Brain imaging. AJNR Am J Neuroradiol 2012; 33: 5–11.

Hofmann B: Simplified models of the relationship between health and disease. Theoretical Med Bioethics 2005; 26: 355–377.

Holtmann M, Bölte S, Poustka F: Rapid increase in rates of bipolar diagnosis in youth: "True" bipolarity or misdiagnosed severe disruptive behavior disorders? Arch Gen Psychiatry 2008; 65: 477.

Hughes JR: A review of the usefulness of the standard EEG in psychiatry. Clin Electroencephalogr 1996; 27: 35–39.

Hunsley J, Bailey JM: Whither the Rorschach? An analysis of the evidence. Psychol Assess 2001; 13: 472–485.

Huntley JD, Howard RJ: Working memory in early Alzheimer's disease: A neuropsychological review. Int J Geriatr Psychiatry 2010; 25: 121–132.

Husain AM, Sinha SR: Nocturnal epilepsy in adults. J Clin Neurophysiol 2011; 28: 141–145.

Husain MM, Rush AJ, Fink M, et al.: Speed of response and remission in major depressive disorder with acute electroconvulsive therapy (ECT): A Consortium for Research in ECT (CORE) report. J Clin Psychiatry 2004; 65: 485–491.

Hyphantis T, Goulia P, Floros GD, et al.: Assessing ego defense mechanisms by questionnaire: Psychometric properties and psychopathological correlates of the Greek version of the Plutchik's Life Style Index. J Pers Assess 2011; 93: 605–617.

IMS Health. 2006-10-24: IMS Health Forecasts 5 to 6 Percent Growth for Global Pharmaceutical Market in 2007. http://www.imshealth.com/ims/portal/front/articleC/0,2777,6025_3665_79210022,00.html.

Institute of Medicine: Primary Care: America's Health in a New Era. Washington, DC, National Academies Press, 1996.

Isaac G: Misdiagnosed bipolar disorder in adolescents in a special educational school and treatment program. J Clin Psychiatry 1992; 53: 133–136.

Isometsa ET, Henriksson MM, Aro HM, et al.: Suicide in bipolar disorder in Finland. Am J Psychiatry 1994; 151: 1020–1024.

Jaffer H, Morris VB, Stewart D, et al.: Advances in stroke therapy. Drug Deliv Transl Res 2011; 1: 409–419.

Jäger M, Haack S, Becker T, et al.: Schizoaffective disorder—an ongoing challenge for psychiatric nosology. Eur Psychiatry 2011; 26: 159–165.

Jáuregui-Lobera I: Neuroimaging in eating disorders. Neuropsychiatr Dis Treat 2011; 7: 577–584.

Jelic V, Kowalski J: Evidence-based evaluation of diagnostic accuracy of resting EEG in dementia and mild cognitive impairment. Clin EEG Neurosci 2009; 40: 129–142.

Jindal RD, Keshavan MS: Neurobiology of the early course of schizophrenia. *Expert Rev Neurother* 2008; 8: 1093–1100.

Kaplan A, Hollander E: A review of pharmacologic treatments for obsessive-compulsive disorder. *Psychiatr Serv* 2003; 54: 1111–1118.

Karege F, Perroud N, Schürhoff F, *et al.*: Association of AKT1 gene variants and protein expression in both schizophrenia and bipolar disorder. *Genes Brain Behav* 2010; 9: 503–511.

Karlsgodt KH, Bachman P, Winkler AM, *et al.*: Genetic influence on the working memory circuitry: Behavior, structure, function and extensions to illness. *Behav Brain Res* 2011; 225: 610–622.

Karnow S: *VietNam, A History*. New York, The Viking Press, 1983.

Katerndahl D, Wood R, Jaen CR: Family medicine outpatient encounters are more complex than those of cardiology and psychiatry. *J Am Board Fam Med* 2011; 24: 6–15.

Keller MB: Remission versus response: The new gold standard of antidepressant care. *J Clin Psychiatry* 2004; 65 (Suppl 4): 53–59.

Kellner CH, Briggs MC, Pasculli RM: "An open letter" to the FDA, further commentary on the reclassification of electroconvulsive therapy (ECT) devices. *J ECT* 2012; 28: 55.

Kellner CH, Knapp RG, Petrides G, *et al.*: Continuation electroconvulsive therapy vs. pharmacotherapy for relapse prevention in major depression: A multisite study from the Consortium for Research in Electroconvulsive Therapy (CORE). *Arch Gen Psychiatry* 2006; 63: 1337–1344.

Kendler KS, Munoz RA, Murphy G: The development of the Feighner Criteria: A historical perspective. *Am J Psychiatry* 2010; 167: 134–142.

Kennedy SH, Giacobbe P, Rizvi SJ, *et al.*: Deep brain stimulation for treatment-resistant depression: Follow-up after 3 to 6 years. *Am J Psychiatry* 2011; 168: 502–510.

Keshavan MS, Morris DW, Sweeney JA, *et al.*: A dimensional approach to the psychosis spectrum between bipolar disorder and schizophrenia: The Schizo-Bipolar Scale. *Schizophr Res* 2011; 133: 250–254.

Kessler RC, Berglund P, Demler O, *et al.*: Lifetime prevalence and age-of-onset distributions of DSM-IV disorders in the National Comorbidity Survey Replication. *Arch Gen Psychiatry* 2005; 62: 593–602.

Kessler RC, Ruscio AM, Shear K, *et al.*: Epidemiology of anxiety disorders. *Curr Top Behav Neurosci* 2010; 2: 21–35.

Khan A, Detke M, Khan SRF, *et al.*: Placebo response and antidepressant clinical trial outcome. *J Nerv Ment Dis* 2003; 191: 211–218.

King NS, Kirwilliam S: Permanent post-concussion symptoms after mild head injury. *Brain Inj* 2011; 25: 462–470.

Kirk SA, Kutchens H: *The Selling of DSM: The Rhetoric of Science in Psychiatry*. Piscataway, NJ, Transaction Publishing, 2008

Kirsch I, Deacon BJ, Huedo-Medina TB, *et al.*: Initial severity and antidepressant benefits: A meta-analysis of data submitted to the Food and Drug Administration. *PLos Med* 2008; 5: e45.

Kirsch I, Moore TJ, Scoboria A, *et al.*: An analysis of antidepressant medication data, submitted to the U.S. Food and Drug Administration. *Prevention Treat* 2002; 5: 1–11.

Kishi Y, Kato M, Okuyama T, *et al.*: Delirium: Patient characteristics that predict a missed diagnosis at psychiatric consultation. *Gen Hosp Psychiatry* 2007; 29: 442–445.

Klingseisen A, Jackson AP: Mechanisms and pathways of growth failure in primordial dwarfism. *Genes Dev* 2011; 25: 2011–2024.

Kotz SA, Schwartze M, Schmidt-Kassow M: Non-motor basal ganglia functions: A review and proposal for a model of sensory predictability in auditory language perception. *Cortex* 2009; 45: 982–990.

Kramer BA: Use of ECT in California 1977–1983. *Am J Psychiatry* 1985; 142: 1190–1192.

Krem MM: Motor conversion disorders reviewed from a neuropsychiatric perspective. *J Clin Psychiatry* 2004; 65: 783–790.

Krimsky S: Journal policies on conflict of interest: If this is the therapy, what is the disease? *Psychother Psychosom* 2001; 70: 115–117.

Kuhn WF, Kuhn SC, Daylida L: Basilar migraine. *Eur J Emerg Med* 1997; 4: 33–38.

Kupfer DJ, Angst J, Berk M, *et al.*: Advances in bipolar disorder: Selected sessions from the 2011 International Conference on Bipolar Disorder. *Ann NY Acad Sci* 2011; 124: 1–25.

Kysar JE: The two camps in child psychiatry: A report from a psychiatrist-father of an autistic and retarded child. *Am J Psychiatry* 1968; 125: 103–109.

LaFranchi SH: Approach to the diagnosis and treatment of neonatal hypothyroidism. *J Clin Endocrinol Metab* 2011; 96: 2959–2967.

Lahmeyer HW: Seasonal affective disorders. *Psychiatr Med* 1991; 9: 105–114.

Lall RR, Eddleman CS, Bendok BR, *et al.*: Unruptured intracranial aneurysms and the assessment of rupture risk based on anatomical and morphological factors: Sifting through the sands of data. *Neurosurg Focus* 2009; 26: E2.

Lapid MI, Rummans TA, Pankratz VS, *et al.*: Decisional capacity of depressed elderly to consent to electroconvulsive therapy. *J Geriatr Psychiatry Neurol* 2004; 17: 42–46.

Large M, Sharma S, Cannon E, *et al.*: Risk factors for suicide within a year of discharge from psychiatric hospital: A systematic meta-analysis. *Aust N Z J Psychiatry* 2011; 45: 619–628.

Lazarus A: Images in psychiatry: Oregon State Hospital, 1883–2008. *Am J Psychiatry* 2009; 166: 151.

Leaf PJ, Brown RL, Manderscheid RW, *et al.*: Federally funded CMHCs: The effects of period of initial funding and hospital affiliation. *Community Ment Health J* 1985; 21: 145–155.

Lee JVV, Kim IO, Kim WS, *et al.*: Herpes simplex encephalitis: MRI findings in two cases confirmed by polymerase chain reaction assay. *Pediatr Radiol* 2001; 31: 619–623.

Lee T-S, Ng B-Y, Lee W-L: Neuropsychiatry—An emerging field. *Ann Acad Med Singapore* 2008; 37: 601–605.

Leichsenring F: Are psychodynamic and psychoanalytic therapies effective? A review of empirical data. *Int J Psychoanal* 2005; 86: 841–868.

Leichsenring F, Hiller W, Weissberg M, *et al.*: Cognitive-behavior therapy and psychodynamic psychotherapy: Techniques, efficacy, and indications. *Am J Psychother* 2006; 60: 233–259.

Leon AC, Solomon DA, Li C, *et al*: Antiepileptic drugs for bipolar disorder and the risk of suicidal behavior: A 30-year observational study. *Am J Psychiatry* 2012; 169: 285–291.

Leuchter AF, Daly KA, Rosenberg-Thompson S, *et al.*: Prevalence and significance of electroencephalographic abnormalities in patients with suspected organic mental syndromes. *J Am Geriatr Soc* 1993; 41: 605–611.

Levey A, Lah J, Goldstein F, *et al.*: Mild cognitive impairment: An opportunity to identify patients at high risk for progression to Alzheimer's disease. *Clin Ther* 2006; 28: 991–1001.

Levin A: FDA advisory panel favors ECT in high-risk category. *Psychiatric News* 2010; 46: 1–31.

Levine MP: Loneliness and eating disorders. *J Psychol* 2012; 146: 243–257.

Levy R, Czernecki V: Apathy and the basal ganglia. *J Neurol* 2006; 253 (Suppl 7): VII54–VII61.

Levy R, Dubois B: Apathy and the functional anatomy of the prefrontal cortex-basal ganglia circuits. *Cereb Cortex* 2006; 16: 916–928.

Lewis C, Clancy C, Leake B, *et al.*: The counseling practices of internists. *Ann Intern Med* 1991; 114: 54–58.

Lezak MD: *Neuropsychological Assessment*, 3rd ed. New York, Oxford University Press, 1995.

Li S, Wang S, Zhao YL, *et al.*: Clinical characteristics and surgical outcomes of intracranial aneurysm: A retrospective study of 3322 cases [in Chinese]. *Zhonghua Yi Xue Za Zhi* 2011; 91: 3346–3349.

Liptzin B, Gottlieb GL, Summergrad P: The future of psychiatric services in general hospitals. *Am J Psychiatry* 2007; 164: 1468–1472.

Lodwick JL, Borries C, Pusey AE, *et al.*: From nest to nest—influence of ecology and reproduction on the active period of adult Gombe chimpanzees. *Am J Primatol* 2004; 64: 249–260.

Loeb KL, Lock J, Grange DL, *et al.*: Transdiagnostic theory and application of family-based treatment for youth with eating disorders. *Cogn Behav Pract* 2012; 19: 17–30.

Loewenstein G, Sah S, Cain DM: The unintended consequences of conflict of interest disclosure. *JAMA* 2012; 307: 669–670.

Lozano AM, Giacobbe P, Hamani C, *et al.*: A multicenter pilot study of subcallosal cingulate area deep brain stimulation for treatment-resistant depression. *J Neurosurgery* 2012; 116: 315–322.

Luck T, Luppa M, Briel S, *et al.*: Incidence of mild cognitive impairment: A systematic review. *Dement Geriatr Cogn Disord* 2010; 29: 164–175.

Luria AR: *The Working Brain: An Introduction to Neuropsychology*. New York, Basic Books, 1976.

Luria AR: *Higher Cortical Functions in Man*, 2nd ed. New York, Basic Books, 1980.

Lurie P, Tran T, Wolfe SM, *et al.*: Violations of exhibiting and FDA rules at an American Psychiatric Association annual meeting. *J Public Health Policy* 2005; 26: 389–399.

Maayan L, Correll CU: Weight gain and metabolic risks associated with antipsychotic medications in children and adolescents. *J Child Adolesc Psychopharmacol* 2011; 2: 517–535.

MacLeod C: The missing link: Evolution of the primate cerebellum. *Prog Brain Res* 2012; 195: 165–187.

Maia TV, Cooney RE, Peterson BS: The neural bases of obsessive-compulsive disorder in children and adults. *Dev Psychopath* 2008; 20: 1251–1283.

Maioli F, Coveri M, Pagni P, *et al.*: Conversion of mild cognitive impairment to dementia in elderly subjects: A preliminary study in a memory and cognitive disorder unit. *Arch Gerontol Geriatr* 2007; 44 (Suppl 1): 233–241.

Maixner D, Taylor MA: The efficacy and safety of electroconvulsive therapy. In Tyrer P, Silk K (Eds.), *Cambridge Handbook of Effective Treatments in Psychiatry*. Cambridge, UK, Cambridge University Press, 2008, pp. 57–82.

Majumdar S, Inui T, Gurwitz J, *et al.*: Influence of physician specialty on adoption and relinquishment of calcium channel blockers and other treatments for myocardial infarction. *J Gen Intern Med* 2001; 16: 351–359.

Mandell AJ: The changing face of chairmen of psychiatry departments in America: An opinion. *Am J Psychiatry* 1974; 131: 1137–1139.

Marazziti D, Baroni S, Faravelli L, *et al.*: Plasma clomipramine levels in adult patients with obsessive-compulsive disorder. *Int Clin Psychopharmacol* 2012; 27: 55–60.

Marazziti D, Consoli G, Picchetti, *et al.*: Cognitive impairment in major depression. *Eur J Pharmacol* 2010; 626: 83–86.

Maris RW: Suicide. *Lancet* 2002; 360: 319–326.

Mark TL, Kassed C, Levit K, *et al.*: An analysis of the slowdown in growth of spending for psychiatric drugs, 1986–2008. *Psychiatr Serv* 2012; 63: 13–18.

Marshall RD, Vaughan SC, MacKinnon RA, *et al.*: Assessing outcome in psychoanalysis and long-term dynamic psychotherapy. *J Am Acad Psychoanal* 1996; 24: 575–604.

Marshall WK: Treatment of obsessional illnesses and phobic anxiety states with clomipramine. *Br J Psychiatry* 1971; 119: 467–468.

Martin JL, Martín-Sánchez E: Systematic review and meta-analysis of vagus nerve stimulation in the treatment of depression: Variable results based on study designs. *Eur Psychiatry* 2012; 27: 147–155.

Martino D, Defazio G, Giovannoni G: The PANDAS subgroup of tic disorders and childhood-onset obsessive-compulsive disorder. *J Psychosom Res* 2009; 67: 547–557.

Masdeu JC: Neuroimaging in psychiatric disorders. *Neurotherapeutics* 2011; 8: 93–102.

Mashour GA, Walker EE, Martuza RL: Psychosurgery: Past, present, and future. *Brain Res Brain Rev* 2005; 48: 409–419.

Maurer K, Maurer U: *Alzheimer: The Life of a Physician and Career of a Disease*. New York, Columbia University Press, 2003.

McCall WV: Physical treatments in psychiatry: Current and historical use in the southern United States. *South Med J* 1989; 82: 345–351.

McDaniel LD, Lukovits T, McDaniel KD: Alzheimer's disease: The problem of incorrect clinical diagnosis. *J Geriatr Psychiatry Neurol* 1993; 6: 230–234.

McDowell AK, Lineberry TW, Bostwick JM: Practical suicide-risk management for the busy primary care physician. *Mayo Clin Proc* 2011; 86: 792–800.

McHugh P: Overestimating mental illness in America, in A Nation of Crazy People? *The Weekly Standard*, 2005; 10: Issue 39, June 27.

McKendrick AM, Sampson GP: Low spatial frequency contrast sensitivity deficits in migraine are not visual pathway selective. *Cephalalgia* 2009; 29: 539–549.

Medawar C, Hardon A: *Medicines Out of Control? Antidepressants and the Conspiracy of Goodwill*. Amsterdam, Aksant Academic Publishers, 2004.

Meeks TW, Culberson JW, Horton MS: Medications in long-term care: When less is more. *Clin Geriatr Med* 2011; 27: 171–191.

Mega MS, Cummings JL: Frontal-subcortical circuits and neuropsychiatric disorders. *J Neuropsychiatry Clin Neurosci* 1994; 6: 358–370.

Meyer GJ, Archer RP: The hard science of Rorschach research: What do we know and where do we go? *Psychol Assess* 2001; 13: 486–502.

Meynert T: *A Clinical Treatise on Diseases of the Fore-Brain Based Upon a Study of Its Structure, Functions, and Nutrition*. Charleston, SC, Nabu Press, 2010.

Meythaler JM, Peduzzi JD, Eleftheriou E, *et al.*: Current concepts: Diffuse axonal injury-associated traumatic brain injury. *Arch Phys Med Rehabil* 2001; 82: 1461–1471.

Michel JP, Herrmann FR, Zekry D: Interference of brain reserve on cognitive disorders. *Rev Med Suisse* 2009; 5 (224): 2190–2194.

Mieli-Vergani G, Vergani D: Autoimmune hepatitis. *Nat Rev Gastroenterol Hepatol* 2011; 8: 320–329.

Miller C: Childhood animal cruelty and interpersonal violence. *Clin Psychol Rev* 2001; 21: 735–749.

Miller L: Neuropsychological assessment of substance abusers: Review and recommendations. *J Subst Abuse Treat* 1985; 2: 5–17.

Misra S, Socherman R, Hauser P, *et al*.: Application of research information in patients with bipolar disorder. *Bipolar Disord* 2008; 10: 635–646.

Misra S, Socherman R, Park BS, *et al*.: Influence of mood state on capacity to consent to research in patients with bipolar disorder. *Bipolar Disord* 2008; 10: 303–309.

Moene, FC, Landberg, EH, Hoogduin, KA, *et al*.: Organic syndromes diagnosed as conversion disorder: Identification and frequency in a study of 85 patients. *J Psychosom Res* 2000; 49: 7–12.

Mojtabai R: Fregoli syndrome. *Aust N Z J Psychiatry* 1994; 28: 458–462.

Moreno C, Laje G, Blanco C, *et al*.: National trends in the outpatient diagnosis and treatment of bipolar disorder in youth. *Arch Gen Psychiatry* 2007; 64: 1032–1039.

Morey LC, Zanarini MC: Borderline personality: Traits and disorder. *J Abnorm Psychol* 2000; 109: 733–737.

Moynihan R: Drug company sponsorship of education could be replaced at a fraction of its cost. *BMJ* 2003; 326/7400: 1163.

Mullen PE: Psychoanalysis: A creed in decline. *Aust N Z J Psychiatry* 1989; 23: 17–20.

Müller-Oerlinghausen B, Ahrens B, Grof E, *et al*.: The effect of long-term lithium treatment on the mortality of patients with manic-depressive and schizoaffective illness. *Acta Psychiatr Scand* 1992; 86: 218–222.

Müller SE, Weijers HG, Boning J *et al*.: Personality traits predict treatment outcome in alcohol-dependent patients. *Neuropsychobiology* 2008; 57: 159–164.

Mulroy E, Murphy S, Lynch T: Alexia without agraphia. *Ir Med J* 2011; 104: 124.

Murrihy R, Byrne MK: Training models for psychiatry in primary care: A new frontier. *Australas Psychiatry* 2005; 13: 296–301.

Nelson JC, Charney DS: The symptoms of major depressive illness. *Am J Psychiatry* 1981; 138: 1–13.

Nelson JC, Kennedy JS, Pollock BG, *et al*.: Treatment of major depression with nortriptyline and paroxetine in patients with ischemic heart disease. *Am J Psychiatry* 1999; 156: 1024–1028.

Nestor L, Roberts G, Garavan H, *et al*.: Deficits in learning and memory: Parahippocampal hyperactivity and frontocortical hypoactivity in cannabis users. *Neuroimage* 2008; 15: 1328–1339.

Noe KH, Locke DE, Sirven JI: Treatment of depression in patients with epilepsy. *Curr Treat Options Neurol* 2011; 13: 371–379.

Northoff G: Neuropsychiatry: An old discipline in a new gestalt bridging biological psychiatry, neuropsychology, and cognitive neurology. *Eur Arch Psychiatry Clin Neurosci* 2008; 258: 226–238.

Nurnberg HG, Raskin M, Levine PE, *et al*.: The comorbidity of borderline personality disorder and other DSM-III-R axis II personality disorders. *Am J Psychiatry* 1991; 148: 1371–1377.

Nyapati R, Rao NR: Recent trends in psychiatry residency workforce with special reference to international medical graduates. *Academic Psychiatry* 2003; 27: 269–276.

Olivers CN, Peters J, Houtkamp R, et al.: Different states in visual working memory: When it guides attention and when it does not. *Trends Cogn Sci* 2011; 15: 327–334.

O'Malley SS, Adamse M, Heaton RK, et al.: Neuropsychological impairment in chronic cocaine abusers. *Am J Drug Alcohol Abuse* 1992; 18: 131–144.

Oquendo MA, Kamali M, Ellis SP, et al.: Adequacy of antidepressant treatment after discharge and the occurrence of suicidal acts in major depression: A prospective study. *Am J Psychiatry* 2002; 157: 1746–1751.

Oquendo MA, Malone KM, Ellis SP, et al.: Inadequacy of antidepressant treatment for patients with major depression who are risk for suicidal behavior. *Am J Psychiatry* 1999; 156: 190–194.

Ottosson J-O, Fink M: *Ethics in Electroconvulsive Therapy.* New York, Brunner-Routledge, 2004.

Palmer BW, Dunn LB, Appelbaum PS, et al.: Assessment of capacity to consent to research among persons with schizophrenia, Alzheimer disease, or diabetes mellitus: Comparison of a 3-item questionnaire with a comprehensive standardized capacity instrument. *Arch Gen Psychiatry* 2005; 62: 726–733.

Pande AC, Sayler ME: Severity of depression and response to fluoxetine. *Int Clin Psychopharamcol* 1993; 8: 243–245.

Papanikolaou K, Richardson C, Pehlivanidis A, et al.: Efficacy of antidepressants in child and adolescent depression: A meta-analytic study. *J Neural Transm* 2006; 113: 399–415.

Paris J: The diagnosis of borderline personality disorder: Problematic but better than the alternatives. *Ann Clin Psychiatry* 2005; 17: 41–46.

Parker G: Evaluating treatments for the mood disorders: Time for the evidence to get real. *Aust NZ J Psychiatry* 2004; 38: 408–414.

Parker G, Fink M, Shorter E, et al.: Issues for DSM-5: Whither melancholia? The case for its classification as a distinct mood disorder. *Am J Psychiatry* 2010; 167: 745–747.

Parker G, Mitchell P, Wilhelm K, et al.: Are the newer antidepressant drugs as effective as established physical treatments? Results from an Australasian clinical pan review. *Aust N Z J Psychiatry* 1999; 33: 874–881.

Parnes B, Smith PC, Gilroy C, et al.: Lack of impact of direct-to-consumer advertising on the physician-patient encounter in primary care: A SNOCAP report. *Ann Fam Med* 2009; 7: 41–46.

Pearce JM: Brain disease leading to mental illness: A concept initiated by the discovery of general paralysis of the insane. *Eur Neurol* 2012; 67: 272–278.

Pehlivanturk B, Unal F: Conversion disorder in children and adolescents: A 4-year follow-up study. *J. Psychosom Res* 2002; 52: 187–191.

Pelkonen M, Marttunen M: Child and adolescent suicide: Epidemiology, risk factors, and approaches to prevention. *Paediatr Drugs* 2003; 5: 243–265.

Perez-Costas E, Melendez-Ferro M, Roberts RC: Basal ganglia pathology in schizophrenia: Dopamine connections and anomalies. *J Neurochem* 2010; 113: 287–302.

Perez-Rincon H: Pierre Janet, Sigmund Freud and Charcot's psychological and psychiatric legacy. In Bogousslavsky J (Ed.), *Following Charcot: A Forgotten History of Neurology and Psychiatry.* Neurol Neurosci Basel, Karger, 2011; 29: 115–124.

Perry PJ: Pharmacotherapy for major depression with melancholic features: Relative efficacy of tricyclic versus selective serotonin reuptake inhibitor antidepressants. *J Affect Disord* 1996; 39: 1–6.

Petersen T, Fava M, Alpert JE, *et al.*: Does psychiatry residency training reflect the "real world" of psychiatry practice? A survey of residency graduates. *Acad Psychiatry* 2007; 31: 281–289.

Petrides G, Fink M, Husain MM, *et al.*: ECT remission rates in psychotic versus nonpsychotic depressed patients: A report from CORE. *J ECT* 2001; 17: 244–253.

Pies R: The psychologist prescribing bill is dead—long live science in the public interest! *Psychiatric Times* 2010; (May) 27: p.1 and 7.

Pincus HA, Tanielian TL, Marcus SC, *et al.*: Prescribing trends in psychotropic medications: Primary care, psychiatry, and other medical specialties. *JAMA* 1998; 279: 526–531.

Pingitore D, Snowden L, Sansone RA, *et al.*: Persons with depressive symptoms and the treatments they receive: A comparison of primary care physicians and psychiatrists. *Int J Psychiatry Med* 2001; 31: 41–60.

Piper A Jr, Merskey H: The persistence of folly: Critical examination of dissociative identity disorder. Part II. The defense and decline of multiple personality or dissociative identity disorder. *Can J Psychiatry* 2004; 49: 678–683.

Pitcher DR: The XYY syndrome. *Br J Psychiatry* 1975; Spec No 9: 316–325.

Plos Medical Editors: Does conflict of interest disclosure worsen bias? *Plos Med* 2012; 9: e10001210

Pollen AA, Hofmann HA: Beyond neuroanatomy: Novel approaches to studying brain evolution. *Brain Behav Evol* 2008; 72: 145–158.

Pollmann W, Feneberg W, Erasmus LP: Pain in multiple sclerosis—a still underestimated problem. The 1 year prevalence of pain syndromes, significance and quality of care of multiple sclerosis inpatients. *Nervnarz* 2004; 75: 135–140.

Price TR, Tucker GJ: Psychiatric and behavioral manifestations of normal pressure hydrocephalus. A case report and brief review. *J Nerv Ment Dis* 1977; 164: 51–55.

Pringsheim T, Lam D, Ching H, *et al.*: Metabolic and neurological complications of second-generation antipsychotic use in children: A systematic review and meta-analysis of randomized controlled trials. *Drug Saf* 2011; 34: 651–668.

Psychiatric GWAS Consortium Coordinating Committee: Genomewide association studies: History, rationale, and prospects for psychiatric disorders. *Am J Psychiatry* 2009; 166: 540–556.

Puig-Antich J, Perel JM, Lupatkin W, *et al.*: Imipramine in prepubertal major depressive disorders. *Arch Gen Psychiatry* 1987; 44: 81–89.

Pusey AE, Pintea L, Wilson ML, *et al.*: The contribution of long-term research at Gombe National Park to chimpanzee conservation. *Conserv Biol* 2007; 21: 623–634.

Rahman B, Meiser B, Sachdev P, *et al.*: To know or not to know: An update of the literature on the psychological and behavioral impact of genetic testing for Alzheimer disease risk. *Genet Test Mol Biomarkers* 2012; 16: 935–942.

Reading P: Parasomnias: The spectrum of things that go bump in the night. *Pract Neurol* 2007; 7: 6–15.

Reynolds EH, Trimble MR (Eds.): *The Bridge Between Neurology and Psychiatry*. Edinburgh, Churchill Livingstone, 1989.

Riggio S: Behavioral manifestations of frontal lobe seizures. *CNS Spectr* 2009; 14: 66–70.

Roberts BW, Walton KE, Viechtbauer W: Patterns of mean-level change in personality traits across the life course: A meta-analysis of longitudinal studies. *Psychol Bull* 2006; 132: 1–25.

Robertson EM: New insights in human memory interference and consolidation. *Curr Biol* 2012; 22: R66–R71.

Robinson RG, Schultz SK, Castillo C, *et al.*: Nortriptyline versus fluoxetine in the treatment of depression and in short-term recovery after stroke: A placebo-controlled, double-blind study. *Am J Psychiatry* 2000; 157: 351–359.

Roffman JL, Simon AB, Prasad KM, *et al.*: Neuroscience in psychiatry training: How much do residents need to know? *Am J Psychiatry* 2006; 163: 919–926.

Roose SP, Glassman AH, Attia E, *et al.*: Comparative efficacy of selective serotonin reuptake inhibitors and tricyclics in the treatment of melancholia. *Am J Psychiatry* 1994; 151: 1735–1739.

Rosazza C, Minati L: Resting-state brain networks: Literature review and clinical applications. *Neurol Sci* 2011; 32: 773–785.

Roselli CE, Stormshak F: The neurobiology of sexual partner preferences in rams. *Horm Behav* 2009; 55: 611–620.

Rosenbach ML, Hermann RC, Dorwart RA: Use of electroconvulsive therapy in the Medicare population between 1987 and 1992. *Psychiatr Serv* 1997; 48: 1537–1542.

Rosenberg PB, Mielke MM, Han D, *et al.*: The association of psychotropic medication use with the cognitive, functional, and neuropsychiatric trajectory of Alzheimer's disease. *Int J Geriatr Psychiatry* 2012; 26: 364–372.

Rosenblatt A: Neuropsychiatry of Huntington's disease. *Dialogues Clin Neurosci* 2007; 9: 191–197.

Rosenblatt R, Hart L, Baldwin L, *et al.*: The generalist role of specialty physicians: Is there a hidden system of primary care? *JAMA* 1998; 279: 1364–1370.

Ross ED, Monnot M: Neurology of affective prosody and its functional-anatomic organization in right hemisphere. *Brain Lang* 2008; 104: 51–74.

Ross ED, Monnot M: Affective prosody: What do comprehension errors tell us about hemispheric lateralization of emotions, sex and aging effects, and the role of cognitive appraisal. *Neuropsychologia* 2011; 49: 866–877.

Rothschild AJ, Winer J, Flint AJ, *et al.*: Study of Pharmacotherapy of Psychotic Depression (STOP-PD) Collaborative Study Group. Missed diagnosis of psychotic depression at 4 academic medical centers. *J Clin Psychiatry* 2008; 69: 1293–1296.

Rouillon F, Gasquet I, Garay RP, *et al.*: Impact of an educational program on the management of bipolar disorder in primary care. *Bipolar Disord* 2011; 13: 318–322.

Roy AK, Rajesh SV, Iby N, *et al.*: A study of epilepsy-related psychosis. *Neurol India* 2003; 51: 359–360.

Ruddle HV, Bradshaw CM: On the estimation of premorbid intellectual functioning: Validation of Nelson and McKenna's formula, and some new normative data. *Br J Clin Psychol* 1982; 21(Pt 3): 159–165.

Rudnick A: Depression and competence to refuse psychiatric treatment. *J Med Ethics* 2002; 28: 151–155.

Ruengorn C, Sanichwankul K, Niwatananun W, *et al.*: Incidence and risk factors of suicide reattempts within 1 year after psychiatric hospital discharge in mood disorder patients. *Clin Epidemiol* 2011; 3: 305–313.

Rush AJ, Trivedi MH, Stewart JW, *et al.*: Combining medications to enhance depression outcomes (CO-MED): Acute and long-term outcomes of a single-blind randomized study. *Am J Psychiatry* 2011; 168: 689–701.

Rush AJ, Trivedi MH, Wisniewski SR, *et al.*, for the STAR*D Study Team: Buproprion-SR, sertaline, or venlafaxine-XR after failure of SSRIs for depression. *New Engl J Med* 2006; 354: 1231–1242.

Ryan LM, Warden DL: Post concussion syndrome. *Int Rev Psychiatry* 2003; 15: 310–316.

Safer DJ: Are stimulants overprescribed for youths with ADHD? *Ann Clin Psychiatry* 2000; 12: 55–62.

Sahin N, Ozturk A, Ozkan Y, *et al.*: What do patients recall from informed consent given before orthopedic surgery? *Acta Orthop Traumatol Turc* 2010; 44: 469–475.

Sandergaard J, Vach K, Kragstrup J, *et al.*: Impact of pharmaceutical representative visits on GPs' drug preferences. *Fam Pract* 2009; 26: 204–209.

Sanders JL: A distinct language and a historic pendulum: The evolution of the Diagnostic and Statistical Manual of Mental Disorders. *Arch Psychiatric Nurs* 2011; 25: 394–403.

Sandifer MG, Hordern A, Timbury GC, *et al.*: Similarities and differences in patient evaluation by U.S. and U.K. psychiatrists. *Am J Psychiatry* 1969; 126: 206–212.

Sandstrom SA, Anschel DJ: Use of serum prolactin in diagnosing epileptic seizures: Report of the Therapeutics and Technology Assessment Subcommittee of the American Academy of Neurology. *Neurology* 2006; 67: 544–545.

Sarbin TR: On the belief that one body may be host to two or more personalities. *Int J Clin Exp Hypn* 1995; 43: 163–183.

Saviano G, Taylor MA, Fensterheim H: Sociopathy, extroversion and social class. In Rubin RD, Franks CM, *et al.* (Eds.), *Advances in Behavior Therapy.* New York, Academic Press, 1971, pp. 7–13.

Savic I, Garcia-Falgueras A, Swaab DF: Sexual differentiation of the human brain in relation to gender identity and sexual orientation. *Prog Brain Res* 2010; 186: 41–62.

Schatzberg AF: Noradrenergic versus serotonergic antidepressants: Predictors of treatment response. *J Clin Psychiatry* 1998; 59 (Suppl 14): 15–18.

Schneeweiss S, Patrick AR, Solomon DH, *et al.*: Comparative safety of antidepressant agents for children and adolescents regarding suicidal acts. *Pediatrics* 2010; 125: 876–888.

Schott GD: Exploring the visual hallucinations of migraine aura: The tacit contribution of illustration. *Brain* 2007; 130: 1690–1673.

Schumann I, Schneider A, Kantert C, *et al.*: Physicians' attitudes, diagnostic process and barriers regarding depression diagnosis in primary care: A systematic review of qualitative studies. *Fam Pract* 2012; 29: 255–263.

Schutter DJ: Antidepressant efficacy of high-frequency transcranial magnetic stimulation over the left dorsolateral prefrontal cortex in double-blind sham-controlled designs: A meta-analysis. *Psychol Med* 2009; 39: 65–75.

Scully JH, Wilk JE: Selected characteristics and data of psychiatrists in the United States, 2001–2002. *Acad Psychiatry* 2003; 27: 247–251.

Seeley WW: Frontotemporal dementia neuroimaging: A guide for clinicians. *Front Neurol Neurosci* 2009; 24: 160–167.

Seltzer A: Multiple personality: A psychiatric misadventure. *Can J Psychiatry* 1994; 39: 442–445.

Selwa LM, Hales DJ, Kanner AM: What should psychiatry residents be taught about neurology? A survey of psychiatry residency directors. *The Neurologist* 2006; 12: 268–270.

Shams PN, Plant GT: Migraine-like visual aura due to focal cerebral lesions: Case series and review. *Surv Ophthalmol* 2011; 56: 135–161.

Sherrill JT, Kovacs M: Nonsomatic treatment of depression. *Child Adolesc Psychiatr Clin N Am* 2002; 11: 579–593.

Sherwood CC, Bauernfeind AL, Bianchi S, *et al.*: Human brain evolution writ large and small. *Prog Brain Res* 2012; 195: 237–254.

Shorter E: *A History of Psychiatry, from the Era of the Asylum to the Age of Prozac*. New York, John Wiley & Sons, 1997.

Shorter E: *A Historical Dictionary of Psychiatry*. Oxford, UK, Oxford University Press, 2005.

Shorter E: *Before Prozac: The Troubled History of Mood Disorders in Psychiatry*. New York, Oxford University Press, 2009.

Shorter E, Healy D: *Shock Therapy: The History of Electroconvulsive Treatment in Mental Illness*. Piscataway, NJ, Rutgers University Press, 2007.

Sidhu KS, Balon R, Ajluni V, *et al.*: Standard EEG and the difficult-to-assess mental status. *Ann Clin Psychiatry* 2009; 21: 103–108.

Siedlecki SL: Normal pressure hydrocephalus: Are you missing the signs? *J Gerontol Nurs* 2008; 34: 27–33.

Sierles FS, Brodkey AC, Cleary LM, *et al.*: Medical students' exposure to and attitudes about drug company interactions: A national survey. *JAMA* 2005; 294: 1034–1042.

Sierles FS, Chen JJ, Messing ML, *et al.*: Concurrent psychiatric illness in non-Hispanic outpatients with post-traumatic stress disorder. *J Nerv Ment Dis* 1986; 174: 171–173.

Sierles FS, Taylor MA: Medical student career choice in psychiatry: The U.S, decline and what to do about it. *Am J Psychiatry* 1995; 152: 1416–1426.

Silver JM, McAllister TW, Arciniegas DB: Depression and cognitive complaints following mild traumatic brain injury. *Am J Psychiatry* 2009; 166: 653–661.

Silverberg ND, Iverson GL: Etiology of the post-concussion syndrome: Physiogenesis and psychogenesis revisited. *NeuroRehabilitation* 2011; 29: 317–329.

Simpson CD, Vega A: Unilateral brain damage and patterns of age-corrected WAIS subtest scores. *J Clin Psychol* 1971; 27: 204–208.

Sirois F: Steroid psychosis: A review. *Gen Hosp Psychiatry* 2003; 25: 27–33.

Skodol AE, Gunderson JG, Pfohl B, *et al.*: The borderline diagnosis I: Psychopathology, comorbidity, and personality structure. *Biol Psychiatry* 2002; 51: 936–950.

Smith EG, Sondergard L, Lopez AG, *et al.*: Association between purchase of anticonvulsants or lithium and suicide risk: A longitudinal cohort study from Denmark, 1995–2001. *J Affect Disord* 2009; 117: 162–167.

Soldatos CR, Paparrigopoulos TJ: Sleep physiology and pathology: Pertinence to psychiatry. *Int Rev Psychiatry* 2005; 17: 213–228.

Sørensen AS, Hansen H, Andersen R, *et al.*: Personality characteristics and epilepsy. *Acta Psychiatr Scand* 1989; 80: 620–631.

Spitzer RL, Fleiss JL: A re-analysis of the reliability of psychiatric diagnosis. *Br J Psychiatry* 1974; 125: 341–347.

Spitzer RL, Williams JBW, Endicott J: Standards for DSM-5 reliability. *Am J Psychiatry* 2012; 169: 537.

Squire LR, Wixted JT: The cognitive neuroscience of human memory since H.M. *Annu Rev Neurosci* 2011; 34: 259–288.

Stein MB, Kirk P, Prabhu V, *et al.*: Mixed anxiety-depression in a primary-care clinic. *J Affect Disord* 1995; 34: 79–84.

Stevens J, Kelleher KJ, Wang W, *et al.*: Research Network on Youth Mental Health: Use of psychotropic medication guidelines at child-serving community mental health centers as assessed by clinic directors. *Community Ment Health J* 2011; 47: 361–363.

Stocholm K, Bojesen A, Jensen AS, *et al.*: Crininality in men with Klinefelter's syndrome and XYY syndrome: A cohort study. *BMJ Open* 2012; Feb 22: 2(1) e000650.

Stone J, Sharpe M, Bimzer M: Motor conversion symptoms and pseudoseizures: A clinical comparison of characteristics. *Psychosomatics* 2004; 45: 492–499.

Strassman RJ: Adverse reactions to psychedelic drugs. A review of the literature. *J Nerv Ment Dis* 1984; 172: 577–595.

Stratton MC, Gregory RJ: After traumatic brain injury: A discussion of consequences. *Brain Inj* 1994; 8: 631–645.

Sturm R, Ringle JS: The role of managed care and financing in medical practices: How does psychiatry differ from other medical fields? *Soc Psychiatry Psychiatr Epidemiol* 2003; 38: 427–435.

Sugarman J, McCrory DC, Hubal RC: Getting meaningful informed consent from older adults: A structured literature review of empirical research. *J Am Geriatr Soc* 1998; 46: 517–524.

Suominen KH, Isometsä ET, Henriksson MM, *et al.*: Inadequate treatment for major depression both before and after attempted suicide. *Am J Psychiatry* 1998; 155: 1778–1780.

Svrakic DM, Whitehead C, Przybeck TR, *et al.*: Differential diagnosis of personality disorders by the seven-factor model of temperament and character. *Arch Gen Psychiatry* 1993; 50: 991–999.

Swigart SE, Kishi Y, Thurber S, *et al.*: Misdiagnosed delirium in patient referrals to a university-based hospital psychiatry department. *Psychosomatics* 2008; 49: 104–108.

Tagariello P, Girardi P, Amore M: Depression and apathy in dementia: Same syndrome or different constructs? A critical review. *Arch Gerontol Geriatr* 2009; 49: 246–248.

Tamburrino MB, Nagel RW, Lynch DJ: Managing antidepressants in primary care: Physicians' treatment modifications. *Psychol Rep* 2011; 108: 799–804.

Tamminga CA, Nemeroff CB, Blakely RD, *et al.*: Developing novel treatments for mood disorders: Accelerating discovery. *Biol Psychiatry* 2002; 52: 589–609.

Tandon R, Keshavan MS, Nasrallah HA: Schizophrenia, "Just the facts": What we know in 2008, Part I: Overview. *Schizophr Res* 2008; 100: 4–19.

Taussky P, Tawk RG, Daugherty WP, *et al.*: Medical therapy for ischemic stroke: Review of intravenous and intra-arterial treatment options. *World Neurosurg* 2011; 76 (6 Suppl): S9–S15.

Taylor MA: *The Fundamentals of Clinical Neuropsychiatry*. New York, Oxford University Press, 1999.

Taylor MA, Abrams R: A critique of the St. Louis psychiatric research criteria for schizophrenia. *Am J Psychiatry* 1975; 132: 1276–1280.

Taylor MA, Abrams R, Gaztanaga P: Manic-depressive illness and schizophrenia: A partial validation of research diagnostic criteria utilizing neuropsychological testing. *Compr Psychiatry* 1975; 16: 91–96.

Taylor MA, Atre Vaidya N: *Descriptive Psychopathology: The Signs and Symptoms of Behavioral Syndromes*. Cambridge, UK, Cambridge University Press, 2009.

Taylor MA, Fink M: Catatonia in psychiatric classification: A home of its own. *Am J Psychiatry* 2003; 160: 1233–1241.

Taylor MA, Fink M: *Melancholia: The Diagnosis, Treatment, and Pathophysiology of Depressive Illness*. Cambridge, UK, Cambridge University Press, 2006.

Taylor MA, Gaztanaga P, Abrams R: Manic-depressive illness and acute schizophrenia: A clinical, family history, and treatment-response study. *Am J Psychiatry* 1974; 131: 678–682.

Taylor MA, Shorter E, Atre Vaidya N, *et al.*: The failure of the schizophrenia concept and the argument for its replacement by hebephrenia: Applying the medical model for disease recognition. *Acta Psychiatr Scand* 2010; 122: 173–183.

Teng EJ, Petersen NJ, Hartman C, *et al.*: Effects of depression and social support on comprehension and recall of informed consent information among Parkinson disease patients and their caregivers. *Int J Psychiatry Med* 2012; 43: 67–83.

Thompson JW, Weiner RD, Myers CP: Use of ECT in the United States in 1975, 1980, and 1986. *Am J Psychiatry* 1994; 151: 1657–1661.

Tolstoy L: *Anna Karenina*. New York, The Modern Library, 1965.

Tondo L, Baldessarini RJ: Long-term lithium treatment in the prevention of suicidal behavior in bipolar disorder patients. *Epidemiol Psychiatr Soc* 2009; 18: 179–183.

Trachtenberg RL: The NAPPH (National Association of Private Psychiatric Hospitals) today—under new management. Interview by John Herrman. *Health Syst Rev* 1992; 25: 31–33.

Tsapakis EM, Soldani F, Tondo L, *et al.*: Efficacy of antidepressants in juvenile depression: Meta-analysis. *Br J Psychiatry* 2008; 193: 10–17.

Tuchman BW: *The March of Folly, from Troy to VietNam*. New York, Alfred A. Knoff, 1984.

Turner B, Amsel Z, Lustbader E, *et al.*: Breast cancer screening: Effect of physician specialty, practice setting, year of medical school graduation, and sex. *Am J Prev Med* 1992; 8: 78–85.

Turner BJ, Laine C: "Differences between generalists and specialists: Knowledge, realism, or primum non nocere?" *J Gen Int Med: Official Journal of the Society for Research and Education in Primary Care Internal Medicine* 2001; 16: 422–424.

Turner EH, Matthews AM, Linardatos E, *et al.*: Selective publication of antidepressant trials and its influence on apparent efficacy. *New Engl J Med* 2008; 358: 252–260.

Vaidya N, Taylor MA: Teaching of psychopathology for neuropsychiatry practice: DSM and beyond. *J Neuropsychiatry Clin Neurosci* 2005; 17: 246–249.

Vaishnavi S, Rosenblatt A, Rabins P, *et al.*: Behavioral neurology and neuropsychiatry fellowship training: The Johns Hopkins Model. *J Neuropsychiatry Clin Neurosci* 2009; 21: 335–341.

Vandenbroucke JP: Do editors live up to the Sept 10, 2001, expectations? *Lancet* 2002; 360: 1605–1606.

Van den Heuvel OA, van der Werf YD, Verhoef KM, *et al.*: Frontal-striatal abnormalities underlying behaviors in compulsive-impulsive spectrum. *J Neurosci* 2010; 289: 55–59.

van Duijn E, Kingma EM, van der Mast RC: Psychopathology in verified Huntington's disease gene carriers. *J Neuropsychiatry Clin Neurosci* 2007; 19: 441–448.

Van Meter AR, Moreira AL, Youngstrom EA: Meta-analysis of epidemiologic studies of pediatric bipolar disorder. *J Clin Psychiatry* 2011; 72: 1250–1256.

Van Voren R: Political abuse of psychiatry—an historical overview. *Schizophr Bull* 2010; 36: 33–35.

Vann SD, Aggleton JP, Maguire EA: What does the retrosplenial cortex do? *Nat Rev Neurosci* 2009; 10: 792–802.

Venna N, Sabin TD: Senile gait disorders. In Joseph AB, Young RR (Eds.), *Movement Disorders in Neurology and Neuropsychiatry*. Boston, Blackwell Scientific Publications, 1992, pp. 301–309.

Verdoux H, Tournier M, Bégaud B: Antipsychotic prescribing trends: A review of phar-
maco-epidemiological studies. *Acta Psychiatr Scand* 2010; 121: 4–10.

Verhoeven WM, Egger JI, Ahmed AI, *et al.*: Cerebellar cognitive affective syndrome and
autosomal recessive spastic ataxia of Charlevoix-Saguenay: A report of two male
sibs. *Psychopathology* 2012; 45: 193–199.

Vigen CL, Mack WJ, Keefe RS, *et al.*: Cognitive effects of atypical antipsychotic
medications in patients with Alzheimer's disease: Outcomes from CATIE-AD.
Am J Psychiatry 2011; 168: 831–839.

Vinik AL: Management of neuropathy and foot problems in diabetic patients. *Clin
Cornerstone* 2003; 5: 38–55.

Vuorilehto MS, Melartin TK, Isometsa ET: Course and outcome of depressive disorders in primary care: A prospective 18-month study. *Psychol Med* 2009; 39:
1697–1707.

Wade JB, Taylor MA, Kasprisin A, *et al.*: Tardive dyskinesia and cognitive impairment.
Biol Psychiatry 1987; 22: 393–395.

Wakefield JC, Schmitz MF, Baer JC: Does the DSM-IV clinical significance criterion for
major depression reduce false positives? Evidence from the National Comorbidity
Survey Replication. *Am J Psychiatry* 2010; 167: 298–304.

Walter P, Ron D: The unfolded protein response: From stress pathway to homeostatic
regulation. *Science* 2011; 334: 1081–1086.

Wang PS, Lane M, Olfson M, *et al.*: Twelve-month use of mental health services in the
United States: Results from the National Comorbidity Survey Replication. *Arch
Gen Psychiatry* 2005; 62: 629–640.

Wang Y, Adelman RA: A study of interactions between pharmaceutical representatives
and ophthalmology trainees. *Am J Ophthalmol* 2009; 148: 619–622.

Watkins K: Developmental disorders of speech and language: From genes to brain
structure and function. *Prog Brain Res* 2011; 189: 225–238.

Watson CG: WAIS profile patterns of hospitalized brain-damaged and schizophrenic
patients. *J Clin Psychol* 1965; 21: 294–295.

Watts BV, Groft A, Bagian JP, *et al.*: An examination of mortality and other adverse
events related to electroconvulsive therapy using a national adverse event report
system. *J ECT* 2011; 27: 105–108.

Wehmeier PM, Schacht A, Wolff C, *et al.*: Neuropsychological outcomes across the day
in children with attention-deficit/hyperactivity disorder treated with atomox-
etine: Results from a placebo-controlled study using a computer-based continuous performance test combined with an infra-red motion-tracking device. *J Child
Adolesc Psychopharmacol* 2011; 21: 433–444.

Weintraub D, Burn DJ: Parkinson's disease: The quintessential neuropsychiatric disorder. *Mov Disord* 2011; 26: 1022–1031.

Weisberg RB, Dyck I, Culpepper L, *et al.*: Psychiatric treatment in primary care patients
with anxiety disorders: A comparison of care received from primary care providers
and psychiatrists. *Am J Psychiatry* 2007; 164: 276–282; erratum *Am J Psychiatry*
2007; 164: 833.

Wen W, He Y, Sachdev P: Structural brain networks and neuropsychiatric disorders.
Curr Opin Psychiatry 2011; 24: 219–225.

Westenberg HG, Fineberg NA, Denys D: Neurobiology of obsessive-compulsive disorder: Serotonin and beyond. *CNS Spectr* 2007; 12 (2 Suppl 3): 14–27.

Whitcomb D: The regulation of electroconvulsive therapy in California: The
impact of recent constitutional interpretations. Gold Gate Law Rev 1989; 18:
469–494.

Whiting BA, Barton RA: The evolution of the cortico-cerebellar complex in primates: Anatomical connections predict patterns of correlated evolution. *J Hum Evol* 2003; 44: 3–10.

Whitley RJ: Herpes simplex encephalitis: Adolescents and adults. *Antiviral Res* 2006; 71: 141–148.

Whitshaw IQ, Kolb B: *Fundamentals of Human Neuropsychology*, 6th ed. New York, Worth Publishers, Inc., 2008.

Wijeratne C, Sachdev P: Treatment-resistant depression: Critique of current approaches. *Aust N Z J Psychiatry* 2008; 42: 751–762.

Wilens TE, Biederman J, Baldessarini RJ, et al.: Cardiovascular effects of therapeutic doses of tricyclic antidepressants in children and adolescents. *J Am Acad Child Adolesc Psychiatry* 1996; 35: 1491–1501.

Wilkinson G: Psychoanalysis and analytic psychotherapy in the NHS—a problem for medical ethics. *J Med Ethics* 1986; 12: 87–90.

Williams BF, French JK, White HD, et al.: Informed consent during the clinical emergency of acute myocardial infarction (HERO-2 consent substudy): A prospective observational study. *Lancet* 2003; 361: 918–922.

Williams HJ, Craddock N, Russo G, et al.: Most genome-wide significant susceptibility loci for schizophrenia and bipolar disorder reported to date cross-traditional diagnostic boundaries. *Hum Mol Genet* 2011; 20: 387–391.

Williamson L: Eating disorders and the cultural forces behind the drive for thinness: Are African American women really protected? *Soc Work Health Care* 1998; 28: 61–73.

Wilson DM: Growth hormone and hypophosphatemic rickets. *J Pediatr Endocrinol Metab* 2000; 13 (Suppl 2): 993–998.

Wilson RS, Leurgans SE, Boyle PA, et al.: Neurodegenerative basis of age-related cognitive decline. *Neurology* 2010; 75: 1070–1078.

Windle C, Bass RD, Gray L: The impact of federally funded CNHCs on local mental health service systems. Community mental health centers. *Hosp Community Psychiatry* 1987; 38: 729–734.

Wolfensberger WP: Construction of a table of the significance of the difference between verbal and performance IQ's on the WAIS and the Wechsler-Bellevue. *J Clin Psychol* 1958; 14: 92.

Wolpe J, Lazarus AA: *Behavior Therapy Techniques*. Oxford, Pergamon Press Ltd., 1966.

Wood JM, Lilienfeld SO: The Rorschach inkblot test: A case of overstatement? *Assessment* 1999; 6: 341–352.

Woodruff R, Goodwin DW, Guze S: *Psychiatric Diagnosis*. New York, Oxford University Press, 1974.

Wun YT, Lam TP, Goldberg D, et al.: Reasons for preferring a primary care physician for care if depressed. *Fam Med* 2011; 43: 344–350.

Yager J, Mellman L, Rubin E, et al.: The RRC mandate for residency programs to demonstrate psychodynamic psychotherapy competency among residents: A debate. *Acad Psychiatry* 2005; 29: 339–349.

Yamamoto D: The neural and genetic substrates of sexual behavior in Drosophila. *Adv Genet* 2007; 59: 39–66.

Yasuhara A: Correlation between EEG abnormalities and symptoms of autism spectrum disorder (ASD). *Brain Dev* 2010; 32: 791–798.

Yeates GN, Gracey F, McGrath JC: A biopsychosocial deconstruction of "personality change" following acquired brain injury. *Neuropsychol Rehabil* 2008; 18: 566–589.

Yerevanian BI, Koek RJ, Mintz J: Lithium, anticonvulsants and suicidal behavior in bipolar disorder. *J Affect Disord* 2003; 73: 223–228.

Young AS, Klap R, Sherbourne CD, *et al.*: The quality of care for depressive and anxiety disorders in the United States. *Arch Gen Psychiatry* 2001; 58: 55–61.

Yudofsky SC, Hales RE: Neuropsychiatry and the future of psychiatry and neurology. *Am J Psychiatry* 2002; 159: 1261–1264

YudofskySC, Hales RE: Neuropsychiatry: Back to the future. *J Nerv Ment Dis* 2012; 200; 193–196.

Zanarini MC, Frankenburg FR, Dubo ED, *et al.*: Axis I comorbidity of borderline personality disorder. *Am J Psychiatry* 1998; 155: 1733–1739.

Zilles K, Amunts K, Smaers JB: Three brain collections for comparative neuroanatomy and neuroimaging. *Ann NY Acad Sci* 2011; 1225 (Suppl 1): E94–E104.

Zima BT, Bussing R, Tang L, *et al.*: Quality of care for childhood attention-deficit/hyperactivity disorder in a managed care Medicaid program. *J Am Acad Child Adolesc Psychiatry* 2010; 49: 1225–1237.

Zimmerman M, Mattia JI, Posternak MA: Are subjects in pharmacological treatment trials of depression representative of patients in routine clinical practice? *Am J Psychiatry* 2002; 159: 469–473.

Zinkin J: *Rosen, John, N. Direct Analysis: Selected Papers*. New York, Grune & Stratton, 1953.

Zipkin DA, Steinman MA: Interactions between pharmaceutical representatives and doctors in training. A thematic review. *J Gen Intern Med* 2005; 20: 777–786.

Zisook S, McQuaid JR, Sciolla A, *et al.*: Psychiatric residents' interest in psychotherapy and training stage: A multi-site survey. *Am J Psychother* 2011; 65: 47–59.

INDEX